THE EUROPEAN UNION AND HUMAN RIGHTS

International Studies in Human Rights

VOLUME 42

The titles published in this series are listed at the end of this volume.

THE EUROPEAN UNION
AND HUMAN RIGHTS

edited by

NANETTE A. NEUWAHL

Lecturer in Law,
University of Leicester

and

ALLAN ROSAS

Director,
Institute for Human Rights,
Abo Akademi University

MARTINUS NIJHOFF PUBLISHERS
THE HAGUE / BOSTON / LONDON

A C.I.P. Catalogue record for this book is available from the Library of Congress.

ISBN 90-411-0124-1

Published by Kluwer Law International,
P.O. Box 85889, 2508 CN The Hague, The Netherlands.

Sold and distributed in the U.S.A. and Canada
by Kluwer Law International,
675 Massachusetts Avenue, Cambridge, MA 02139, U.S.A.

In all other countries, sold and distributed
by Kluwer Law International,
P.O. Box 85889, 2508 CN The Hague, The Netherlands.

Printed on acid-free paper

TABLE OF CONTENTS

FOREWORD

As the European Union is moving from an economic to a "political" constitution, one may ask what future there is for human rights protection in the Union. The Treaty on European Union for the first time includes treaty articles requiring the respect for human rights in the Union, but their potential is reduced to the extent that an involvement of an independent court to secure their respect is not guaranteed. What potential is there for improvement of the human rights protection in the European Union?

This book examines the human rights implications of the European Union in a forward-looking perspective. Seventeen experts from nine different countries inside and outside the Community have been asked to give their opinion on the potential for development in different spheres of activity of the Union. Is Maastricht a step forward in the protection of human rights? How does judicial protection under Union Law compare with standards of protection under the European Convention for the Protection of Human Rights and Fundamental Freedoms, or with national constitutional law? Which rights, and whose rights are being protected?

These questions are to some extent underlying all the contributions to this book. Apart from the general reflective contributions a broad range of specific issues of particular topicality is dealt with, including property rights, the freedom of expression for commercial actors, the principle of governmental openness, the right to vote and to be elected, freedom of movement, social rights as general principles of Community law, workers' rights of participation, family rights and the position of women in the family, expulsion and extradition in and from the European Union, the protection of minorities, the protection of cultural heritage, foreign policy and extraterritoriality. A select bibliography on the topics dealt with is also included.

This publication is the result of collaboration between the Law Department of the University of Leicester, England, and the Department of Law and the Institute for Human Rights of Åbo Akademi University in Turku, Finland, where substantial research is at present being done both in the field of human rights and in the field of European Community law. The Law Department and the Institute for Human Rights jointly provided the infrastructure and the necessary financial support.

The editors wish to thank Professor *David O'Keeffe*, University College London, and Dr. *Joerg Monar*, Director of the Institut für Europäische Politik,

Bonn, for their suggestions in the preliminary stages of this project. We also would like to thank Mr Md. *Parvez Sattar,* Leicester, for doing useful research and preparing the select bibliography.

Very special thanks go to Ms *Johanna Bondas* and Ms *Raija Hanski* of the Institute for Human Rights, who established the camera-ready proofs and who, as always, did quite a bit more than that.

The Editors

CONTRIBUTORS

Catherine Barnard, City Solicitor's Educational Trust Lecturer in Law, Jean Monnet Chair of European Integration, University of Southampton.

Fiona Campbell-White, law graduate of University of Leicester.

Deirdre Curtin, Professor of the Law of International Organisations, Europe Institute, University of Utrecht.

Tamara K. Hervey, Jean Monnet Lecturer in European Law, Assistant Director of Durham European Law Institute, University of Durham.

María Amor Martín Estébanez, A.S.I.R., Research Fellow, EC Human Capital and Mobility Programme, Institute for Human Rights, Åbo Akademi University.

Herman Meijers, Professor Emeritus of International Law, University of Amsterdam.

Daniela Napoli, Head of the Human Rights Unit, Directorate General of External Political Relations, Commission of the European Communities.

Nanette A. Neuwahl, Lecturer in Law, University of Leicester.

Siofra O'Leary, Visiting Fellow, University of Cadiz. In charge of a project on "Subsidiarity and the Regions in the EC".

David Pollard, teaches Public Law at the University of Leicester.

Allan Rosas, Armfelt Professor of Law, Director of the Institute for Human Rights, Åbo Akademi University.

Malcolm Ross, Jean Monnet Senior Lecturer in EC Law, University of Leicester.

Henry G. Schermers, Professor of the Law of International Organisations, University of Leiden. Member of the European Commission of Human Rights.

Erika Szyszczak, Senior Lecturer in Law, London School of Economics and Political Science.

Paul L.C. Torremans, Lecturer in Law, Assistant Director for Postgraduate Research, University of Leicester.

Patrick M. Twomey, Lecturer in Law, International and European Law Unit, University of Liverpool.

Joseph H.H. Weiler, Manley Hudson Professor of Law, Harvard Law School. Co-director of the Harvard European Law Research Center. Co-director of the Academy of European Law, European University Institute in Florence.

ABBREVIATIONS

ACP	Asian, Caribbean and Pacific States
AJIL	American Journal of International Law
Bull. EC	Bulletin of the European Communities
BYIL	British Yearbook of International Law
CCPR	International Covenant on Civil and Political Rights
CFSP	Common Foreign and Security Policy
CLJ	Cambridge Law Journal
CMLR	Common Market Law Reports
CML Rev.	Common Market Law Review
COM	Commission
COREPER	Comité des représentants permanents
CSCE	Conference on Security and Cooperation in Europe
DG	Directorate General
EAEC	European Atomic Energy Community
EC	European Community
ECHR	Convention for the Protection of Human Rights and Fundamental Freedoms
EHRR	European Human Rights Reports
ECJ	Court of Justice of the European Communities
ECLR	European Competition Law Review
ECR	European Court Reports
ECSC	European Coal and Steel Community
EEA	European Economic Area
EEC	European Economic Community
EIRR	European Industrial Relations Review
EJIL	European Journal of International Law
EL Rev.	European Law Review
ETS	European Treaty Series
EU	European Union
Eu GRZ	Europäische Grundrechte Zeitschrift
HRLJ	Human Rights Law Journal
ICLQ	International and Comparative Law Quarterly
ICR	Industrial Court Report
ILO	International Labour Organisation

ILRM	Irish Law Reports Monthly
IR	Industrial Relations
IRLR	Industrial Relations Law Reports
JCMS	Journal of Common Market Law Studies
JHA	Justice and Home Affairs
KEA	Kraft Export Association (the Pulp, Paper and Paper Board Export Association of the United States)
LIEI	Legal Issues of European Integration
MLR	Modern Law Review
NILR	Netherlands International Law Review
NLJ	New Law Journal
O.J.	Official Journal
OJLS	Oxford Journal of Legal Studies
OSCE	Organization for Security and Cooperation in Europe
P.C.I.J.	Permanent Court of International Justice
RCDIP	Revue Critique de Droit International Privé
Rev. Inst. Eur.	Revista de Instituciones Europeas
RGDIP	Revue Générale de Droit International Public
RMC	Revue du marché commun et de l'union européenne
RTDE	Revue Trimestrielle de Droit Européen
SEA	Single European Act
SEC	Document of the Secretariat-General of the Commission
TEU	Treaty on European Union
YB ECHR	Yearbook of the European Convention on Human Rights
YEL	Yearbook of European Law
ZaöRV	Zeitschrift für ausländisches öffentliches Recht und Völkerrecht

1 THE TREATY ON EUROPEAN UNION: A STEP FORWARD IN THE PROTECTION OF HUMAN RIGHTS?

Nanette A. Neuwahl

1 INTRODUCTION

With Europe being on the move from an "economic constitution" to a "political constitution", it is legitimate to ask: what about human rights? Both as a guarantee of democracy, as a limit to the power of public authority, and as legitimation of that authority in terms of the rule of law, human rights are a key notion. This is well understood by the drafters of the Treaty on European Union (TEU), who took care to devote specific Treaty articles to human rights. In particular, Article F(2) TEU provides that:

> the Union shall respect fundamental rights, as guaranteed by the European Convention for the Protection of Human Rights and Fundamental Freedoms signed in Rome on 4 November 1950 and as they result from the constitutional traditions common to the Member States, as general principles of Community law.

As the Treaties establishing the European Communities did not contain any specific provision on fundamental rights, one may ask whether the TEU constitutes or can provide the basis for a real step forward in the protection of human rights. In order to cast somewhat more clarity on this issue the practice of the Community institutions before the conclusion of the TEU has to be examined just as much as the new provisions and the prospects for the future.

2 THE REASONS FOR A GENUINE HUMAN RIGHTS CONCERN IN THE COMMUNITY

The original Community Treaties were not concerned with human rights. They were of a relatively narrow (economic) scope and at the time one could still

1

N. A. Neuwahl and A. Rosas (eds.), The European Union and Human Rights, 1–22.

consider it unlikely that the Community could infringe human rights at all. However this may be, this context has now changed.

First of all, because of the evolution of the Community legal order and the growth of activity of the institutions, people's daily lives are more and more affected by Community law; rights of individuals are increasingly at issue and more and more different human rights can become threatened.

The creation of the Single Market is only one case in point: the abolition of frontier controls within the Community and the concomitant intensification of controls at its external borders and also within Member States raise questions of human rights, especially in relation to matters such as terrorism and organized crime, drug traffic, AIDS, refugees, racism and xenophobia.

In addition, the transformation of industry taking place since the entry into force of the Founding Treaties, with on the one hand increased competition and on the other hand the emergence of trans-European industries with enormous economic power and social impact—in itself beneficial—raises fears that weaker elements of society may be exploited. Consequently, there is an increased concern with the "social dimension" of market integration.

Also technological changes have come to raise new transboundary questions. Satellite television, for instance, poses the question of freedom of information and expression; and also the trans-border flow of information through electronic mailing systems and multinational databases raises questions which a national legislator alone is insufficiently equipped to solve.

Another reason for the Community to take fundamental rights into account is that the protection of human rights furthers the evolution of a European identity: Even if many people in these Western societies will live their lives without ever experiencing a violation of their fundamental human rights, the knowledge that one's rights are being protected and that one lives in a political society which takes such rights seriously stimulates the emergence of a group consciousness, which may go beyond national frontiers. From the viewpoint of a citizens' Europe of course the protection of human rights can be seen as one of the aspects which make Europe "meaningful".

Furthermore, an adequate protection of human rights also strengthens the Community in the relations with its Member States. The protection of human rights is a primary task which all the Member States set themselves. If the Community does not actively protect human rights the Community legal order may come under pressure because the national courts, who regard fundamental human rights as inalienable, might refuse an application of Community law allegedly inconsistent with such principles. So much is clear from the case law of the constitutional courts of Germany and Italy on the matter (see below, Section 3).

Finally, if the Court of Justice of the European Communities (ECJ) in Luxembourg assumes full responsibility for ensuring the respect for human rights, it is in a position to construe the relevant Community law and its meaning in the light of such fundamental principles, and can thus ensure the uniform application of the law in the same way as it does with European Community law in general. The ECJ's concern with human rights can therefore also have a unifying effect as regards the law which is being applied. The same is true, of course, of an active stand by the Community legislator.

For all those reasons a concern with human rights in the European Community is amply justified.

3   THE PRESSURE BY MEMBER STATES' COURTS

The concern of the Community institutions, including the ECJ, with human rights arose largely in response to the preoccupation voiced by the constitutional courts of Germany and Italy that Community law and its implementation, if it were not to go unchecked, might have to be reviewable in some way or another before national courts.[1] Since the latter would have impeded the uniform and harmonious development of Community law, the ECJ had little choice but to assert its jurisdiction in matters of human rights.

That the Italian and German courts played this part may be explained by the fact that the experience of these countries with human rights violations under their former fascist regimes made them most conscious of the issue. After the Second World War both Germany and Italy had introduced new constitutions with charters of rights and constitutional courts to define and interpret them. Over the years these courts had built up a fine body of constitutional law and they were perhaps more sensitive than the courts of countries with a happier constitutional history to the importance of defending constitutional rights. Thus, when the ECJ was making claims to authority to override the constitutions of the Member States in the name of the Treaty of Rome, the fact that it did so without reference to rights guaranteed in national constitutions was considered most disturbing.

The matter culminated in 1974 in the *German Internationale Handelsgesellschaft* case[2] (the *first "solange"* case). A German firm

---

[1] See Jacobs, "The Protection of Human Rights in the Member States of the European Community: The Impact of the Court of Justice", in O'Reilly (ed.), *Human Rights and Constitutional Law* (1992), pp. 243–250.

[2] *Internationale Handelsgesellschaft* case, 29 May 1974, [1974] 2 CMLR 551.

challenged before a German *Verwaltungsgericht* (administrative court) the import and export licensing system provided for under the common organization of the grain market. The grant of licences was conditional upon the lodging of a deposit, which was forfeited if the licence was not or not totally used during its period of validity. In the view of the plaintiffs this was against the principle of the protection of private property guaranteed by the German Constitution. The case went all the way up to the ECJ and down again. When the matter came before the German Constitutional Court (the *Bundesverfassungsgericht*), this court stated that as long as the Community is not endowed with a catalogue of fundamental rights, adopted by a directly elected and representative European Parliament and equivalent to the one in the German *Grundgesetz*, German courts should not apply Community legislation which conflicts with the *Grundgesetz*. If a German court considers that a provision of Community legislation clashes with a fundamental right recognized in the Basic Law and is therefore inapplicable, it must use the procedure for the control of constitutionality before the German Constitutional Court.

It is worth noting that the Constitutional Court in this judgment reaffirms its earlier case law that the Community legal order is a distinct legal order, separate from that emanating from the German authorities, and that therefore Community law cannot be assessed on its validity by a German court. This can be done only by the ECJ—in a preliminary ruling under Article 177 EEC Treaty or otherwise. However, the *Bundesverfassungsgericht* rejects the idea that acts of implementation or execution of Community law by the German authorities, including the courts, could be contrary to human rights recognized in the German Basic Law. German authorities may therefore not give application to Community law if this would conflict with the *Grundgesetz*.

This judgment of the *Bundesverfassungsgericht* was not supported by all the judges, and it was highly criticized by scholars as well as by the Commission of the EC. Its implications are on strain with the principle of supremacy of Community law. Whereas many thought it was unlikely that Community law could infringe human rights, this judgment implied that parties could now challenge the constitutionality of Community law before German courts. These would then consider whether or not they should bring the matter before the Constitutional Court, if appropriate after a reference to the ECJ for a preliminary ruling. All this would delay the full application of Community law in Germany and would detract from its authority.

Understandably, the attitude of the German Constitutional Court caused dismay in the European Community. The ECJ in the same year affirmed in the *second Nold* case[3] that the law which it was called to interpret drew inspiration from common constitutional traditions of the Member States. The ECJ thereby acknowledged that the delegation by Governments of wide-ranging powers to Community institutions entailed that these could not be exercised otherwise than in a constitutional manner. The ECJ also stated that in searching for the common constitutional values of the Community, it would look at treaties and conventions entered into by the Member States, and in particular at the Convention for the Protection of Human Rights and Fundamental Freedoms (European Convention on Human Rights; ECHR).

Three years later the European Parliament, the Council and the Commission, in their Joint Declaration on Human Right dated 5 April 1977[4] declared themselves bound in their actions by the general principles contained in the constitutions of the Member States and in the ECHR. Other important documents related to or specifically dealing with human rights would follow.[5] The approach of the Community was also "endorsed" by the Member States in the Single European Act (SEA), which refers in its preamble to "the fundamental rights recognized in the constitutions and laws of the Member States, in the Convention for the Protection of Human Rights and Fundamental Freedoms and the European Social Charter, notably freedom, equality and social justice".

Eventually, in 1986 the *Bundesverfassungsgericht* was "mollified" and revised its position. In the *second "solange"* case[6] it found that the Community was offering a protection of human rights comparable to that of the German Constitution. By consequence, the German Constitutional Court ruled that it would not exercise its jurisdiction on the question whether Community legislation was sufficiently in conformity with German consti-tutional requirements, *as long as* (in German: *"solange"*) the Community itself continued to protect fundamental rights at the present level. Like the *first*

---

[3] Case 4/73, *Nold v Commission,* [1974] ECR 491.

[4] O.J. 1977, C 103/1.

[5] E.g., the Declaration Against Racism and Xenophobia of 11 June 1986 adopted by the European Parliament, the Council and the Representatives of the Member States within the Council; the European Parliament Declaration of Fundamental Rights and Freedoms of 12 April 1989; the Resolution on the Fight Against Racism and Xenophobia adopted by the Council and the Representatives of the Member States meeting within the Council on 29 May 1990, and the Resolution on Human Rights, Democracy and Development of 28 Nov. 1991 adopted by the Council and the Member States meeting within the Council. A compilation of these and other human rights documents can be found in Duparc, *The European Community and Human Rights,* Commission of the European Communities, Luxembourg, 1992.

[6] *Internationale Handelsgesellschaft* case, 22 Oct. 1986, [1987] 3 CMLR 225.

"solange" case, this decision is conditional, this time in the sense that the Constitutional Court will not exercise its jurisdiction as long as an appropriate standard of protection of fundamental rights is maintained. This condition is fulfilled at present, but the Constitutional Court reserves its power to exercise its jurisdiction should the situation change.

4   THE EVOLUTION OF THE CASE LAW OF
THE COURT OF JUSTICE OF THE EUROPEAN COMMUNITIES

The following overview of the case law of the ECJ will show to what extent the human rights protection offered by the ECJ could develop without explicit Treaty articles dealing with the matter. It will be seen that the jurisdiction of the ECJ in matters of human rights has been continually expanding.

4.1 Establishing a concern with human rights

One of the first timid references to human rights can be found 1969 in the *Stauder* case.[7] This concerned a Decision of the Commission, who, in the light of the Community's surplus of butter, had authorized Member States to allow the sale of this particular product at reduced prices to certain categories of persons in need. In order to prevent the abuse of this privilege by fraud, applicants had to produce certain documents, which in the German language version of the Decision included their identity card. One of the recipients, who considered this requirement to be contrary to human dignity, challenged the validity of this requirement before a German administrative court.

When the matter was referred to it in a preliminary ruling, the ECJ denied a breach of human rights on the facts, but it stated in an *obiter dictum* that "fundamental rights are enshrined in the general principles of Community law and protected by the Court".

This may have been new, but it was not a very bold innovation. No legal system can do without general principles to fill in gaps in the positive law. Also, it should be recalled that Article 164 (then) EEC Treaty provides: "The Court of Justice shall ensure that in the interpretation and application of this Treaty the law is observed." The expression "the law" can be understood as including the general principles of law to be observed in the Community. It does, however, not answer the question where these principles are to be taken from.

---

[7] Case 29/69, *Stauder* v *Ulm,* [1969] ECR 419.

The picture becomes clearer in the *Internationale Handelsgesellschaft* case,[8] the preliminary ruling by the ECJ preceding the *first "solange"* judgment of the *Bundesverfassungsgericht*. As will be recalled, in this case it was submitted that the Community Decision in question, laying down the deposit system referred to earlier on, was void for infringing a basic guarantee of the German Constitution, the protection of property rights. The ECJ denied that it could apply a guarantee contained in the German Constitution. However, the ECJ reaffirmed the *Stauder* case ("fundamental rights are enshrined in the general principles of Community law and protected by the Court"), specifying in addition that the protection of such (fundamental) rights, whilst "inspired by the constitutional traditions common to the Member States", must be ensured "within the framework of the structure and objectives of the Community". The ECJ examined whether the deposit system infringed fundamental rights and found that it did not.

If *Stauder* confirmed the existence of fundamental rights in Community law and *Internationale Handelsgesellschaft* identified their primary source as the constitutional traditions of the Member States, the landmark *second Nold* case referred to earlier on[9] introduced a secondary source: international treaties for the protection of human rights. This case, also involving property rights, became one of the leading cases on human rights because the ECJ for the first time clearly announced that it would quash any provision of Community legislation which was contrary to the fundamental principles enshrined in the constitutions of the Member States.

The *second Nold* case is therefore important for two reasons: first, the ECJ affirms that it would strike down any provisions of Community legislation which were contrary to the fundamental rights protected by the constitutions of the Member States, and second, it adds that international treaties for the protection of human rights can supply guidelines which should be followed within the framework of Community law. The following quote from the judgment neatly summarizes the position of the ECJ on human rights:

> In safeguarding these rights, the ECJ is bound to draw inspiration from constitutional traditions common to the Member States, and it cannot therefore uphold measures which are incompatible with fundamental rights recognized and protected by the Constitutions of those States.

---

[8] Case 11/70, *Internationale Handelsgesellschaft* v *Einfuhr- und Vorratsstelle Getreide*, [1970] ECR 1125.

[9] Case 4/73, loc. cit., note 3.

7

Similarly, the ECJ continues, "international treaties for the protection of human rights on which the Member States have collaborated or of which they are signatories can supply guidelines which should be followed within the framework of Community law".

After this case the ECJ repeatedly referred explicitly to the ECHR, and later also to other treaties on which the Member States have collaborated or of which they are signatories. The following are only the most well-known examples.

In *Hauer*[10] the ECJ tested a Council Regulation prohibiting the planting of vines against the right to property, which, it stated, was guaranteed in the Community legal order in accordance with the ideas common to the constitutions of the Member States, and also reflected in Protocol No. 1 to the ECHR.

In *National Panasonic*[11] the ECJ considered whether it was contrary to fundamental rights for the Commission to carry out investigations—provided for by a Community Regulation—on the premises of a firm without prior warning. The ECJ referred to Article 8 ECHR, which allows exceptions to the right to privacy in cases where interference with this right is necessary in view of the public interest. No infringement was established. Later the ECJ established explicitly that the right to privacy was restricted to private dwellings of private persons.[12]

In the *second Defrenne* case[13] the ECJ stated that the elimination of discrimination based on sex formed part of fundamental rights, and inspiration was drawn from the European Social Charter and Convention No. 111 of the International Labour Organisation. However, the ECJ held that at the time the question was referred to it the Community had not assumed any responsibility for supervising the observance of this principle by the Member States.

In other cases the ECJ has also accepted, for instance, the freedom to practice one's religion,[14] the right of respect for private life,[15] the inviolability of the domicile,[16] the freedom of expression,[17] the right to

---

[10] Case 44/79, *Hauer* v *Land Rheinland-Pfalz,* [1979] ECR 3727.

[11] Case 136/79, *National Panasonic* v *Commission,* [1980] ECR 2033.

[12] Joined Cases 97–99/87, *Dow Chemical Ibérica and Others* v *Commission,* [1989] ECR 3165, at 3185, para. 15.

[13] Case 149/77, *Defrenne* v *Sabena (No. 2),* [1978] ECR 1365.

[14] Case 130/75, *Prais* v *Council,* [1976] ECR 1589.

[15] Case 165/82, *Commission* v *United Kingdom,* [1983] ECR 3431.

[16] I.a., Joined Cases 97–99/87, loc. cit., note 12.

freely pursue trade and professional activities,[18] the right to form trade unions,[19] as well as the principle of "democracy" or rather, the safeguarding of the representation of interests in the Community.[20]

4.2 Expansion of the field of protection

The concern of the ECJ for ensuring observance of human rights is now a longstanding one. But there have recently been some significant developments.

The earlier decisions of the ECJ were primarily concerned with the validity of Community provisions. More recently the issue has arisen of the ways in which provisions of Community law are implemented in the law of the Member States. In fact this is but a logical development from the earlier case law. The idea is, that Member States who interpret Community law in such a way that it would infringe human rights would thereby infringe Community law. Broadly speaking, therefore, whereas the earlier case law was largely concerned with the protection of human rights against the Community institutions, the concern of the more recent case law seems to be the principle that throughout the entire field of Community law human rights must be protected at the level of the Member States as well.

Wachauf[21] is the leading case in this respect. The issue was again the compatibility of Community provisions with fundamental rights, but the ECJ held that "those requirements are also binding on the Member States when they implement Community rules". The point in this case was that in Germany, Community legislation was implemented in such a way that people who transferred their agricultural business could be deprived of their milk quota without being able to realize its economic value. In these circumstances the ECJ centred on the issue, not whether the Community provision in question was invalid, but whether the adoption by the Member State of such a mode of implementation was in conformity with the principle of the protection of the right to property. As a result, the holder of the quota might in such a case be entitled to receive compensation from the Member State as a matter of Community law.

---

[17] Case C-100/88, *Oyowe and Traore* v *Commission,* [1989] ECR 4285.

[18] Case 249/83, *Hoeckx* v *Openbaar Centrum voor Maatschappelijk Welzijn, Kalmthout,* [1985] ECR 973, at 982.

[19] Case 175/73, *Union Syndicale, Massa and Kortner* v *Council,* [1974] ECR 917.

[20] Case 139/79, *Maizena GmbH* v *Council,* [1980] ECR 3393. For a more recent example see Case C-300/89, *Commission* v *Council (Titanium Dioxide),* [1991] ECR I-2867.

[21] Case C-5/88, *Wachauf* v *Federal Republic of Germany,* [1989] ECR 2609.

So in *Wachauf* we see that the ECJ not merely supervises Community action, but also Member State action on its conformity with human rights.

However, not in all areas in which Community law is relevant the protection of human rights against infringements by Member State action can be required. In *Cinéthèque*[22] the ECJ had to consider the compatibility with the EEC Treaty of a French law which temporarily restricted the issue in videocassette form of films released for the cinema. Having examined the compatibility of that law with the Treaty, the ECJ also referred to an argument raised during the proceedings to the effect that the French measure was in breach of Article 10 ECHR (freedom of expression). In this connection the ECJ states that:

> although it is the duty of the Court to ensure observance of fundamental rights in the field of Community law, it has no power to examine the compatibility with the European Convention of national legislation which concerns, as in this case, an area which falls within the jurisdiction of the national legislator.

By so providing, the ECJ therefore establishes a distinction between cases where Member States are implementing Community law and cases where the matter is within the jurisdiction of the Member States themselves, even if questions of Community law may also arise. In the latter case the ECJ will not intervene. Similarly, in *Demirel*[23] the ECJ found that:

> the national rules at issue did not have to implement a provision of Community law. In those circumstances, the Court does not have jurisdiction to determine whether national rules such as those at issue are compatible with the principles enshrined in Article 8 of the ECHR.

Again there appears to be a difference between areas which are within what one may call the primary competence of the national legislator—because they fall outside the scope of Community law—and areas where the national legislator is confined to implementing Community legislation on the subject.

A further extension of the jurisdiction of the ECJ occurred, however, in the *ERT* case,[24] where the ECJ interpreted *Wachauf* in broader terms. In this case the Greek Government defended the Greek television broadcasting

---

[22] Joined Cases 60 and 61/84, *Cinéthèque* v *Fédération nationale des cinémas français*, [1985] ECR 2605.

[23] Case 12/86, *Demirel* v *Stadt Schwäbisch Gmünd*, [1987] ECR 3719.

[24] Case C-260/89, *Elliniki Radiophonia Tileorassi (ERT)*, [1991] ECR I-2925.

monopoly as a public policy derogation from the free movement of services under Article 66 EC Treaty.

The ECJ stated that the restrictions on the freedom to provide services and the justification of such restrictions under Articles 56 and 66 EC Treaty for reasons of public order, public security and public health must be understood in the light of the general principle of freedom of expression, enshrined in Article 10 ECHR.[25] In other words, the national legislation in question may only benefit from the exceptions provided for by the combined provisions of Articles 56 and 66 EC Treaty if it is acting in conformity with fundamental rights.

As a result the jurisdiction of the ECJ is now affirmed, not only in respect to national measures taken in implementation of Community law, but also in respect to measures taken in the exercise of discretionary powers foreseen by Community law, since they are considered to be within the scope of Community law. In terms of the ECJ, "Measures which are incompatible with respect for human rights, which are recognized and guaranteed in Community law, could not be admitted in the Community."[26]

To summarize, the case law of the ECJ in this area appears to be evolving. The review by the ECJ of compliance with human rights has developed from review of measures adopted by the Community institutions themselves (the *second Nold* case) to "review" of measures adopted by Member States in implementing Community measures (*Wachauf*) and more recently to "review" of measures adopted by the Member States which, in one way or another, fall within the scope of Community law (the *ERT* case). The concern with human rights is recognized in the Community, and the case law of the ECJ is flourishing, even though there is no bill of rights nor any general guarantee of fundamental rights in the Community Treaties.[27]

4.3 The limits of protection

In its present state European Community law does not play a significant role with regard to the protection of human rights within the sphere of the residual powers of the Member States. This makes that the ECJ is rather vulnerable to

---

[25] Para. 41 of the judgment.

[26] Ibid.

[27] Some questions which are still open are, e.g., what would happen in case of conflicts, should these exist, of the Founding Treaties with fundamental human rights principles, or to what extent rights protected in only one of the Member States but not in the other can be relevant in the Community legal order.

criticism:[28] sometimes the ECJ is being reproached not to take human rights seriously, at other times it is reproached of encroaching on Member States' powers.

In this context it is instructive to dwell on a case decided by the ECJ in 1985:[29] Mrs *Diatta,* a Senegalese national, was the wife of a Frenchman working in Berlin, and therefore entitled under Community law to reside in Germany. However, the couple separated and intended to divorce. When the residence permit of Mrs Diatta came up for renewal, the Berlin Chief Commissioner of Police declined to do so on the grounds that Mrs Diatta was no longer a member of the family of a Community national, and hence she no longer enjoyed the right to reside in Germany. The administrative court in Berlin upheld the refusal, even though it considered that formally Mrs Diatta was still married.

The matter was then referred to the ECJ in a preliminary ruling relating to the interpretation of Regulation 1612/68 on the free movement of workers and their families. The ECJ held that under that Regulation it is not necessary for a member of the family of a migrant worker to live with the worker permanently under the same roof. In addition, the marriage cannot be regarded as dissolved as long as it has not been terminated by the competent authority. However, the ECJ went on to find that the Regulation in question did not confer on members of a migrant family an independent right of residence, even if they wished to pursue an activity as employed person in the territory of the host Member State.

The implication of the ruling was therefore that once the divorce was complete, Mrs Diatta was likely to be expelled. Had she been a Community national, she would have had rights of free movement of her own; however, because she had the nationality of a non-Member State, her position was precarious.

In view of this implication, the judgment has been severely criticized as showing insufficient regard for human rights. In the opinion of Weiler,[30] a construction of Community law that empowered a husband to coerce his wife to do things under threat from which followed the consequence that she could be expelled, could compromise the right to human dignity (encapsulated in Article 1 of the European Parliament Declaration of Fundamental Rights and

---

[28] See, e.g., Coppel and O'Neill, "The European Court of Justice: Taking Rights Seriously?", 29 CML Rev. (1992), 669–692.

[29] Case 267/83, *Diatta* v *Land Berlin*, [1985] ECR 567.

[30] Weiler, "Thou Shalt Not Oppress a Stranger: On the Judicial Protection of the Human Rights of Non-EC Nationals—A Critique", 3 EJIL (1992), 65–91.

Freedoms), or it could compromise the right to family life if the husband gained custody over the children and such expulsion could severe the relationship between mother and child. According to Weiler the ECJ should have said that the spouse may not be expelled if such expulsion would compromise his or her fundamental rights.[31]

Again, if the ECJ would have done this it would be reproached by some to interfere with the remaining powers of the Member State, while it would probably not change anything about the legal situation of Mrs Diatta. It is important to accept, I think, that the Community legal order is characterized by a distribution of law-making powers between the Community and the Member State. This may not always be immediately clear, as it depends on substantive criteria (relating to the subject-matter involved) as well as on normative criteria (legislative function for the Community, executive function for the Member States), but it is nevertheless a reality of the present state of integration.

5   THE TREATY ON EUROPEAN UNION

We now come to the TEU. The object is to see whether Maastricht is a step forward or not, and which problems are left to be resolved for the future.

First of all, according to Article F(2) TEU:

> the Union shall respect fundamental rights, as guaranteed by the European Convention for the Protection of Human Rights and Fundamental Freedoms signed in Rome on 4 November 1950 and as they result from the constitutional traditions common to the Member States, as general principles of Community law.

What does this article add? At first sight it is merely a restatement of what the ECJ has been establishing as from the late 1960s. However, some apparent novelties can also be observed.

In particular, we may observe that the reference to human rights and the ECHR is now contained in a Treaty article, not merely in a paragraph of a preamble, as was the case in the SEA. In the view of some scholars this implies that the material provisions of the ECHR have been introduced into the Community legal order, and the TEU therefore gives rise to a strict legal obligation to observe the ECHR. In the past the ECJ has only used the ECHR

---

[31] Ibid., at 88.

13

as a source of inspiration. The ECJ would establish on a case-by-case basis whether any rights contained in the ECHR, or rather similar rights, would be applicable in the Community legal order, but the Community was not legally bound by the convention as such. This would now be different.

I do not think, however, that it can be maintained that the Community moved from "no obligation" to obligation. The Community and the Member States are bound to observe human rights in so far as they are part of the general principles of Community law. The ECHR is part of those principles to the extent that it is expressive of the common constitutional traditions of the Member States. In other words, there already exists a strict legal obligation to observe human rights, including those enumerated in the ECHR. It is difficult to see what Article F(2) could add to this. Are there perhaps any principles in the ECHR which are not part of the common constitutional traditions of the Member States?

Another matter of interest is that Article F(2) provides that fundamental rights must be respected "as they are guaranteed by the ECHR", suggesting that the TEU brings along a change in the protection of human rights in so far the interpretation of the rights contained in the ECHR is concerned: these rights must be protected as they are guaranteed by the European Commission of Human Rights rather than as they would be interpreted in the Community context. However, it can hardly be assumed that this would be the intention of the parties to the Maastricht Treaty, since such an interpretation might be objectionable. If the ECHR is incorporated in the TEU, surely the interpretation which is applicable in the context of the Union should prevail, rather than the one which would apply in the wider European context, for the latter could mean that, in some cases at least, a more lenient interpretation may be given to the provisions of the ECHR than the one which it could have in the context of the Community. Such an interpretation could therefore be counterproductive. The better view seems to be that, while the article reaffirms the obligation to observe the ECHR, the interpretation to be given to the rights contained in the Convention may be different from that given to it in the wider European context. In principle, a lower human rights protection than that under the ECHR should of course be excluded. Also in this respect, therefore, Article F(2) seems to reaffirm the status quo.

One step forward under the TEU is that the obligation under Article F(2) covers a much larger area than the EC Treaties. This is due to the fact that the TEU itself covers a much larger area, including also the two intergovernmental "pillars" of the Union, the Common Foreign and Security Policy (CFSP) regulated in Title V and Justice and Home Affairs (JHA) in Title VI. Because Article F(2) is contained in the Common Provisions, it is applicable to all the pillars.

However, the practical importance of this is not immediately clear, because the parts of the Maastricht Treaty concerned with these other two pillars, Title V and Title VI, contain their own specific references to human rights. I shall come back to this later on.

A final apparent novelty introduced by the Maastricht Treaty is that by virtue of its Final Provisions, and more specifically Article L, all the articles contained in the section "Common Provisions" have been excluded from the jurisdiction of the ECJ, as have Titles V and VI.

In this respect, two questions need to be asked. First, if the ECJ's jurisdiction is excluded for matters dealt with in the Common Provisions, does this affect the jurisdiction of the ECJ as exercised in connection with the EC Treaty? Second, what is the sense of laying down an obligation to respect the ECHR and then not make it justiciable?

As regards the first question, I think one can rest assured. That the jurisdiction of the ECJ over human rights matters in connection with the European Community is not restricted by the Final Provisions can be seen from a comparative study of the relevant provisions. First of all, Article M TEU provides that:

> Subject to the provisions amending the [Treaties establishing the European Communities] and to these final provisions, nothing in this treaty shall affect the Treaties establishing the European Communities or the subsequent Treaties and Acts modifying or supplementing them.

This can be taken to mean that in so far as Article F(2) does not amend the EC Treaty, including Article 164, the powers of the ECJ under that Treaty remain unaffected. In addition, it should not be forgotten that Article L explicitly affirms the jurisdiction of the ECJ in matters relating to, *inter alia,* the EC Treaty. Again, this may be deemed to include the application of that Treaty in the light of the fundamental principles on which it is based. Thus, from the explicit reference to areas of law in Article L one may conclude *a contrario* that the jurisdiction of the ECJ is only excluded in matters not mentioned or implied in that Article.

In sum, the jurisdiction of the ECJ to consider matters in connection with the EC Treaty remains intact. What is excluded by Article L, so it seems, is that the ECJ exercises jurisdiction in human rights (and other) cases involving *exclusively* Titles V and VI relating to CFSP and JHA. But if, for instance, the ECJ would annul a Council Regulation imposing sanctions on a developing country on the grounds of infringement of human rights, one would think it should be able to do so even if the consequence of this were that a joint action in the field of CFSP must remain ineffective. Any other conclusion would have as a result that the jurisdiction of the ECJ would indeed be curtailed, and this would conflict with the interpretation of Article L presented above.

As regards the other question (what sense does it make to lay down a strict legal obligation and refuse to adjudicate it, in the field of CFSP and JHA), opinions may differ. Some would say the provision thereby loses all its meaning. Others would hold that an involvement by the ECJ in matters of intergovernmental co-operation is objectionable. This is not sustainable, if only because there are institutional overlaps between the different pillars. If the ECJ is not willing or not able to exercise its jurisdiction over acts of the Community institutions in the intergovernmental pillars, one may ask which authority will be able to do so.

However this may be, the following *interim* conclusion is due: by incorporating the ECHR, the Maastricht Treaty broadens the human rights concern in the Union as opposed to that of the EEC, since it also applies to fields covered by the intergovernmental pillars. However, this innovation is considerably scaled down by the fact that a control of the observance of human rights in these fields by the ECJ is in principle excluded.

Another thing which regrettably has remained the same is that the TEU does not contain a catalogue of human rights. The Commission, who has been considering since long the possibility of drawing up such a catalogue, has expressed doubts that a satisfactory list of rights could ever be established because there are differences in the fundamental rights protection of the Member States. This would make it difficult for some of them to accept a codification of fundamental rights as binding in its entirety. Indeed, especially economic and social rights are protected in different ways in different Member States. For the same reason it is feared that the Community, when attempting to draw up a list of human rights, would by necessity take a minimalist approach and be able to agree only on the lowest common denominator of such rights.

The European Parliament Declaration of Fundamental Rights and Freedoms of 12 April 1989[32] was a first attempt to produce a charter of fundamental rights for the Community. It centres around fundamental rights recognized by the ECJ in its case law, with some minor additions.

It proclaims a number of classic concepts such as human dignity, the right to life, equality before the law, freedom of thought and expression, the right to privacy, etc., as well as social rights such as freedom of association, freedom to choose an occupation, the right to strike, social security rights, the

---

[32] O.J. 1989, C 120/51.

right to education and training, etc. Then there follow a number of administrative type rights which already have a recognized place in the Community legal order: access to the courts, the principle of *ne bis in idem,* non-retroactivity. There is also a provision for the right to petition the European Parliament and a declaration that environmental and consumer protection form an integral part of Community policy. Finally, Article 25(1) provides: "This declaration shall afford protection for every citizen in the field of application of Community law."

The impact of the Declaration of Fundamental Rights and Freedoms is mostly symbolic. It is a non-legislative resolution of Parliament. Moreover, until now neither the Commission nor the Council have taken up Parliament's invitation to issue a declaration in support of the Declaration. This may be due to the fact that the Declaration presented some compromising features. For instance, the proposed right of all Member States' citizens to move freely within the Community and the principle of democracy are open to restrictions in conformity with the Community Treaties (Article 8(3) and 17(5)), so that the absence of these two rights is implicitly admitted. For other rights, such as the right to equality between men and women before the law, and for environment and consumer protection, legislative action was required (Article 3(4) and 24(2)), and this was taken as an encroachment on Member States' powers. Possibly, whereas for some Member States the Declaration does not go far enough, for others it does go too far.

The Community Charter on the Fundamental Social Rights of Workers of 9 December 1989[33] illustrates how difficult it is to get the agreement of the Member States on matters of social rights. This Charter, which similarly has no binding legal effect, was adopted by the Heads of State or Government of eleven Member States. The United Kingdom did not adopt the Charter because it considered that many of the matters addressed by it were within the competence of the Member States and it could not agree to a convention which provides for implementation in accordance with the principle of subsidiarity.[34]

The advantages of having a Community catalogue of human rights can be taken from a report of the Commission of 4 February 1974,[35] since they are still valid: It would emphasize the importance of fundamental rights and remove any doubt about their relevance for Community law. It could be tailor-

---

[33] In Clapham, *Human Rights and the European Community: A Critical Overview* (1991), pp. 230–236.

[34] Ibid., Art. 27 of the Charter.

[35] Commission Memorandum on Community Accession to the European Convention for the Protection of Human Rights and Fundamental Freedoms, 4 April 1979. Supplement 2/79 – EC Bull.

made for use in the Union. It would enhance legal certainty. It would be of support to the judiciary, and it would facilitate the exercise of economic and social rights, most of which would require legislative measures to take effect. The establishment of a catalogue of human rights would therefore be valuable.

The chance to append a catalogue of human rights to the TEU has, however, been missed, and the European Parliament's Resolution or the Community Charter cannot aspire to fulfill a comparable role. The Draft Constitution of the European Union elaborated by the Human Rights Committee of the European Parliament contains a list of human rights to be protected by the Union. The following legal guarantees are contained in Title VIII of the Draft Constitution: the right to life, human dignity, equality before the law, freedom of conscience, freedom of expression and information, the right to privacy, the right to family life, the freedom of association, the freedom to join trade unions, the right to property, the freedom to choose a profession and conditions of work, collective social rights, social protection, the right to education, the right of access to information, the right to form political parties, access to justice, *ne bis in idem,* non-retroactivity, the right of petition, and the right to respect for the environment. There are also provisions on limitations of human rights, the level of protection, and abuse of rights. However, so far the Draft Constitution has not yet been adopted by the European Parliament.

Another thing which is to be regretted is that the TEU does not make up for the absence of an enforcement mechanism in matters of human rights which is independent of the Community institutions. The Community is not a party to the ECHR and therefore, it is not subject to its control mechanisms. The European Commission of Human Rights has rejected as inadmissible applications of human rights violations by Community institutions by stating that the Community is not a party to the ECHR. Thus, for instance, applications against the European Parliament have failed because of a lack of jurisdiction *ratione personae* of the European Commission of Human Rights.[36] Civil servants of the Community therefore have no other remedies against infringements of their human rights by their employer than those which are provided by himself, and individuals in Member States whose rights are infringed by the Community cannot complain in Strasbourg against the

---

[36] Cf. Applications No. 8030/77, *Confédération Française Démocratique du Travail* v *European Communities,* Decision of 10 July 1978, Decisions and Reports 13 (1979); No. 11574/85, *Associazione spirituale per l'unificazione del mondo* v *Italy,* Decision of 5 Oct. 1987; No. 13258/87, *M. & Co.* v *Federal Republic of Germany*, Decision of 9 Feb. 1990, Decisions and Reports 64 (1990); No. 13539/88, *Christine Dufay* v *European Communities, subs., the collectivity of Member States,* Decision of 19 Jan. 1989.

Community institutions. Acts promulgated by the Community enjoy a sort of "immunity from the Convention".

Claims against the Community Member States for breach of the Convention by the Community have hitherto also been unsuccessful. In 1988, for instance, an applicant[37] who alleged breach of the ECHR by the Community institutions subsidiarily made a claim against all the Community Member States. The Commission of Human Rights explicitly left open the question whether a breach of the ECHR by the Community could entail the responsibility of its Member States, but it stated that the legal remedies available from the ECJ were to be counted as local remedies the exhaustion of which was required under Article 26 ECHR before an application could be considered. The question therefore seems both unresolved and removed from the agenda.

The possibility of challenging the national implementation or execution of Community provisions for non-compliance with the ECHR is also uncertain. In 1987 a private firm launched an application against Germany because the courts of that country had confirmed the execution of a decision by the Commission, supported by the ECJ, to impose a fine against it.[38] In the opinion of the applicant the German authorities breached the ECHR by executing a decision of the ECJ which offended against the ECHR.

First, the Commission of Human Rights established its jurisdiction, arguing that the German authorities had acted in their capacity of organs of a State Party to the ECHR rather than as quasi-Community authorities. By virtue of Article 1 ECHR, the States Parties to the European Convention on Human Rights are responsible "regardless of whether the act or omission in question is a consequence of domestic law or regulations or of the necessity to comply with international obligations". Then the Commission of Human Rights observed that such states remain free to transfer competencies to an international organization, as long as it is ensured that this organization provides an equal protection of human rights. As this condition appeared to be fulfilled in the case of the Community, witness the practice of the ECJ concerning the guarantes of the ECHR and also the Declaration of 1977, the Commission felt it may not assess whether the execution of a decision of the ECJ by a Member State court is contrary to the ECHR.

With this decision the European Commission of Human Rights has therefore taken a position comparable to the German *Bundesverfassungsgericht* in the *second "solange"* case. As a result, next to Community acts also their

---

[37] Application No. 13539/88, loc. cit., note 36.

[38] Application No. 13258/87, loc. cit., note 36.

implementation and execution by the Member States is in principle excluded from the control by the Strasbourg institutions.

In my opinion, because the Community itself is excepted *de facto* and *de jure* from the jurisdiction of the Strasbourg institutions, it is indispensable that it adhere to the ECHR. This is not so much because perhaps the Member States might be held responsible for breaches of human rights by the Community institutions. It is basically just for the same reasons as the Member States have for being parties to this Convention. In addition, however, being a party to the ECHR would also enhance the Community's image on the international plane; since the Community supports the protection of human rights in other societies (notably in the context of the OSCE) and the Member States refer to the ECHR as a model for the protection of human rights, it is difficult to understand why the Community would not adhere to the Convention.

There are said to be several inconveniences to this option. First, the ECHR is more than 40 years old and is not entirely representative of contemporary European standards, particularly as economic and social rights are lacking.[39] Also, the accession of the Community to the ECHR would take much of the wind out of the sails of those who would prefer to see the Community establish its own charter of human rights. This is not the context to assess these criticisms in depth, but one could say that, since a more stringent protection of human rights within the Community is not excluded by the accession to the ECHR, this argument is not wholly convincing.

Also, it is said to be doubtful whether the Community has the capacity to accede to the ECHR. Admittedly, there are technical problems involved in an accession of the Community to the Convention, *inter alia,* because the ECHR is open to states only. However, these problems, of a technical rather than a political nature, can be overcome.

A more serious difficulty is that there are objections by some of the Member States, notably the United Kingdom and to a lesser extent Ireland and Denmark. If the Community would accede to the ECHR, that Convention would become part of the internal legal order of the Member States. The problem is that in the United Kingdom, a dualist Member State, the ECHR has not been introduced into the national legal order. Therefore, this country fears that accession to the ECHR would mean the introduction (through Community

---

[39] Schermers and Waelbroeck, *Judicial Protection in the European Communities* (1987), 4th edn, at p. 40.

law) of the ECHR into the British legal order.[40] The same would be true for Ireland and Denmark.

These arguments can, however, be countered, because accession by the Community would concern only areas covered by Community law. It would not affect the legal systems of the Member States outside this scope, and it would not mean giving the Community general powers in the area of human rights. Since the United Kingdom is already obliged to give effect to those human rights which are binding via the Community legal order in the way established by the ECJ, it is not clear what the United Kingdom would lose.

In sum, therefore, the TEU should have provided for the accession of the Community to the ECHR by a simple majority of votes in the Council. Instead, a decision on accession can now only be taken under Article 235 EC Treaty, and this requires the unanimity of the Member States.[41] In the case of the CFSP and JHA, no treaty-making power seems to have been given.

It has been remarked that the Titles of the TEU relating to the other two pillars of the Union, CFSP and JHA, contain their own references to human rights. Of these, Article K.2(1) provides that:

> The matters referred to in Article K.1 shall be dealt with in compliance with the European Convention for the Protection of Human Rights of 4 November 1950 and the Convention relating to the Status of Refugees of 28 July 1951 and having regard to the protection afforded by Member States to persons persecuted on political grounds.

We have seen that the new obligations to respect human rights in the case of CFSP and JHA are withdrawn from the jurisdiction of the ECJ. At least in one respect this is puzzling: there is an institutional overlap between the pillars, as the Commission, the Council and to some extent the European Parliament act in all three fields. Now, if a Community institution breaches human rights under one of the intergovernmental pillars, there may be no remedy available. Human rights could be enforced only within the individual Member States, if necessary in the context of the supervisory mechanisms in Strasbourg. No remedy would, however, be available against the Community as such. One may therefore ask if the ECJ in Luxembourg should not be willing to exercise a jurisdiction *ratione personae* over the Community institutions in cases where they act contrary to human rights on the basis of Title VI or V. Since the

---

[40] See the comments of the House of Lords' Select Committee on the European Communities, 73rd report 1979–80, HL 326, and 3rd report 1992–93, HL 10.

[41] Also the fact that it merely requires the consultation of European Parliament is to be regretted as this is undeniably a matter of importance to the European citizen.

Council does not seem to have any treaty-making power on matters relating to the CFSP or JHA—and the Union has no such power whatsoever—this matter can not be solved by an accession to the ECHR or other treaties. If the Community pretends to be bound by the ECHR, one may argue, it should at least provide access to justice in accordance with the rule of law, the more so if an action against the Member States jointly does not exist.

It is, however, far from clear whether the ECJ would exercise a jurisdiction *ratione personae* over the Community institutions acting under the intergovernmental pillars, even in the event they would act contrary to human rights. Although there are signs that the ECJ considers that it has to some extent an "inherent" jurisdiction (Case C-2/88, *Zwartveld*[42]), there is considerable opposition against this, and it is therefore unlikely that the ECJ would expand its jurisdiction outside the context of the EC Treaty, especially since its jurisdiction is explicitly excluded from the intergovernmental pillars if the EC Treaty is not concerned. As regards JHA this problem can be overcome either by using the bridge provision of Article K.9 or by concluding conventions under Article K.2(3) with appropriate provisions giving the ECJ the authority to interpret the rules concerned, combined with Community accession to the ECHR. In the case of the CFSP no solution seems available.

6   PROSPECTS

At this stage many questions are still open. The ECJ has been invited to deliver its opinion under Article 228 EC Treaty on the implications of Community accession to the ECHR, and it is hoped that this will provide the institutions with the necessary impetus to go ahead. But even this would not solve everything. To what extent will the ECJ be willing to take the position of a constitutional court? With or without accession to the ECHR, there is the question of the relationship between the case law of the ECJ and decisions taken in Strasbourg. Besides the question which jurisdiction is supreme, one may ask, is there any mutual influence, any friction or practical competition? And, most of all, how will the political institutions take up the exhortation in Article F(2) and elsewhere in the TEU to respect human rights? What will be done to guarantee the respect for human rights not only in the Community, but also in the intergovernmental pillars? All in all, there is a lot to be done in this field, and a lot to be learnt from lawyers and politicians alike.

---

[42] Case C-2/88, *Zwartveld and Others,* [1990] ECR I-3365.

2 ASPECTS OF THE RELATIONSHIP BETWEEN COMMUNITY LAW AND NATIONAL LAW

Siofra O'Leary

1 INTRODUCTION

This chapter revisits the relationship between the Court of Justice of the European Communities (ECJ) and Member State courts as regards the protection of fundamental rights in the context of Community law. It first analyses the content and consequences of a decision of the ECJ (*Grogan*) which located the service of abortion within the scope of the Community's free movement regime and which has subsequently been the subject of considerable and diverse academic comment.[1] The object here is to underline with reference to that case the different legal and political perspectives which may influence the two legal orders in their protection of fundamental rights. What was the effect at national level of the reference of the *Grogan* case[2] to the Court? Thereafter, with reference to new provisions and amendments introduced by the Treaty on European Union (TEU) we discuss the potential for conflict between the national and supranational legal orders. We examine the basis for the symbiotic legal relationship which has existed between the two to date and comment on the possible future of that relationship in the light of these changes. What are the future prospects for harmonious judicial co-operation in the protection of fundamental rights when issues which are highly sensitive at national level increasingly come within the field of Community

---

[1] See Colvin, "Irish Abortion Law and the Free Movement of Services in the European Communities", 15 *Fordham International Law Journal* (1991–1992), 476–526; Coppel and O'Neill, "The European Court of Justice: Taking Rights Seriously?", 29 CML Rev. (1992), 669–692; annotations of the *Grogan* case by Curtin, 29 CML Rev. (1992), 585–603; de Búrca, "Fundamental Human Rights and the Reach of European Community Law", 13 OJLS (1993), 283–319; O'Leary, "The Court of Justice as a Reluctant Constitutional Adjudicator: An Examination of the Abortion Information Case", 17 EL Rev. (1992), 138–157; Phelan, "Right to Life of the Unborn *v.* Promotion of Trade in Services", 55 MLR (1992), 670–689.

[2] Case C-159/90, *Society for the Protection of Unborn Children Ireland* v *Grogan*, [1991] ECR I-4685.

N. A. Neuwahl and A. Rosas (eds.), The European Union and Human Rights, 23–49.

law and therefore subject to the Community's fundamental rights standards?

This chapter would neither be original nor alone in suggesting that the Community and the Union's increased range of competences will increasingly impinge on a wider field of social activities.[3] Indeed, parts of the TEU are the result of the Community's previously expanding competences in areas such as justice and home affairs, education, health and consumer policy, to name but a few.[4] It is argued that the abortion information issue which arose in *Grogan* will not be alone in reflecting the sensitive moral, ideological and political issues which may arise in the context of Community law and which may create tension between the three legal orders in which human rights can be protected in the European Union—national, Community and Council of Europe. Contemporary issues such as the relationship between the broadcasting of pornography and the free provision of services,[5] the Community legal position regarding the social, cultural and religious aspects of Sunday trading,[6] or the relationship between the rights of Union citizens, the free movement of persons and the availability of political asylum, will continue to embroil Community law and the ECJ in the type of issue with respect to which it was once thought to lack competence and with which it was once thought to be badly equipped to deal. Will Article F(2), which contains a specific reference to the Convention for the Protection of Human Rights and Fundamental Freedoms (European Convention on Human Rights; ECHR) and constitutional traditions common to the Member States, or other relevant provisions of the TEU, excite any judicial departure in the manner in which fundamental rights are protected therein? Will it alter the manner in which Member States accept and interact with Community law pursuant to Article 177 EC Treaty, in particular with respect to the protection of fundamental rights? It is still arguable that the absence of a bill of rights in Community law deprives the

---

[3] See, e.g., de Búrca, loc. cit., note 1, at 284; and O'Higgins, "The Constitution and the Communities—Scope for Stress?", in O'Reilly (ed.), *Human Rights and Constitutional Law. Essays in Honour of Brian Walsh* (1992), pp. 227–241, at p. 240.

[4] See Lane, "New Community Competences Under the Maastricht Treaty", 30 CML Rev. (1993), 939–979.

[5] See, for example, *Regina v Secretary of State for National Heritage, ex parte Continental Television BV and Others,* [1993] 2 CMLR 333; and Coleman and McGurtrie, "Too Hot to Handle", 143 NLJ (1993), pp. 10–11.

[6] Case C-145/88, *Torfaen Borough Council v B&Q Plc.,* [1989] ECR 3851.

Treaties of a constitutional status.[7] We must ask, therefore, whether Article F(2) was the appropriate means to provide for the first specific reference to the protection of fundamental rights in the Treaties, given the latter's development into a "constitutional charter based on the rule of law".[8] Does Article F(2) involve the "transposition" of the jurisprudence of the European Court of Human Rights to the Community legal order?

This chapter reintroduces the early criticism by some national constitutional courts of the weakness in the protection of fundamental rights in the Community legal order. In the 1970s, the fear expressed by some Member States was that the Community institutions were not bound by fundamental rights in the exercise of their activities. By making a specific reference to the protection of fundamental rights in Article F(2), the TEU may have finally disposed of the type of national judicial opposition to the principle of supremacy which was witnessed in the *"first solange"*. Nevertheless, the TEU marks a fundamental step in the development of a "closer union" among the peoples of Europe and it has altered a number of the components of the "socio-legal" contract which it has been suggested exists between the Member States and the Community.[9] With reference to the reaction of the Irish Supreme Court in the *Grogan* case it is clear that Member States' fears now revolve around the extent to which Community law (Community institutions now being acceptably bound by fundamental rights), will interfere with the protection of fundamental rights at national level. The smooth legal interaction between national courts and the Community legal order may be threatened by the extent to which national protection of fundamental rights is brought within the jurisdiction of the ECJ. It is generally accepted that a fundamental aspect of Community law is that Member States have transferred sovereignty in numerous fields to the latter and that:[10]

---

[7] See Diaz, *Estado de Derecho y sociedad democratica* (1981); and Diez Picazo, "¿Una Constitucion sin Declaracion de Derechos? (Reflexiones constitucionales sobre los derechos fundamentales en la Comunidad Europea)", 32 *Revista Española de Derecho Constitucional* (1991), 135–155.

[8] See *Opinion 1/91, Re the Draft Treaty on a European Economic Area*, [1992] 1 CMLR 245, at 272.

[9] See Weiler, "Journey to an Unknown Destination: A Retrospective and Prospective of the Court of Justice in the Arena of Political Integration", 31 JCMS (1993), 417–446, at 439, who regards this "socio-legal contract" as the ECJ's provision that "the Community constitutes a new legal order ... for the benefit of which the states have limited their sovereign rights, *albeit within limited fields*". See further *infra*, Section 3.1.

[10] Weiler, "The Transformation of Europe", 100 *The Yale Law Journal* (1991), 2403–2483, at 2414.

in the sphere of application of Community law, any Community norm, be it an article of the Treaty ... or a minuscule administrative regulation enacted by the Commission, "trumps" conflicting national law whether enacted before or after the Community norm.

It remains to be seen whether Member State courts will continue to obediently accept this principle of supremacy now that some of the variables of the "socio-legal contract" which is the basis for the transfer of national sovereignty are changing and now that "the field of Community law" and, therefore, the ambit and scope for the Community's protection of fundamental rights is far less certain and, as regards the Member States, far more intrusive.

2   DELIMITING THE PROTECTION OF FUNDAMENTAL RIGHTS IN COMMUNITY LAW

2.1 Background to the Grogan decision

It was a criminal offence in Ireland to unlawfully procure or assist in the procurement of an abortion.[11] This legislative provision was supported by a constitutional article, inserted following a popular referendum in 1983, which guaranteed the right to life of the unborn child.[12] In 1985, injunctions were sought and granted against welfare clinics which provided non-directive counselling to pregnant women setting out the options, amongst them abortion, available in the case of unwanted pregnancy.[13] In the event that a woman was interested in considering the option of abortion further, the clinics would refer her to medical clinics in Great Britain. Various students' associations in Ireland subsequently issued welfare guides to their members which included information as to the identity, location and method of communication with abortion clinics in the United Kingdom. In *Society for the Protection of Unborn Children* v *Grogan*, the plaintiff sought a declaration in the High Court to the effect that any publication of the aforementioned information was contrary to Article 40.3.3. In refusing to grant the interlocutory relief sought, the High Court judge, exercising her discretion under Article 177 EC Treaty,

---

[11] Sections 58 and 59 of the Offences against the Person Act, 1861.

[12] Art. 40.3.3 of the Irish Constitution provides that "The State acknowledges the right to life of the unborn and, with due regard to the equal right to life of the mother, guarantees in its laws to respect, and, as far as practicable, by its laws to defend and vindicate that right."

[13] [1987] ILRM 477, upheld on appeal in the Supreme Court, [1988] ILRM 19.

decided to refer a number of questions to the ECJ for a preliminary ruling.[14] Both the High Court and Supreme Court had denied the need for a preliminary ruling in *Open Door*.[15] In the *Grogan* case, the High Court judge distinguished *Open Door* on the basis that:

> the single question of entitlement to receive information about the availability or existence of abortion services outside the State, taken on its own, without being associated with assistance to obtain an abortion, was not an issue in that case.

In the Court's view the issue which arose in *Grogan* was the right to impart and receive information and a preliminary ruling on the matter was necessary for the Court to give a final judgment. While not interfering with the lower judge's decision to refer, the Supreme Court was clearly critical of her choice to do so.[16] Given the controversies stirred by the issue of abortion in Ireland and the very explicit challenge to the supremacy of Community law by the highest national court, the importance of the reference of the abortion issue to the ECJ cannot be underestimated. As Weiler points out:[17]

> When a national court *seeks* the Reference it is with few exceptions acknowledging that, at least at face value, Community norms are necessary and govern the dispute. This very issue may be of huge political significance and the subject of controversy among governments or between the Member State as a whole and, say, the Commission. But, the very fact that "their own" national courts make a Preliminary Reference to the European Court of Justice, forces governments to "juridify" their argument and shift to the judicial arena in which the Court of Justice is pre-eminent (*so long as it can carry with it the national judiciary*).

---

[14] [1989] IR 734, [1990] CMLR 689.

[15] The High Court judge concluded that the proceedings related to the activities of the defendants within the state, rendering the provisions of Community law inapplicable. In the Supreme Court, having stated that what was sought to be restrained was assistance to pregnant women to travel abroad and obtain an abortion, the Chief Justice excluded a role for Community law on the ground that this assistance did not amount to a corollary right to whatever rights Irish women could claim under the Treaty.

[16] According to Walsh J., "any judge of first instance who decides to refer a case for a preliminary opinion must bear in mind that such power does not give a completely free and untrammelled power in respect of all other issues in the case", [1990] 1 CMLR 689, at 702. See also the comments by Murphy, "Maastricht, Implementation in Ireland", 19 EL Rev. (1994), 94–104, at 96; and de Búrca, loc. cit., note 1, at 286.

[17] Weiler, loc. cit., note 9, at 422. Emphasis added.

Whether the ECJ and national courts will continue to cohabit in such splendid harmony is the focus of this contribution to the debate on the protection of fundamental rights in the light of the TEU.

2.2 *The decision of the ECJ in* Grogan

The questions referred by the national court sought to establish whether the activities of the abortion clinics constituted services within the meaning of Article 60 EC Treaty and, if so, whether the Treaty provisions on the freedom to supply services precluded a national rule prohibiting the provision of information concerning abortion services legally carried on in another Member State. The ECJ held that the medical termination of pregnancy covers a number of services which are normally provided for remuneration and which fall within the scope of Article 60 EC Treaty.[18] The ECJ failed, however, to dispose of the substantive issue referred to it by the national court pursuant to Article 177 EC Treaty, namely, whether a prohibition on the distribution of information about a service performed in another Member State constituted a restriction within the meaning of Article 59 EC Treaty. The ECJ held that since the link which existed between the providers of the information and the providers of the service operating in another Member State was extremely tenuous, the prohibition could not be regarded as a restriction on services within the meaning of Article 59 EC Treaty. Since the impugned national prohibition fell outside the scope of Community law, the ECJ did not proceed to assess the said prohibition for compliance with the fundamental human rights to which the ECJ adheres.

Many reasons may be put forward for the ECJ's reluctance or failure to address the fundamental rights issue in the *Grogan* case—awareness of national public and judicial resistance to such a step,[19] caution in giving a decision when parallel proceedings had not yet been concluded in the European Court of Human Rights,[20] weakness in its protection of fundamental

---

[18] Art. 60 EC Treaty provides that "Services shall be considered to be 'services' within the meaning of this Treaty where they are normally provided for remuneration, in so far as they are not governed by the provisions relating to freedom of movement of goods, capital and persons." It further provides that services shall include in particular "(a) the activities of professionals".

[19] See *infra,* Section 3.2; and Walsh, "Reflections on the Effects of Membership of the European Communities in Irish Law", in Capotorti et al. (eds), *Du Droit international au Droit de l'intégration* (1987), pp. 805–820, at p. 819.

[20] Following the *Open Door* case, the defendant clinics complained to the Commission of Human Rights that the injunctions prohibiting the dissemination of information constituted breaches of their rights under Arts. 8, 10 and 14; see Applications Nos. 14234/88 and 14235/88, the

rights in the Community context given this apparent deference to external political and legal factors.[21] Some authors criticize the *Grogan* decision, incorrectly in this author's opinion, precisely because it includes abortion within the scope of Article 60 EC Treaty and because it left open the possibility of a more far-reaching decision in future in the event that an economic or contractual link did exist between the provider of the information and the provider of services.[22] They argue that the Court has allowed a slippage between economic freedoms and fundamental rights which, in the case of the right to life, was protected in Ireland in a chosen form in the Constitution. We would disagree that the Court in *Grogan* admitted such a slippage. It defined abortion as a service which it was entitled to do given that it is a lawful activity lawfully performed in certain circumstances by the medical profession, normally for consideration and therefore falls squarely within the definition of services in Article 60 EC Treaty and as defined in the subsequent case law of the Court of Justice.[23] This did not mean that the ECJ was depriving a Member State of its right to determine that the protection of the unborn is a fundamental principle of law to be guaranteed by the Constitution.[24]

The Treaty specifically provides for instances when Member States may derogate from their Treaty obligations.[25] The ECJ has additionally devised a justification for national legislation which is incompatible with the Treaty but

---

Commission of Human Rights' report in [1992] 14 EHRR 131 and the decision of the Court of Human Rights in Eur. Court H. R., *Open Door Counselling and Dublin Well Woman Centre Ltd. v. Ireland* judgment of 29 October 1992, Series A no. 246.

[21] For a commentary which incites the ECJ to display greater immunity to such factors see de Búrca, loc. cit., note 1, at 304: "... unless it is content to be perceived and to act entirely as an instrumental court, determining the cases in which it will monitor the states' treatment of human rights and values largely by reference to a receptive political climate, it must develop a consistent and principled justification for both the development and the limitation of its 'human rights role'".

[22] See, e.g., Phelan, loc. cit., note 1, at 673; and Coppel and O'Neill, loc. cit., note 1.

[23] See, in particular, Joined Cases 286/82 and 26/83, *Luisi and Carbone v Ministero del Tesoro*, [1984] ECR 377; for a discussion of the provision of services for no charge, such as for example, the provision of medical services in a national health system, see Curtin, loc. cit., note 1, at 592.

[24] On this point see, for example, Schermers' concurring opinion in the Report of the Commission of Human Rights on the *Open Door* case, 7 March 1991, [1992] 14 EHRR at 143: "... although for internal legislation on abortion Irish society may be of decisive importance, the European (Community) society should be paramount when the question of necessity concerns the movement of people or the performance of services across borders".

[25] Since abortion was regarded as a service within the meaning of Community law, the Treaty obligation in the instant case was the duty to refrain from posing obstacles to the free movement of services. For the provision of derogations see Arts. 56 and 66 EC Treaty.

which pursues an imperative requirement of public interest and is justifiable on that basis.[26] The fact that the Court is now willing to examine these derogations and justifications of national legislation in the light of its general principles, fundamental rights in particular, does not necessarily mean that it is championing its own fundamental economic freedoms over the legal and constitutional choices made by Member States.[27] It is not surprising that national legislative or constitutional provisions, to the extent that they impinge on the fields of activity of the Community, fall to be considered by the ECJ. What was at issue in *Grogan* was not the constitutional choice of the Irish people in Article 40.3.3, but the restriction of the ancillary rights of persons wishing to avail of services lawfully provided in other Member States. The Member States have accepted international commitments beyond their borders, not only in the Community but also as signatories of the ECHR. The delicate balance to be achieved given this intertwining of legal orders is surely that the Member States accept the supremacy of the legal order to which they have bound themselves and that the Community institutions, the ECJ included, keep their actions within the limits of their legitimate competence. The protection of fundamental rights by the ECJ is part of its duty to uphold the rule of law and the democratic principles on which the Community is founded.[28] However, it is in determining the limits of Community competence that the ECJ is and will increasingly be confronted with major difficulties.[29] The adoption of the TEU could have been used to clarify some aspects of the ECJ's jurisdiction in the field of fundamental rights, but the content and

---

[26] See, e.g., Case 205/84, *Commission* v *Germany,* [1986] ECR 3755; Case C-353/89, *Commission* v *Netherlands,* [1991] ECR I-4069; and briefly, Lenaerts, "Some Thoughts About the Interaction Between Judges and Politicians in the European Community", 12 YEL (1992), 1–34, at 12–15.

[27] In support of this position, see de Búrca, who argues that "Human rights concerns have been asserted by the ECJ ... as an independent rather than merely a functional means of promoting EC economic aims", loc. cit., note 1, at 299. Cf. Phelan, loc. cit., note 1, at 677, citing *Opinion 1/91,* loc. cit., note 8, at 268 and 272, to the effect that general principles are "merely means of achieving [the Community's] objectives" and that the provisions from which they are extrapolated "far from being an end in themselves are only means for attaining those objectives."

[28] See the Preamble to the Treaty where the Member States "[Confirm] their attachment to the principles of liberty, democracy and respect for human rights and fundamental freedoms and the rule of law" and Art. F(1) TEU, which provides that "The Union shall respect the national identities of its Member States, whose systems of government are founded on the principle of democracy."

[29] See Weiler, loc. cit., note 10, at 2414, regarding the issue of the Community's supposed "*Kompetenz-Kompetenz*". See also de Witte, "Community Law and National Constitutional Values", (1991) LIEI, 1–22, at 2, where he claims that "one of the conditions of Member States accepting supremacy is that the Community is competent to act".

position of Article F(2) suggests that this challenge was not taken up by the Member States.

2.3 The decision of the Court of Human Rights in Open Door

The European Court of Human Rights subsequently handed down its decision in *Open Door* to the effect that the injunctions restraining the complainant welfare clinics from providing non-directive counselling constituted an impermissible restriction of the freedom of expression guaranteed by Article 10(1) ECHR.[30] Having accepted that the prohibition pursued the legitimate aim of the protection of morals, the Court asked "whether there was a pressing social need for the measures in question and, in particular, whether the restriction complained of was proportionate to the legitimate aim pursued".[31] It concluded that the injunctions were not "necessary in a democratic society". The ban on counselling was overbroad, since it applied to all women regardless of their age, health, or reasons for seeking advice. The Court accepted that the counselling was a means of setting out options, that it did not direct women to have abortions and that a link could not definitely be established between counselling and abortion. Furthermore, similar information was still available from other sources in Ireland and the effectiveness of the prohibition was also undermined by the fact that the number of women obtaining abortions in the United Kingdom was rising. Finally, the restrictions on the activities of the clinics were having a disproportionate effect, causing a health risk to women who now sought abortions later and who no longer could avail of the back up medical and counselling services previously on offer.[32] The Court of Human Rights emphasized that state authorities may be in a better position than an international court to determine the requirements of morals but that their power of appreciation was not unfettered and unreviewable.[33] Indeed, it held that "careful scrutiny" was called for in the circumstances of a prohibition which related to an activity tolerated by the national authorities of other Contracting States.

In the light of the *Grogan* decision the Irish Government hastily attached a protocol to the Maastricht Treaty soon before its conclusion. It provided that "Nothing in the Treaty on European Union, or in the Treaties establishing the

---

[30] *Open Door Counselling and Dublin Well Woman Centre Ltd v. Ireland,* loc. cit., note 20.

[31] Ibid., at para. 70.

[32] Ibid., at paras 70–78.

[33] For the contrary view of some of the national judges, at least in the context of the review of national constitutional provisions by the ECJ, see *infra*, Section 3.2.

European Communities ... shall affect the application in Ireland of Article 40.3.3 of the Constitution of Ireland." National controversy followed when an Irish woman wishing to obtain an abortion in the United Kingdom was prevented from doing so by an injunction of the Irish High Court.[34] There was considerable fear in Ireland that the Maastricht Protocol would not only safeguard the constitutional position on abortion but would also deprive Irish women of their rights to travel and receive information (if indeed the latter existed). The Government was forced to revise the Protocol but this solution was rejected by fellow Member States who were unwilling to reopen the intergovernmental negotiations, thereby exposing the TEU to the possibility of further amendment. It succeeded only in adding an addendum to the Protocol.[35] A constitutional referendum was later held to guarantee the protection of the right to travel and the freedom to provide information in certain circumstances.[36] Commentators[37] and Community institutions[38] alike had previously thought that the issue of abortion did not touch the Communities. The way it arose in *Grogan*, indirectly linked to the free movement of services brought the potential conflict between three separate but related legal orders—national, Community and Council of Europe—clearly and dramatically to the fore. Furthermore, within one year of the *Grogan* decision, the Irish Government had been forced to clarify the right to travel and the right to receive information. Since no legislative position had been formulated on these issues since the right to life amendment in 1983, it is arguable that the ultimate resolution of this problem in Irish law owed no small part to the involvement of supranational legal orders and the decisions of the European Court of Human Rights and the ECJ.

---

[34] *Attorney General* v. *X and Others,* [1992] IR 1.

[35] The addendum eventually provided that "This protocol shall not limit the freedom to travel between Member States or to obtain or make available in Ireland legislative information relating to services lawfully available in a Member State." See also EP Debates. No. 3–416/207–218, 12 March 1992, where the European Parliament supported the attempt to revise the protocol; and Curtin, "The Constitutional Structure of the Union: A Europe of Bits and Pieces", 30 CML Rev. (1993), 17–69, at 47–49.

[36] Following the 13th amendment to the Constitution (25 Nov. 1992), the limitations on the right to travel and the right to receive information have been removed.

[37] See, for example, Weiler, "Protection of Fundamental Rights in the Legal Order of the European Communities", in Bernhardt and Jolowicz (eds), *International Enforcement of Human Rights: Reports Submitted to the Colloquium of the International Association of Legal Science*, Heidelberg, 28–30 Aug. 1985, pp. 113–142, at pp. 128–129.

[38] See, e.g., the answers to Written Questions Nos. 655/88 (O.J. 1989, C 111/21) and 319/88 (O.J. 1989, C 111/16).

3 THE RECEPTION OF THE COMMUNITY'S FUNDAMENTAL RIGHTS STANDARDS AT NATIONAL LEVEL

3.1 The Grogan conundrum and beyond

With hindsight, the ECJ's cautious response to the issue in *Grogan* is understandable. If indeed the Court had disregarded the absence of an economic link it would probably have reasoned along the lines pursued by the Advocate General who accepted that the substantive issue in the case (the prohibition of information on a service) fell within the scope of Community law, although in coming to this conclusion he regarded the existence of an economic relationship between the defendants and the providers of the service as irrelevant. The Advocate General also accepted that a restriction on information, even if not discriminatory, could compromise the freedom of a recipient to go to another Member State to avail of the services there. However, the restriction, in his view, was justified by an imperative require-ment of public interest, namely, the protection of the unborn. He accepted that the latter was justifiable under Community law as a moral and philosophical judgment which Ireland was entitled to make and which was proportionate to the aim sought to be achieved. The Advocate General proceeded to examine the prohibition for conformity with the general principles of Community law, fundamental rights and freedoms included. In his view, an objective which needed to be justified in order not to impermissibly infringe Community law, *a priori*, fell outside the exclusive jurisdiction of the Member State in question and was therefore susceptible to review by the ECJ. However, he concluded that the prohibition and its stated objective to protect unborn life were not incompatible with the general principles of Community law and were framed in a manner proportionate to the objective sought to be achieved.

If indeed the ECJ had reasoned in this manner[39] it would have found itself in a curious position *vis-à-vis* the European Court of Human Rights. The ECJ's protection of fundamental rights and freedoms is based on its obligation

---

[39] The subsequent decision of the Court in Case C-260/89, *Elliniki Radiophonia Tileorassi* (hereinafter referred to as the *ERT* case), [1991] ECR I-2925, demonstrates that the ECJ is not adverse to the reasoning employed by the Advocate General in *Grogan* as regards the examination of derogations from Community law and justifications for the exclusion of national legislation from Community law for compatibility with the Community's general principles, fundamental rights included.

to ensure respect for the law.[40] Ever since *Nold* it has accepted that the ECHR and other international conventions on which the Member States have collaborated or of which they are signatories, are sources from which the Court may draw inspiration in protecting fundamental rights, which form an integral part of the general principles of Community law.[41] The ECHR has been explicitly cited by the ECJ on a number of occasions.[42] Much debate has surrounded whether the interpretations of the ECHR by the Court of Human Rights do or should take preference over the "indirect" interpretations of its provisions by the ECJ. It has been argued that the latter is bound to adopt previous interpretations of the Convention by the Court of Human Rights and that its explicit reference to such interpretations shows an increasing willingness on its part to do so.[43] It has also been argued that the ECHR binds the European Communities as a prior obligation of international law.[44] We will not attempt to conclusively answer these questions here. For the purposes of this chapter it is sufficient to reiterate that the ECJ accepts that in ensuring respect for the law it must ensure that the Community (and in certain circumstances the Member States) respect the fundamental rights principles which it derives variously from the Convention and from the constitutional traditions common to the Member States. In this way the fundamental rights principles which inform the Convention could be said to apply via the Community legal order to the activities of the Community institutions and the

---

[40] Art. 164 EC Treaty provides that "The Court of Justice shall ensure that in the interpretation and application of this Treaty the law is observed."

[41] See Case 4/73, *Nold* v *Commission,* [1974] ECR 491, at 507.

[42] See, i.a., Case 249/86, *Commission* v *Germany,* [1989] ECR 1263 (Art. 8); Case 44/79, *Hauer* v *Land Rheinland-Pfalz,* [1979] ECR 3727 (Art. 1 Protocol No. 1); Case 222/84, *Johnston* v *Chief Constable of the RUC,* [1986] ECR 1651 (Art. 13); Case 374/87, *Orkem* v *Commission,* [1989] ECR 3283 (Art. 6); and Joined Cases 46/87 and 227/88, *Hoechst* v *Commission,* [1989] ECR 2859 (Art. 8(1)).

[43] See Lenaerts, "Fundamental Rights to Be Included in a Community Catalogue", 16 EL Rev. (1991), 367–390, at 378; and Grief, "The Domestic Impact of the European Convention of Human Rights as Mediated Through Community Law", (1991) *Public Law,* 555–567, at 566; Cf. Diez Picazo, loc. cit., note 7, at 152, who is less convinced that the ECJ is bound by the decisions of the Court of Human Rights.

[44] Art. 234 EC Treaty provides that "The rights and obligations arising from agreements concluded before the entry into force of this Treaty between one or more Member States on the one hand, and one or more third countries on the other, shall not be affected by the provisions of this Treaty."

Member States when acting within one of the fields of activity of the Communities.[45] It is true that the protection of fundamental rights in the Communities does not amount to incorporation of fundamental rights at national level, which would thereby involve a genuine control of the constitutionality of national legislation along the lines of the US Fourteenth amendment.[46] However, the *ERT* decision has expanded the extent to which the ECJ can examine national legislation for compatibility with its fundamental rights standards, as it covers derogations and simply refers to situations covered by Community law, as has the fact that it is increasingly difficult to define such situations.

In the context of the abortion information and counselling issues which arose in *Grogan* and *Open Door*, a very peculiar result would have followed from a decision of the ECJ along the lines expressed in the Opinion of the Advocate General. On the one hand, the ECJ could have denied the existence of any impermissible infringement of Community law (on the basis of a restriction which was justifiable by an imperative requirement of public interest, namely, the protection of unborn life) or the fundamental rights principles to which it adheres (on the grounds that the prohibition was a proportionate and justified exercise of the state's discretion), while on the other, the Court of Human Rights (from whose legal order the Community draws inspiration in its adherence to fundamental rights) would have determined that an infringement of freedom of expression did occur in the *Open Door* case in circumstances very similar to *Grogan*. Does the manner in which fundamental rights are protected in the Community legal order not suggest that the interpretation of the fundamental right of freedom of expression handed down by the Court of Human Rights should apply by implication in the Community context?[47] Or does the ECJ's proviso that fundamental rights should be guaranteed "within the framework of the structure and objectives of the Community" indicate that fundamental rights

---

[45] See, however, O'Higgins, loc. cit., note 3, at p. 237, who claims that general principles have taken into account, in particular, the ECHR, but that it is not true to say that the Convention "has been taken over and has become a part of Community law".

[46] See Diez Picazo, loc. cit., note 7, at 140.

[47] Lenaerts further suggests in a case where no interpretation of a Convention provision is available that Community cases involving infringement of a fundamental right by a Community institution which can be challenged before a national court should be revised if they differ with a subsequent interpretation of the ECHR by the Court of Human Rights. Where such an infringement can only be challenged in the Court of Justice or First Instance, he argues that a procedural bridge should be negotiated between the two legal orders to ensure a full and coherent system of judicial enforcement. Lenaerts, loc. cit., note 43, at 378–380.

standards are employed in Community law in a different qualitative sense?[48] However, the essential element of the judgment of the Court of Human Rights in *Open Door* was the meaning of what was "necessary in a democratic society". Given that the ECJ in *Rutili* specifically referred to this aspect of the Convention,[49] surely it would be difficult to argue against the applicability of this interpretation of a Convention principle in Community law.[50]

In the opinion of this author, herein lies the crux of the problem as regards the protection of fundamental rights in the European Community. Community law claims to adhere to the principles which inform the Convention and the constitutional traditions common to the Member States.[51] Yet Community law is informed by different objectives and relies on different legal mechanisms than the ECHR. The latter applies to "everyone resident within the territory of a Contracting State" (Article 1 ECHR), its objective is to uphold the fundamental rights which it enshrines and the function of the Court of Human Rights is to determine whether a fundamental right is infringed and,

---

[48] See, e.g., Case 11/70, *Internationale Handelsgesellschaft* v *Einfuhr- und Vorratsstelle Getreide,* [1970] ECR 1125, where behind the ECJ's protection of fundamental rights lay the preservation of the supremacy of Community law; Weiler, "Eurocracy and Distruct", (1986) *Washington Law Review,* 1105, at 1111; Diez Picazo, loc. cit., note 7, at 141; and Dauses, "The Protection of Fundamental Rights in the Community Legal Order", 10 EL Rev. (1985), 398–419, at 408. See also Case C-5/88, *Wachauf* v *Federal Republic of Germany,* [1989] ECR 2609, at 2639, para. 18: "restrictions may be imposed on the exercise of these [fundamental rights recognized by the ECJ] in particular in the context of the common organization of the market, provided that those restrictions in fact correspond to objectives of general interest pursued by the Community"; and Case 155/79, *AM and S* v *Commission,* [1982] ECR 1575, at 1610–1611. See also the discussion of Community citizenship in a framework of fundamental rights by O'Leary in CML Rev. (forthcoming).

[49] See Case 36/75, *Rutili* v *Minister for the Interior,* [1975] ECR 1219, at para. 32: "[the limitations on Member State action] ... are a specific manifestation of the more general principle enshrined in Articles 8, 9, 10 and 11 of the Convention for the Protection of Human Rights and Fundamental Freedoms ... which provide[s] in identical terms that no restrictions in the interests of national security or public safety shall be placed on the rights secured by the above quoted articles other than such as are necessary for those interests 'in a democratic society'". The latter was defined by Sir Basil Hall in the report of the Commission of Human Rights in the *Open Door* case as something which "correspond[s] to a pressing social need". Similarly, in the context of Community law, see Case 30/77, *Regina* v *Bouchereau,* [1977] ECR 1999, at para. 35.

[50] See also Art. F(1) TEU; and Perez, "El Tratado de la Union Europea y los Derecho Humanos", 2 Rev. Inst. Eur. (1993), 459–484, at 476.

[51] As we shall discuss in Section 4, Art. F(2) could imply that the ECJ must now explicitly adhere to the Convention *per se* and not simply to the principles underlying it.

if so, to assess a state's justification for the infringement.[52] The European Community seeks to achieve an ever closer union among the peoples of Europe and fulfil the objectives of the Community, many of which are principally economic. In doing so it is based on a transfer of competences from the Member States to the Community, supposedly however, "within limited fields". Although these fields have been extended recently there are limits on the extent to which the Community can substitute itself for the Member States. The constitutional protection of the rights and principles construed as fundamental by a given community is precisely one of these fields, since "it is not possible to find in the legal and social orders of the Contracting States a uniform European conception of morals".[53] Thus, essential to the operation of derogations and justifications in Community law is the acceptance that the national measure in question infringes Community law, but that "at the present stage of development" the Court feels that it must permit Member States a margin of appreciation in difficult areas since political consensus for further integration in that field may be lacking. This reasoning also formed the basis for the development of mandatory requirements in the ECJ's *Cassis de Dijon* line of case law with respect to the free movement of goods. Yet, to go too far in accepting the sensitivity of certain issues for certain Member States would be to allow that famous coach and four to be driven through the provisions of Community law, the fulfilment of its objectives, its uniform application and the supremacy of its laws. This partial stage of Community integration involves the ECJ in a delicate balancing of the objectives and values of the supranational and national orders. Its legitimacy may depend on getting the balance right and on not arrogating the sovereignty which Member States still retain, while the continued effectiveness of Community law requires that Member State sovereignty cannot act as an obstacle to the fulfilment of Community objectives in areas which it does cover. The ECJ's contributions to the constitutional development of Community law are reknowned—*Van Gend en Loos, Costa v ENEL, Stauder, Gravier, Francovich* and *ERT* testify to an active and pro-integration court. Indeed as regards the *ERT* decision:[54]

---

[52] For a comparison of the different functional techniques of the two courts, see de Búrca, loc. cit., note 1, at 315.

[53] See the decision of the European Court of Human Rights in *Open Door,* loc. cit., note 20, at para. 68.

[54] See Mancini and Keeling, "From *CILFIT* to *ERT:* The Constitutional Challenge Facing the European Court", 11 YEL (1991), 1–13, at 12.

Anyone who reflects for a moment about how intimately some of those derogations (public policy, security and morality) are bound up with the fundamental notions governing the relationship between States and their citizens cannot fail to appreciate the potential incidence of that judgment *(ERT)* on national sovereignty.

But in the absence of an explicit political and constitutional step it is difficult, and indeed unwise in some areas, for the Court to go further.[55] To advance on *ERT* and further incorporate Community fundamental rights standards with respect to the action of Member States requires a degree of political integration which the Community has not yet reached, or as is evident from the TEU, which Member State governments are not yet willing to admit. When the Court does assert jurisdiction in politically or constitutionally difficult cases, the legitimacy of its authority will be subject to considerable scrutiny.[56]

3.2 Article 177 EC Treaty and the supremacy of Community law

In the event that the ECJ did treat the prohibition on information as contrary to its fundamental rights standards (probably on the grounds that the means chosen were disproportionate to the aim sought to be achieved), how would that decision have been received at national level? As Lenaerts has pointed out, the ECJ's system of judicial review under Article 177 heavily relies on the authority of national judicial systems and their willingness to work in tandem with the ECJ before and after a reference. At least as regards national provisions of constitutional law which enshrined rights viewed as fundamental under Irish law, this view did not seem to be shared by the Irish Supreme Court which granted an interlocutory injunction against the defendants while *Grogan* was pending before the ECJ. In the opinion of the Supreme Court there could be "no question of a possible or putative right to travel so as to avail of 'services'". Furthermore:[57]

if and when a decision of the European Court of Justice rules that some aspect

---

[55] See Curtin, "Prospects for a European Social Policy", in Betten (ed.), *The Future of European Social Policy* (1991), pp. 163–169, at p. 165: "The case law of the Court of Justice is showing elements of minimalism: In other words, where the political will is lacking to take concrete legal steps, the philosophy is that it is not for the Court to step in and creatively fill the gaps." See also Mancini, "The Making of a Constitution for Europe", 26 CML Rev. (1989), 595–614, at 613.

[56] See de Búrca, loc. cit., note 1, at 304; and Weiler, loc. cit., note 9, at 434.

[57] This preemption by the Supreme Court of the ECJ's ruling was questionable, particularly in view of the sanctity of the reference procedure which it itself had emphasized in *Campus Oil,* [1983] IR 82.

of European Community law affects the activities of the defendants impugned in this case, the consequence of that decision on these constitutionally guaranteed rights and their protection by the [national] courts will fall to be considered by these courts.

According to Walsh J. "any answer to the reference received from the ECJ will have to be considered in the light of our own constitutional provisions" and "the interpretation of the Constitution of Ireland is within the exclusive competence of the courts of Ireland". He also alluded to the possibility that the eighth amendment to the Constitution qualifies the amendment of Article 29 which was necessary to permit the adhesion of Ireland to the Treaties. Are these correct statements of the relationship between Community law and national law? Though constitutional adjudication and interpretation is a matter falling to the Irish courts, the role of Community law in matters falling within its scope cannot be discounted. Furthermore, Article 29.4.3 of the Irish Constitution states that:

> No provision of the Constitution invalidates laws enacted, acts done or measures adopted by the State *necessitated* by the obligations of membership of the Communities or prevents laws enacted, acts done or measures adopted by the Communities, or institutions thereof, from having the force of law in the State.

It is contended that comprehensive abortion legislation is not a measure "necessitated" by membership of the Communities. Nevertheless, a ruling by the ECJ invalidating a prohibition on abortion information as a disproportionate exercise of the state's margin of discretion, is within the bounds of possibility. In such circumstances, would a discontinuance of the ban, given its disproportionate effect on free movement, not be "necessitated" by Ireland's obligations under the Treaty?[58] The Supreme Court judgment suggests that a serious constitutional crisis would have arisen in such a situation and that a certain resistance exists at national level to the supremacy of Community law and to the extent of a Member State's obligations under Article 5 EC Treaty.[59]

National judicial mutiny with respect to the protection of fundamental rights and the supremacy of Community law is not a new phenomenon. The German Federal Constitutional Court had been confronted with and accepted

---

[58] See O'Higgins, loc. cit, note 3, at 234, for his views on the jurisdiction of the Irish Courts and what is "necessitated" by Community law under Art. 29.4.3.

[59] See also commentators in *The Irish Times,* 5 Oct. 1991.

the autonomy and supremacy of Community law over national decisions.[60] However, since Article 24 of the Basic Law was the basis of German accession to the Communities, membership of the latter could not, it was argued, involve the infringement of fundamental rights.[61] In the absence of a Community Bill of Rights, the protection of fundamental rights and the control of Community legislation for compatibility with German fundamental rights was said to lie with the Federal Constitutional Court.[62] The German Constitutional Court now accepts that the protection of fundamental rights in the Communities satisfies the requirement laid down by it in 1974 (namely, that there exist a Bill of Rights). It based the reversal of its earlier decision, *inter alia,* on the accession of all Member States to the ECHR, the developing case law of the ECJ and the 1977 Joint Declaration.[63] Nevertheless, the German court did not *exclude* its jurisdiction to review Community law for compatibility with fundamental rights in the Basic Law, nor did it deny that such jurisdiction exists, it simply provided that it would no longer exercise it as long as the present conditions remain.[64] Frowein is loathe to criticize this assertion of ultimate jurisdiction by national courts. He notes that the German Constitutional Court has accepted the priority of Community law and claims that this preservation of its final authority "to intervene where real problems concerning the protection of fundamental rights in Community law could arise" is to be expected as long as the Community does not enjoy a federal structure. Given this fact, he argues that questions about sovereignty or final supremacy as to the sources of law are not totally clear or resolved.[65] In the 1970s the Italian Constitutional Court also expressed reservations about the protection of

---

[60] See annotation of the Court's decisions by Frowein in 5 CML Rev. (1967–1968), 481–487, at 484–485.

[61] Art. 24 permits the transfer of sovereignty to supranational organizations, but it is subject to the guarantee in Art. 79 that no amendment of the Constitution may diminish the protection of human rights and therefore, it cannot permit a transfer of sovereignty which would diminish fundamental rights.

[62] See [1974] *Bundesverfassungsgericht,* 37, p. 271.

[63] O.J. 1977, C 103/1.

[64] *Solange II,* [1986] *Bundesverfassungsgericht* 73, 339; and Frowein, *"Solange II"* (BVerfGE 73. 339). Constitutional Complaint Firma W.", 25 CML Rev. (1988), 201–206, at 203.

[65] In support of this line of reasoning see Schermers, "The European Communities Bound by Fundamental Human Rights", 27 CML Rev. (1990), 249–258, at 255, who cites the *Nold* case (loc. cit., note 41, at 507: "it [the Community] cannot therefore uphold measures which are incompatible with fundamental rights recognised and protected by the Constitutions of those States") to the effect that "a Community act is void whenever it infringes a national constitutional requirement".

fundamental rights in the Community.[66] It has since left the door open on national scrutiny of Community law with respect to the fundamental principles for the protection of human rights that are contained in the Italian Constitution.[67]

These cases reflected the concern of Member States that the Community institutions might infringe fundamental rights in the exercise of their activities. In the light of the German Constitutional Court's satisfaction with the Community's commitment to the protection of fundamental rights, most commentators regarded the threat to the supremacy of Community law as having been adverted.[68] In the next section it is suggested that the relationship between the European Communities and the Member States in the protection of fundamental rights has shifted in recent years. It is argued that the threat of Member State opposition to supremacy in the field of fundamental rights now stems from the possibility that the ECJ might excessively extend its scope of review, so that Member States find themselves and their protection of fundamental rights as the targets of judicial scrutiny, (a) because *ERT* refers broadly to situations covered by Community law, and (b) because through expansive interpretations of the scope of Community law and a further transfer of competence to the Communities, it is arguable that the content of the "socio-legal contract" on which respect for the principle of supremacy was once based has changed.

4   FUNDAMENTAL RIGHTS POST-MAASTRICHT

4.1 Article F(2) and the protection of fundamental rights in the Treaty on European Union

Article F(2) TEU provides that "the Union shall respect fundamental rights, as guaranteed by the European Convention of Human Rights and Fundamental

---

[66] See *Frontini,* Decision No. 183, 27 Dec. 1973, [1974] CMLR 386.

[67] See *Spa Fragd v Amministrazione delle Finanze,* Decision No. 232, 21 April 1989, 34 *Giurisprudenza Costituzionale,* 1984 I, 1098, 21 CML Rev. (1984), 756. See also Gaja, "New Developments in a Continuing Story: The Relationship Between EEC Law and Italian Law", 27 CML Rev. (1990), 83–95, at 94–95; and generally, on the relationship between national courts and Community law, see Schermers, "The Scales in Balance: National Constitutional Court *v.* Court of Justice", 27 CML Rev. (1990), 97–105.

[68] In the United Kingdom and Ireland, the question of supremacy seemed to be resolved by the terms of their acts of accession, s. 3(1) of the (UK) European Communities Act, 1972 and Art. 29.4.3 of the Irish Constitution, respectively.

Freedoms ... and as they result from the constitutional traditions common to the Member States, as general principles of Community law".

This is not the first time that a Community Treaty refers to the Community's adherence to fundamental rights. The preamble of the Single European Act (SEA) similarly expressed the Member States' determination to "promote democracy on the basis of the fundamental rights recognized in the constitutions and laws of the Member States, in the Convention for the Protection of Human Rights and Fundatmental Freedoms and the European Social Charter, notably freedom, equality and social justice".

It is, however, the first time that a specific provision has been introduced into a Treaty text referring to the protection of fundamental rights in the European Communities and making an explicit reference to the sources of the Community's inspiration in the field of fundamental rights. Article F(2) is not alone in this regard in the TEU. Article J.1(2) similarly provides that "[the] objectives of the common foreign and security policy shall be: to develop and consolidate democracy and the rule of law, and respect for human rights and fundamental freedoms" and Article K.2 provides that the matters dealt with under Article K.1 (asylum, external borders, immigration and third-country nationals, drugs, fraud, judicial co-operation in civil and criminal matters, police co-operation):

> shall be dealt with in compliance with the European Convention for the Protection of Human Rights and Fundamental Freedoms ... and the Convention relating to the Status of Refugees ... and having regard to the protection afforded by Member States to persons persecuted on political grounds.

Titles V and VI of the TEU are not amendments of the European Community Treaties. They are regarded as additional pillars which, along with Title II, principally combine to form the TEU.

Like Article F(2) and the other common provisions in Title I of the TEU, Articles J and K are excluded from the jurisdiction of the ECJ pursuant to Article L.[69] What is the effect of this exclusion on the future protection of fundamental rights in the Community and Union? It cannot be contended that fundamental rights themselves no longer fall to be reviewed by the ECJ. One

---

[69] Art. L provides that "The provisions of the Treaty establishing the European [Communities] ... shall apply only to the following provisions of this Treaty: (a) provisions amending the Treaty establishing the [EEC] with a view to establishing the [EC] ... ; (b) the third subparagraph of Article K.3(2)(c) [conventions regarding the matters listed in Article K.1 which the Council may draw up and recommend to the Member States for adoption, only however when such review is stipulated]; (c) Articles L to S."

of the objectives of the TEU is to maintain in full the *acquis communautaire* and to build on it.[70] The latter is defined by the Commission as:[71]

> the contents, principles and political objectives of the Treaties ... the legislation adopted in implementation of the Treaties and the jurisprudence of the court; the declarations and resolutions adopted in the Community framework; the international agreements; and agreements between Member States connected with the Community's activities.

Furthermore, Article M, which is justiciable, provides that:

> Subject to the provisions amending the Treaty establishing the [EEC] with a view to establishing the [EC] ... and to these final provisions [Title VII], nothing in this Treaty shall affect the Treaties establishing the European Communities or the subsequent Treaties and Acts modifying or supplementing them.

Although Article M does not negate the exclusion of jurisdiction in Article L, the former being "subject to" the latter, it nevertheless reaffirms the Union's commitment to the existing *acquis*.

But, both the European Parliament and the Commission initially proposed that protection of and respect for fundamental rights should be included within the scope of the TEU provisions on citizenship.[72] The fact that these proposals were rejected and the exclusion of Article F(2) from the jurisdiction of the ECJ suggest a reluctance on the part of the Member States (or rather their personal representatives in the intergovernmental negotiations) to facilitate or admit future extensive interpretations of Community law and Member State obligations, under the guise of the mandate of the ECJ to protect fundamental

---

[70] Art. B, para. 5, provides that the Community shall set itself the objective "to maintain in full the *acquis communautaire* and build on it with a view to considering, through the procedure referred to in Article N(2) [further intergovernmental conferences], to what extent the policies and forms of cooperation introduced by this Treaty may need to be revised with the aim of ensuring the effectiveness of the mechanisms and the institutions of the Community".

[71] Commission report on the criteria and conditions for accession of new members to the Community, *Europe Documents* No. 1790, 3 July 1992, at 3.

[72] See Union Citizenship. Contributions of the Commission to the Intergovernmental Conferences, SEC (91) 500, Supplement 2/91, Bull. EC; and Bindi Report on Union Citizenship, PE Doc. A-30139/91, 23 May 1991.

rights.[73] Weiler has suggested that a similar attempt by Member States to foreclose judicial review in the areas covered by Titles V and VI may in fact turn out to be singularly unsuccessful in this regard.[74] His argument is that although judicial review by the ECJ is curtailed in general, this does not negate or lessen the legal obligations which flow from Articles J and K, nor is the exclusion of the jurisdiction of the ECJ possible in all cases.[75] A parallel could be drawn between this reasoning and the protection and development in the ECJ of the principle of the judicial effectiveness of Community law. In a series of cases the Court has underlined that lack of direct effect does not imply the absence of legal obligations.[76] The criteria laid down for direct effect simply indicate the provisions of Community law which are susceptible to being directly enforced in the national courts. Those provisions which are not directly effective carry the same legal weight, although they must be enforced and vindicated in a different way. Although judicial review is excluded for the common provisions of the TEU and Titles V and VI in general, this does not mean that the legal obligations enshrined in those provisions are any less.

Regarding the express adherence to fundamental rights in Article F(2), the Community and the Member States have thereby expressly committed themselves to the fundamental rights standards displayed in the ECHR and the constitutional traditions common to the Member States. Looking closely at the text of Article F(2), it provides that the Union will respect fundamental rights,[77] as guaranteed by the ECHR and as they result from the constitutional

---

[73] See Jacobs, "The Protection of Human Rights in the Member States of the European Communities—The Impact of the Court of Justice", in O'Reilly, op. cit., note 3, pp. 243–250, at p. 250; Weiler, loc. cit., note 9, at 444: "The express attempt at judicial exclusion from the two Maastricht non-Community 'pillars' [Articles J and K] should be read as a illustration of the same type of reticence *vis-à-vis* the Court." Note that he refers to the "attempt" to exclude judicial review under Art. L. See also Curtin, loc. cit., note 35, at 18–19.

[74] Weiler, "Neither Unity Nor Three Pillars—The Trinity Structure of the Treaty on European Union", in Monar, Ungerer and Wessels (eds), *The Maastricht Treaty on European Union* (1993), pp. 49–62, at pp. 51 and 55.

[75] Similarly, see the decision of the German Federal Constitutional Court on the TEU, 2 *Bundesverfasssungsrecht* 2134/92 and 2 *Bundesverfassungsrecht* 2159/92, 12 Oct. 1993, where it provided that Art. L only excludes the jurisdiction of the ECJ with respect to measures which do not directly affect fundamental rights.

[76] See, e.g., Joined Cases C-6/90 and C-9/90, *Francovich and Others,* [1991] ECR I-5357; and generally, Steiner, "From Direct Effect to *Francovich:* Shifting Means of Enforcement of Community Law", 18 EL Rev. (1993), 3–22.

[77] See previously Case 29/69, *Stauder v Ulm,* [1969] ECR 419.

traditions common to the Member States,[78] as general principles of Community law. The effectiveness of Article F(2) and the Community's continued adherence to fundamental rights surely lies in this last reference to general principles. Not only does this aspect of the provision expressly confirm the source and legitimation of the protection of fundamental rights in the Community and now the Union but, by doing so, it ensures, in our view, that the attempt to exclude the jurisdiction of the ECJ is rendered null and void.[79] We have noted that Article 164 EC Treaty provides that in the interpretation and application of the Treaty, the ECJ is to ensure that "the law" is observed. It was using this tool in *Stauder* that the ECJ confirmed the existence of general principles—a set of unenumerated principles and rights which act as "a canon of the validity of the acts of the institutions ... constituting a limit which they must respect".[80] Fundamental rights were said to belong to this category which the ECJ felt bound to protect in order to fulfil its aforementioned duty to protect "the law".[81] To conclude that fundamental rights are not justiciable general principles would detract from the existing *acquis*, there never before having been non-justiciable general principles.[82] It would also undermine one of the essential and established aspects of general principles in Community law which are recognized as a primary source of law in the European Communities, independent of the Treaties. General principles are said to:[83]

> define the structural foundation of the legal system and of life in a society

---

[78] See Case 4/73, loc. cit., note 41; and Twomey, "The European Union: Three Pillars Without a Human Rights Foundation", in O'Keeffe and Twomey (eds), *Legal Issues of the Maastricht Treaty* (1993), at p. 121–132.

[79] See also Perez, loc. cit., note 50, at 477.

[80] See Diez Picazo, loc. cit., note 7, at 141 (my translation); and Dauses, "La Proteccion de los Derechos Fundamentales en el Orden Juridico Comunitario", D-14 *Gaceta Juridica de la CEE* (1991), 359–388, at 367.

[81] See Lenaerts, loc. cit., note 26, at 1, who notes that what constitutes "the law" has never been specified; Weiler, loc. cit., note 48, at 1117 argues that it could mean a higher law; while Jacobs, loc. cit., note 73, at p. 243 suggests that it is "the common legal heritage of the Member States, including the general principles in the national legal system".

[82] See Jacobs, loc. cit., note 73, at p. 244, who points out that the language of *Stauder* to the effect that "les principes generaux du droit communautaire, dont la Cour assure le respect" emphasizes that general principles of law, including fundamental rights, are part of "the law" referred to in Art. 164.

[83] See Dauses, loc. cit., note 48, at 406, citing Lecheler, *Die Europäische Gerichtshof und die allgemeinen Rechtsgrundsätze*, (Dissertation, Berlin, 1971), at p. 45.

which is subject to the rule of law, with the result that a general principle of law, unlike a simple 'rule' of law, cannot be ignored without simultaneously bringing into question the foundations of the legal order.

Fundamental rights are to be respected as general principles of Community law and the TEU has thereby specified that they are to be enforced and protected in the same manner and vindicated when necessary before the ECJ.[84] It would be unacceptable in the light of the Court's duty pursuant to Article 164 that fundamental rights which form part of its generally justiciable general principles and which now form part of the Treaty text which ratifies and to some extent specifies the Community fundamental rights standards, should be excluded from the competence of the very Court which first recognized their applicability in Community law and which is said to be guided in the exercise of its duties by the rule of law.[85] Just as the reference in Article B to the principle of subsidiarity and the role of citizens in the European Union must influence how other relevant justiciable provisions of the Treaty are interpreted so must the scope and content of Article F(2) influence the Community's protection of fundamental rights.[86] It is to be remembered that the Community/Union is obliged to build on the existing *acquis* and it is not, we may presume, to detract from it. Since the ECJ is charged to police its own exclusion, it would not be surprising to come across references to Article F(2) in its future judgments which formally exclude its review but which more strictly adhere to its content.

4.2 Judicial co-operation in the field of fundamental rights following the Treaty on European Union

We noted in the introduction that the TEU confirms Community involvement in various fields such as justice and home affairs, health, education, citizenship-like rights, etc. The legal nature of this involvement ranges from the

---

[84] Art. F(3) provides that "The Union shall provide itself with the means necessary to attain its objectives and carry through its policies."

[85] The ECJ itself has indicated the essential role which respect for the rule of law plays in the Communities generally and in the exercise of its judicial task in particular. See 294/83, *Les Verts* v *Parliament,* [1986] ECR 1339; and *Opinion 1/91,* loc. cit., note 8.

[86] In a similar vein, see Lenaerts, "Education in Community Law After Maastricht", 31 CML Rev. (1994), 7–41, at 8. Some authors go further, however, e.g., Perez, loc. cit., note 50, at 469, who argues that Art. F(2) is "the reception or incorporation by reference of the normative part of the European Convention of Human Rights, constitutionalising its content in the Community plane" and that Art. F(2) "determines the obligation to respect fundamental rights as they are guaranteed in the European Convention of Human Rights" (my translation).

power to enact binding legislation, to co-operation, to the formulation of common policies. The TEU has also built the principle of subsidiarity into the legal structure of the Union and into some specific Treaty provisions.[87] The Treaty reflects the concern of Member States that the Community "act within the limits of the powers conferred upon it by this Treaty".[88] The Community principles of supremacy and direct effect were previously based on the fact that the "Community constitutes a new legal order ... for the benefit of which the states have limited their sovereign rights, *albeit within limited fields*".[89] With only a few minor hiccups, national courts have accepted these principles. It has also been said that "although it has never been stated explicitly, the Court of Justice has the '*Kompetenz-Kompetenz*' in the Community legal order, i.e., it is the body that determines which norms come within the sphere of application of Community law".[90]

But the "limited fields" in which this transfer has taken place now appear far less limited and the division of competence upon which Member State loyalty in Article 5 EC Treaty is surely based is becoming an increasingly essential aspect of the Union's constitutional development and an increasingly blurred one at that. If, as seems to be the case, the German Constitutional Court did not actually deny its jurisdiction to examine whether Community law infringed fundamental rights recognized as inviolable in national constitutional law, it remains to be seen whether it will reopen this jurisdiction at some later date when the facts of a case cause sufficient controversy at national level to merit it.[91] The reasoning of the Irish Supreme Court, as it awaited the preliminary ruling in *Grogan*, indicated that if it regarded the ECJ's decision to be contrary to the protection of fundamental rights in the national legal order, it would assess the ruling with reference to provisions of national constitutional law. The Irish Court was clearly unwilling to cede the authority to determine whether the principles of Community or national law applied and seemed willing to engage in battle with the ECJ over which court was to

---

[87] See variously Arts. B, 3b, 126, 127, 128, etc.

[88] Art. 3b.

[89] See Case 26/62, *Van Gend en Loos* v *Nederlandse Administratie der Belastingen*, [1963] ECR 1; Case 6/64, *Costa* v *ENEL*, [1964] ECR 585; and Weiler, loc. cit., note 9, at 439.

[90] See Weiler, loc. cit., note 10, at 2414; and Temple Lang, "The Sphere in Which Member States are Obliged to Comply with the General Principles of Law and Community Fundamental Rights Principles", (1992) LIEI, 23–35, at 35.

[91] See Perez, loc. cit., note 50, at 469; and de Witte, loc. cit., note 29, at 5.

adjudicate the limits of the scope of Community versus Member State law.[92]

This trend has been reaffirmed in remarkably clear terms by the German Federal Constitutional Court in its decision on the TEU.[93] The Federal Constitutional Court there held that the TEU satisfies the requirement that the sovereign rights which Member States have transferred to the latter are identifiable. In coming to this conclusion, however, it has identified the constitutional basis of the Treaty as the principle of a singular and restricted attribution of competences. The Court expressly rejected the idea that Article F(3) (to the effect that the Union shall provide itself with the means necessary to attain its objectives and carry through its policies) was an expression of "Kompetenz-Kompetenz". It was clearly concerned about the development of the "socio-legal contract" on which the judicial and legislative co-operation of the national and Community orders has been based and referred specifically to the "excessively wide use which had been made of Article 235 EC" (author's own translation), as well as certain interpretative principles which have been coined in the Community, namely, "inherent and implicit powers" and *"effet utile"*. The German Court has thus indicated not only limits to the interpretation of the competences attributed to the Community but, more importantly, it sees itself as the authority competent if not to determine the validity of a Community act then to interpret the application of the Treaties themselves in Germany. Similarly, although the Court rejected the admissibility of a claim that the TEU failed to sufficiently guarantee fundamental rights, it did so only by partially returning to its position in the *"first solange"* case.[94] Thus, the protection of fundamental rights in Germany is said to be based on a relationship of co-operation between the Federal Constitutional Court and the ECJ and the former will only interfere with the latter's jurisdiction over the applicability of Community law in Germany in cases where the ECJ fails to satisfy the level of protection considered indispensable by the Federal Constitutional Court. In the *"second solange"* case the German Court appeared to have expressed global satisfaction with the Community's fundamental rights standards. It now appears to be willing to resort to a case-by-case assessment of whether in fact the Community's standards are sufficiently high. Once again the authority to determine whether in fact those standards are sufficiently high lies with the national court. Although the German Court ultimately gave its

---

[92] See Weiler, loc. cit., note 9, at 439.

[93] See *supra*, note 75; and Bacigalupo, "La Constitucionalidad del Tratado de la Union Europea en Alemania (La Sentencia del Tribunal Constitucional Federal de 12 octubre de 1993)", D-21 *Gaceta Juridica de la CE y de la Competencia* (1994), 7–45.

[94] See also Bacigalupo, loc. cit., note 93.

approval to ratification of the TEU, it did so in the context of a decision which attempts to clarify some of the more blurred aspects of the national/supra-national legal relationship. With particular respect to the protection of fundamental rights, it is arguable that the cases when the ECJ is thought not to be exercising a sufficiently high standard will be few and far between.[95] The important aspect of the German case is, however, the clear message to the ECJ and Community institutions that Member States regard a two-way relationship based on judicial *co-operation* as an essential element of the "socio-legal contract" on which supremacy and the effective and uniform application of Community law is based.

5   CONCLUSION

The protection of fundamental rights in Community law is intimately bound up with the relationship of judicial co-operation which exists between the ECJ and national courts. This relationship is particularly crucial at the present stage of partial integration in the Community, when the transfer of competences from the national to the supranational level is limited, but nevertheless far-reaching and subject, in recent years, to steady expansion. National courts are now clearly signalling that they are uncomfortable with the extent to which the Community institutions can now intrude in areas previously thought to be the preserve of the Member States. The latter have now incorporated the principle of subsidiarity explicitly into the Community's legal structures, but they have also reiterated a desire to maintain and build on the existing *acquis*. It will be to the detriment of both national law and the coherent development of Community law if the relationship of judicial co-operation which exists between the two legal orders is marred by a "hijacking" of existing Commun-ity law and the *acquis communautaire*, as Member States make special pleas in the form of derogating protocols from unpopular judgments of the ECJ.[96] Far preferable is a principled approach of the ECJ to the limits of Community competence and its role in the protection of fundamental rights and a disciplined acceptance by Member State courts that national constitutional provisions and their protection of fundamental rights can no longer exist in splendid isolation.

---

[95] See, however, de Witte, loc. cit., note 29, for an excellent discussion of when and how such cases could occur.

[96] See Curtin, loc. cit., note 35, at 49 et seq.

3 FUNDAMENTAL RIGHTS AND FUNDAMENTAL BOUNDARIES: ON STANDARDS AND VALUES IN THE PROTECTION OF HUMAN RIGHTS

Joseph H.H. Weiler

1   INTRODUCTION

Judicial protection of fundamental human rights by the Court of Justice of the European Communities (ECJ) may operate as a source of both unity and disunity in the dialectical process of European integration. There is, of course, the classical vision which regards a commitment to fundamental human rights as a unifying ideal, one of the core values around which the people and peoples of Europe may coalesce. When the ECJ, in the very well-known story, held itself out as the guarantor of fundamental human rights in the field of Community law, it was, on this view, merely giving judicial expression (and teeth!) to that core value. But judicial protection by the ECJ, both of Union measures and Member State measures, can also be a source of tension.

First, and this goes to the heart of this chapter, beyond a certain core, reflected in Europe by the Convention for the Protection of Human Rights and Fundamental Freedoms (European Convention on Human Rights; ECHR), the definition of fundamental human rights often differs from polity to polity. These differences, I will argue, reflect fundamental societal choices and form an important part in the different identities of polities and societies. They are often that part of social identity about which people care a great deal. What menu and flavour of human rights are chosen in the Community context matters, and it can become a source of tension even in the absence of a direct conflict of norms. The choice of human rights is about the choice of fundamental values, so the stakes are rather high. In the first part of this chapter I shall explore these situations of conflict and tension and, from a distance, try to explain how the ECJ has attempted to mediate the tensions and blunt the conflicts.

Second, judicial review of Community measures but especially Member State measures can be seen, and have been seen, as part of a relentless and highly problematic extension of jurisdiction into areas of social regulation

N. A. Neuwahl and A. Rosas (eds.), The European Union and Human Rights, 51–76.
© 1995 *Kluwer Law International. Printed in the Netherlands.*

which are, or ought to be, the prerogative of the Member States. I will deal in some detail with this extension of jurisdiction and its roots.

I should clarify that my focus is not on the problems which result from the fact that it is judge made law—an issue with which I have dealt elsewhere. I am concerned with the meeting of European rights with national rights. I should also explain that in this chapter I shall remain firmly within the liberal rights paradigm, leaving for another occasion the rights-critique apparatus. Before turning to the actual jurisprudence I will explore a little deeper the notion of human rights as societal values and their potential for conflict in the European architecture.

Modern liberal states, taking their cue principally from the American rather than British democratic tradition, increasingly acknowledge a higher law —typically a constitution, and in more recent time, international treaties—binding even the legislature of the state. In an increasing number of modern democracies the higher law is backed up by courts and a system of judicial review which give it, so to speak, teeth. Within this constitutional ethos judicial protection of fundamental human rights has a central place. Constitutionalism, despite its counter-majoritarian effect is regarded as a complimentary principle to majoritarianism rather than its negation. One formulation which describes the complex relationship between the two is the notion of protection against a tyranny of the majority—seemingly an oxymoron. I think the appeal of rights has to do with two roots. The first of these two roots regards fundamental rights (and liberties) as an expression of a vision of humanity which vests the deepest values in the individual which, hence, may not be compromised by anyone. Probably one of the oldest and most influential sources of this vision is to be found in the Pentateuch: *And God created man in His own image, in the image of God created He him.* (Gen. I:27). With this trademark, what legislator has the authority to transgress the essential humanity of the species? Naturally, there are secular, humanist parallels to this vision a plenty.

The other root for the great appeal of right, and part of the justification, even if counter-majoritarian, looks to them as an instrument for the promotion of the *per se* value of putting constraints on power. Modern democracy emerges, after all, also as a rejection of absolutism—and absolutism is not the prerogative of kings and emperors. Similar sentiments inform the great appeal of fundamental boundaries in non-unitary systems such as federal states and the European Union. I use the term Fundamental Boundaries as a metaphor for the principle of enumerated powers or limited competences which are designed to guarantee that in certain areas communities (rather than individuals) should be free to make their own social choices without interference from above. If you wish, if fundamental rights are about the autonomy and self-determination of the individual, fundamental boundaries are about the autonomy and self-determination of communities. The appeal of fundamental boundaries rests as well on two parallel roots. First as an expression of a vision of humanity which vests the deepest values in communities (potentially existing within larger polities) which, thus, must be protected. This Community vision of humanity derives from an acknowledgment of the social nature of humankind, as a counterbalance to the atomistic view of the individual which is reflected in the concept of individual rights and liberties. It too finds a powerful Biblical expression in the Pentateuch: *And the Lord God said: It is not good that man should be alone* (Gen. II:18). Fundamental boundaries around communities-of-value become the guarantee against existential aloneness—the protection of the *Gemeinschaft* against the *Gesellschaft.* Its second root is a reflection at the level of social organization of that same *per se* value of non-aggregation of power. Fundamental boundaries constitute and thus ensure different realms of power.

At first blush it would seem that these two basic principles need not clash at all. There could be, it would seem, a neat, tidy way to situate fundamental rights and fundamental boundaries within the constitutional architecture of Europe. For example, one set of norms and institutions, national-constitutional and/or transnational, would take care of human rights: Ensuring that no public authority at any level of governance would violate the basic autonomy and liberty of the individual. Another set of norms, national-constitutional and/or transnational, would take care of boundaries: ensuring that transnational governance would not encroach on fundamental societal choices of, principally, states.

The adoption of the ECHR by the Member States of the Council of Europe is a reflection of this tidy arrangement: The High Contracting Parties of the ECHR retain their full prerogatives as sovereign states. State boundaries constitute thus, *par excellence,* fundamental boundaries which guarantee full autonomy of their respective national societies. The one self-limiting exception concerns the core fundamental human rights given expression in the ECHR which may not be transgressed in any of these societies. Thus, the universalism of human rights and the particularism of fundamental boundaries may rest together like the Wolf and Sheep.

You will note, however, that I used the term "core fundamental rights" in drawing this idyll. The neat arrangement which the ECHR may be said to represent can only work in relation to a core which gives expression to those "rights", or to those "levels of protection", which are said to be universal, transcending any legitimate cultural or political difference among different societies in, at least, the universe of Europe. The ECHR is premised on this understanding.

Critically and crucially the ECHR does not exhaust the spectrum of human rights. By its own self-understanding, whereas the ECHR provides the "minimum standard" of protection "below" which no state may fall, the High Contracting Parties are free, perhaps even encouraged, to offer "higher" standards of protection to individuals. Indeed, part of the uniqueness of states, part of what differentiates them from each other may be the very way they give protection beyond the core universal standard. Thus, the commitment to, and the acceptance of, the ECHR as a universal, culturally transcendent core of human rights is, surely, an expression of a very important aspect of the political culture of a state which brings it together with other states and societies. When this is backed up by submission to transnational machinery of enforcement the commitment is all the more expressive.

But, I would argue, the differences in the protection of human rights in these societies within the large band which exists beyond the universal core, are no less an important aspect of the political culture and identity of societies. Human rights constitute thus both a source of, and index for, cross-national differentiation and not only cross-national assimilation.

Here is a banal example to illustrate the point. Freedom of expression is a fundamental right in relation to which a transcendent universal core of protected speech may be defined across national divides in the framework of, say, the ECHR. But there is, evidently, a large margin for rights discourse beyond that core of protected speech. In America, a band of neo-nazis may march with full regalia in the neighbourhood of Holocaust survivors. An attempt by the local authorities to ban such a march will be struck down as compromising the fundamental right to freedom of expression of the marchers. In many European countries, and clearly in, say, Germany, such speech would be prohibited without that prohibition being construed in violation of core freedom of expression. I would make three comments on the example.

First, we do not capture the contrast of values inherent in this example by simply saying that in America you get a little bit more protection of freedom of expression than in, say, Germany. Often, there is much more to these differences. It is through these differences, and others like them, that societies at times define some of their core values which go to their very self-understanding—their particularized identity rooted in history, and social and political culture. America is saying something very important about itself (good and/or bad) when it insists on the right of the individual to engage in such extremist, even injurious speech. Germany says something very important about itself (good and/or bad) when it would deny the individual such a right.

It may even be saying something rather profound about a different emphasis on individualism and communitarianism in the respective polities.

Secondly, there is another sense in which it would be simplifying these societal choices to articulate them as a "mere" difference between level of protection of human rights. Human rights are almost invariably the expression of a compromise between competing social goods in the polity. In liberal democracies, the most typical is an accommodation between, on the one hand, the various interests of the collectivity represented by governmental authority and, on the other, the interest of the individual in autonomy and individual liberty. Society may find it very important to empower the individual against government authority. That is how we normally think of human rights. But society may find it very important too to empower government authority against the individual. The fight against crime comes, perhaps, first to mind. Alternatively, in the context, say, of rights to private property and land reform, as differences between capitalist-liberalism and the gamut of socialist world views show the need to look at human rights as a looking-glass reflection of government or public rights is evidenced. The extent of government power (as well as the desirability) to interfere with private property rights (for example, programmes for nationalization) was for long a dividing line between governments of left or right persuasion within European liberal democracies.

Critically, when a society strikes that balance between these competing interests and characterizes that balance as a fundamental right or liberty (to property, to free speech, etc.) it is the balance which is fundamental: The fundamental right of the individual to be protected against government power set against the fundamental right of the public through government to act in accordance with the general interest. Note that it is as injurious to the social choice involved in this balance to compromise the right of the individual as it would be to limit the rights of government. This balance is an expression, then, of core values, of basic societal choices. This is the point where the distinction between rights and boundaries collapses since fundamental rights—beyond the core—become an expression of the kind of particularized societal choice of which fundamental boundaries are an expression. Fundamental boundaries are designed, thus, to allow communities and polities to make and live by those differing balances which they deem fundamental. Beyond the agreed core, to foist a fundamental right on a society is, arguably, to tamper with its fundamental boundaries.

Finally, the position of the ECHR in relation to this tension is, once more, worth defining. Imagine that the example of the neo-nazi march were transported into Europe. Imagine further one ECHR state following the American solution. So now we would have one state prohibiting the march and one state protecting it. The jurisprudence of the ECHR would not hold the prohibition on the march as a violation of freedom of expression protected by the ECHR. But, in this type of case, it would also not interfere with the state which protected the rights of the marchers. In relation to freedom of expression the ECHR would be concerned to define a core of protected speech, a minimum level of protection. Once it was decided (for good or for bad) that the neo-nazi hate speech did not fall within this core, states would be free to protect it or to ban it and to part define themselves and differentiate themselves in terms of the choice they made on this issue. This is part of the famous margin of appreciation which the ECHR allows. States might, as I mentioned, even constitutionalize such a choice, and make it a "fundamental" part of their self-understanding. The difference between the states would thus become fundamental. By contrast, in relation to speech found to be within the core protected by the ECHR, states would not be able to make that choice. They would be bound by a shared view, namely, that the protection of that particular speech vindicated a right which was transcendent and to which all were bound. In this case the commonality between the states would be fundamental.

Another way of describing the play of the ECHR in this context is to say that it defines the margin within which states may opt for different fundamental balances between government and individuals. It defines the area within which fundamental boundaries may be drawn. However, certain balances, tilted too much in favour of government are not permitted. It is against this background that I turn now to the protection of fundamental rights in the legal order of the Union.

2   HUMAN RIGHTS IN THE UNION LEGAL ORDER

2.1 Judicial protection of fundamental human rights and European Community measures: The conundrum of "high" and "low" standards

Neither the Treaty of Paris nor the Treaty of Rome contained any allusion to the protection of fundamental human rights. And yet, once the ECJ put in place its constitutional jurisprudence in cases such as *Van Gend en Loos*[1] and *Costa* v *ENEL*[2] it became legally and politically imperative that a way be found to vindicate fundamental human rights at the Community level. How

---

[1] Case 26/62 *Van Gend en Loos* v *Nederlandse Administratie der Belastingen,* [1963] ECR 1.

[2] Case 6/64, *Costa* v *Enel,* [1964] ECR 585.

could one assert the direct effect and supremacy of European law—vesting huge constitutional power in the political organs of the Community—without postulating embedded legal and judicial guarantees on the exercise of such power? After all, the effect of direct effect and supremacy would be to efface the possibility of national legislative or judicial control of Community law. This imperative was all the more urgent given the notorious democratic deficiencies of European governance, in some respects more acute in the 1960s than in the 1980s and 1990s. How could one expect the constitutional and other high courts of the Member States, especially of those Member States with national constitutional orders and judicial review such as, at the time, Germany and Italy, to accept the direct effect and supremacy of Community norms without an assurance that human rights would be protected within the Community legal order and, critically, that individuals would not lose any of the protections afforded under national constitutions?

Protecting human rights became a joined legal and political imperative. The response to this imperative, the story of *Stauder* and *Nold* and all the rest is well-known, and there is no need to recapitulate. The investigation into the legal basis and formal constitutional legitimacy of this act of so-called judicial activism by the ECJ whereby the Court put in a place, or discovered, an unwritten Bill of Rights against which to check the legality of Community measures.[3]

It is the perspective of Rights-as-Values that is of interest to me in this chapter. The issues can be drawn out at their sharpest by imagining the ECJ's jurisprudence as a dialogue with, or a monologue at, its national counterparts.

Let us take the *Hauer* case[4] as our basic factual matrix: Imagine (following *Hauer*) a Community measure, say a Regulation, which restricts the use of agricultural land, prohibiting its exploitation as a vineyard by its owner, a German national, and, thus, arguably compromising her right to "private property". States differ in the extent to which they will protect private property against governmental authority. Imagine therefore further, merely for the sake of argument, that in Germany the constitutional norm and practice afford greater protection to private property than, say, in Italy and that both offer more protection than the core guaranteed under the ECHR. Let us, finally, imagine that Germany affords protection of private property greater than any other Member State in the Community.

---

[3] See, for instance, Chapters 1 and 2 in this volume.

[4] Case 44/79, *Hauer* v *Land Rheinland-Pfalz*, [1979] ECR 3727.

Direct effect and supremacy mean that the national legal orders must uphold the Community measure restricting the use of agricultural land and potentially compromising the fundamental human right to private property. It therefore falls to the ECJ to check the Community regulation. The potential conflict of values emerges, classically, in response to the question: Which standard of protection should the ECJ adopt? Given the legal and political imperatives I suggested above, there would seem to be a ready and easy answer: The ECJ should adopt the high, German, standard.

Several reasons argue for this "maximalist" approach. First, it may be argued with an idealistic turn, that the Community should always seek to adopt the highest standard of human rights around. If, in the field of property rights it is a German standard, so be it. After all, it is often asserted in the regulatory area that European political decision-making creates the danger of a race to the bottom, of lowest common denominator choices. Why, then, not have in the field of human rights a race to the top? Idealism would, in this instance, be complemented by expediency: How would you expect the German Constitutional Court to accept less? From the German perspective, it would not be enough that the ECJ undertake in principle to scrutinize Community legislation for violation of human rights. Its yardstick for scrutiny must be "up to standard"—the German standard. It is only the combination of the procedural with the material, of the institutional with the constitutional, that will give the necessary assurances necessary to accept supremacy and all the rest.

The virtue of the maximalist approach goes even further since, it is argued, while it would satisfy the German legal order, it would not dissatisfy the other legal orders. For, if the ECJ were to adopt the "high" German standard in this area, what would be the reaction of, say, the Italian legal order and that of the other Member States? They, the argument goes, would not and should not object since the measure to be judged by the high German standard would be a Community measure. Their own legislation would not be touched. And in other areas the ECJ would be looking to their standards, always choosing the highest around.

And yet the maximalist approach does not work, cannot work and, for good reason, has been rejected by the Court. The maximalist approach would be satisfactory neither from an individual Member State perspective nor from a Community or Union perspective. In some cases it is not achievable at all.

To explain why, consider first another hypothetical example. Imagine a Member State like Ireland, with relatively little heavy industry. Imagine further that the Member State adopts a constitutional amendment which introduces a fundamental human right to clear air which was then interpreted by the domestic constitutional court as requiring a very high level of purity. To impose these standards on, say, heavy coal and steel industries would be to render them economically non-viable, but this is a matter which need not concern the Irish political and legal policy-maker since Ireland has no coal and steel industries. Imagine now that at some stage the Community adopts an industrial policy which in combination with its environmental protection policy allows certain levels of factory emissions which exceed the strict ("high") Irish standard. If, at this point, the European policy were challenged before the ECJ, would it, under the maximalist approach be obliged to adopt the Irish standard for the entire Community and strike the policy down? Let us now move beyond the hypothetical case and articulate in more abstract terms the high/low conundrum.

If, on the one hand, the Community's constitutional architecture which includes direct effect and supremacy should not compromise the protection of individual rights guaranteed in the various Member States; and if the ECJ is to secure and maintain the loyalty of its national counterparts to the EU constitutional structure, then, it would seem, the Court would have to adopt the maximalist approach—in each case it would have to choose the highest level of human rights protection which exists among the Member States.

No wonder that the ECJ in *Hauer* said the following:[5]

> fundamental rights form an integral part of the general principles of the law, the observance of which it ensures; that in safeguarding those rights, the Court is bound to draw inspiration from constitutional traditions common to the Member States, *so that measures which are incompatible with the fundamental rights recognized by the constitutions of those States are unacceptable in the Community*; and that, similarly, international treaties for the protection of human rights on which the Member States have collaborated or of which they are signatories, can supply guidelines which should be followed within the framework of Community law.

If, on the other hand, the ECJ were to adopt in each case the highest standard of protection it would mean, as in our hypothetical "Irish" case, that it would be subject to the constitutional dictate of individual Member States even when these national standards of protection may be considered as entirely unsuitable for the Community as a whole. No wonder that in the same case the ECJ said as follows:[6]

---

[5] Case 44/79, loc. cit., note 4. Recital 15, emphasis added.

[6] Recital 14, emphasis added.

the question of a possible infringement of fundamental rights by a measure of the Community institutions can only be judged in the light of Community law itself. *The introduction of special criteria for assessment stemming from the legislation or constitutional law of a particular Member State would, by damaging the substantive unity and efficacy of Community law, lead inevitably to the destruction of the unity of the Common Market and the jeopardizing of the Cohesion of the Community.*

The problem is even more complex calling into question the very utility of using the "high" and "low", maximal/minimal nomenclature in this context.

Consider first the situation when at issue is a fundamental human right which seeks to protect rights as between individuals *inter se*. No clearer is the case in relation to abortion as emerged in the *Grogan* case.[7] *Grogan* provides a classic illustration why the maximalist approach was rejected and why it cannot both as a matter of policy and logic be accepted in this type of case. In Ireland there was a very "high" level of protection for the unborn. What if in another Member State, the "opposing" right of a woman to autonomy over her body was constitutionally guaranteed including the right to abort a foetus in certain circumstances? Which of the two rights would the ECJ choose to recognize as a Community right? Is there any meaning to a maximalist approach in this situation? In the case of abortion how can the Court recognize the near to absolute right of the unborn in the Irish Constitution and at the same time uphold a woman's right to self-determination, which, say, in another Member State permits abortion in some situations?

It could, however, be argued that the abortion situation is special, pitting as it were one individual against another. In most situations, it could be argued, the philosophy of rights pits the individual against public authorities. In those cases, the vast majority, it still does make sense to talk about high and low standards of protection, and, consequently, the maximalist approach would be feasible and desirable. To understand the fallacy of this argument we have to recall the introductory remarks on human rights as an expression of a fundamental balance between rights of the individual and rights of public authorities. To say, as we did in our hypothetical case based on *Hauer* that Germany has the highest level of protection of private property among the Member States is also to say that Germany, in this area, places the largest number of restrictions on public authorities to act in the general interest. The rights of the public at large have the "lowest" level of protection. Even if this is so, we could still ask why it would matter to the Italian legal order that in

---

[7] Case C-159/90, *Society for the Protection of Unborn Children Ireland,* [1991] ECR I-4685.

the area of private property rights the ECJ adopts the "high" German standard? After all, as we already mentioned, that choice does not interfere with the conduct of Italian socio-economic policies by Italian public authorities. This very question represents a failure to grasp that what is fundamental in fundamental rights is the balance struck between individual and public interests.

If this is understood, surely the answer to the question is that it could and should matter to the Italian legal order that the ECJ adopts the German standard simply because it is the "highest". The fallacy rests in the unstated assumption that "higher" standards are always desirable. But we know better. We know that to adopt the "higher" German standard (or that of another Member State, as the case may be) is to adopt for the Community as a whole the societal *Weltanschauung* struck in a particular Member State between individual and the public at large. It is to adopt for the Community as a whole the fundamental values of a particular Member State. At least two things are problematic with such an outcome.

The Community is comprised of many Member States and peoples. Its basic values should be an expression of that mixture. The maximalist approach would always privilege the core values of one Member State, the one which happened to accord the "highest" level of protection to the individual, the "lowest" level of protection to the public and the general interest.

Further, when applied across the board, the "maximal" approach could lead to an interesting result. In all Member States there would tend to be a balance among different human rights—some privileging the individual, others the public and the general interest. If the ECJ were to adopt a maximalist approach this would simply mean that for the Community in each and every area the balance would be most restrictive on the public and general interest. A maximalist approach to human rights would result in a minimalist approach to Community government. This, in the eyes of some, would be a fine choice of socio-economic values. It may be so, or may not. But it should not happen as the unintended consequence of a (non-workable) policy of protecting human rights.

How, then, can one solve, if at all, this conundrum? How can one square the need to prevent that the Union's constitutional architecture be bought at the expense of compromising individual rights hitherto protected by national constitutions, which points towards a maximal standard policy, with the realization that such a policy is inherently flawed, and in some instances simply not workable? How has the ECJ sought to square this vicious circle? Again *Hauer* can provide the clues. Let us here move from the hypothetical to the actual judgment and see how the Court attempts to resolve the conundrum.

The ECJ first repeats its basic philosophy and methodology in this specific context: The right to property is guaranteed in the Community legal order in accordance with the ideas common to the constitutions of the Member States, which are also reflected in Protocol No. 1 to the ECHR.[8] Whereas earlier it said that "measures which are incompatible with the fundamental rights recognized by the constitutions of those States are unacceptable in the Community",[9] there is now a subtle change: the ECJ is insisting that the right to property will be guaranteed in accordance with *ideas* common to the constitutions of the Member State. I interpret that as the ECJ itself edging away from the vocabulary of standards. Interestingly, the Court deals first with the protection afforded through the ECHR. Referring to Article 1 of the Protocol,[10] the ECJ simply notes that the Council Regulation at issue would come within the right of a state "to enforce such laws as it deems necessary to control the use of property in accordance with the general interest". Further, the provisions in the ECHR, in the eyes of the ECJ, do not enable a sufficiently precise answer to be given to the question submitted by the German Court.[11]

It is clear that for the purposes of its decision the ECJ regards itself subject to the requirements of the Protocol despite the fact that the Community as such is not a signatory. Secondly, it is in my view evident that the ECJ regards the ECHR and its Protocols as mere starting-points, as the first and not most difficult steeplechase which the Community regulation has to pass. It is hugely important to note that although the Court regards the Community as bound by the Convention it does not regard the Convention as setting "The" standard of protection for the Community. Like a state, the Community may not violate the Convention but may go beyond it.

The ECJ then moves to define its own balance. Its starting-point seems to respect the rhetoric employed earlier: "[I]n order to be able to answer [the question], it is necessary to consider also the indications provided by the

---

[8] Case 44/79, loc. cit., note 4. Recital 17.

[9] Recital 15.

[10] Every ... person is entitled to the peaceful enjoyment of his possessions. No one shall be deprived of his possessions except in the public interest and subject to the conditions provided for by law and by the general principles of international law. The preceding provisions shall not, however, in any way impair the right of a State to enforce such laws as it deems necessary to control the use of property in accordance with the general interest or to secure the payment taxes or other contributions or penalties.

[11] Recital 19.

constitutional rules and practices of the nine [as they then were] Member States".[12] In practice the ECJ gives only three textual examples (from the German, Italian and Irish Constitutions) but then goes on to declare that:

> ... those [constitutional] rules and practices permit the legislature to control the use of private property in accordance with the general interest .... In all the Member States, numerous legislative measures have given concrete expression to that social function of the right to property. Thus in all the Member States there is legislation on agriculture and forestry, the water supply, the protection of the environment and town and country planning, which imposes restrictions, sometimes appreciable, on the use of real property.
> More particularly, all the wine-producing countries of the Community have restrictive legislation, albeit of differing severity, concerning the planting of vines [etc.] ... [which is not] considered to be incompatible in principle with the regard due to the right to property.

This, in my view, is the most critical juncture in the decision. If all the ECJ was doing was to ensure that "measures which are incompatible with the fundamental rights recognized by the constitutions of those States are unacceptable in the Community", it could have reached a rapid conclusion to its decision at this point. Surely the above analysis proves beyond doubt that the Community regulation in question is not incompatible with the fundamental rights recognized by the constitutions of the Member States. But there would have been a huge price to pay had the ECJ ended its decision at this point. The implication could have been that had it discovered that a similar measure were held unconstitutional in one of the Member States, the Community measure too would have to be struck down. At a stroke we would be back to the Maximal Standard trap.

Instead, the ECJ reverts to the second strand in its reasoning, that the right to property is guaranteed in the Community legal order in accordance with the *ideas* common to the constitutions of the Member States. The constitutional practices of the Member States are not used by the ECJ as a test for the constitutionality of the Community measure but simply as a source for culling the "ideas" inherent in the right to private property.

This the ECJ defines, not surprisingly, as a requirement that interference with private property "correspond[s] to objectives of general interest pursued by the Community" and, in a cumulative test (though the ECJ uses the word "or") the measure must not "constitute a disproportionate and intolerable

---

[12] Recital 20.

interference with the rights of the owner, impinging upon the very substance of the right to property".

These two tests of substantive and procedural policy good faith and proportionality, are of course known in virtually all systems of administrative and legislative review. It is worth noting that in substance the ECJ has not really developed criteria which are in any way more precise than those enumerated in the ECHR and which it had earlier dismissed rather curtly as not enabling it to give an answer.

Since we are not interested in the substance of property law in the EU, it is not necessary to go into the detailed assessment by the ECJ of the aims of the agricultural policy at the basis of the contested regulation, nor into its assessment of the reasonableness of the measure itself, save to make some general comments on the method as a whole.

First it is clear that in assessing what is the "general interest" which the measure must serve the ECJ makes reference to the *Community* general interest and not to an aggregate or cumulative Member State interest. In adducing the general interest the Court looks at the preamble of the regulation and at the general objectives of the Common Agricultural Policy as enunciated in the Treaty.

Proportionality is also discussed in terms of the Community policy. The ECJ makes reference to the temporary nature of the regulation and the conjunctural situation of the Community as a whole suffering from a surplus in the vine sector. In the light of its analysis of these factors the ECJ concludes:[13]

> the measure criticized does not entail any undue limitation upon the exercise of the right to property. Indeed, the cultivation of new vineyards in a situation of continuous over-production would not have any effect, from the economic point of view, apart from increasing the volume of the surpluses; further, such an extension at that stage would entail the risk of making more difficult the implementation of a structural policy at the Community level in the event of such a policy resting on the application of criteria more stringent than the current provisions of national legislation concerning the selection of land accepted for wine-growing.
> ... the restriction ... is justified by the objectives of general interest pursued by the Community and does not infringe the substance of the right to property in the form in which it is recognized and protected in the Community legal order.

---

[13] Recitals 29 and 30.

What does this have to tell us on the way the ECJ addresses the issue of "high" and "low" standards? The following is my interpretation of this case and the general jurisprudence. It is clear that the ECJ rejects the maximal approach. To repeat:[14]

> the question of a possible infringement of fundamental rights by a measure of the Community institutions can only be judged in the light of Community law itself. *The introduction of special criteria for assessment stemming from the legislation or constitutional law of a particular Member State would, by damaging the substantive unity and efficacy of Community law, lead inevitably to the destruction of the unity of the Common Market and the jeopardizing of the cohesion of the Community.*

But the ECJ's move is even bolder. It rejects, in my view, any attempt at some mathematical averages approach to this issue. In its dialogue with its national counterparts its claim is jurisdictional: Only the ECJ is in a position to make the determination on the compatibility of a Community measure with fundamental human rights.

I will explain this in two steps. Assume first that the ECJ were to adopt the "German" standard (or that of any other Member State). It would still have to apply that standard to the facts of the case and to the material, geographic, social and other matrix of the Community, which is different from that of any Member State. Imagine that the German Government were to pass an identical measure restricting the growth of vineyards in its territory. Imagine further that *on the German market* planting such a vineyard would make economic sense. It is conceivable that German Constitutional Court would find that the state could not prove a sufficiently strong general interest to outweigh the interest of the individual in his or her unrestricted use of their private property. But in the Community geographic and socio-economic context it is possible that planting the vineyard in Germany could put someone out of work in Sicily. The ECJ's first claim is that only it, given its position, is able meaningfully to assess the claims of general interest and proportionality in the Community as a whole.

The second implicit claim in *Hauer* is even bolder. The language of the constitutional provisions it cites from the German, Italian and Irish Constitutions is as bland as the text of Protocol No. 1 to the ECHR. It is the respective ECJ in each of these systems which translates the bland language into the societal choice, the fundamental balance between the individual and the general public. To the best of their ability judges will give expression to the

---

[14] Recital 14, emphasis added.

constitutional ethos of the constitutional text and of the polity in those decisions. Why we should entrust such a fundamental choice to our judges is a different question, but that we do so entrust them with the task is beyond dispute. The care we take in choosing judges to constitutional courts is an acknowledgment of that function we give to them. The ECJ's implicit claim in *Hauer* is that the Community legal order can do no better or worse than its national counterparts. It inevitably falls to a court itself to make that fundamental balance for the Community legal order. But clearly the ECJ, when fleshing out the bland language of general interest and proportionality should try to give expression to a constitutional ethos which derives from its controlling texts—not the constitution of one Member State but of all of them. Just as in the geographical-political sense the Community constitutes a polity different from its Member States with a general interest which must include Bavaria and Sicily, so too its constitutional ethos should reflect the various Member State constitutions as well as the Union's own founding Treaties. It is a new polity the constitutional ethos of which must give expression to a multiplicity of traditions. The implicit claim of the ECJ is that in the field of Community law a Community law balance will have to be struck which derives from the specificity of the Community. The Court is calling on its national counterparts to accept that it, the ECJ, will do or has to do, within the Community legal order what they, national courts, do or have to do, within the national realms. It is not about high or low standards. It is a call to acknowledge the Community and Union as a polity with its own separate identity and constitutional sensibilities which has to define its own fundamental balances—its own core values.

2.2 Protection of fundamental human rights: review of Member State measures

My starting-point here is the well-known development in the jurisprudence of the ECJ from a practice which focused on Community measures to a jurisprudence which is willing to scrutinize some Member State measures too.

Here too the general story is well-known. The material landmarks are *Rutili, Cinéthèque, Klensch, Wachauf,* Advocate General in *Grogan, ERT.* I do not consider it necessary to recapitulate fully the facts of these cases or their principal holdings. Briefly stated, the ECJ, who regards it its duty to ensure the protection of fundamental rights within the field of Community law, has construed that field to include Member State measures implementing Community law as well as Member State measures adopted in derogation from the prohibition on restricting the free movement of the four factors of production.

In the first part of this chapter we saw how even the review of *Community* measures may create a tension with fundamental values of the various Member States. Here the "assault" is more direct since at issue are *Member State* measures normally thought to be subject to the scrutiny and control of Member State courts.

Now, returning to the issue of standards: we have seen that in relation to Community measures the possible concern of Member State courts was that the Community standards might not be high enough thus letting stand Community measure which, but for the doctrine of supremacy would be struck down by national courts. In relation to Member State measures the principal concern would be reversed, namely that in reviewing Member State measures, the ECJ strike down acts authorized by the domestic jurisdiction and possibly even sanctioned by the ECHR.

The first and most pressing issue that has to be addressed in this context is the very justification for review of Member State measures by the ECJ. If, as I argued in the introduction to this chapter, constitutionally protected human rights express core societal choices as to the balance between individual and community interests (and visions), an "encroachment" by the ECJ would be a direct challenge to the fundamental boundaries of the Member States. There has already been considerable protest in this regard. What then is the justification for this jurisdictional drive?

The ECJ has extended, so far, the exercise of its human rights jurisdiction to Member State measures in two types of situation: (1) The "agency situation"—when the Member State is acting for and/or on behalf of the Community and implementing a Community policy (*Klensch*[15] and *Wachauf*[16]); and (2) When the state relies on a derogation to fundamental market freedoms (*ERT*).[17] How is this to be evaluated from a narrower "legal" point of view?

2.2.1 The rationale for "agency" review. All of us often fall into the trap of thinking of the Community as an entity wholly distinct from the Member States. But of course, like some well-known theological concepts, the Community is, in some senses, its Member States, in other senses separate from them. This, as two thousand years of Christian theology attest, can at times be hard to grasp. But in one area of Community life it is easy. In the

---

[15] Joined Cases 201 and 202/85, *Klensch* v *Secrétaire d'État,* [1986] ECR 3477.

[16] Case C-5/88, *Wachauf* v *Federal Republic of Germany,* [1989] ECR 2609.

[17] Case C-260/89, *Elliniki Radiophonia Tileorassi (ERT),* [1991] ECR I-2925.

Community system of governance, to an extent far greater than any federal state, the Member States often act as and indeed are the executive branch of the Community. When, to give an example, a British customs official collects a Community imposed customs duty from an importer of non-Community goods, he or she is organically part of the British customs service, but functionally he or she is wearing a Community hat. If the ECJ's human rights jurisdiction covers, as it clearly does, not merely the formal legislative Community normative source, but its *mise-en-œuvre,* is it not really self-evident, as Advocate General Jacobs puts it in *Wachauf,* even on a narrow construction of the ECJ's human rights jurisdiction, that it should review these "Member State" measures for violation of human rights? In this case the very nomenclature which distinguished Member State and Community acts fails to capture the reality of Community governance and the Community legal order. Not to review these acts would be legally inconsistent with the constant human rights jurisprudence and, from the human rights policy perspective, arbitrary: If the Commission is responsible for the *mise-en-œuvre* review will take place but if it is a Member State, it will not?

2.2.2 The rationale for ERT *type review.* The development in *ERT,*[18] foreshadowed by the Opinion of the Advocate General in *Grogan*[19] is more delicate. The Treaty interdicts Member State measures which interfere with the fundamental free movement provisions of the Treaty. This interdiction applies to any Member State measure, regardless of its source. The mere fact that the interference may emanate from a constitutional norm is, in and of itself, irrelevant. Likewise, the fact that the constitutional measures may be the expression of deeply held national societal mores or values is, in and of itself, irrelevant. If, say, a Member State, even under widespread popular conviction and support, were to adopt a constitutional amendment which, "in the interest of preserving national identity and the inalienable fundamental rights of our citizens" prohibited an undertaking from employing foreigners, including Community nationals, ahead of Member State citizens or to purchase foreign goods ahead of national products, such a constitutional provision would be in violation of Community law.

Community law itself defines two situations which may exculpate such a national measure from the Treaty interdiction. First, the national measure itself must be considered as constituting an illegal interference with the market

---

[18] Case C-260/89, loc. cit., note 17.

[19] Case C-159/90, loc. cit., note 7. See also Chapter 2 in this volume.

freedom. The Treaty is very vague on this and the ECJ has developed a rich case law in this regard. Not every measure which on its face seems to interfere will necessarily be construed as a violation of one of the market freedoms. Second, even a national measure which on its face constitutes a violation of the interdiction may, under Community law, be exculpated if it can be shown to fall under derogation clauses to be found in the Treaty. Article 36, for example, speaks of measures "justified" on grounds of public morality, health, etc.

The crucial point is that defining what constitutes a violation of the basic market freedoms is, substantively and jurisdictionally, a matter of Community law and for the ECJ to decide, as is the exculpatory regime. Substantively the ECJ will interpret the language of the Treaty, which is often opaque: What, for example, does (or should) "justified" mean or "public order"? Jurisdictionally, the ECJ (in tandem with national jurisdictions) will supervise that the Member States are in fact fulfilling their obligations under the Treaty.

One way of explaining the "extension" of human rights jurisdiction to Member State measures in the *ERT* situation is simple enough. Once a Member State measure is found to be in violation of the market freedoms, *but for* the derogation it would be illegal. The scope of the derogation and the conditions for its employment are all "creatures" of Community law, Treaty and judge made. Now, it could be argued in opposition, and I would not consider this a specious argument, that one should look at the derogations as defining the limit of Community law reach. I am not persuaded. Even from a formalist perspective, the very structure of, say, Articles 30–36 indicates the acceptance of the Member States that the legality or otherwise of a measure constituting a prima-facie violation of the prohibition on measures having effect to quantitative restrictions becomes a matter for Community law. From a policy perspective it could hardly be otherwise. Imagine the state of the common market if each Member State could determine by reference to its own laws and values—without any reference to Community law—what was or was not covered by the prohibition and its derogation. Surely how wide or narrow the derogation is, should be controlled by Community law. The concomitant consequence of this is that once it is found that a Member State measure contravenes the market freedom interdictions such as Article 30, even if it is exculpated by a derogation clause in the Treaty, the Community's legislative competence is triggered and it may become susceptible to harmonization.

Let us illustrate this by taking the most telling instance: The rule of reason doctrine developed principally in *Cassis de Dijon*,[20] of which *Cinéthè-*

---

[20] Case 120/78, *Rewe v Bundesmonopolverwaltung für Branntwein,* [1979] ECR 649.

que[21] is an example. Here the ECJ has carved out new circumstances, not explicitly mentioned in the Treaty derogation clause, which would allow the Member States to adopt measures which otherwise would be a violation of Article 30. I do not recall any protest by Member States complaining about the ECJ's rather audacious construction of Articles 30–36 in this regard. But, obviously the Member States are not given a free hand. The ECJ will have to be persuaded that the Member State measures seeking to benefit from the rule of reason are, for example, as a matter of Community law, in the general interest and of sufficient importance to override the interest in the free movement of goods, that they are proportionate to the objective pursued, that they are adopted in good faith and are not a disguised restriction to trade. So, the ability of the Member States to move within the derogations to the free movement provisions are subject to a series of limitations, some explicitly to be found in the Treaty, others the result of judicial construction of the Treaty.

In construing the various Community law limitations on the Member States' ability to derogate from the Treaty and in administering these limitations in cases that come before it, should the ECJ insist on all these other limitations and yet adopt a "hands off" attitude towards violation of human rights? Is it so revolutionary to insist that when the Member States avail themselves of a Community law created derogation they also respect the fundamental human rights, deriving from the constitutional traditions of the Member States, even if the European Community construction of this or that right differs from its construction in this or that Member State? After all, *but for* the judicially constructed rule of reason in *Cassis,* France would not be able to justify at all its video cassette policy designed to protect French cinematographic culture. To respect the Community notion of human rights in this scenario appears to us wholly consistent with the earlier case law and the policy behind it.

It could be argued that in supervising the derogation the ECJ should not enter into the policy merits of the Member State measure other than to check that it is proportionate and not a disguised restriction to trade. Human rights review, on this reading, is an interference with the merits. Again, I am not persuaded. First it must be understood that the doctrine of proportionality also involves a Community imposed value choice by the ECJ on a Member State. Each time the Court says, for example, that a label informing the consumer will serve a policy adequately compared to an outright prohibition, it is clear that at least some consumers will, despite the label, be misled. There are ample

---

[21] Joined Cases 60 and 61/84, *Cinéthèque* v *Fédération nationale des cinémas français,* [1985] ECR 2605.

studies to demonstrate the limited effectiveness of labels. Thus, in the most banal proportionality test "lurks" a judicial decision by the ECJ as to the level of risk society may be permitted to take with its consumers.

Second, even if human rights review may be more intrusive than proportionality review in some cases, it need not always interfere with the actual merits of the policy pursued and could still leave considerable latitude to the state to pursue their own devices. Provided they do not violate human rights, the ECJ will not interfere with the content of the policy. Admittedly this may sometimes thwart their wills, but that, after all, would also be the case under the ECHR. That on some occasions it might give teeth to the ECHR in those countries which have after decades not yet incorporated it into national law, we assume must be welcomed by all those who profess to take rights seriously.

2.3 The double scrutiny of Member State measures: institutional considerations and the question of standards

Even if there is a doctrinal and policy justification for extending human rights review of Member State measures, would it not be overly transgressing the prerogatives of Member State courts? This very question might suggest a view which sees the relationship between the ECJ and its national counterparts in the area of human rights as consisting of a zero-sum game (powers granted to one are taken away from the other) or, worse, confrontational. It suggests perhaps a view which considers a tug-of-war between a *transnational* court and a *national* court. This might be so in some instances, but the relationship is far more complex and in other cases it could, and in my view should, be seen as a relationship between a transnational *court* and a national *court*. A co-operative relationship wherein the critical sense of identity results not from one body being national and the other transnational but from their sense of both belonging to the judicial branch, not confrontational but mutually reenforcing their ability to uphold the law (as they see it). Not, then, a zero-sum game, but a positive sum game with both parties better off.

The institutional dimension is particularly intriguing in relation to the domestic application of the ECHR, especially in those states where the Convention has not been incorporated into domestic law. Consider, for example, the United Kingdom.

By extending its jurisdiction to Member State measures the ECJ may be stepping into areas which previously were reserved to a national court. But that domain may be more illusory than real. What was reserved to UK courts previously? The "power" to tell hapless individuals that, for example, since successive British Governments for their own reasons have refused to incorporate the ECHR into domestic law, courts were unable to give them relief (except, *à la Wachauf*, as an aid in interpretation) even in the face of egregious violations of the ECHR to which their country is a party? One can, of course, take the view that British constitutional arrangements and the denial of power to British courts to apply the ECHR are matters which should be left to Britain. But in anybody's book that would hardly qualify as a position which takes human rights seriously. Moreover, is not the extension of jurisdiction of the ECJ, at least in some respects, an *empowerment* of the United Kingdom courts and a strengthening of the protection of human rights in Britain in that at least in those areas coming within the scope of Community law as defined by the ECJ, British domestic courts would have gained the right and the power, hitherto denied them, to give human rights relief to individuals?

At least as fundamental is the pertinent issue of standards of review. What is the potential there for conflict of fundamental values? My reflections in this respect are very speculative, suggesting at most a possible interpretation of the scant case law. More realistically they should be taken as prognosis of future developments. Let us examine first the *Wachauf* situation: review of a Member State measure implementing Community law or acting for the Community. This review arises only in those situations when the Community norm or policy leaves some discretion to the Member State so that national authorities are choosing from several possible executing or implementing options.

2.3.1 Human rights standards in the Wachauf *situation.* In order to judge the potential for conflict, one has to distinguish between several scenarios.

A. If the measure is in violation of the ECHR, it should be struck down either by the national court or by the ECJ, but there would be no conflict of values since both Community and Member State regard the ECHR as a basic core which cannot be transgressed.

B. In a second scenario the measure clears the ECHR hurdle but is in violation of a more stringent Member State standard though it would not be in violation of the Community standard. In this case, the measure should be struck down by the national court. Since the Community gives the Member State discretion in execution or implementation, provided the Community norm is executed or implemented by one way or another, Community law does not require that Member State standards be violated. There is no conflict of values either.

C. In a third scenario the measure clears both the ECHR hurdle and national standards of human rights but fails the Community standard. Again the measure should be struck down, but there is a conflict of values since the public authorities of the Member State are prohibited from exercising a power in a manner which under domestic constitutional standards would be permitted. However, the conflict is not acute since the Member State public authorities are, *ipso facto* and *ipso jure* acting for and on behalf of the Community.

2.3.2 Human rights standards in the ERT *situation.* The evaluation of the *ERT* situation can be done on the basis of similar scenarios.

A. If a Member State measure violates the ECHR, the measure should be struck down either by national court or by the ECJ. There is no substantive conflict of values since both legal orders accept the ECHR as a basic core which cannot be transgressed. There could, of course, be a difference in interpreting the ECHR minimal standard. The mistake will inevitably fall in favour of human rights.

B. In the second scenario the Member State measure clears the ECHR standard but violates the national standard though it would clear the Community standard. I would submit that the result should be a striking down of the measure. There is no Community interest in overriding a national human rights standard applied by a national court against a Member State *derogating from the Treaty.*

C. In the last scenario the Member State measure clears the ECHR, clears the Member State standard but violates the Community standard. I have come to believe that in the *ERT* situation the Community should not impose its own standard on the Member State measure but allow a wide margin of appreciation, insisting only that the Member State not violates the basic core encapsulated in the ECHR.[22] Unlike the *Wachauf* situation, where the Member State is merely the agent of the Community and the Member State measure is in truth a Community measure, here we are dealing with a Member State measure in application of a Member State policy. The interest of the ECJ and the Community should be to prevent a violation of core human rights but to allow beyond that maximum leeway to national policy. This would essentially equate situation C with situation A with practical effects limited essentially to those jurisdictions, such as the United Kingdom, where national courts are not empowered to enforce under national law the ECHR. They would, as suggested above, be empowered through European Union law. It would also mean that should the Community harmonize disparate Member State derogation measures to, say, Article 30, the standard of human rights

---

[22] This seems to be consistent with the Opinion of Advocate General Van Gerven in *Grogan*, loc. cit., note 7.

review of the harmonized measure may be higher than the standard applied by the ECJ to reviewing the previous Member State measures.

2.4 Concluding remarks

Finally, in the *ERT* situation and more generally, even when the standard for review imposed by the ECJ may be no different than that applying in a Member State I confess to a bias, rebuttable to be sure, in favour of human rights judicial review by courts not directly part of the polity the measures of which come under review. That is why, for example, I favour accession of the Community to the ECHR which would subject even the jurisprudence of the ECJ to a second outside scrutiny. As I noted in the introduction, transnational protection of human rights frequently involves the painful tension between the universal and the particular. So far I have insisted on the value of the particular as encapsulating a fundamental choice of the polity. It is trite to recall, however, that regularly, states defend alleged human rights violations on the grounds of respect for deeply held local cultural practices. Sometimes there is merit in the argument. Often, as in the case of, say, the Southern States in the United States defending in the 1950s and 1960s discrimination against blacks, or some countries today defending the ghastly practice of female mutilation, or corporal punishment of adults (hand chopping) and children (whippings, canings and the like) the defense is specious, a mockery of the transcendental notion of human dignity. In our impressionistic view, local courts, close to local culture, are overly susceptible to this type of argument. We are particularly suspicious of these claims when they emanate in contexts, such as Europe, of considerable common cultural affinity among peoples and with a shared concept of the state and public authority. Adjudicating these competing claims between the particular and the universal is never easy and may not ultimately have a "right" answer. On balance, from the perspective of my own human rights sensibilities, I prefer, in this respect, the bias of the transnational forum to that of the national one, tempered as it is by the doctrine of margin of appreciation and mindful that the transnational forum is, as noted, often a second bite at the apple, the national jurisdiction having already had its say.

Having said that, the principal permutations of review for violation of human rights and the relationship between the different standards of review which have been the object of this chapter can, by way of summary, be set out as follows in tabulated form.

Principal permutations of human rights review in Union legal order

Type of measure	Conformity with ECHR	Conformity with EC Human Rights Standards	Conformity with National Human Rights Standards	Constitutionally Correct Result
Community measure	Violates	(Necessarily) violates	(Necessarily) violates	Should be struck down by ECJ
Community measure	Does not violate	Violates	Does not violate	Should be struck down by ECJ
Community measure	Does not violate	Does not violate	Violates	Should be upheld and not struck down by either ECJ or Member State court
Member State measure: Agency Situation where Member State has discretion	Violates	(Necessarily) violates	(Necessarily) violates	Should be struck down by ECJ or Member State court
Member State measure: Agency Situation where Member State has discretion	Does not violate	Violates	Does not violate	Should be struck down by ECJ or Member State court
Member State measure: Agency Situation where Member State has discretion	Does not violate	Does not violate	Violates	Should be struck down by Member State court and implemented another way

Member State measure: *ERT* situation	Violates	(Necessarily) violates	(Necessarily) violates	Should be struck down by ECJ or Member State court
Member State measure: *ERT* situation	Does not violate	Violates (i.e., EC standard when applied to Community measure goes beyond core ECHR)	Does not violate	Should not be struck down. ECJ should not enforce own standard beyond ECHR core
Member State measure: *ERT* situation	Does not violate	Does not violate	Violates	Should be struck down by Member State court and implemented another way

4 ACCESS TO EUROPEAN UNION INFORMATION: AN ELEMENT OF CITIZENSHIP AND A NEGLECTED CONSTITUTIONAL RIGHT

Deirdre Curtin and *Herman Meijers*

1 INTRODUCTION

Freedom of information, "the great public school of political education",[1] is a central freedom within the democratic model of government. The major justification for granting freedom of information a special status is precisely its role in linking citizen to representative and ensuring accountability of administration, government and legislature.[2] As long ago as 1946 the General Assembly of the United Nations passed a resolution which stated that "Freedom of information is a fundamental human right and is the touchstone for all the freedoms to which the United Nations is consecrated".[3]

Freedom of information can be subdivided into two closely connected but yet free-standing aspects. First, there is the basic principle of the openness of the legislative process—a universal principle recognized by all non-totalitarian regimes and considered a *sine qua non* of the democratic system of governance. Indeed, the adjective "democratic" can hardly be applied where legislative proceedings are secret. This fundamental principle applies in all the Member States of the Union. Article F(1) of the Treaty on European Union (TEU) recognizes that the systems of government of the Member States are founded upon the "principles of democracy" and guarantees to respect them. Moreover, the TEU refers to the respect for fundamental rights as guaranteed

---

[1] Thorbecke, quoted by Ribberink, "Openheid en openbaarheid in Europa", *Overheidsdocumentatie* (1991), p. 236.

[2] See Boyle, "Freedom of Expression and Democracy", in Heffernan (ed.), *Human Rights: A European Perspective* (1994), pp. 211–219.

[3] Resolution of the UN General Assembly 59(I), 14 Dec. 1946. This was followed in 1948 by the Universal Declaration of Human Rights, Art. 19 of which states that: "Everyone has the right to freedom of opinion and expression; this right includes freedom to hold opinions without interference and to seek, receive and impart information and ideas regardless of frontiers."

N. A. Neuwahl and A. Rosas (eds.), The European Union and Human Rights, 77–104.

by the Convention for the Protection of Human Rights and Fundamental Freedoms (European Convention on Human Rights; ECHR) and as they result from the constitutional traditions of the Member States, as general principles of Community law.

It cannot be denied that the fundamental principle of the openness of the legislative procedure present in the constitutional system of every single Member State is just such a general principle. Finally the preamble and the provisions of Protocol No. 1 to the ECHR are particularly instructive in this connection. The preamble to the ECHR states that the "fundamental freedoms" which it lays down "are best maintained ... by an effective political democracy ...". Protocol No. 1 elaborates in that connection—in its Article 3—the duty on the parties to the Convention to organize regular free elections "under conditions which will ensure the free expression of the people in the choice of the legislature". It enshrines a characteristic principle of democracy regarded as of prime importance in the Convention system.[4]

Second, and in addition to this fundamental principle at the root of democracy itself, an increasing number of the Member States of the Union have recognized the fact that the imperatives of democracy *also* demand that the business of the executive arm should be subject to the scrutiny of the general public. Out of the 15 Member States of the Union only four of these countries have neither a constitutional provision on the general principle of access to administrative documents nor specific legislation thereon (Austria, Germany, the United Kingdom and Ireland).[5] The belief underlying these developments is that the quality of the ultimate decisions will be improved not only by the public contribution to the decision-making process itself but perhaps even more by the knowledge of the decision-makers that they are acting in the public view. General understanding and acceptance of their purpose may thereby be increased. Nevertheless all democracies exclude *certain* aspects of public administration from the public eye. This is for example the case with regard to security matters and privacy. Does the ECHR refer to this borderline between the general requirements of openness in a democracy and the exceptions which can validly be made to this general principle? Freedom of information is dealt with in Article 10 ECHR and this freedom is indeed framed in such a fashion that its primary function is to ensure freedom of expression as to the functioning or otherwise of the

---

[4] See, e.g., Eur. Court H. R., *Mathieu-Mohin and Clerfayt* judgment of 2 March 1987, Series A no. 113, p. 22.

[5] For a more detailed account of, *inter alia,* the situation in the Member States, see Curtin and Meijers, "Open Europa", *Nederlands Juristenblad* (forthcoming 1995).

administration. Freedom of expression over unknown administrative practices is, of course, a virtual *contradicto in terminis*. How can an individual realistically and effectively exercise his freedom to express himself fully and without unwarranted hindrance if he is denied by the public authorities any access to information about the functioning in practice of the administration? Suppression of the right to seek information would obviously paralyse the right to receive and communicate information. It can therefore be argued that the very premise on which Article 10 ECHR implicitly rests is that considerable openness must prevail, since if this is not the case what sense is there in solemnly guaranteeing "freedom of expression"?

As is well known, and much documented,[6] the European Union suffers from a "democracy deficit". The preoccupation in this respect has been too exclusively focused on the role of the European Parliament[7] (and its corresponding interaction with national parliaments). Other aspects have as a result been neglected, aspects which deserve particular attention because of the widespread transformation of law-making activity, from the national sphere to that of the Union. However, it is not simply the case that one of the primary means of engaging the interest and loyalty of the people in the European Union as a progressive political system would be to ensure that they are empowered in terms of political debate and opinion formation. In other words, granting the people access to the information necessary for intelligent participation in the process of decision-making is indisputably a vital part of the democratization process of the governing system of the Union.

The issue of freedom of information at the Union level has, however, even more far-reaching implications. These are quite simply that at present the widescale transformation of Union law-making activity, stretching way beyond the classic economic and social terrains of the European Economic Community, has actually brought about a *retrogression* in the quality of democracy prevailing at the national level, and this in clear violation of the explicit wording of Article F(1) TEU. It is not only that the world of the European Union is populated by paper curtains, closed intergovernmental circuits, high civil servant secretive committees, autocratic *Herren der Verträge*, executive

---

[6] See, most recently, Ress, "Democratic Decision-Making in the European Union and the Role of the European Parliament", in Curtin and Heukels (eds), *The Institutional Dynamics of European Integration. Liber Amicorum Henry Schermers* (1994), Vol. II, pp. 153–176; and Weiler, "Parliamentary Democracy in Europe 1992: Tentative Questions and Answers", in Greenberg, Katz, Beth Oliviero and Wheatley (eds), *Constitutionalism and Democracy: Transitions in the Contemporary World* (1993), pp. 249–263.

[7] See also Joerges, "European Economic Law, the Nation-State and the Maastricht Treaty", in Dehousse (ed.), *Europe After Maastricht: An Ever Closer Union?* (1994), pp. 29–62.

specialist agencies, management committees and so forth. It is above all the fact that the actual process of legislation takes place to a high degree in secret, behind closed doors (with the corollary that the documentation on the basis of which the decisions are being taken and the outcome of the voting process in many cases do not enter the public domain)—a fact which grievously offends the tradition and practice of the democratic systems of government as they operate in all 15 Member States.

Freedom of information and the right to freedom of expression have a crucial role to play in strengthening the imperfect democratic order of the European Union. Moreover, the unacceptable face of the process of European integration needs to be recognized once and for all for what it is. This concern is particularly topical with the accession of two Nordic countries where systems of open government are not only deeply entrenched and accepted in the political culture but where access to official documents are regarded as something like a natural right with a counterpart in all civilized societies.[8] As the contradictory declarations made by Sweden and the existing Union Member States annexed to the Accession Treaty[9] graphically illustrate, the issue of openness and transparency in the decision-making process, considered essential by a large part of the Unions citizens,[10] is a time-bomb slowly ticking away. Adequate diffusion requires recognition of the fundamental nature of the principle at stake and a mentality revolution.

2   THE EUROPEAN UNION'S FIRST TENTATIVE STEPS TOWARDS OPENNESS

Even before the Treaty of Maastricht there was a trickle of interest shown by the European Parliament and the European Commission on the question whether democracy demands that the business of the legislative and executive

---

[8] See Herlitz, "Publicity of Official Documents in Sweden", *Public Law* (Spring 1958), pp. 53, 58.

[9] The declaration by the Kingdom of Sweden on open government (O.J. 1994, C 241) reads: "Sweden welcomes the development now taking place in the European Union towards greater openness and transparency. Open government and, in particular, public access to official records as well as the constitutional protection afforded to those who give information to the media *are and remain fundamental principles which form part of Sweden's constitutional, political and cultural heritage*" (emphasis added). A counter-declaration made by the present Member States in response states: "The present Member States of the European Union take note of the unilateral Declaration of Sweden concerning openness and transparency. They take it for granted that, as a member of the European Union, Sweden will fully comply with Community law in this respect."

[10] See the Presidency Conclusions, European Council, Corfu Summit, 24–25 June 1994.

arms should be subject to the glare of publicity and scrutiny and a dual active and passive information supply initiated. Not surprisingly given its vested interest in improving the existing democratic deficit, the European Parliament showed a pioneering interest in the subject more than a decade ago adopting a resolution in 1984 calling for the introduction of legislation on openness of government;[11] two further resolutions in very similar terms were adopted in 1988 and in 1994 respectively.[12] Interestingly the Legal Affairs Committee in its opinion annexed to the Report finally adopted in 1988 by the Committee on Youth, Culture, Education, Information and Sport stressed the link with citizenship. In its view the right to be informed, as a corollary of an over-all duty on the part of public authorities to supply information, should be clearly recognized in Community law as one of the "basic rights" of citizens.

The Commission's only concrete initiative has been taken in the specific field of environmental information and has related to the duty of *Member States* to provide information in their possession on request.[13] However, the Commission recognized, as early as 1988, that free access to information (on the environment) must not be only imposed on the public authorities but also "on the Community institutions and the Commission in particular. The reasons for the need to broaden the possibilities of access to information held by national, regional or local administrations apply equally to Community institutions".[14] It included a hortatory statement to the effect that it would take specific follow-up proposals "designed to introduce the same transparency within the Community institutions as proposed for the national authorities in the Member States", but did not do so. The Economic and Social Committee in its opinion on this proposal[15] went further stating more generally that

> if the need for a Directive of this kind is recognized, there is an equally strong need for Community bodies and authorities to provide access to information.

---

[11] Resolution on the compulsory publication of information by the European Community, O.J. 1984, C 172/176.

[12] Resolution on the compulsory publication of information by the European Community, O.J. 1988, C 49/174 and Resolution on the transparency of Community legislation and the need for it to be consolidated, O.J. 1994, C 205/514.

[13] See Proposal for a draft directive on the freedom of access to information on the environment, O.J. 1988, C 335/5. In 1990 the Council of Ministers adopted the Directive (O.J. C 1990, L 158/56) and it entered into force on 1 Jan. 1993. The rules apply to environmental information held by the competent authorities of the Member States and not to environmental information held by the Community institutions.

[14] See Explanatory Memorandum to the proposal for a Council Directive, ibid.

[15] O.J. 1989, C 139/46.

The Committee sees no reason for putting off this legislation until a later date.

In fact not only did the Commission not actively seek to open up access to its own documents in practice, it positively balked at the idea of freely providing information on request from its archives.

This point is most graphically emphasized by the facts which gave rise to an order of the Court of Justice of the European Communities (ECJ) in the *Zwartveld* case in 1990.[16] The Commission refused to supply a Dutch *Rechter-commissaris* (investigating magistrate) with information (such as internal and inspection reports drawn up by EEC inspectors) sought by him so as to assist him in the conduct of a fraud investigation in The Netherlands. In so doing the Commission relied, *inter alia,* on Article 2 of the Protocol on the Privileges and Immunities of the European Communities, annexed to the EC Treaty, which states that the archives of the Community are inviolable. Article 2 does not define the terms "archives" and "inviolable" but in practice this is explained by the Commission in the broadest sense, with "archives" meaning all documents held by the institutions and their members and officials and "inviolable" meaning "top secret" if the documents are less than 30 years old. This interpretation was codified in 1983 in a Decision of the Commission[17] and a Directive of the Council,[18] laying down uniform rules about the access to the archives of the Communities older than 30 years and the general exceptions to this rule. These highly restrictive rules oblige the Member States to keep secret those national documents which reproduce the content of documents of the Community institutions, even if these national documents would be open to the public under that Member State's national legislation. The Commission relied moreover before the Court on the fact that the reports drawn up by its inspectors were documents which of their nature could not be used except for internal information. The Court gave short shrift to these arguments and ruled that "it is incumbent upon every Community institution to give its active assistance to such national legal proceedings, by producing documents to the national court and authorizing its officials to give evidence in the national proceedings".[19] The Court's innovative judgment[20] was

---

[16] Case C-2/88, *Zwartveld and Others,* [1990] ECR I-3365.

[17] No. 359/83, O.J. 1983, L 43/14.

[18] Directive 354/83, O.J. 1983, L 43/1.

[19] Case C-2/88, loc. cit., note 16, cons. 22.

[20] It comes close to admitting that the ECJ in fact enjoys inherent jurisdiction; see further, Arnull, "Does the Court of Justice Have Inherent Jurisdiction?", 27 CML Rev. (1990), 683–708.

widely hailed at the time as the first step towards creating greater openness in the administration of the Community in general.[21] But it was an imposed first step, contested to the bitter end by the Commission itself.

3   THE EMERGENCE OF THE CODE
OF CONDUCT AND IMPLEMENTING DECISIONS

The first sign of any serious Member State interest in the subject of openness surfaced during the Intergovernmental Conference preceding the signing of the Maastricht Treaty when the Dutch tabled in January 1991 a proposal to amend the Treaty of Rome by inserting an express provision, a new Article 213 bis.[22] Their idea was to confer an explicit Treaty competence on the Council to adopt by qualified majority vote a regulation on the access to the information held by the Community institutions and organs (excluding specifically the ECJ, the Court of Auditors, the European Investment Bank and the European Central Bank for imperative reasons tied to their independence from political interference).

This regulation would be adopted on the legal basis of Article 213 bis EC Treaty obliging the relevant Community institutions to allow access to information retained by them, subject of course to detailed provisions on the permitted exceptions from the principle of access to information as well as the methods of recourse in event of refusal. In making this proposal, modelled along the lines of the parallel provision of the Dutch Constitution, the primary concern of the Dutch appears to have been to emphasize the fact that it is not so much a matter of the internal working procedure of the institutions but rather the paramount importance of the *public* aspect of access to information (viz. enforceable legal rights for *third parties*). The departure point of this Treaty amendment proposal was clearly meant to copperfasten the principle of openness, subject only to necessary and desirable restrictions. The exclusion of certain institutions and organs seems to be premised on the assumption that their tasks do not directly entail public administration as such. In any event this proposal to give the subject a specific Treaty base as such was not

---

[21] See in particular, Mortelmans, *Ars Aequi* (1990), pp. 974, 989; Keurentjes, (1990) *Nederlands Juristenblad*, 1282; Brouwer, *Staatscourant* (1990), p. 5; and Watson, 28 CML Rev. (1991) 428, 442.

[22] See van Poelgeest, "Secrecy and the Right of Access to Information in Europe", in De Graaff and Jonker (eds), *The Optimum Formula for a Foreign Policy Document Series. Proceedings of the Second Conference of Editors of Diplomatic Documents* (1992), pp. 121–126.

successful and does not appear to have been taken up by either the Commission or the European Parliament in their submissions to the Intergovernmental Conference.

There was, however, a consolation prize for the Dutch tucked away in the small print of the voluminous Treaty of Maastricht which was finally published at the end of 1991. This was packaged in the wrapping of a "declaration" on transparency promising further study and action in the not too distant future. Here for the first time was a statement by the Contracting Parties to the effect that they considered that:

> transparency of the decision-making process strengthens the democratic nature of the institutions and the public's confidence in the administration. The Conference accordingly recommends that the Commission submit to the Council no later than 1993 a report on measures to improve the public access to the information available to the institutions.

In the period between the signing of the Maastricht Treaty in December 1991 and its entry into force (November 1993), political difficulties in ensuring ratification in several countries (in particular Denmark and France) ironically ensured that the seemingly innocuous declaration on transparency, regarded at the time as a "sop" to the Dutch demands for open administration, assumed a pivotal place in the politicians' efforts to reassure potential voters that winds of change were blowing and to inject the Union enterprise with renewed credibility in the eyes of its citizens. Having placed such reliance on the follow-up to be given to the transparency declaration, in the context of attempts to change the minds of the Danish voters concrete steps had indeed to be proposed. Alongside hortatory statements at both the Birmingham and Edinburgh European Council Summit meetings to the effect that the Community had to be brought closer to its citizens,[23] specific Commission measures were noted and welcomed which operated so as to increase transparency (for example, the production of work programmes in October of each year, wider consultation on the basis of green papers, codification of legal texts). Moreover, the Commission was asked to complete by early 1993 its work in application of the declaration to the Maastricht Treaty on improving public access to the information available to the institutions.[24]

---

[23] See in particular, the declaration by the Heads of State or Government entitled "A Community Close to Its Citizens", European Council, Birmingham, 16 Oct. 1992 and the chapter "A Community Close to Its Citizens" in the conclusions of the European Council Summit, Copenhagen, 22 June 1993.

[24] See conclusions of the Copenhagen European Council, ibid.

The result was two relatively superficial communications by the Commission to the Council and the European Parliament in May and June 1993 respectively.[25] Despite the fact that what was at issue was a novel and important matter of policy, the Commission did not undertake independent research for the specific purpose of studying the relevant access legislation, practice and pitfalls in the various Member States and applicant Member States. Rather the approach was to largely cull information from an earlier report undertaken in the different context of the information market,[26] presenting its overall findings in a very cursory fashion indeed. Moreover the Commission entirely glossed over an issue which is terribly important in the context of EU transparency, namely the practice of the Council of Ministers *legislating* behind closed doors and access to information relating to the legislative process as such. Given this crucial difference with the national situation where legislation in principle takes place in public, it would have been relevant for the Commission to undertake (or commission) a comparative study of the situation in the various Member States and other relevant democratic systems with regard to parliamentary openness, plenary sessions, parliamentary committees and related matters. The fact that this preliminary study has not been undertaken does not facilitate the discussion. Arguably the Commission has not fully complied with the mandate imposed upon it by the Maastricht Declaration on openness since "measures designed to improve public access to the information available to the institutions" must necessarily include information pertaining to legislative measures, relevant preparatory documents, minutes and voting records of meetings where the decisions were actually taken.

The proposal of the Commission advanced in its communications of 1993 was the adoption of an inter-institutional agreement containing a minimum set of requirements. These were essentially the adoption of a document based system, that a member of the public would not be required to identify an interest and permitting only limited grounds of refusal (i.e., personal privacy, industrial and financial confidentiality, public security and information passed to the institution in confidence). If the request was refused then the institution would be obliged to reason such refusal. The Commission did not opine as to the appropriate form which the putative act implementing the rights of access of third parties should take.

The Copenhagen European Council of 22 June 1993 invited the Council

---

[25] See COM (93) 191 final, *Public Access to the Institutions Documents,* 5 May 1993; COM (93) 258 final, *Openness in the Community,* 2 June 1993.

[26] PUBLAW 1991.

and the Commission to continue their work "based on *the principle of the citizens having the fullest possible access to information*".[27] The aim, the European Council stated, was to have all the necessary measures in place by the end of 1993. In the period July to December 1993 the Council and the Commission separately continued their work on this subject. The main subjects of these discussions were the form of the instrument to be adopted as well as its legal effect, the scope of the concept of information as well as the permissible grounds of exemption and the judicial protection of the citizen.

With regard to the form of the putative instrument it was ultimately decided that a common instrument would be adopted by both the Commission and the Council, the provisions of which would then be separately implemented in legally binding "decisions" by the respective institutions.[28] More or less around the same time an inter-institutional declaration on democracy, transparency and subsidiarity was signed by the Parliament, the Commission and the Council, reaffirming their attachment to the implementation of transparency by the institutions. The European Parliament recalled that in amending its Rules of Procedure on 15 September 1993 it confirmed the public nature of the meetings of its committees and its plenary sessions.

It subsequently transpired that a majority of Member States within the Council preferred to implement the inter-institutional instrument (the Code of Conduct, as it was finally to be known) via the Council's *Rules of Procedure*. It so happened that at precisely the same moment in time the Council's Rules of Procedure were, in any event, undergoing thorough revision as a result of the substantial changes introduced by the Maastricht Treaty. The decision-making on the Code of Conduct and the Rules of Procedure took place during the General Affairs Council of 6 December 1993. By virtue of the provisions of Article 151 EC Treaty and the link made between the Rules of Procedure and the Code of Conduct, a simple majority voting procedure was followed for both measures. In both cases the Dutch delegation voted against the adoption of the measures in question. When on matters of openness, one of the basic values of democracy, decisions could be taken by simple majority vote, this meant ultimately that a rule could be introduced by a majority to the effect that one Member State could frustrate openness on, for example, any decision taken by the Council under Article K.3 of the Maastricht Treaty. And that is exactly what happened in practice.

Whereas the Code of Conduct largely followed the Commission's

---

[27] Emphasis added. Bull. EC 6–1993, point 1–22, 16.

[28] See Resolution of the European Parliament, 17 Nov. 1993.

approach to the matter, stressing the general principle that the public have the widest possible access to documents held by the Commission and the Council, followed by an outline of the procedure for handling applications, it provided for more extensive exceptions to be made to the general principle than those originally suggested by the Commission during its preparatory studies.[29] Alongside five mandatory exceptions (public interest, privacy, commercial and industrial secrecy, protection of the Community's financial interests and protection of confidentiality as requested by private parties or as required by the legislation of the Member States supplying the information) one facultative exception made its first stealthy outing. The institutions could also refuse access in order to protect the institutions interest in the confidentiality of its proceedings. It is that lone sentence which explains the otherwise cryptic Council statement at the end of the inter-institutional Code of Conduct as adopted on 6 December 1993:

> This code of conduct and the decisions which the Council and the Commission will severally adopt on the basis thereof are intended to allow public access to Council and Commission documents.
> They alter neither the existing practices nor the obligations of Member States Governments toward their parliaments.

This Council statement was included at the insistence of the (out-voted) Dutch Government which genuinely feared that the Code of Conduct would operate in practice so as to *deprive* the Dutch Parliament of rights which it currently enjoyed by virtue of the operation of more generous provisions of national legislation. Given the obvious aim of the Code to increase the public's rights of access and expressly to guarantee them the *widest* possible access, the effect of actually worsening currently enjoyed access (at least in the context of the operative Dutch legislation) was obviously unacceptable. The fact remained, however, despite the Council's explanatory statement as to the intended effect of the Code *vis-à-vis* national legislation, that the fear of the Dutch in particular was not without foundation.

The inter-institutional agreement cast in the form of a Code of Conduct enabled institutions to deny access where their interest was in protecting "the confidentiality" of their own proceedings. In other words, access could continue to be denied to minutes, voting records, etc. of Council meetings. Where national parliaments, such as the Dutch one, obtained such information

---

[29] Code of Conduct concerning public access to Council and Commission documents, O.J. 1993, L 340/41.

from national ministers as a matter of national law, such existing obligations prevailed. What, however, of the circumstances where national access legislation might enable individuals to obtain information on documents or events restricted as a matter of European Union law? The fear in this respect was that by finally adopting an (inadequate) Union measure it operated so as to override the provisions of national access laws and other provisions of national constitutional law irrespective of whether hierarchically superior Union law was also qualitatively superior in the sense of being more progressive in terms of obtaining and improving freedom of information or not.

4   THE COUNCIL'S RULES OF PROCEDURE

4.1 The meetings

Article 4(1) of the Council's Rules of Procedure provides that: "Meetings of the Council shall not be public except in the cases referred to in Article 6". Article 6(1) states that "The Council shall hold policy debates on the six-monthly work programme submitted by the Presidency and, if appropriate, on the Commission's annual work programme. These debates shall be the subject of public retransmission by audiovisual means."

A comparison with the Council's previous Rules of Procedure dating from 1979 reveals that the Council's policy has softened—but only marginally—regarding the closed nature of its meetings. Article 3(1) of the 1979 rules had only provided the possibility of public meetings in the event of a unanimous decision of the Council to that effect. Henceforth "policy debates" and "annual work programmes" are subject to the mandatory (and largely symbolic) glare of public (and televised) meetings—providing the not very inspiring spectacle of ministers reading to one another from set scripts.

It seems that post 1993 the possibility for other meetings of the Council to be opened up to the public is by an unanimous decision to that effect. Article 6(2) of the Council's Rules of Procedure provides that:

> The Council may decide unanimously and on a case-by-case basis that some of its other debates are to be the subject of retransmission by audiovisual means, in particular where they concern an important issue affecting the interests of the Union or an important new legislative proposal. To that end it shall be for the Presidency, any member of the Council, or the Commission to propose issues or specific subjects for such a debate.

This provision is really little more than a dressed-up restatement of the old rule of public meetings by unanimous decision with the explicit gloss of audiovisual technicolour.

4.2 The votes

What of the possibilities for members of the public to know—despite the meetings which take place behind closed doors—how the various Government Ministers actually voted on a given issue? The Council's 1993 Rules of Procedure are quite explicit on this and do represent some movement forward as compared to earlier Rules of Procedure. Article 7(5) states in mandatory terms that:

> The record of the votes shall be made public:
> — when the Council is acting as legislator within the meaning of the term given in the Annex to these Rules of Procedure, unless the Council decides otherwise. This Rule shall apply when the Council adopts a common position pursuant to Article 189b or 189c of the Treaty establishing the European Community,
> — when they are cast by the members of the Council or their representatives on the Conciliation Committee set up by Article 189b of the Treaty establishing the European Community,
> — when the Council acts pursuant to Titles V and VI of the Treaty on European Union by a unanimous Council Decision taken at the request of one of its members, in other cases, by Council Decision taken at the request of one of its members.

Two points are particularly noteworthy. First, a unanimous decision of the Council can keep secret the record of votes when the Council is acting as a legislator. Second, the much stricter rule which applies in the context of Second and Third Pillar matters: publication of voting records on decisions taken in this context can be prevented by a single Council member.

Finally where the record of a vote in Council is made public in accordance with Article 7(5), Article 5(1) provides that "the explanations of vote made when the vote was taken shall also be made public at the request of the Council members concerned, with due regard for these Rules of Procedure, legal certainty and the interests of the Council".

The wording used makes it clear that such publication of the explanations of vote presumably contained in the minutes of the relevant Council meeting is largely discretionary, not only subject to the initiative of the member concerned but also to the amorphous catch-all proviso of being in "the interests of the Council", these (interests) being probably determined by majority vote.

4.3 Publication of decisions

Article 15 of the Council's Rules of Procedure states the general rule that Regulations, Directives and Decisions adopted in accordance with the Article 189b procedure as well as Regulations and Directives of the Council or the Commission addressed to the Member States are to be published in the Official Journal. Common positions adopted by the Council in accordance with the procedures referred to in Articles 189b and 189c EC Treaty and the reasons underlying those common positions are also to be published. This represents an improvement in the discretion enjoyed by the Council (acting by unanimous decision only) regarding the publication of Directives and Decisions for the purposes of information. Article 18(5) continues such discretion in the case of "directives other than those referred to in Article 191(1) and (2) EC Treaty, Council Decisions and Recommendations" as well as "conventions signed between the Member States".

What is remarkable is the restrictive attitude of the Council in its Rules of Procedure to publication of decisions (common positions defined in the Joint Actions, implementing measures thereof and measures implementing K.3(2) conventions) in the new policy areas enshrined in the Second and Third Pillars. Article 18(3) categorically provides that the decision to publish in the Official Journal "shall in each case be taken by the Council acting unanimously when the said instruments are adopted". In practice this of course means that any single Member State can object to publication and prevent it. The situation prevailing with regard to the Second and Third Pillars is therefore much worse in terms of openness than the normal rule prevailing in the context of the First Pillar that all decisions are more or less automatically published in the Official Journal. Only conventions drawn up by the Council in accordance with Article K.3(2) must be published in the Official Journal (Article 18(4)).

4.4 Access to documents

The ultimate step, at least for the time being, along the road of Union initiative in the field of access to information was the follow-up adoption by the Council and Commission respectively of a decision implementing the Code of Conduct with regard to their separate institutional set-ups. They were supposed to do so by the end of 1993. The Council succeeded; the Commission did not manage to adopt the relevant decision until 8 February 1994.[30]

Different approaches were followed. The Commission simply declared

---

[30] O.J. 1994, L 46/58.

that the Code of Conduct had been adopted in Article 1 of the Decision and then proceeded to elaborate briefly the *procedural rules* on how applications for access to documents shall be dealt with by the Commission.[31] The Council's approach differed in an important respect. The Council Decision adopted on the basis of Article 151(3) (which enables it to adopt its Rules of Procedure) of the EC Treaty does not confine itself to elaborating the necessary procedural rules in order to implement the principles set out in the Code of Conduct but lays down instead all the rules and conditions governing public access to Council documents, thus repeating in the process, with some modifications, a large number of provisions already contained in the Code of Conduct.[32]

The Council Decision, being based on Article 151 EC Treaty and the Council's Rules of Procedure, was adopted pursuant to a majority vote. The clear implication of the choice of legal basis was that this was primarily a matter of the *internal* rule-making procedure of the institutions themselves and that the issue of legal rights for third parties was an ancillary side-effect. The philosophy followed was that access to documents and transparency were simply an extension of the requirements of good administration rather than the outcome of any belief in the value of participatory democracy. The Dutch voted—yet again—against the Decision (this time joined by the Danes) on the grounds that its provisions were too restrictive and that it was adopted pursuant to an incorrect legal basis, but they were once more outvoted. The Dutch felt that the measures being adopted "did not bring about any meaningful transparency for the citizens and that they therefore would not contribute towards a positive opinion formation about the Union, which is so badly needed at the moment".[33]

The (loaded) dice were finally cast and the game of cat and mouse that was to follow could finally begin in earnest. This game has concentrated above all on the playing field of the Council decision-making and behaviour, the Commission Decision having to date given rise to considerably less controversy and no legal challenges. It is of course indisputable that the principles on which the Commission Decision are based are the same: those contained in the inter-institutional Code of Conduct and a legal basis permitting the

---

[31] See Art. 2 of its Decision.

[32] E.g., in Art. 8 it effectively added another ground of exemption additional to those already found in the Code of Conduct by providing that "this Decision shall apply with due regard for provisions governing the protection of classified information". See further, *infra*.

[33] See the letter from the Minister of Foreign Affairs, *Handelingen Tweede Kamer*, 1993–1994, 21, 501–02, No. 106.

adoption of internal rules of procedure (respectively Articles 151 and 163 EC Treaty). For that reason the discussion which follows of the Council Decisions can to a certain extent be regarded as applying to the Commission Decision with the *caveat* that due regard be paid to the different nature and tasks of the two institutions concerned.

5   LEGAL CHALLENGES TO THE UNION'S
POLICY ON PUBLIC ACCESS TO COUNCIL DOCUMENTS

5.1 Internal rules of procedure v. access rights for third parties

Within six weeks of the adoption by the Council of its implementing Decision the Dutch Government had lodged an Article 173 EC Treaty procedure before the ECJ seeking the annulation of the Council Decision of 20 December 1993, Article 22 of the Council's Rules of Procedure and the inter-institutional Code of Conduct to the extent that legal consequences may be ascribed to it.[34] The main grounds advanced were violation of Treaty rules (Articles 4, 151 and 190 EC Treaty) and misuse of powers. One of the main arguments advanced by the Dutch Government was that the legal basis of Article 151(3) EC Treaty and Article 22 of the Council's Rules of Procedure is wrong, since these provisions are concerned solely with the Council's internal organization.[35] The disputed Council Decision contains pivotal provisions on a matter directly affecting Community citizens, going well beyond the scope of the Council's internal organization and budget. In the view of the Dutch Government the Rules of Procedure as an instrument with a purely internal working cannot form a sufficient legal basis for the adoption of a Council Decision which expressly purports to create legal rights for citizens.

This is a technical case with the Dutch Government relying heavily on the fact that the rules of procedure of an institution are not apt to include provisions or to provide the legal basis for provisions which confer rights on third parties. The ECJ's judgment in *Commission* v *BASF*[36] makes it clear, albeit in an entirely different context, that certain provisions in an institution's

---

[34] O.J. 1994, C 90/11, Case C-58/94, *Netherlands* v *Council,* pending.

[35] Art. 22 of the Council's Rules of Procedure provides that "the detailed arrangements for public access to Council documents disclosure of which is without serious or prejudicial consequences shall be adopted by the Council".

[36] Case C-137/92P, *Commission* v *BASF and Others,* [1994] ECR I-2555. See also Joined Case T-79/89, *BASF and Others* v *Commission,* [1992] ECR II-315.

rules of procedure can give rights to third parties and in the event of failure to respect them can lead to the annulment of legal measures at the suit of interested third parties. But the Dutch case raises much broader issues in our view. This is the question whether it is acceptable that the Council approaches the issue of freedom of information purely from the perspective of the administration of its own services (in the interests of good administration). The chosen approach by the Council, encasing the principle in its Rules of Procedure, negates the fundamental nature of the principle which has to be seen in the light of the nature of the democratic process itself (see in particular the preamble to the Treaty, Article F and the ECHR and its Protocol No. 1, discussed *supra*). In other words, the legal right for individuals (citizens) to obtain access to documents (subject, of course to the necessary restrictions) is of a fundamental nature which should preferably be regulated in the Treaty itself.

This is precisely what the Council (and implicitly the Commission) have steadfastly refused to recognize. Starting from the debate on the Dutch proposal to include a specific Treaty provision in the Maastricht Treaty in 1990, a majority of Member States pugnaciously stuck to their line that a Treaty provision was unnecessary and that a much less formal regulation of the matter of access to official records was desirable.[37] The Dutch plea that a Treaty provision was necessary to underline the fundamental importance of the general principle towards the institutions fell on deaf ears; the Commission finally came up with the proposal to lay down the general principle of access to information in a (non-legally binding) declaration to be appended to the new Treaty, a proposal apparently accepted without difficulty. Even in the difficult post-Maastricht epoch the Council in particular departed from the premise that the basic rule remained the one enshrined in Article 5(1) of its Rules of Procedure, that of the confidentiality of its procedure. As a matter of policy orientation it became possible (once the Code of Conduct and implementing Decision were agreed) in certain circumstances, and at the entire discretion of the Council itself, to decide to allow access to certain documents to be decided upon a case-by-case basis and depend upon the establishment of consensus within the Council itself thereon. The cleverness of this approach is the claim that the Council Decision of 20 December 1993 must be understood in its context of the other provisions of the Council's Rules of Procedure and as a coherent body of rules: it putatively does not override any of the provisions set out in the Council's Rules of Procedure, including the basic and pre-eminent rule of confidentiality: it is only subject to the Council otherwise

---

[37] See van Poelgeest, loc. cit, note 22, at p. 124.

93

deciding! That at any rate is the view of the Council on the matter. Obviously given this hidden agenda of the Council—the correctness or otherwise which can only be established by the ECJ itself—the adoption of a specific Treaty provision or a measure of secondary legislation (for example based on Article 235 EC Treaty and making some—satisfactory—provision for the Second and Third Pillars) would have squarely placed the rights of the individuals concerned foremost. In such circumstances the more technical resulting amendment of the Council's Rules of Procedure would then have been relegated to its rightful subsidiary place.

The parameters of the dispute between the Dutch and the other members of the Council is therefore the difference of opinion regarding the legal nature of the principle of freedom of information in the Union context: the Dutch emphasize the fundamental (at least from the perspective of democratic philosophy) nature of the principle and maintain that the primary purpose of the Decision was to regulate the openness of the administration for third parties. On the other hand, the other members of the Council (with the probable exception of the Danes[38]) are convinced that the Code of Conduct and Council Decision constitute a simple policy orientation adopted by the Council in a mood of paternalism and restrained altruism, subject as a matter of course to the other rules of its Rules of Procedure as well as the stringent and discretionary exceptions outlined in the Decision itself and that these normative instruments did not create a legal right of a fundamental nature. Rather the Code and Conduct simply enable the Council in certain circumstances to permit access but do not in any way affect the basis upon which it operates as an institution.

In any event it seems clear that rules of procedure of a Community (Union) institution cannot—given the democratic character of the Union Treaty and its antecedents in the ECHR—*reduce* national law regarding freedom of information and openness, especially for those Member States enshrining that openness in their constitution. When it comes to legislation and the openness of parliamentary documents all 15 Member States have such constitutional guarantees. It follows from such openness that individuals everywhere have the right to have access to all parliamentary documents which are part of the legislative process. This right and the generally prevailing openness with regard to documents of a legislative nature is an essential component of the democratic systems of government prevailing in the Member States. The Union is bound in accordance with the terms of Article F(1) to respect "the national

---

[38] See their intervention in Case T-194/94, *Carvel and Guardian Newspapers Ltd. v Council*, pending.

identities of the Member States, whose systems of government are founded on the principles of democracy".

5.2 The Council's stewardship of its access decision

The Council Decision of 20 December 1993 entered into force on 1 January 1994. It was not explicitly stated whether its provisions were intended to have retroactive effect. In any event its provisions appear to have been interpreted in this sense by the Council which has given access to documents dated from before that period.

The Council Decision grants the public access to Council documents, not information, which must be specified in a sufficiently precise manner enabling the document or documents in question to be identified. The procedure which applies is that an initial application for access to a Council document is examined by the relevant departments which then suggest what action is to be taken. The applicant is informed within one month of the success or rejection of the claim by the department in question. In the event that the response is negative the applicant is to receive a reasoned reply. In this event the applicant has a further one month during which to make a so-called "application" for the initial position of the Council department to be reconsidered. Finally the Decision equates a failure to reply with a negative response and the time limits operate in the same fashion as with an explicit response.

Although this is not stated explicitly in the Decision, it seems that a decision to reject a confirmatory application is taken by the Council itself. The practice evolved early on of having the draft reply to the confirmatory application established by the Secretariat-General and rubber-stamped by the Council itself. The problem soon emerged that the Danish and Dutch delegations objected to the procedure of putting such replies on the Council's Agenda as "A" points (hence no discussion) and quickly insisted on discussing several of the initial replies before the Council as a whole despite the fact that a majority of the delegations (in practice the other 10 delegations) had already agreed to the replies to be issued at the level of the relevant COREPER Working Group (the so-called "GAG" Group: *Groupe des Affaires Generales*[39] and subsequently by the *Amis de la Presidence* and then the so-called

---

[39] There has been a proposal by COREPER, which, if adopted, would literally "gag" members of the Council in that it forced them to adopt the opinion of the relatively low-level GAG Group. Member States who did not agree with a draft reply but were outvoted at the level of the "GAG" Group would be deemed to "approve without discussion in the Permanent Representative Committee and in the Council draft replies on which a majority has emerged within the Working Party or regarding which no delegation has requested reference to the Working Party". See *The Guardian*,

Information Working Group). The result of this practice was that the Council reached its decision to confirm the reply drafted by the Secretariat-General by a simple majority vote (given the legal basis of the Council Decision itself) and that the Danish and Dutch had no recourse other than to issue declarations (unilateral or joint) objecting to the majority decision and the manner in which the decision was reached. Moreover it emerged that in the event of one or more Member States objecting to the content of a draft negative reply, there was a greater likelihood of the mandatory time limits imposed in the Decision not being respected, and hence that the refusal by virtue of Article 7(4) would be deemed implicit.[40] The attraction of the latter course of events, it has been suggested, is that not only does the Council not need to reason its refusals but moreover it does not then need to alert applicants to their possibilities of legal recourse or of initiating a complaint to the Ombudsman.[41]

When the Secretariat-General or relevant department of the Council is considering the question of the appropriate reply to be given to an individual application for documents, Article 4 of the Council Decision assumes paramount importance. The application of the first paragraph, although including broader exceptions than those initially suggested by the Commission in its preparatory work on the matter (viz. the protection of the public interest and the protection of the Community's financial interests) is mandatory and would appear not to have given rise to substantial difficulties in its application thus far. The same fate has not, however, been reserved to the discretionary second paragraph of Article 4 pertaining to the protection of "the confidentiality of the Council's proceedings". Basically the most significant problems in this respect seem to have arisen with regard to requests from individuals for Council minutes, voting records and preparatory documents.

For the first six months of the application of the Code and Council

---

"Ambassadors Agree to Eurocrats' Gag", 11 June 1994. See also *Agence Europe,* 17 June 1994. Fortunately, this COREPER proposal—with all its totalitarian overtones—appears to have been abandoned for the moment.

[40] This less than satisfactory evolution of the practice of the Council in granting/refusing access to documents led the Dutch and Danish delegations to call for an in-depth debate on the entire matter. However, their proposed draft guidelines to the Council Secretariat on the procedure to be followed once a decision has been taken to reject a confirmatory application in a given instance were rejected by a slim majority of 7:5 at the General Affairs Council of 19 July 1993. Interestingly, those delegations voting in favour included, for the first time, not only the Dutch and the Danish but also the British, Irish and Spanish. See *The Guardian,* 19 June 1994. See further, *Agence Europe,* 23 July 1994.

[41] See Wopereis, "De EuroWOB: Teruggeschrokken voor Werkelijke Openbaarheid", (1994–5) *Mediaforum,* 54, 55.

Decision the Council appeared to *systematically* refuse applications for Council minutes and voting records on the grounds that documents cannot be released which might identify the positions which various national governments might have taken on any particular issue. The first case in which this issue arose is also the first case to have availed of the option explicitly conferred in the Decision to enable an unsuccessful individual applicant to bring an action for annulment against a refusal before the Court of First Instance in Luxembourg. This is the case of The Guardian Newspapers and John Carvel, its European Editor against the Council. They were refused access to Justice and Agricultural Council minutes and voting records and told that similar documents which had been previously sent on the Social Affairs Council in October and November 1993 were sent pursuant to an "administrative error".[42] The negative reply was agreed upon by a majority of delegations at the level of COREPER and placed on the "A" level of the General Affairs Council Agenda. At this stage the Danish insisted that the matter be debated, thereby ensuring that no agreement could be reached as to the content of the reply until after the deadline of one month specified in the Decision had expired. When the reply was finally adopted both the Danish and the Dutch delegations entered formal reservations[43] which stated as follows:

> the Danish and Dutch Governments would like to point out that no comparative analysis has taken place of, on the one hand, the interests of the citizens seeking information, and, on the other hand, the criteria of secrecy of Council deliberations, as is required in the opinion of the Dutch and Danish Governments in case the Council bases its rejection on this specific criteria. Had such a comparative analysis taken place, this should have been communicated to The Guardian.

When the reply was finally received by the applicant (after the deadline had expired) it simply stated that:

> the Council takes the view that access to these documents cannot be allowed since they refer directly to the deliberations of the Council and its preparatory instances. If it did allow such access, the Council would fail to protect the confidentiality of its proceedings. *The documents contain confidential information relating to the position taken by the members of the Council*

---

[42] Presumably access had been granted by the respective departments within the Council and the "mistake" was discovered when COREPER/the General Affairs Council considered the "confirmatory application".

[43] The declarations were made available in press releases subsequent to the Council meeting.

during its deliberations [emphasis added].

The last sentence is the critical one. The Council effectively admits that it is applying a systematic policy of refusing access to all documents which might reveal Member State positions, thereby effectively eliminating any possible (national) parliamentary scrutiny. In practice it has indeed not granted access to any Council minutes or other related documents other than those released pursuant to an "administrative error" as detailed above[44] and—in July 1994—in two Danish cases.[45] This comes close to the imposition of an *absolute* criterion whereby access to minutes will be refused automatically, since the very purpose of minutes is to reflect the content of the proceedings covered by confidentiality.

A different approach is based on a *relative* assessment of the confidentiality of proceedings.[46] Each case would be examined to see whether confidentiality needs to be protected, and the decision to release a document would be taken by a majority.

In other words, a case-by-case assessment must be made. This process of *ad hoc* balancing the interest in confidentiality and the public's right to information is perhaps not without its own drawbacks. It can be argued that the subjective approach is vague and somewhat unpredictable, allowing a majority of the members of the Council to reach any conclusion it wishes. This is not of necessity the case and what needs to be developed is a common unit of measurement to place upon the opposing side of the scale.

In any event it seems clear that the Council is currently *de facto* applying an objective approach systematically refusing to make available minutes on the grounds of the confidentiality of its proceedings (Article 5(1) of its Rules of Procedure). This view is supported not only on the case evidence available (all applications for minutes thus far having being turned down on grounds of confidentiality and one "administrative error"), but also by the fact that no evidence exists of a serious "weighing" of the conflicting interests involved, as would be essential in the more subjective approach to the matter. On the

---

[44] See further, *Agence Europe,* 25 May 1994, at 12.

[45] These concerned the confirmatory applications made by the journalist Ms Bundegaard and the student Mr Ravin who were successful in their request for minutes at the ECOFIN Council of 27 July. Having examined the documents supplied by the Council it may be validly doubted whether it amounts to a precedent indicating future grant of such minutes. In any event it seems clear that the minutes actually released contained no information other than that which had been included in the press releases of the respective Council meetings at the time.

[46] See further *Agence Europe,* 25 May 1994, at 12.

contrary, the fact that serious weighing of the different interests involved has *not* taken place has been precisely the complaint of the Dutch and Danish delegations throughout the entire period of application of the Council Decision, witness their explicit reservations to many of the Council Decisions refusing access thus far.

The other issue which has been the subject of persistence is that of obtaining access to the voting records of the Member States. This issue was tested by a Financial Times journalist, David Gardner, who requested selected voting records of the Member States since 1989 on foreign affairs, the Single Market, social affairs and agriculture and was turned down in first instance. On appeal this approach was confirmed: the voting records requested were actually turned down on the rather extraordinary ground that the Secretariat-General has not compiled lists of voting records "and is not in possession of any such statistics". It followed that the request for access to documents did not fall within the terms of the Council Decision since the latter only covers actual texts held by the Council. However, the Council did appear to hold out a carrot for the future. It stated that since the adoption of the Code of Conduct (and pursuant to its new Rules of Procedure) most of the votes taken in the Council have been made public in the press release issued after every meeting, and, for the future, the Council intends to arrange for statistics on votes made public under Article 7(5) of the Rules of Procedure of the Council to be periodically published.[47] But this latter hint of a compromise is not quite as generous as it might appear at first blush: after all, it simply states that the Council will compile statistics (the Legal Service will keep a register of votes on legislative issues of future sessions[48]) for those voting records that it is already obliged to release in accordance with its own Rules of Procedure. For other agenda items on which the Council is not acting as legislator *stricto sensu* (Second and Third Pillars?) no attempt to increase transparency will presumably be made. The Danish delegation abstained from voting on this compromise solution and the Dutch voted against it. According to The Netherlands, the Council should have made it clear to the applicant that the information is not yet available in the form he has requested but needs to be extracted from various sources. It felt that the applicant should be communicated that the Council is willing to start research in its files in order to compile a list of votes, of which the applicant will be given a copy in due time.[49] It

---

[47] See "EU to Compile Record of How Ministers Vote", *Financial Times,* 4 July 1994.

[48] *Agence Europe,* 6 July 1994, at 9–10.

[49] *Agence Europe,* 18 May 1994, at 11.

is submitted that this would indeed have been a preferable approach and one enabling the Council to take a significant first step in implementing the conclusions of the Corfu European Council of 1994 on transparency and open governance, thereby showing a commendably serious and result orientated approach.

Finally, the last category of cases to have arisen concern several attempts to force the Council to disclose the preparatory documents pertaining to how it operates its openness policy, including details of the types of documents sought by the various applicants under the Code and Council Decision as well as details of the replies given by the Council to the applications and confirmatory applications. In one of the first such cases the Council ordered that the lid was to be kept on the workings of the public access rules and that related documents were themselves covered by the secrecy rules![50] It stated that "this is a particularly sensitive file and the preparatory documents which it contains are covered by the obligation of professional secrecy, as provided by Article 5(1) of the Rules of Procedure of the Council". Shortly thereafter, in another case initiated by the Guardian Newspaper, the Council nuanced its reply somewhat, apparently sensitive to the ridicule it was exposing itself on this particular refusal. It was also prompted to do so by the confirmatory application in question which actually suggested different options to the Council in order not to infringe the privacy of those persons who had actually submitted the applications in question and pointed out that this was customary in countries operating freedom of information policies. The most helpful option, involving copies of applications and confirmatory applications with the names blanked out, was not chosen but rather the tortuous option involving the Council Secretariat writing to all the authors of the applications (some 27 by now) to obtain their permission that either their names be revealed or blanked out.[51] Once such permission has been received, copies of the relevant (doctored) applications are to be forwarded along with the replies issued by the Council. At least the approach which has been ultimately adopted here constitutes some evidence of a willingness to take small, albeit hesitant, steps in the direction of greater openness.

---

[50] See *Financial Times*, 8 July 1994.

[51] See *The Guardian*, 19 July 1994.

6 SOME PRELIMINARY CONCLUSIONS
ON THE UNION'S POLICY ON OPENNESS

After the tricky ratification process of the Maastricht Treaty in several Member States of the Union, the focus by the European Council on the obvious alienation of the citizens from the decision-making process by the political *élite* in Europe was understandable. The key to the opening of the hearts and minds of the citizens of the European Union was much greater transparency and openness of the Community institutions. Sadly, it must be concluded that the heady and spirited declarations as to the Union's position as a community of democracies,[52] the resultant need to ensure that citizens had the fullest possible access to information,[53] thereby ensuring a better informed public debate on the activities of the Union,[54] were mocked by the substantive content of the measures actually adopted and in particular by the Council Decision itself as well as its manner of implementation thus far.

The fifth Section of this chapter has attempted to highlight the banalization of the issue by the Council in particular. This is illustrated not only by its choice of legal basis for its Access Decision—its Rules of Procedure—but also by the extremely restrictive manner in which it has implemented the Decision since its entry into force. The implementing decisions which it has taken thus far, especially its replies to a few notorious confirmatory applications, have shown to what extent the Council itself was unprepared to make anything resembling a quantum leap in terms of the evolution of its existing philosophy on the paramount confidentiality of its proceedings.

The stakes are high and it is crucial that the citizen-critic remains vigilant. It is of critical importance that the focus of attention is not too exclusively on access documents but that vigilance is maintained as regards connected developments. For example, at the same time that the Declaration on transparency was included in the Maastricht Treaty, Working Parties of COREPER were busy debating a proposal on the security measures *applicable to classified* information exchanged between Member States.[55] At the Edinburgh EC Summit in December 1992 the Commission's draft secrecy

---

[52] Birmingham Declaration, loc. cit., note 23.

[53] Copenhagen Council, loc. cit., note 23.

[54] Birmingham Summit, loc. cit., note 23.

[55] Under a draft Regulation of Feb. 1992 officials in Brussels and their counterparts in the Member States would have been able to classify documents on Community proposals and policies. This was a blanket provision applicable to any area of EC policy.

regulation was one of the proposals withdrawn under the subsidiarity clause. But a little remarked provision in the Council's Decision on Access to Documents provides that the Decision applies "with due regard for provisions governing the protection of classified information". In other words, this is designed to constitute a *further* exception to the principle of access to Council documents: once a document is "classified" no access is possible. The classification issue has, however, resurfaced (in 1994) in COREPER's Working Parties but this time in the context of an amendment to the Council's Rules of Procedure and covering Justice and Home Affairs (the Third Pillar of the Maastricht Treaty).[56] Very little of this issue has reached the public domain, being debated entirely in secret and not on the basis of a draft Commission proposal. The problem with the entire classification issue is that the Council itself (or a Working Party of COREPER or a Member State) decides when a document must be classified and what precise classification it must receive and no provision has to date been made for independent control over this classification process nor the operation of declassification in suitable circumstances. It is vital that this entire issue be considered in *tandem* not only with the existing archives rules[57] but also with the question of third-party access if the basic principle that citizens be given the fullest possible access is not to be hollowed out even further.

Another part of the basic background canvas on which access legislation is highlighted is the question of the role of the European Parliament and the failure by Ministers to "regularly inform" the European Parliament of discussions in the areas covered by Title VI (as *per* Article K.6). As a rule the public availability of information is as important to the European Parliament in its various roles as to the public. Without an adequate flow of information, even *ex post facto,* accountability is meaningless. The point is that the European Parliament is supposed to receive draft Title VI decisions as well before the Council takes its decision. Otherwise it will not be possible for the European Parliament to influence the decision—hence it will not be possible that "the views of the European Parliament are duly taken into consideration"

---

[56] See for further details, *Statewatch*, Jan.–Feb. 1994, 15. The current proposals seek to ensure that no documents on foreign policy (including Europol) or immigration and related matters will be released before all Member State governments are collectively committed to specific policies. Thus the government favouring the lowest level of "openness" will determine the general European level of public access to information on European decision-making and documents. Such a restrictive policy is in line with Art. 7(5), third indent of the Council's Rules of Procedures which provides that when the Council acts pursuant to Titles V and VI of the Treaty the record of votes taken can only be made public where all the Member States *unanimously* agree.

[57] See notes 17 and 18.

(see the wording of Article K.6, second paragraph).

The disrepute which has ensued for the Council as a result of the manner in which it has chosen to implement in practice the declarations by the European Council can only result in further alienation of the citizens from the political élite, an entirely self-defeating result. The saga thus far underlines the need for a much more fundamental approach to be adopted in future. The material is too important to be left to national civil servants and government ministers habituated to operating—at least in the Union context—in the cushioned twilight of ministerial, diplomatic and administrative ante-chambers. It must be included as a fundamental constitutional right enshrined explicitly in the TEU (or an amended version thereof) and the connection must finally be made with citizenship of the Union itself. The reason for its inclusion in the entire Union system is not of course to facilitate the institutions in their internal regulation of procedural matters, but rather as a critical aspect of the democratic foundations of the Union, a "community of democracies". Such explicit constitutional copper-fastening is desirable at the 1996 Intergovernmental Conference. An important consequence of a fundamental right status is that in restricting the right to public access more rigorous standards have to be met than with respect to legal rights generally. Limitations on a fundamental right of access should only be permitted if prescribed by law and if they are necessary in a democratic society for the protection of specified public or private interests. "Necessary" should imply the existence of a pressing social need and the denial of access should be narrowly tailored to serve this interest.

It is not meant to suggest that it would not be feasible for the ECJ, were it so minded and were a suitable case to present itself, to construe such an unenumerated constitutional right from the specificity of the entire Community legal system as well as from existing provisions contained in international human rights treaties, in particular the provisions of the ECHR and its Protocol No. 1.[58] Even if the European Court of Human Rights has not yet explicitly deduced a specific right of access from the provisions of Article 10 ECHR[59]

---

[58] See also Art. 19 of the Universal Declaration of Human Rights 1948 and Art. 19 of the International Covenant on Civil and Political Rights 1966, both of which expressly envisage the possibility for persons to "seek" information.

[59] This remains controversial. Some authors maintain that the right to "seek" information which was not expressly included in Art. 10 ECHR, nevertheless, implicitly follows from the right to "receive" and "impart" information and rely on an encouraging trend in the case law of the European Commission of Human Rights and the Court of Human Rights. See in particular, Malinverni, "Freedom of Information in the European Convention on Human Rights and in the International Covenant on Civil and Political Rights", (1983) *Human Rights Law Journal*, 443–460; Germer,"Administrative Secrecy under the European Convention on Human Rights", in *Secrecy and*

and despite the fact that not *every* Member State of the European Union has specific access legislation or constitutional provision, surely the ECJ in its construction of a new autonomous legal order on the very basis of democratic principles may indeed be moved to recognize the fundamental value of participatory democracy? After all, it can be argued that it is the very specificity of the Community legal order and decision-making process which bolsters recognition of the fundamental nature of enabling citizens to have access to the information necessary for the free and democratic formation of opinions. It could be an effective way to confer more "social legitimacy"[60] on the European Union and to imbue real substantive content to a notion of European "citizenship".

Openness: Individuals, Enterprises and Public Administration (1988), pp. 61–75; Pinto, *La liberté d'information et d'opinion en droit international* (1984), p. 96.

[60] The term was coined by Joseph Weiler.

5   RIGHTS OF FREE MOVEMENT

David Pollard

1   INTRODUCTION

The addition by the Treaty on European Union (TEU) of a new Part II
(Citizenship of the Union) to the Treaty of Rome illustrates and emphasizes
the developing and transient nature of the relationship between the original
European Economic Community (EEC), the subsequent European Community
(EC) and, now, the European Union (EU) and the nationals of the individual
Member States constituting the Community or Union. The TEU has established
a citizenship of the Union and has conferred some of the features of
citizenship of a nation-state. Citizenship usually relates to a nation-state with
geopolitical characteristics. For the purposes of a chapter which discusses the
free movement rights of citizens, it is proposed to refer to the Union in terms
of a nation-state, because although the Union does not yet possess all the
political characteristics of a nation-state, it is undoubtedly a geographical area.

It would be normal, with regard to rights of free movement, perhaps
contained in a Bill of Rights within a written constitution, to think in terms of
such "physical" rights as encompassing the right to leave (and not be refused
entry into) the Union, the right not to be extradited or deported from the Union
to another state except in accordance with restrictive rules based on international law, the right, irrespective of status, political affiliation, health or
financial situation, to travel across any "national" boundary and to reside in
every region of the Union for as long as one wished (together with "associated" rights, such as social assistance for subsistence and housing guaranteed
equally to all, but which do not, however, come within the scope of this
chapter). Indeed, lip-service is given to such rights in the new wording of the
Treaty of Rome, whereby the activities of the Community shall include "an
internal market characterized by the abolition, as between Member States, of
obstacles to the free movement of ... persons"[1] and citizens are given "the

---

[1] Art. 3(c) EC Treaty.

N. A. Neuwahl and A. Rosas (eds.), The European Union and Human Rights, 105–118.
© 1995 *Kluwer Law International. Printed in the Netherlands.*

right to move and reside freely within the territory of the Member States".[2]

One might be forgiven for thinking that the peoples of Europe are now entitled to comprehensive rights of free movement if one looks at documents now emanating from the Community institutions and praising this "first" right of citizenship. The truth is somewhat different, because the new Part II of the Treaty of Rome contains two "opt-outs" (agreed, naturally, by federalist politicians), namely that there is no mirroring within the Union of comprehensive principles relating to the acquisition of Union citizenship and that such rights as are granted to such of the peoples of Europe who possess Union citizenship are themselves drastically limited. This chapter maintains that not all of the peoples of Europe are citizens of the Union; that of those persons who are citizens, not all are entitled to move freely within the territories of the Union; and that of those who are entitled to move, not all are entitled to remain permanently wherever they wish. When measured against the normal political ideals that all members of a state should possess rights equally and that those rights should be absolute, the peoples of Europe can rightly feel betrayed by the new provisions, unless much is done by the Union legislators and done soon.

Although "Citizenship of the Union is hereby established" and "Every person holding the nationality of a Member State shall be a citizen of the Union",[3] this results in a mere compilation of the several nationalities of the Member States having such citizenship. Furthermore, according to the Member States:[4]

> wherever in the Treaty establishing the European Community reference is made to nationals of the Member States, the question whether an individual possesses the nationality of a Member State shall be settled solely by reference to the national law of the Member State concerned.

In a nation-state, one would expect that the right to Union citizenship would be based on uniform rules, such as birth in the Union *(ius soli)*, by reason of Union parentage *(ius sanguinis)* or by naturalization in accordance with rules treating all applicants for Union nationality in an equal manner. However, the peoples of Europe are still, therefore, held hostage to the lowest common denominator of the least liberal Member State. Furthermore, although "Every citizen of the Union shall have the right to move and reside freely within the

---

[2] Art. 8a EC Treaty.

[3] Art. 8(1) EC Treaty.

[4] TEU, Declaration on Nationality of a Member State.

territory of the Member States", this is "subject to the limitations and conditions laid down in this Treaty and by the measures adopted to give it effect"[5] (that is, the mere anodyne preservation of the status quo), and, instead of an obligation to ensure such rights within a specified timetable, the only implementing Treaty provision with regard to such rights is that the "Council may adopt provisions with a view to facilitating the exercise of" those rights.[6]

This state of affairs has arisen and been maintained in existence for three reasons: first, the peoples of Europe are still considered primarily as a factor of economic production and greater rights are given to those who are economically active; second, nationalistic interests of greed are such that Member States are only willing to accept as residents persons whose economically productive activity has ended if such persons will not be a financial burden on the host Member State; third, individual Member States insist on their own right to refuse entry to or to deport from what may be termed "their region of the Union" persons whom they deem to be "undesirables" or "marginals" (and, therefore, in need of social exclusion). This chapter maintains that the European Community or Union must do more than merely facilitate the exercise of free movement rights and must create a welcoming Statute of Liberty, unless Part II of the Treaty of Rome is to be no more than another example of "Euro-hypocrisy".

2   PROVISIONS FOR THE ECONOMICALLY ACTIVE

Persons who are economically active were given considerable rights to move by a European Economic Community designed to integrate the economies of the Member States, since it was necessary to abolish restrictions on factors of production. Treaty provisions and secondary legislation on workers, establishment and services were designed to eliminate discrimination based on nationality. The Court of Justice of the European Communities (ECJ) supported this by presumptions of broad interpretation and minimal exclusion but of necessity had to work within the regressive statutory restraints of those provisions dominated as they are by the notion of economic activity as opposed to social liberalism.

---

[5] Art. 8a(1) EC Treaty.

[6] Art. 8a(2) EC Treaty.

The ECJ gave a broad interpretation to the concept of "worker",[7] but emphasized that the advantages which Community law confers in the name of freedom of movement for workers may be relied upon only by persons who actually pursue or seriously wish to pursue activities as employed persons.[8] The ECJ accepted the right of a national of a Member State to move freely and to stay for a reasonable time in the territory of another Member State in order to seek employment there, but made this subject to the provision by that person of evidence that he or she is continuing to seek employment and that he or she has genuine chances of being engaged.[9] Of special importance in the development of rights of workers, in particular, towards recognition of the migrant worker as a citizen integrated with the citizens of the host Member State has been the emphasis on non-discrimination in respect of "social advantages",[10] which, whether or not linked to a contract of employment and including those granted on a discretionary basis, are generally granted to national workers primarily because of their objective status as workers or by virtue of the mere fact of their residence on the national territory and the extension of which to workers who are nationals of other Member States therefore seems suitable to facilitate their mobility.[11] The ECJ has emphasized the importance of the integration of migrants (and family) into the host Member State without any difference in treatment in relation to nationals of that state[12] and created a basis in Community law for the view that persons who have previously pursued in the host Member State an effective and genuine activity as an employed person but who are no longer in an employment relationship are nevertheless considered to be workers under certain provisions of Community law and are guaranteed certain rights linked to the status of worker.[13] However, such social benefits belong to the actively engaged worker (and dependent family) and not to any "non-dependent family"

---

[7] Case 75/63, *Hoekstra v Bedrijfsvereniging Detailhandel,* [1964] ECR 177; Case 66/85, *Lawrie-Blum v Land Baden-Württemberg,* [1986] ECR 2121; Case 139/85, *Kempf v Staatssecretaris van Justitie,* [1986] ECR 1741; Case 53/81, *Levin v Staatssecretaris van Justitie,* [1982] ECR 1035.

[8] Case 53/81, loc. cit., note 7; Case 344/87, *Bettray v Staatssecretaris van Justitie,* [1989] ECR 1621.

[9] Case C-292/89, *Antonissen,* [1991] ECR 745.

[10] Regulation 1612/68, Arts. 7(2), 10, 11.

[11] Case 207/78, *Ministère Public v Even,* [1979] ECR 2019; Case 65/81, *Reina v Landeskreditbank Baden-Württemberg,* [1982] ECR 33; Case 59/85, *Netherlands v Reed,* [1986] ECR 1283.

[12] Case 249/86, *Commission v Germany,* [1989] ECR 1263; Case 9/74, *Casagrande v Landeshauptstadt München,* [1974] ECR 773.

[13] Case 39/86, *Lair v Universität Hannover,* [1988] ECR 3161.

or to nationals of Member States who move in search of employment.[14]

The message from both statutory provisions and jurisprudence is, therefore, that whilst a citizen is economically active, much is conferred, but those citizens whose status is on the wrong side of the "margin" receive at the very best very little.

3   THE RIGHT TO REMAIN

If a person has availed him or herself of the right to engage in economic activity in another Member State, "the right to move and reside freely within the territory of the Member States" (plural) should grant that person a choice, namely whether to return to his or her original state (which cannot be denied by international law, below) or whether to stay in the host state. It is normal for a person who has engaged in economic activity in another Member State and who has indeed integrated him or herself (and any family) in the host state by forming socio-cultural and property and financial attachments there at least to desire the opportunity of long-term or permanent residence in the territory of that host Member State by remaining there. The absence of an absolute right so to remain in such circumstances is an obstacle to the attainment of freedom of movement and current Community legislation denies that absolute right.

Partial recognition of what may be called "the right to remain" is achieved by Community legislation[15] and Member States, therefore, are under a duty to abolish restrictions on the right to remain in their territory in favour of nationals of another Member State who have pursued activities as workers or self-employed persons in their territory, and members of their families, but the duty is a limited one. Apart from certain persons who "live" in one state and "work" in another, the right to remain permanently in the territory of another Member State is limited to persons (workers and self-employed) whose termination of economic activity is as a result of old age or of permanent incapacity to work and who, in specified circumstances, have already fulfilled conditions as to length of residence and activity, together with the members

---

[14] Case 316/85, *Centre public d'aide sociale de Courcelles* v *Lebon,* [1987] ECR 2811.

[15] Regulation 1251/70 (on the right of workers to remain in the territory of a Member State after having been employed in that state); Directive 75/34 (on the right of nationals of a Member State to remain in the territory of another Member State after having pursued therein an activity in a self-employed capacity).

of the person's family (even after the death of the person concerned).[16] Special, but very limited, rules apply if the worker or the self-employed person dies during his or her working life and before having acquired the right to remain in the territory of the state concerned, permitting the members of his or her family to be entitled to remain there permanently.[17] Perhaps the cynic may be forgiven for pointing out that provisions which so often terminate the right to remain contemporaneously with the ending of economic activity are directed towards those already economically rewarded and those who have contributed towards the provision of social security benefits for invalidity and retirement, and away from those with little resources—and this "thinking" is reinforced below.

4   THE "RESIDENCE" DIRECTIVES

Some small measure of progress towards the right "to move and reside freely within the territory of the Member States" had already been made by the adoption, significantly under Article 235 EC Treaty, of what may be termed the "Residence Directives".[18] The recitals to both directives refer to the fact that the deadline (31 December 1992) for the establishment of an internal market comprising an area without internal frontiers in which the free movement of persons is ensured, together with the abolition, as between Member States, of obstacles to freedom of movement for persons, was perilously close. Under the directives, Member States were obliged to grant the right of residence to nationals of Member States who either do not enjoy the right under other provisions of Community law[19] or who have pursued an activity as an employee or self-employed person (the latter even if they have not exercised their right to freedom of movement during their working lives).[20] Since "this right can only be genuinely exercised if it is also granted to members of the family",[21] the following must, irrespective of their nationality, have the right to install themselves in another Member State with

---

[16] Regulation 1251/70, Arts. 2, 3(1); Directive 75/34, Arts. 2, 3(1).

[17] Regulation 1251/70, Art. 3(2); Directive 75/34, Art. 3(2).

[18] Directive 90/364 (on the right of residence); and Directive 90/365 (on the right of residence for employees and self-employed persons who have ceased their occupational activity).

[19] Directive 90/364.

[20] Directive 90/365.

[21] Directives 90/364, 90/365, Recitals.

the holder of the right of residence, namely, his or her spouse and their descendants who are dependants, together with dependent relatives in the ascending line of the holder of the right of residence and his or her spouse.[22]

This seems to be a Brave New World, foretelling of the right "to move and reside freely within the territory of the Member States", but nationalism reared its ugly head in the statement that "beneficiaries of the right of residence must not become an unreasonable burden on the public finances of the host Member State".[23]

Consequently, to be a beneficiary a Member State national (and his or her family) must either be covered by sickness insurance in respect of all risks in the host Member State and have sufficient resources to avoid becoming a burden on the social assistance system of the host Member State during their period of residence[24] or be both recipients of an invalidity or early retirement pension, or old age benefits, or of a pension in respect of an industrial accident or disease of an amount sufficient to avoid becoming a burden on the social security system of the host Member State during their period of residence and also be covered by sickness insurance in respect of all risks in the host Member State.[25] In both cases, these resources will only be deemed sufficient if they are higher than the level of resources below which the host Member State may grant social assistance to its nationals, taking into account the personal circumstances of the applicant and, where appropriate, the personal circumstances of persons admitted as family members and, if this rule cannot be applied in a Member State, the resources of the applicant will only be deemed sufficient if they are higher than the level of the minimum social security pension paid by the host Member State.[26] Furthermore, Member States are entitled to derogate from the provisions of the directives on grounds of public policy, public security or public health.[27]

---

[22] Art. 1(2).

[23] Directives 90/364, 90/365, Recitals.

[24] Directive 90/364, Art. 1(1).

[25] Directive 90/365, Art. 1(1).

[26] Art. 1(1).

[27] Art. 2(2).

5   DEROGATIONS FROM THE FREE MOVEMENT PRINCIPLE

Current Community provision for derogations from the free movement principle blatantly does not mirror, within the Community (or Union), the rights which may be accorded to citizens by a national state. It is a principle of international law that a national state cannot deny its citizens access to and residence in the territory of the state, even if these citizens commit criminal offences, are a financial burden on the state or present some form of health risk. Although the Treaty cannot be assumed to disregard this principle of international law,[28] Community law applies it still in the context of relations between Member States (as opposed to a real Union). Member States are not obliged to accept or permit to reside on their territory every Community (or Union) national and derogations from the free movement principle, allowing European citizens to be refused entry to (and to be deported from) one constituent part of the Union to another, are permitted on the grounds of public policy, public security and public health.[29] The ECJ has admitted that this permits Member States to adopt, with respect to the nationals of other Member States, measures which they cannot apply to their own nationals.[30]

There are, it is true, legislative restrictions on the derogation rules, which are a specific manifestation of the principle enshrined in the Convention for the Protection of Human Rights and Fundamental Freedoms (European Convention on Human Rights; ECHR) that no restrictions in the interests of national security or public safety can be placed on the rights secured by the ECHR other than such as are necessary for the protection of those interests "in a democratic society"[31] and which are capable of producing direct effects.[32] These have been restrictively interpreted, and generously supplemented, by the Court.

First, measures taken on grounds of public policy or of public security

---

[28] Case 41/74, *Van Duyn* v *Home Office,* [1974] ECR 1337.

[29] Treaty of Rome, Arts. 48(3), 56 and 66; Directive 64/221 (on the coordination of special measures concerning the movement and residence of foreign nationals which are justified on grounds of public policy, public security or public health).

[30] Joined Cases 115 and 116/81, *Adoui and Cornuaille* v *Belgium,* [1982] ECR 1665.

[31] Case 36/75, *Rutili* v *Minister for the Interior,* [1975] ECR 1219.

[32] Case 41/74, loc. cit., note 28; Case 48/75, *Royer,* [1976] ECR 497; Case 131/79, *Regina* v *Secretary of State for Home Affairs,* [1980] ECR 1585.

must be based exclusively on the personal conduct of the individual concerned,[33] the mere existence of previous criminal convictions may not automatically constitute grounds for deportation measures and can, therefore, only be taken into account in so far as the circumstances which gave rise to that conviction are evidence of personal conduct constituting a present threat to the requirements of public policy, as opposed to the purpose of deterring other aliens by measures of a general preventive nature.[34] In so far as it may justify certain restrictions on the free movement of persons subject to Community law, recourse by a national authority to the concept of public policy presupposes, in any event, the existence, in addition to the perturbation of the social order which any infringement of the law involves, of a genuine and sufficiently serious threat to the requirements of public policy affecting one of the fundamental interests of society[35] and conduct may not be considered as being of a sufficiently serious nature to justify restrictions on the admission to or residence within the territory of a Member State of a national of another Member State in a case where the former Member State does not adopt with respect to the same conduct on the part of its own nationals repressive measures or other genuine and effective measures intended to combat such conduct.[36] The mere failure by a national of a Member State to complete the legal formalities concerning access, movement and residence of aliens does not justify a decision ordering expulsion or temporary imprisonment for that purpose.[37]

Second, diseases or disabilities justifying refusal of entry or refusal to issue a first residence permit are limited to diseases which, by their infectious or contagious nature, might endanger public health and to those which might threaten public policy or public security (such as drug addiction and profound mental disturbance), and it is specifically stated that diseases or disabilities occurring after a first residence permit has been issued can not justify refusal to renew the residence permit or expulsion from the territory.[38]

Third, in each Member State, nationals of other Member States who may be refused a residence permit or may be expelled must have adequate legal

---

[33] Case 41/74, loc. cit., note 28.

[34] Directive 64/221, Art. 3; Case 30/77, *Regina v Bouchereau,* [1977] ECR 1999; Case 131/79, loc. cit., note 32; Case 67/74, *Bonsignore v Stadt Köln,* [1975] ECR 297.

[35] Case 30/77, loc. cit., note 34; Joined Cases 115 and 116/81, loc. cit., note 30.

[36] Joined Cases 115 and 116/81, loc. cit., note 30.

[37] Case 48/75, loc. cit., note 32.

[38] Directive 64/221, Art. 4(1)(2), Annex.

remedies available to them in respect of administrative decisions in such matters. These include the right to be informed of the grounds upon which the decision taken is based,[39] the right to be allowed a period of time for leaving the territory (which must be stated),[40] the same legal remedies (and certainly not lesser safeguards) as are available to nationals of the state concerned in respect of acts of the administration[41] and (if there is no right of appeal to a court of law, or where such appeal may be only in respect of the legal validity of the decision, or where the appeal cannot have suspensory effect) the right to obtain and be notified of an opinion from a separate and independent authority before a decision refusing renewal of a residence permit or ordering the expulsion of the holder of a residence permit is made and assessed at the very time when the decision is made (because the factors to be taken into account, particularly those concerning conduct, are likely to change in the course of time).[42]

However, despite the restrictions outlined above and although the concept of public policy, in particular where it is used as a justification for derogating from the fundamental principle of freedom of movement, must be interpreted strictly, so that its scope cannot be determined unilaterally by each Member State,[43] nevertheless that concept may vary from one Member State to another and Member States are allowed "an area of discretion". Community law does not impose upon the Member States a uniform scale of values as regards the assessment of conduct which may be considered as contrary to public policy and such difference of treatment must therefore be allowed.[44] It is ironic that the conduct for the public policy derogation has to be "a genuine and sufficiently serious threat to the requirements of public policy affecting one of the fundamental interests of society",[45] whereas under the public health derogation one only has to be the victim of tuberculosis or syphilis, and,

---

[39] Ibid., Art. 6. Such notification must be sufficiently detailed and precise to enable the person concerned to defend his or her interests: Joined Cases 115 and 116/81, loc. cit., note 30.

[40] Ibid., Art. 7.

[41] Ibid., Art. 8; Case 98/79, *Pecastaing* v *Belgium*, [1980] ECR 691: Joined Cases C-297/88 and C-197/89, *Dzodzi*, [1990] ECR 3763.

[42] Ibid., Art. 9; Joined Cases C-297/88 and C-197/89, loc. cit., note 41; Case 131/79, loc. cit., note 32.

[43] Case 41/74, loc. cit., note 28; Case 36/75, loc. cit., note 31; Case 30/77, loc. cit., note 34.

[44] Case 41/74, loc. cit., note 28; Case 30/77, loc. cit., note 34. Joined Cases 115 and 116/81, loc. cit., note 30.

[45] Case 30/77, loc. cit., note 34.

furthermore, in view of the disguised free movement derogation based on the exclusion of economically non-active marginals, one only has to be workless or resourceless.

The very existence of free movement derogations, irrespective of how narrowly they may be drafted and interpreted and irrespective of the procedural safeguards which they contain, should be an anathema to those who believe in, as opposed to those who merely mouth pious platitudes towards, true citizenship rights of movement throughout the totality of territory of the Member States which constitute the Union. For there to be true free movement for the peoples of Europe, it is apparent that much must be done to liberalize the current situation and this must be done by the Union legislators.

6 COMMUNITY (OR UNION) ACTION (OR INACTION)

Until the insertion of the new Part II of the Treaty of Rome, Community action on the free movement of persons was limited to the achievement of the internal market (with all the imperfections discussed above) by concentrating on moves to improve the lot of those already granted rights under existing provisions. Even before then, as the Commission itself recently admitted, while the elimination of frontier controls on goods has become something of a reality, the same was not true for the removal of identity checks, which "is behind schedule to a worrying extent", and the application of the Convention implementing the Schengen Agreement on frontier controls has not been achieved.[46] Once it had become clear that free movement of persons had not been fully achieved by 1 January 1993, the Commission took steps to exert pressure on defaulting Member States and undertook to decide on measures to be taken, in particular by way of legislation prompted by the fact that the TEU would provide the Commission with new opportunities in fields which were previously covered by intergovernmental co-operation.[47] The Commission's Legislative Programme for 1993 admitted that "the thorniest problem is the abolition of controls on people at the Community's internal frontiers" and pledged that, within the limits of its powers, it would "contribute to an overall strategy to be put in place in 1993 to remedy the situation".[48] The Commission noted that once the TEU came into force, protection of the rights and

---

[46] "The Community Internal Market", 1993 Report (COM (94)) 55 final, 14 March 1994), para. 55.

[47] Ibid., paras 56, 57.

[48] Supplement 1/93 – Bull. EC, 17.

115

interests of Member States' "nationals" (that is, taking the limited view of citizenship) "will have to be strengthened by gradually giving substance to Union Citizenship to supplement [but not replace] national citizenship, which will include the right to travel and settle freely in the territory of the Member States".[49] This was repeated in the Commission's Legislative Programme for 1994, but it should be noted that the Commission specifically emphasized the limited wording of the new Charter in that the right to move and reside freely throughout the territory of the Member States was dependent "on the terms set out in the Treaty and in secondary legislation".[50] In any event, the free movement provisions remain as they are, a paper declaration, and perhaps it is significant that the European Parliament, in response, proposed "that the Commission proposal be complemented by measures for the freedom of movement of persons, with a view to finally achieving the most powerful symbol of completion of the internal market".[51] Perhaps the Commission will be goaded into action by the European Parliament's recent resolution, referring to both Universal and European Declarations on Human Rights and calling upon the Commission to achieve "free circulation of persons".[52]

Some elements of a common Union policy towards immigration have evolved. First, the Commission has adopted a new draft proposal for a decision by the Council of the European Union establishing a convention on controls on persons crossing the external frontiers of the Member States.[53] The Commission has also sent the Council, on the basis of the (new) Article 100c, a proposal for a regulation determining the third countries whose nationals must be in possession of a visa when crossing the external borders of the Member States.[54] The exercise in mutual recognition will list more than 120 third countries whose nationals will have to have a visa and the list is the same as that agreed by the nine Member States which are signatories to the Schengen Agreement. With regard to other third countries, Member States will remain free to require a visa or not. The Commission proposes that this option be subject to a time-limit (the Commission suggests 30 June 1996). Second, under the TEU, asylum is designated as a subject of common interest, since

---

[49] Ibid., 30.

[50] COM (93) 588 final.

[51] Supplement 1/94 – Bull. EC.

[52] Debates of the European Parliament, 8 March 1994 (O.J. 1994, C 91/316–317). See also Parliament's reaction to passport checks by airlines (EP Doc. A3–0081/94).

[53] COM (93) 684 final.

[54] Ibid.

it concerns both aspects of foreign and security policy and of justice and home affairs. This, it is hoped, will result in a common asylum policy for the Union, commenced (albeit in a spasmodic manner) by the Dublin Convention of 15 June 1990 (determining the Member State responsible for examining applications for asylum made in one of the Member States and already ratified by six Member States). A recent initiative by the Commission highlights the need for action on the causes of migration pressure, action on controlling migration flows, and action to strengthen immigration policies for legal immigrants in order "to assimilate their rights with those of citizens of Member States".[55] One hopes that this means that both legal third-country immigrants and national "marginals" are to be accorded full citizenship rights of movement.

On recent development in Community thinking which could augur well for the liberal approach advocated in this chapter relates to the educational policies to be adopted by the Community *vis-à-vis* children of citizens and non-citizens alike. A policy for socio-cultural integration for both groups is a key element in the struggle against social exclusion. Although strictly speaking, the free movement of Union citizens and their families must be distinguished from the integration of nationals of third countries, the Commission has recently reaffirmed that:

> such distinctions cannot apply to education policy, the struggle against social exclusion and for equal opportunities. Indeed, ever since the Action Programme for Education of 9 February 1976[56] it has been clear for the Community that all measures to promote the education of migrant children will include the children of nationals of other Member States and the children of third country nationals.[57]

Perhaps, one day, the free movement provisions of the TEU will be implemented and, one day, there will be a Charter of Free Movement Rights for the

---

[55] Communication from the Commission to the Council and the European Parliament on Immigration and Asylum Policies (COM (94) 23 final, 23 Feb. 1994).

[56] O.J. 1976, C 38.

[57] Report on the Education of Migrants' Children (COM (94) 80, 25 March 1994). See also, Resolution of the Council of Ministers of Education meeting within the Council of 14 Dec. 1989 (O.J. 1990, C 27): "Policies on immigration and social integration of immigrants in the European Community", expert report drafted at the request of the Commission (28 Sept. 1990, SEC (90)) 1813 final), para. 42; and Report of the European Parliament on cultural plurality and the problems of cultural education for children of immigrants in the European Community (EP Doc. A3–0399/92, 21 Jan. 1993).

Citizens of the Union. A number of criticisms of substance have already been made in this chapter and it is hoped that the Union will succeed where the Community failed. In addition to the granting of more liberal substantive rights, is the need, in the interest of legal certainty for so many potential beneficiaries, for a change, perhaps a drastic change, in the manner in which such a Charter might be promulgated. First, such a Charter should be clearly drafted in detail, without the obvious gaps and fudged language that has characterized this area up to now and has resulted in the delays and uncertainties of having to submit Article 177 references to (or to await the results of Article 169 proceedings before) the ECJ. Second, citizenship rights of free movement are too important to be left to a directive and should be in the form of a regulation. Under the Community regime, Member States could hide behind their own inactivity. By 31 October 1993 (over a year after the due date of 30 June 1992), neither Germany nor France, great Europeans both, had yet transposed Directives 90/364 or 90/365.[58] The adoption of a regulation would obviate the constant need for establishment of rights by means of the doctrine of direct effect. It would ensure real and practical enjoyment of the law of the Union by facilitating actions for damages or judicial review (or any other legal remedies) in the same way as individuals can rely on national laws, properly so-called.

Finally, so, Commission, Council and European Parliament, so then our European masters, think again, as you guzzle from your troughs of gravy. The Union, in the context of free movement rights, is as yet a myth, a cosmetic device which gives superficial pleasure to federalist politicians but ignores the peoples of Europe. Have the courage to be real Europeans. By the time 1996 comes and further progress is made towards a European Constitution, think of your statements about human rights, think about a European Bill of Rights, and think of a real free movement of citizens, which will confer absolute rights for all of Europe's peoples.

---

[58] Commission Report on National Implementing Measures to give effect to the White Paper of the Commission on the completion of the internal market—situation at 31 Oct. 1993, 404, 405.

6 HUMAN RIGHTS OF ALIENS IN EUROPE

Henry G. Schermers

1 INTRODUCTION

Europe is faced with many problems concerning admission, expulsion and extradition of aliens. The Treaty on European Union (TEU) provides for citizenship of the Union. Each person holding the nationality of a Member State shall be a citizen of the Union.[1] Does this mean that citizens from other Member States are no longer aliens, so that the national laws on aliens no longer apply to them? The TEU makes no such demand, but the existing rules on European integration do have an enormous impact on the rights of citizens coming from other Member States. In particular the freedom of movement of persons provided for in several articles of the EC Treaty and in the Schengen Agreement necessarily has an impact on national rules concerning admission, expulsion and extradition of aliens. Gradually, the regime applicable to nationals of other Member States of the Union has become so different from the regime applicable to other aliens that one must distinguish between internal and external expulsion and extradition, expulsion or extradition from one Member State of the European Union to another being internal and expulsion or extradition to a third country being external.

European Community law does not contain any specific rules on the admission of aliens, nor on expulsion or extradition. These are regulated by national rules. All Member States of the European Union are bound by treaties on extradition with numerous other states. Under these treaties the European states have undertaken to extradite suspected and condemned criminals to other states, but in all cases under certain conditions. Normally, people will not be extradited for political offences, nor will they be extradited for acts which are not criminal in the extraditing state or when threatened with penalties unacceptable to that state, in particular with the death penalty. In order to verify whether the conditions for expulsion are

---

[1] Art. G 8 (Art. 8 EC Treaty).

N. A. Neuwahl and A. Rosas (eds.), The European Union and Human Rights, 119–131.

fulfilled persons whose extradition has been requested may appeal to a court. Judicial proceedings in the European states protect individuals against unjustifiable extradition.

Though they are usually rather similar, extradition treaties may vary from one state to another. Apart from them there are some treaties affecting admission, expulsion and extradition, which bind all Member States of the Union in the same way. They therefore contribute to rules which are uniform throughout the Union. The most important of them is the Convention for the Protection of Human Rights and Fundamental Freedoms (European Convention on Human Rights; ECHR) to which all Member States of the Union are parties. This Convention applies to everyone within the jurisdiction of a participating state, which means throughout the entire Union. Expulsion or extradition contrary to the ECHR is prohibited to all Member States of the Union. The European Commission of Human Rights is of the opinion that expulsion or extradition to a State Party to the ECHR is not restricted by any Convention rules as the receiving state is equally bound by these rules so that the individual can bring a complaint against that state when the expulsion or extradition would lead to a situation contrary to the ECHR. The only exception ever made to this policy concerned the expulsion of Kurds to Turkey. Even though also Kurds can lodge a complaint against Turkey whenever they would be treated there in a way contrary to the ECHR, the Commission was not sufficiently sure that such complaints would actually reach her in time. This exception does not, however, concern states of the European Union. With respect to them the European Convention on Human Rights is relevant only to external expulsion and extradition and to the admission of aliens from outside the Union. The ECHR will be discussed, therefore, below in Section 3.

Individuals may be expelled from a Member State of the European Union in three different situations. First, immigrants who illegally enter the country can be expelled at any time. Secondly, the admission of foreigners can be refused which means that they are detained when trying to enter the country and that they are subsequently returned to where they came from. Legally this may not be expulsion but in practice the refusal of an entry permit will have the same consequence that the person concerned is sent back to a foreign country.

Thirdly, persons who are legally inside a Member State may be expelled if they do not fulfil the conditions under which they were admitted. One of these conditions generally is that no crime will be committed. All European countries expel foreigners who have committed serious crimes such as dealing in drugs. It also happens that people are admitted for the reason that they are married to a national. If subsequently the marriage is broken up the foreigner may be expelled.

Like in the case of extradition judicial remedies are foreseen in cases of expulsion. Whenever a decision to expel has been taken to a foreigner he has the right to bring his case before a court which will rule upon the validity.

2   INTERNAL EXPULSION AND EXTRADITION

Internal expulsion is practically unworkable in a union where persons can move freely. Already in 1960 free movement of persons inside Benelux was achieved. Still, it happened a number of times that the Dutch authorities expelled people from The Netherlands to Belgium. Usually these people were ordered subsequently to move to a further destination and in some cases Belgian police took the persons over at the border and brought them outside Benelux territory. It has also happened, however, that there was no Belgian police to take the person over at the Dutch-Belgian border and the Dutch police limited itself to sending the persons into Belgium. In practice, most of these persons took the next train back into The Netherlands. As there was no border control this could not be prevented. After the acceptance of free movement of persons under the TEU any expulsion from one European country to another will be equally ineffective as the expelled person can freely move back into the country from which he was expelled. His situation is similar to that of a citizen who is banished from a province of his own state. For nationals of third states rules will have to be developed for creating the possibility to expel them out of the territory of the entire Union. This means that Member States either have to send undesired aliens directly to a third country or they have to seek co-operation of neighbouring Union members in order to guarantee that they will further the foreigner concerned over the external borders of the Union.

Internal extradition also leads to practical problems. The freedom of movement within the European Union also applies to criminals. A bank-robber may, for example, rob a bank in a country other than his own. The freedom of movement of persons facilitates a quick return to his own country after the robbery. For bringing the bankrobber to trial, the Member State, where the robbery took place, has to request extradition and extradition proceedings have to be started in the state of the bankrobber. These proceedings may take a long time and may even be unsuccessful. The net result is a serious unbalance in the sense that criminals can easily move out of the country where the crime is committed whilst their return to that country is usually difficult. This unbalance may become a serious barrier to the maintenance of law and order. There would be good reason to move any arrested criminal back to the place of crime without any extradition proceedings, in the same way as persons are moved from one province to another in a unified state. Still, this may lead to problems in cases of acts which are not in all states recognized as criminal. For example, abortion may under certain circumstances be a crime in one Member State whilst under the same circumstances it is not a crime in other countries.

Even after recent amendment of the law homosexual acts with a consenting boy between 16 and 18 years of age is a criminal offence in the United Kingdom and not in many other countries. In such cases most countries object against automatic extradition. The main ground for such objection is that one does not want to subject nationals to prosecution for acts which one does not accept as being criminal. If Dutch law permits a Dutchman to have sexual intercourse with a consenting 16 or 17-year-old boy, then the Dutch authorities refuse to co-operate in a prosecution elsewhere which may lead to punishment for such intercourse. The argument is ineffective and unconvincing. It is ineffective because in many cases it leads to long detention on remand which does not help the national. Knowing the difficulty of extradition the state where the crime is committed will keep the person in detention for fear that he may leave the country. The argument is unconvincing because we accept the cultural differences between the Member States of the European Union. We also accept that each national society is entitled to make legislation for its own territory. If the British society decides that they want, for example, to punish sexual intercourse with 16 and 17-year-old boys, then it is their right to do so and anyone committing such acts in Britain should be equally prosecuted and punished.

To consider a person subject to his own criminal law, irrespective where he goes, denies the right of each society to decide for itself what acts are to be tolerated on its territory. The traditional rule of international law that a state does not extradite for facts which it does not itself consider criminal is based on distrust in foreign legislation. Whereas such distrust may be justified with respect to alien cultures which make the use of the word "Kurd" or any criticism of religion into a criminal offence, it should not prevail in a European Union.

To find a reasonable balance between the free movement of criminals throughout the European Union and the needs of criminal prosecution extradition should in any case be facilitated. If free extradition by the police without judicial review is still unacceptable, then one might limit judicial review to a number of exceptional situations.

When extradition on request without further judicial control would be permitted between the Member States of the European Union specific problems might arise with respect to third countries. When, for example, The Netherlands would not agree to the extradition of a certain person to Latin America, but Spain would have no objection against such extradition the Spanish authorities could ask for the delivery of the person to Spain and subsequently extradite him to Latin America. To prevent such situations extradition procedures and extradition treaties with third countries should be harmonized as much as possible. As long as discrepancies remain, some judicial control should be possible also for internal extradition.

In order to facilitate prosecution of freely moving criminals close co-operation between national authorities and some harmonization of criminal law will increasingly be necessary.

3   EXTERNAL EXPULSION AND EXTRADITION

So far, the Member States of the European Union are free to decide whether to expel or extradite persons to a third country. Great divergencies between national policies may lead to confusion and will limit the freedom of movement within the European Union, but they are not necessarily contrary to any rule of European Community law. In the long run harmonization will be desirable. Up to now some harmonization is achieved by international treaties to which all Member States of the Union are bound. The most important treaty which prescribes rules common to all Member States of the Union is the European Convention on Human Rights. Under this Convention the European Court of Human Rights has refined the meaning of several of its articles. Especially the interpretation of Articles 3 and 8 has developed rules on expulsion and extradition which apply to all Member States of the Union.

Most important are the interpretations of Article 3. Under this article the Court established that neither expulsion nor extradition is permitted towards a country where the person concerned may be subject to a serious violation of his most fundamental human rights. In the *Soering* case the Court held:[2]

---

[2] Eur. Court H. R., *Soering* judgment of 7 July 1989, Series A no. 161, para. 91, p. 35.

the decision by a Contracting State to extradite a fugitive may give rise to an issue under Article 3, and hence engage the responsibility of that State under the Convention, where substantial grounds have been shown for believing that the person concerned, if extradited, faces a real risk of being subjected to torture or to inhuman or degrading treatment or punishment in the requesting country.

Seen from the perspective of human rights it is unacceptable to expel or extradite a person to a country where he will be tortured or killed. Such extradition or expulsion would be inhuman treatment contrary to Article 3. Under European standards of human rights there is no alternative to this ruling of the European Court of Human Rights. Under a convention set up to protect minimum rights of individuals it must be unacceptable to send a person into his death or into torture. Still, the ruling may lead to a number of practical problems which can be illustrated by the following, partly hypothetical, cases.

Some countries, such as Singapore and Malaysia, have a compulsory death penalty for drug-dealers. This means that a Singaporean or Malaysian drug-dealer arrested in the European Union would risk the death penalty when he is expelled or extradited to his own country in cases where it is clear that he traded in drugs in that country. So far, persons punished for drug-dealing in Europe and subsequently sent back to Malaysia have not been sentenced to death there, but this policy could change. If any drug-dealer sent back from Europe would be automatically sentenced to death, would that prohibit Europe to expel or extradite drug-dealers to Malaysia or Singapore? If there was such a prohibition would that then open a practical possibility for migrants who otherwise would not be admitted to Europe to force admission by trading in drugs? Having a restricted immigration policy it must be difficult for Europe to be forced to keep all drug-dealers from countries like Malaysia and Singapore within its borders.

In the *Soering* case the European Court of Human Rights held that the death row phenomenon in the state of Virginia was of such character that extradition of Mr Soering to the United States, whilst knowing that he would most likely be subjected to the death row would be inhuman treatment contrary to Article 3 ECHR under the circumstances of the case, especially the age and mental state of Mr Soering.[3] This raises a number of questions of borderline. Usually when a person is sentenced to imprisonment for life, there is at least a fair chance that he may come free after a

---

[3] *Soering*, loc. cit., note 2, para. 111, pp. 44, 45.

certain period of time. This prospect, this element of hope, may make treatment in prison bearable. In some legislations, however, a life sentence may be imposed with the express provision that no release will ever be possible. Is that inhuman? Would extradition to a state which has such legislation be inhuman treatment violating Article 3 ECHR?

The same question may be posed with respect to long sentences which are to be executed in prisons or labour camps where the conditions may be considered inhuman.

Another problem under Article 3 may be imposed by the general conditions existing in a particular area. May a European state send people back to Rwanda, Somalia, Southern Sudan, Iran or Iraq, if no extradition is requested, nor personal persecution claimed, solely because life in these areas is extremely difficult? If it is inhuman treatment to send people to these areas, does that mean that all people from there must be granted asylum? In practice, European states do not grant asylum but neither do they send people back as long as they consider the situation unbearable. Some kind of temporary right to stay is given. One may expect that the European Court of Human Rights will consider expulsion to such areas in violation of Article 3 ECHR in extreme cases only.[4]

Some people from Africa need expensive medical care which is not available in their home country. So they, legally or illegally, migrate to Europe and receive medical care there, often at the expense of the receiving country. Subsequently, they claim that expulsion to their home country is impossible because there they would die or become seriously handicapped for lack of sufficient medical care. Morally European states are compelled to receive and care for these immigrants, but will that remain possible if their quantity increases when transport facilities become cheaper?

In some African countries the future is so dim that parents who care for their children send these children without papers to family or friends in Europe. The European Commission of Human Rights has established that sending children to a country where there is no one to receive them is inhuman treatment. Does this mean that Member States of the European Union have to accept all children when they cannot find family in the children's home country where the children can be sent to?

There is also a stream of political refugees. All European states grant asylum to people prosecuted in their home country for political reasons. In

---

[4] See Eur. Court H. R., *Cruz Varas and Others* judgment of 20 March 1991, Series A no. 201, paras 75, 76, 83; and Eur. Court H. R., *Viljavarah and Others* judgment of 30 October 1991, Series A no. 215, paras 102–116.

practice, a large number of foreign immigrants apply every year for political asylum. Usually they illustrate their request with awful stories about the treatment undergone in the home country. In practice, it is usually difficult to verify these stories. Sometimes immigrants have documentation proving the political risks they run, sometimes the papers are false and other times such papers are totally lacking. A person fleeing from his home country may be unable to take all kinds of papers with him. In all European countries immigration services scrutinize people seeking political asylum and no European authority is able to separate the wheat from the chaff with absolute certainty. Some alien services collect extensive documentation on false documents. Pooling all available documentation on falsifications and on the different letters of typewriters and handwriting of both false and genuine documents into one central European institution may strengthen the control by immigration services.

Article 8 ECHR stipulates respect for private and family life. Expulsion or extradition of a person does not necessarily infringe his family life as in many cases family members may follow the expelled or extradited person. Private life will most likely be affected by any expulsion or extradition, but this is not necessarily in violation of Article 8 ECHR. The second paragraph of the Article permits interference with both private and family life if that is in accordance with the law and necessary in a democratic society in the interests of national security, public safety or the economic well-being of the country, for the prevention of disorder or crime, for the protection of health and morals, or for the protection of the rights and freedoms of others. Again the problems which may arise with respect to this Article in cases of expulsion and extradition may be best illustrated by a number of, partly hypothetical, examples.

A Chinese from Hongkong has lived for 20 years in Amsterdam as a cook in a Chinese restaurant. His children, born in The Netherlands, went to Dutch schools. When the children were some 10 to 14 years of age, the Chinese restaurant went bankrupt and the father became unemployed. To gain some income, he started trading in drugs, got caught and punished. After completion of his prison sentence he was expelled from The Netherlands. The expulsion clearly affected the family life of all members of the family. For the children it was almost impossible to follow their father to Hongkong which was a completely foreign country to them. Does that mean that the expulsion of the father was a violation of Article 8? In this kind of cases the human rights institutions in Strasbourg will normally not consider expulsion contrary to Article 8 as it will be justified for the prevention of disorder or crime and for the protection of the rights and freedoms of others (the victims of drugs). The interest of society to be protected against drug-dealers outweighs the interests of family life, not only of the drug-dealer, but also of his next of kin.

The situation is more difficult in the case of second generation immigrants, that is, when it concerns a person born in Europe as child of legal or illegal immigrants or a person who has come to Europe at a very young age. When, subsequently, that person has had his full education in Europe, but has not obtained any European nationality, may he then still be expelled to the country whose nationality he has, even if he is a total stranger to that country? The question arose for the first time in the case of Moustaquim. Moustaquim had come from Morocco to Belgium before his second birthday. While still a minor he committed a substantial number of crimes, mainly theft and robbery. After coming of age he served a prison sentence of eighteen months. He was released in 1984 at the age of 20. Before his release an order was served on him to leave Belgium and not to return for ten years. Within 30 days of leaving prison he had to comply with the order. Both the Commission and the Court of Human Rights found the expulsion order in violation of the respect for family life required by Article 8.[5]

Similar cases were brought by Mr Djeroud[6] and Mr Beldjoudi[7] against France. In the case of Beldjoudi, however, the family ties were considerably weaker. When a deportation order was issued against him, Mr Beldjoudi was 29 years old and had left his parental home for more than 10 years. His wife was French but there were no clear reasons why she could not follow him in exile. Both the Commission and the Court found a lack of respect for family life, rather than for private life, probably in order to limit the effect of the case as infringements of private life will more clearly arise in all cases of expulsion and extradition. Still it seems better to consider cases of this kind under private life. The ties of a second generation immigrant to the country where he grew up and where he lived all his life or almost all his life do not become weaker when his parents die and when he has no brothers or sisters. Also, the family-life argument would equally apply to an immigrant who has lived in the country for only a short time, provided that his family lives there. Special treatment of second

---

[5] Eur. Court H. R., *Mustaquim* judgment of 18 February 1991, Series A no. 193.

[6] Eur. Court H. R., *Djeroud* judgment of 23 January 1991, Series A no. 191-B, pp. 25–39.

[7] Eur. Court H. R., *Beldjoudi v. France* judgment of 26 March 1992, Series A no. 234-A, pp. 1–52.

generation immigrants should be based on their own position rather than on that of their family.[8]

Another question which arose a number of times concerns the composition of a family. It is generally accepted that admission to a European country must be granted to the wife and the minor children of persons who lawfully reside in the country. In a number of cases against The Netherlands, the Commission held that the ECHR does not prohibit a state to refuse admission to a second (and further) wife of a polygamous immigrant and her children. With respect to the children difficult questions may arise. If an alien was married to one wife and after her death to another, the second wife and the minor children of both wives must be admitted once the father is legally in the country. If an alien was married to one wife and during the valid existence of that marriage he married a second wife then either the first wife and her children or the second wife and her children must be admitted. Both the other wife and her children may be refused. But what happens to the children when the not admitted wife dies? In the most extreme situation the children have no other relatives than their father. But even if there are uncles or aunts, should the children not be entitled to stay with their father? Much depends on factual circumstances, such as the age of the children, their attachment to either society, their previous contacts with the father (did he, for instance, support them financially?) and the availability of family in their country of origin.

How heavily should one weigh relationship in blood? In the *Berrehab* case the European Court of Human Rights did not consider cohabitation as a *sine qua non* of family life between parents and minor children. It had held in a previous case that the relationship created between spouses by a lawful and genuine marriage has to be regarded as "family life".[9] In the *Berrehab* case the Court concluded from the concept of family on which Article 8 is based that a child born of such a union is *ipso jure* part of that relationship; hence, from the moment of the child's birth and by the very fact of it, there exists between him and his parents a bond amounting to "family life", even if the parents are not then living together. The Court accepted as a matter of course, that subsequent events may break that tie.[10]

---

[8] See also my concurring opinion in the *Beldjoudi* case, loc. cit., note 6, pp. 48, 49.

[9] Eur. Court H. R., *Abdulaziz, Cabales and Balkandali* judgment of 28 May 1985, Series A no. 94, p. 32, para. 62.

[10] Eur. Court H. R., *Berrehab* judgment of 21 June 1988, Series A no. 138, p. 14, para. 21.

In principle, one should accept that under Article 8 ECHR minor children have a right to stay with the remaining parent when one of the parents die.

Duties of care may also exist between adult children and their parents. Especially in states with little social security it may be a generally recognized duty of children to look after their parents when the latter become old and disabled. So far, the European Commission of Human Rights has not accepted a duty of Member States under Article 8 ECHR to admit parents of aliens regularly present in their territory. As the Commission declares cases of this kind inadmissible, they never come before the Court.

In a case in England a homosexual family was at stake. Since the age of 17, an Austrian girl had recognized herself to be a lesbian. Her acknowledgement of her sexuality caused estrangement from her parents and she moved to England. She was given temporary leave to stay and work there. She entered into a lesbian relationship with a British woman (Ms E.) resident in the United Kingdom. Her application to remain in the United Kingdom as a lesbian cohabitee was rejected, this not being a status recognized by a statement of changes in the immigration rules. Pending her appeal against this rejection she became pregnant by artificial insemination. She wanted to have her child in the family unit of herself and Ms E., and she claimed that the splitting up of such a family unit would be contrary to Article 8 ECHR. The Home Office did not consider the pregnancy to be a sufficient reason to depart from the immigration rules. After having given birth to a daughter the Australian girl applied to the European Commission of Human Rights submitting disrespect of her family life in violation of Article 8 ECHR.

At the time of her complaint she had been living together with Ms E. for almost five years, during the last year in a property which they owned jointly. Since confinement and the birth of the child she was financially dependent on Ms E. and parenting tasks were shared between them. She claimed that she would be homeless, destitute, and have to rely on social security payments for the maintenance of herself and her child, if she were deported to Australia. The European Commission of Human Rights had to decide whether there was an infringement of family life.

In the light of its previous case law, the Commission found that a lesbian partnership involved private life, within the meaning of Article 8 ECHR but not family life. It further held that, although lawful deportation will have repercussions on such relationships, it cannot, in principle, be regarded as an interference with the ECHR, given the state's right to impose immigration controls and limits. In the case the Commission found no exceptional circumstances to justify a departure from these considerations. It, therefore, concluded by majority vote that there had been no interference with the applicant's right to respect for private life ensured by Article 8 ECHR and that this aspect of the case was manifestly ill-founded within the meaning of Article 27(2) ECHR.

The Australian girl also complained of discrimination on the grounds of sexual preference, in so far as British immigration policy gave better protection to heterosexual couples than to homosexual couples.

The Commission, however, was of the opinion that the difference in treatment between the applicant and somebody in the same position whose partner had been of the opposite sex be objectively and reasonably justified. It accepted that the immigration rules in the UK gave priority and better guarantees to traditional established families, rather than other established relationships like a lesbian partnership.[11]

4   SOLUTIONS

All problems will never be solved. Unavoidably some places will be more attractive as residence than others and some measures to prevent excessive immigration will remain necessary. That is not an international issue. The same goes within national communities. Many large cities restrict immigration of people from elsewhere and also some regions, such as the Channel Islands have severe restrictions for residence.

Quantitatively, problems of extradition, composition of families, family reunion and even second generation immigrants are of a minor character. The most real problem facing Western Europe concerns admission and expulsion of aliens seeking refuge in Europe for the reason that living in their own countries becomes unbearable. This creates a continuously growing stream of people who come to Europe from other parts of the world. The growth of this stream is caused by several developments. Radio and television make Europe known to other parts of the world; air traffic brings Europe within easier reach than ever before; both economically and politically, Europe—with a few exceptions—is a very good place to live.

This stream cannot be stopped. There is only one possibility to mitigate it. Only improvement of the standard of living in the other parts of the world will diminish the need of people to migrate to Western Europe. Medical refugees can be stopped by making medical care available in other

---

[11] Application No. 14753/89 by Christine and Lauren Moss against the United Kingdom, Decision of the Commission of 9 Oct. 1989.

parts of the world, political refugees can be stopped by improving the political climate elsewhere and economic refugees will be less numerous when the economic situation elsewhere improves. All other means for limiting immigration into Western Europe will remain ineffective if no very severe border control can be set up. A border control sufficiently severe to prevent illegal immigration into Europe will require enormous investments, will hamper legal trade and legal movements of persons and isolate Western Europe from the rest of the world. Even with a perfect co-operation between the European states such border control will remain defective in practice.

7 THE PROTECTION OF NATIONAL OR ETHNIC, RELIGIOUS AND LINGUISTIC MINORITIES

María Amor Martín Estébanez

1 INTRODUCTION

European states have traditionally considered national or ethnic, religious and linguistic minorities as a "problem" for their well-being rather than a source of enrichment. Western European states have preferred to keep the minority issue within the domestic domain where it has tended to be ignored, minority protection being rare and usually lacking a comprehensive character. This is why international frameworks and organizations play a very important role in the protection of European minorities. In particular the security aspects of this question have caused regional and international concern. Relevant precedents exist for regional and international involvement in the minority question in Europe (such as that provided under the League of Nations) and recent initiatives of the European Union in this field should not lose sight of existing experience.

The reluctance of the Member States of the European Union to recognize the rights of minorities or even their existence is also reflected in the international arena. Vivid expressions of this reluctance are the reservation made by France to Article 27 of the International Covenant on Civil and Political Rights[1] (which has been the main international legal provision concerning minority protection since 1976), and the fact that Greece has not even become a party to the Covenant. Whereas the reports of the United Kingdom to international human rights bodies tend to concentrate on the "ethnic minorities" which comprise both citizens and non-citizens originating,

---

[1] For the text of the French reservation see *Human Rights. Status of International Instruments* (1987), pp. 34–35. See also Nowak, *UN Covenant on Civil and Political Rights—CCPR Commentary* (1993), p. 755.

N. A. Neuwahl and A. Rosas (eds.), The European Union and Human Rights, 133–163.

mainly, from the States of the Commonwealth,[2] Germany is unwilling to grant minority status to groups of non-citizens legally resident within its territory.[3]

Notwithstanding this, the UN Declaration on the Rights of Persons Belonging to National or Ethnic, Religious and Linguistic Minorities (UN Declaration) has recently been adopted by consensus with the active participation of the Member States of the European Union.[4] Both within the framework of the Organization for Security and Cooperation in Europe (OSCE) and within the Council of Europe the Member States of the Union have undertaken or are in the process of undertaking international commitments to protect minorities.

The Treaty on European Union (TEU) does not include any reference to minorities. Attempts in the European Parliament to introduce an article into the Treaty providing for the Community and the Member States to "recognise the existence on their territory of minority ethnic and/or linguistic groups" and "take the necessary measures for the preservation and free development of their linguistic and cultural identity" were not seriously considered at the intergovernmental level.[5]

The question arises as to whether an effective system of minority protection already exists or should be provided for in the European Union.[6] The characterization of the TEU in its Article A as "a new stage in the process of creating an ever closer union among the peoples of Europe, in which decisions are taken as closely as possible to the citizen", and the proclamation

---

[2] Thornberry, "The ICCPR and Minority Rights in the UK", in Harris (ed.), *The International Covenant on Civil and Political Rights and the United Kingdom* (forthcoming 1995, Oxford University Press).

[3] In the report of the working group for the drafting of the UN Declaration on the Rights of Persons Belonging to National or Ethnic, Religious and Linguistic Minorities during the Forty-seventh session of the UN Commission on Human Rights, a declaration by the German Government was placed on record in which it reasserted its reluctance to grant minority status to distinct groups other than those well-defined and long-established on the territory of a state and especially to groups settled in the territory of a state, particularly under the term of immigration laws (UN Doc. E/CN.4/1991/53, at 4, para. 17). In the same working group report the French Government reasserted its reluctance to recognize the existence of "groups whose particular features are based on racial, linguistic and religious criteria" by reference to the French Constitution, ibid., at 6, para. 30.

[4] General Assembly resolution 47/135 of 18 Dec. 1992. See also Phillips and Rosas (eds), *Universal Minority Rights* (1995).

[5] De Witte, "The European Communities and its Minorities", in Brölman et al. (eds), *Peoples and Minorities in International Law* (1993), pp. 167–185, at p. 179.

[6] In the recent European Parliament initiative for a draft Constitution of the European Union, Title VIII of which is dedicated to the human rights guaranteed by the Union, specific reference to the rights of minorities is limited to a prohibition of discrimination on the grounds of membership of a national minority (1994, A3–0064/94, at 36, para. 3(b)).

in the same Article of the Union's task "to organise in a manner demonstrating consistency and solidarity, relations between the Member States and between their peoples" set out the innovative approach of the Union to relations between the individuals, peoples and Member States involved. The need for this innovative approach is especially urgent with regard to minority questions. Appropriate action is a responsibility not only for the Member States, but also for the Community institutions.

No general policy with regard to minority protection within the borders of the Union has been adopted so far, initiatives in this area being confined to action by the European Parliament. Until recently, the only binding provisions within the Community legal order concerning minorities could be found in some of the legal instruments of accession. Initiatives taken in the context of the process for peace and reconciliation in Northern Ireland seem to open new ground regarding a comprehensive approach to minority questions. However, with the exception of those references contained in merely declaratory statements, such as that made by the European Council on human rights in Luxembourg in 1991,[7] the heading "minority protection" continues to be confined to the international agenda of the Union. The appropriateness of the restriction of this issue to the external activity of the European Union should be assessed in the light of the provisions of the TEU and of international law and security demands. Furthermore, several concepts, provisions and procedures introduced by the TEU have a direct impact on minorities. New areas for Community competence have been established which previously belonged to the states' exclusive jurisdiction, thus opening a new spectrum of possibilities and responsibilities for Community action relevant to the protection and promotion of the rights of minorities.

European Union involvement in the protection of minorities becomes particularly relevant in the light of the international obligations acquired by the Member States in other international fora. On the one hand, effective compliance with these commitments could result in the derivation of obligations on the Community organs to act, given the extended field of their competence. Additionally, relevant experience acquired in other international fora may be applied in the design and implementation of Community policies with regard to minorities. This must be balanced with the Treaty provisions and derived legislation relevant to minority protection. On the other hand, the necessity for the European Union to provide for a specific framework for

---

[7] Duparc, *The European Community and Human Rights,* Annex: Human rights and fundamental freedoms—Texts containing commitments made by the Community and its Member States and by the institutions (1993), at p. 48.

minority protection should be assessed on the basis of the applicability of existing international standards, in order that the protection of the rights of minorities by the Union can be adequately guaranteed and made effective.

Existing Community law and legislative initiatives relevant to the protection of the rights of minorities will be analysed in the following pages, including those areas of Community policy which provide wider possibilities for Community action. The minority question has been addressed directly by the Union only in the field of Common Foreign and Security Policy. Consequences for the protection of minorities within the Union are derived from this and from the participation of Member States in other international fora in which they have acquired commitments with regard to minorities. These elements constitute the basis for the protection of minorities in the European Union, the scope of which will be analysed.

2   COMMUNITY LAW AND LEGISLATIVE
INITIATIVES CONCERNING MINORITIES

The only references to collective human rights within the constitutional order of the Union can be found in some of the Accession Treaties. Article 2 of Protocol No. 3 of the Treaty of Accession of the United Kingdom to the EEC refers to the preservation of the rights enjoyed by Channel Islanders or Manxmen.[8] In Protocol No. 2 of the Act of Accession of Austria, Sweden, Finland and Norway, restrictions on the right of establishment, the provision of services and the holding of real property are imposed on those who do not enjoy regional citizenship in Åland or have not obtained permission from the competent authorities of the Åland Islands. Similarly, Protocol No. 3, includes the possibility of granting exclusive rights to reindeer husbandry within traditional Sami areas to the Sami people.[9]

---

[8] Documents concerning the accessions to the European Communities of the Kingdom of Denmark, Ireland and the United Kingdom of Great Britain and Northern Ireland, the Hellenic Republic, the Kingdom of Spain and the Portuguese Republic (1988), Office of Official Publications of the European Communities, at 69.

[9] O.J. 1994, C 241/352. Norway made a declaration included in the Final Act, stating that it would continue to fulfil its obligations and commitments to the Sami people. It also declared that in the written use of Norwegian as an official language of the institutions of the Communities, equal status must be given to Bokmal and Nynorsk (O.J. 1994, C 241/395). The fact that Norway, after the recent referendum where the majority of the citizens voted against EU membership, chose to stay outside the EU, diminishes the possibilities for the relatively progressive attitude of the Norwegian policies towards indigenous peoples and minority rights to find reflection in EC policies. The different positions of the Nordic States with regard to EU membership may also create new divisions

The Luxembourg Council referred in 1991 to "the importance of respecting the cultural identity as well as rights enjoyed by members of minorities which such persons should be able to exercise in common with other members of their group".[10] Nevertheless, the only Community initiative for a support programme dealing with minority questions in a comprehensive manner has been taken as a result of a situation of violence. In the context of the peace process in Northern Ireland, a special Commission Task Force was created, in particular "to consider ways to develop and refocus the policies of the European Union to help those people who have been most affected by the conflict to live together in mutual respect and economic prosperity".[11] Areas for priority Community action, such as urban and rural regeneration, cross-border development and social inclusion have been identified, as well as activities which offer particular scope for bringing communities and individuals together. The appropriate involvement of local and grass root organizations in shaping and implementing the programmes and the creation of consultative platforms have been recommended. However, the emphasis placed on economic considerations and on the cessation of violence as a basis for an initiative which deals, mainly, with a minority situation, does not necessarily follow the spirit of the new framework for Community action established under the TEU. Equally, the "exceptional" character attributed to the initiative seems to contradict this spirit.

Although the minority question has not been directly addressed in the TEU, several of its concepts and provisions have a direct impact on minorities. Besides Article A, Article F of the Common Provisions establishes Union respect for the national "identities" of the Member States. Article 3 EC Treaty indicates that "the activities of the Community shall include: ... p) a contribution to education and training of quality and to the flowering of the cultures of the Member States". Article 126 establishes that the Community shall contribute to the development of quality education "while fully respecting the responsibility of the Member States for ... the organization of education systems and their cultural and linguistic diversity". Article 128 uses the plural term "cultures" of the Member States and the expression "culture and history of the European peoples" while proclaiming the need to respect "regional diversity". With the TEU, the cultural pluralism characterizing European states

---

among the Sami.

[10] Duparc, op. cit., note 7, at p. 49.

[11] Communication from the Commission to the Council and the European Parliament on "A Special Support Programme for Peace and Reconciliation in Northern Ireland", COM (94) 607 final, p. 3.

has been acknowledged and become object of protection. The different identities of European minorities must be protected in the future because of their contribution to the richness of the European Union, and not only in the framework of solutions to situations of violence.

The European Parliament has been the only Community organ which has focused its attention on minority protection within the Union and has adopted several resolutions concerning the fate of minorities. Since 1983, a European Parliament "intergroup" has been meeting during the plenary sessions to examine Community initiatives which favour regional languages and cultures and at its annual vote on the budget, the European Parliament allocates sums to Community activities in support of minority languages.[12] As far back as 1987, in a resolution "on the languages and cultures of regional and ethnic minorities in the European Community",[13] the European Parliament regretted the lack of Commission proposals for the implementation of its previous resolutions of 1981 and 1983 "on a Community charter of regional languages and cultures and on a charter of rights of ethnic minorities" and on "measures in favor of minority languages and cultures".[14] In these resolutions the European Parliament called on national governments and regional authorities to implement a policy in these fields and to adopt specific measures regarding education, the media and public life and social affairs. It established a framework for Community action with regard to minorities by referring to measures in educational and cultural programmes and financial assistance for projects designed to support regional and folk culture and for the financing of regional economic projects.

At its meeting of 20 December 1989, the European Parliament Committee on Legal Affairs and Citizens' Rights decided to draw up a report calling on the governments of the Member States:[15]

> by means of the insertion of an appropriate title in the TEU at the next Intergovernmental Conference on the amendment of the Treaties to be concluded by 1996, to give recognition, binding guarantees and lasting

---

[12] The budget line (B3–1006) for 1994 was ECU 3.5 million (O.J. 1994, L 34/799). The Communication from the Commission on "Lesser Used Languages of the European Union—Report of Activities 1989–1983" COM (94) 602 final, contains a table showing the evolution of the budget allocations for the period 1983–1994 (p. 3) and refers to the problems derived from the annual character of such allocations (p. 10).

[13] Doc. A2–150/87 (O.J. 1987, C 318/161).

[14] Resolution of 16 Oct. 1981 (O.J. 1981, C 287/106) and Resolution of 11 Feb. 1983 (O.J. 1983, C 68/103) respectively.

[15] 1993, A3–0000/93, at 6, para. K.1.

protection to the rights of ethnic groups and their members as defined in the
following Charter of rights of ethnic groups.

These groups, together with their members, are the holders of the rights
granted under the proposal. The large scope given to the collective aspect is
striking, bearing in mind the traditional reluctance of European states to grant
rights to collectivities which was reflected during the drafting of the UN
Declaration and in its final text. The provision of a specific definition and the
negative delimitation (qualifications and restrictions) of the subjects protected,
which excludes migrant workers and their families, other immigrants resident
in the Member States, refugees, persons granted asylum or displaced persons,
contrasts with the approach which has been adopted in the UN Declaration,
where considerations of legal certainty have given way to a pragmatic
approach in which flexibility and adaptability to concrete situations prevail.
The exclusion of these groups cannot be based on a defined Community
position, since a specific concept of "minority" has not yet been established
in the Union.[16] In addition, such an approach may indeed prove too restrictive,[17] because benefiting from minority protection may help these groups to
overcome their vulnerable position until specific protection has been granted.
Other proposals include the right for ethnic groups and their members to
appeal to the Court of Justice of the European Communities (ECJ) after
exhausting all courses of legal action in the Member States, and establishing
the jurisdiction of the Member States' Supreme Courts with regard to actions
brought forward by ethnic groups, as well as the possibility of the creation of
an "ethnic group" Ombudsman at the level of the Member States. No provision
is made for a similar figure at the Community level.

After the failure of this initiative to provide a general framework of
minority protection within the Union due to lack of political support, the
European Parliament adopted a narrower approach.[18] On 9 February 1994, a
resolution "on linguistic and cultural minorities in the European Community"

---

[16] Even in the motion for a resolution (B3–0475/90) annexed to the draft Report containing the
Charter the subjects referred to are the "black, Asian and other ethnic minority residents living
within the Community" which would seemingly not be comprised within the limitative approach
adopted in the Charter proposal.

[17] "Community and Ethnic Relations in Europe". Final report of the Community Relations
Project of the Council of Europe, Doc. MG–CR (91) 1 final E, p. 2.

[18] This is the case with the Resolution on languages in the Community and the situation of
Catalan (O.J. 1991, C 19/43) and the Resolution on the situation of gypsies in the Community
adopted on the basis of the Report 1994, A3–0124.

was adopted.[19] This resolution has reemphasized the importance of the application of the previous resolutions and especially the necessity for Member States to recognize their linguistic minorities, declaring that "all peoples have the right to respect for their language and culture and must therefore have the necessary legal means to protect and promote them". This curious declaration of the "peoples" right to culture and language may result from an attempt to place the resolution within the framework of the terminology used by the TEU and particularly Article A of the Common Provisions, while avoiding the recognition of any specific rights for minorities. Other provisions are devoted to proposing specific measures addressed to the Community institutions and to the Member States, aimed at the protection and development of minorities' languages and cultures. The resolution supports and builds upon the substantive provisions of the European Charter for Regional or Minority Languages adopted within the framework of the Council of Europe[20] by calling on the Member States and local and regional authorities to encourage and support specialized associations, and to create transfrontier linguistic institutions. The resolution also refers to several initiatives in areas of Community competence which are highly relevant to minorities.

With the adoption of the TEU, some of these areas of Community competence have been established or developed. Article 128(1) has inaugurated a Community responsibility not only for respecting the national and regional diversity within the Union, but also for contributing to the flowering of the cultures of the Member States. Accordingly, the Community must take positive action to facilitate the development of minority cultures and identities. This is largely affected by the Community regional policies and the position of the local and regional representative organs with regard to Community decision-making. Furthermore, the concepts of subsidiarity and citizenship enshrined in the TEU have important repercussions with regard to minority participation. Finally, the title of the TEU dealing exclusively with culture and some of the treaty provisions on education open a wide range of possibilities regarding minority protection. The analysis of the specific scope of these areas of competence, their achievements and possibilities for future action with regard to the protection of minorities is undertaken below.

---

[19] A3–0042/94 (O.J. 1994, C 61/111).

[20] ETS No. 148.

3 MINORITIES AND UNION CITIZENSHIP

No clear-cut connection can be established between the concept of Union citizenship and the rights it comprises—as presented in the TEU—and the rights of minorities. On the contrary, this concept could be considered to be a means of excluding from minority protection at the Union level those who do not have Union citizenship. Vulnerable (and especially ethnic) groups who do not enjoy minority protection in some of the Member States on the basis of their citizenship could also be deprived of minority protection at the Union level because the citizenship of one of the Member States is a requirement for Union citizenship. However, as already indicated, the concept of minority has not been exactly delimited at the level of the European Union and at the universal level a wide approach has prevailed.[21] Limitative approaches by particular Member States should not necessarily be reflected at the Union level, although a restrictive approach has predominated in recent intergovernmental initiatives in the Council of Europe, where the text of a Framework Convention for the Protection of National Minorities has been adopted by the Committee of Ministers on 10 November 1994.[22]

With regard to those who enjoy Union citizenship, Article 8a grants "the right to move and reside freely within the territory of the Member States". This freedom of movement and residence implies the putting of different ethnic, religious and linguistic identities into contact. It also implies the placing of some of those identities, which used to be majoritarian in their communities of origin, in a "minority situation". Today, some five million nationals of Member States of the Union are living in a Member State of which they are

---

[21] Besides the text of the UN Declaration, the UN Human Rights Committee, in its General Comment 23 (Fiftieth Session, 1994) has indicated that in order to enjoy the protection granted under Art. 27 of the International Covenant on Civil and Political Rights, no requirements concerning nationality or permanent residence are necessary. Migrant workers or even visitors in a State Party constituting ethnic, religious and linguistic minorities are entitled not to be denied the exercise of those rights granted under Article 27. The existence of an ethnic, religious or linguistic minority in a given State Party does not depend upon a decision by that State Party but requires to be established by objective criteria. (UN Doc. CCPR/C/21/Rev.1/Add.5). See also Wolfrum, "The Emergence of 'New Minorities' as a Result of Migration", in Brölman et al., op. cit., note 5, pp. 153–166, at p. 165.

[22] The declaration resulting from the Council of Europe Summit held in Vienna in Oct. 1993 contains a request by the Heads of State and Government to the Committee of Ministers to draft with minimum delay a framework convention to assure the protection of "national" minorities and to begin work on drafting a protocol complementing the ECHR in the cultural field by provisions guaranteeing individual rights, in particular for persons belonging to "national" minorities.

not nationals.[23] They and the small communities in which they tend to gather are in a minority situation with regard to the larger communities in which they live. In fact, these groups can be regarded as Union-induced minorities.[24] As submitted above with regard to non-citizens, minority protection should be granted on the basis of the need for the provision of such protection, rather than on the basis of legal status and historical title. Groups of European citizens originating from one Member State and living in the territory of another should qualify for those aspects of minority protection relevant to them.

The two specific levels at which voting rights have been granted to European citizens forming a minority within the territory of another Member State have a limited influence on most of the policies which directly affect them. As the size of these communities is often relatively small, their aspirations are not properly reflected under most of the electoral regimes. The granting of the right to vote and to stand as a candidate in municipal elections—the level of government closer to the citizen, where the particular identity of minorities ought seemingly to be better expressed—does not necessarily suffice to reflect their aspirations. Specific measures to facilitate minority participation should be provided, such as the creation of advisory and decision-making bodies in which minorities are represented, in particular with regard to education, culture and religion.[25] In this context, the responsibility of political parties at the European level—they are considered in Article 138a EC Treaty as an instrument for the expression of "the political will of the citizens of the Union"—should also be stressed as a means for the channelling of minority concerns.

4   CULTURE AND EDUCATION

Highly relevant not only for the protection, but also for the projection of the identity of minorities within the framework of the Union has been the

---

[23] Proposal for a Council Directive laying down detailed arrangements for the exercise of the right to vote and to stand as a candidate in municipal elections by citizens of the Union residing in a Member State of which they are not nationals, COM (94) 38 final, p. 3.

[24] De Witte, loc. cit., note 5, at p. 180.

[25] These possibilities are presented in the final report submitted by Asbjørn Eide to the UN Sub-Commission on Prevention of Discrimination and Protection of Minorities and contained in UN Doc. E/CN.4/Sub.2/1993/34/Add.4, para. 17. These types of initiatives have been supported in Recommendation R (92) 12 of the Committee of Ministers of the Council of Europe and during the First European Parliament—EU Local Authorities Conference.

introduction of new EC competences in the field of Education, Vocational Training and Youth within Title VIII, as well as Title IX, which specifically deals with culture.

Before the adoption of the TEU, the Community supported vocational training and educational projects and youth or university exchanges, which occasionally—but only as an indirect consequence—may have facilitated the knowledge of minority cultures of the Member States. The Community has also placed on its agenda issues such as the education of children of migrant workers[26] but mainly as a means to accomplish the economic objectives of the common market. The LINGUA programme was set up to facilitate knowledge of the official languages of the Member States and comprised only those minority languages (such as Irish or Letzeburgesch) which due to their official status already enjoy a certain level of recognition and protection.

The Council Directive regulating television broadcasting activities does not provide for specific action in favour of minority cultures, leaving open the possibility for states "in order to allow for an active policy in favor of a specific language ... to lay down more detailed or stricter rules in particular on the basis of language criteria ...".[27]

Nevertheless, the level of concern for purely cultural aspects has been on the rise in recent years. This has been illustrated by the support given to multilingualism in television programmes by the Council Decision on the implementation of an action programme to promote the development of the European audiovisual industry.[28] The control exercised by the Commission on the application by Member States of Articles 4 and 5 of Directive 89/552/EEC "Television without frontiers" the objective of which "is not only to ensure the transmission of a majority proportion of European works but also to encourage the movement of programmes between the Member States and so to promote the emergence of economically viable secondary markets for all European productions, in particular those created by the independent sector"[29] also seems a step forward. Financial support to "Community measures in favor

---

[26] The first directive specifically dealing with this issue dates back to 1977 (O.J. 1977, L 199/32). On this issue consult the recent Commission report, COM (94) 80 final.

[27] Council Directive on the coordination of certain provisions laid down by law, regulation or administrative action in Member States concerning the pursuit of television broadcasting activities (O.J. 1989, L 298/25).

[28] Cf. the different attitude maintained in the Commission proposal (O.J. 1990, C 127/6) and in the Council Decision (O.J. 1990, L 380/38) with regard to cultural and linguistic diversity.

[29] COM (94) 57 final, p. 19.

of minority languages and cultures"[30] has been channelled mainly through the European Bureau for Lesser Used Languages, a non-profit making association which among other activities coordinates Mercator, a group of four computerized information and documentation networks on minorities' issues. The setting-up of a five-year pilot scheme to provide financial aid for translations of contemporary literary works, in which priority is given to works written in one of the Community minority languages, has been another improvement.[31]

A similar evolution has been experienced by the jurisprudence of the ECJ in fields of education and culture of special relevance to minorities. The decisions of the Court from being based mainly on economic considerations, and in particular the achievement of the four freedoms and its exceptions on the basis of general mandatory requirements,[32] have started to give increasing consideration to strictly cultural aspects.[33]

According to Articles 126 and 128 EC Treaty, Community action in the fields of education and culture shall aim, *inter alia,* at the teaching and dissemination of the languages of the Member States and at the improvement of the knowledge and dissemination of the culture and history of the European peoples. Action will be based on the adoption of incentive measures and recommendations and will encourage co-operation between the Member States.

Although the Community competence in these fields has been enshrined in the TEU, Member States continue to bear primary responsibility for developing educational and cultural policies. Apart from the promotion of state

---

[30] *Supra*, note 12.

[31] O.J. 1992, C 56/15.

[32] Illustrations of this are: Case 155/73, *Sacchi,* [1974] ECR 409, at 431; Case 52/79, *Procureur du Roi* v *Debauve,* [1980] ECR 833, at 853; Case 229/83, *Leclerc* v *Au blé vert,* [1985] ECR 1; Joined Cases 60 and 61/84, *Cinéthèque* v *Fédération nationale des cinèmas français,* [1985] ECR 2605; Cases 281, 283–285 and 287/85 *Germany, France, Netherlands, Denmark and United Kingdom* v *Commission,* [1987] ECR 3203. For an analysis of the content of the latter see Plender, "Competence, European Community Law and Nationals of Non-Member States", 39 ICLQ (1990), 599–610, at 605; and on the preceding cases see Lomman et al. (eds), *Culture and Community Law before and after Maastricht* (1992).

[33] Examples are: Case 379/87, *Groener* v *Minister for Education and the City of Dublin Vocational Education Committee,* [1989] ECR 3967; Case 352/85, *Bond van Adverteerders* v *Netherlands State,* [1988] ECR 2085; Case C-154/89, *Commission* v *France,* [1991] ECR I-659; Case C-180/89, *Commission* v *Italy,* [1991] ECR I-709; Case C-198/89, *Commission* v *Greece,* [1991] ECR I-727; Case C-353/89, *Commission* v *The Netherlands,* [1991] ECR I-4069. For an analysis of the first case see de Witte, "Surviving in Babel? Language Rights and European Integration", in Dinstein and Tabory (eds), *The Protection of Minorities and Human Rights* (1992), pp. 277–300, at pp. 295–297. For an analysis of the former and the rest of the cases mentioned see Lomman et al., op. cit., note 32.

co-operation, the Community's role will extend if necessary to "support" and "supplement" the action of the Member States in several pre-defined areas.[34] This corresponds with a strict application of the principle of subsidiarity as established in Article 3b EC Treaty to educational and cultural policies. Also, the TEU makes no express reference to Community action at levels of government other than the state level.

The Treaty provisions should be analysed in the light of already existing initiatives for EC action. There is, for example, the less restrictive interpretation of the principle of subsidiarity under the Community action programme in the field of education, i.e., SOCRATES. Here "the principle of subsidiarity on which Community action is based is a common sense principle and means that action at the Community level is only undertaken *if it cannot be done by the Member States themselves or if, in the opinion of the Member States or for reasons of scale,* such action can be better performed at the Community level".[35] In contrast, the Commission Communication on "New Prospects for Community Cultural Action", requesting the Council and the Parliament to decide on a new reference framework for Community cultural action, indicates that "the Community will encourage cultural cooperation *only when it complements action by the Member States and, if necessary, continue to support their action in the areas listed* in the [EC Treaty] Article on culture".[36] Similarly, the Commission Communication on "European Community Action in Support of Culture" specifies that "the guiding principles for Community intervention in the cultural field are subsidiarity and the requirement that it supplements Member States' action. *The object is to encourage cooperation between Member States and, where necessary, support and supplement their action in the areas of intervention indicated*".[37] The EC Treaty uses a similar formula, in Articles 126(1) and 128(2) respectively, to establish the division of competence between the Community and the Member States both with regard to education and culture. The reason for this different

---

[34] Arts. 126(2) and 128(2) with regard to educational and cultural policy, respectively.

[35] "Proposal for a European Parliament and Council Decisions establishing the Community action programme 'Socrates'" COM (93) 708 final, p. 10. In addition, the objective is set of "a higher degree of decentralisation of administrative and financial responsibilities ... whenever possible provided decentralised management is genuinely seen to achieve greater effectiveness ..." (Ibid., p. 12). Emphasis added.

[36] COM (92) 149 final, p. 3. Emphasis added.

[37] Communication from the Commission to the European Parliament and the Council of the European Union on "European Community Action in Support of Culture", COM (94) 356 final, p. 4.

approach of the Commission may lie in the fact that far more consolidated precedents exist for Community action along the lines established by the TEU in the field of education than in the cultural field.[38]

Also the interpretation given to the concepts "European dimension" and "value added" which are frequently used in the context of these programmes of action, may be relevant when determining the possibilities of Community initiative and involvement, especially with regard to promotional aspects of minority education and culture. Of the Titles of the TEU dealing with education and culture, Titles VIII and IX, only Article 126(1) contains a reference to the "European dimension". This reference simply serves to delimit one of the several aims at which Community action should intend in the educational field. Nevertheless, several references to this concept have been introduced in the development of Community action in the cultural field, conveying a limiting approach which could be detrimental to minority protection.

The Green Paper on the European Dimension of Education[39] considers that one of the specific objectives—and, through these, the "added value" of Community action in the sphere of education is: contributing to European citizenship "respecting different cultural and ethnic identities, and combating all forms of chauvinism and xenophobia ... Europe is not a dimension which replaces others, but one which enhances them".[40] Yet, the only promotional activities of minority education and culture of the Action "on the promotion of the 'European dimension' in higher education institutions" under the SOCRATES programme are the references to language teaching and learning in the lesser used languages and "the incorporation into curricula of elements designed to enhance understanding of the cultural, political, economic and social characteristics of other Member States...".[41] So far, however, the "European dimension" and "value added" concepts incorporated to the Community educational policies do not seem to have had a detrimental effect regarding minority protection.[42]

---

[38] See, e.g., O.J. 1991, C 284/17; O.J. 1991, C 314/1 2 and 3; O.J. 1992, L 231/26; O.J. 1992, L 395/1 and 6; O.J. 1994, L 63/28; O.J. 1994, C 235/1.

[39] COM (93) 457 final.

[40] Ibid., p. 5.

[41] Amended proposal for a European Parliament and Council Decision establishing the Community action programme SOCRATES, COM (94) 180 final, pp. 19 and 20.

[42] A cautious attitude should be mantained in this respect. The Economic and Social Committee had criticized the lack of clearness of the Commission in the delimitation of the concept "European dimension" in the Green Paper on the European Dimension of Education as well as the fact that no

The same does not necessarily apply to cultural policies. In the Communication from the Commission on "European Community Action in Support of Culture",[43] three priority areas of intervention have been identified: cultural heritage; books and reading; and artistic activities. Specific proposals have been put forward for the development of the second and third areas. The use of the concepts "European dimension" and "value added" both in the draft decision[44] and the conditions of participation of the proposal for a "programme to support artistic and cultural activities having a European dimension—Kaleidoscope 2000", serves as a support for a framework giving prevalence to projects which by their very nature tend to exclude the promotion of minority cultures and minority participation.[45] In contrast, the proposal for a "support programme in the field of books and reading—ARIANE"[46] places its emphasis on the dissemination of works of contemporary literature while giving priority to works in the lesser used languages of the Community. The concept of "European dimension" is referred to only in the context of the stimulating and supporting role to be played by the Community with respect to the efforts of competent authorities in the

---

emphasis is placed on culture and cultural diversity, while providing for its own delimitation of the concept (CES (94) 563 p. 3). In the Opinion of the Committee on the proposal for a European Parliament and Council Decision establishing the SOCRATES programme, the Committee adopts a somewhat confusing approach to the implications of the concept "European Dimension" with regard to lesser used languages teaching and the role to be played by the SOCRATES programme in this respect [CES (94) 564] p. 2, paras. 3.4 and 3.4.1.

[43] COM (94) 356 final.

[44] In this draft decision reference is made to the fact that "Community action in support of *artistic and cultural events with a 'European dimension', and cultural projects with a Europe-wide scope and symbolic nature,* promote the spread of different cultures whilst bringing artists and creators closer to the European public, and can also create added value at a socio-economic level by encouraging operational synergies and partnership" (emphasis added) (Ibid., p. 21).

[45] As a way of example, the programme Action 1 "Promotion and spread of culture in Europe" is open to *"large scale cultural projects with a European dimension and of an emblematic nature"* (emphasis added) further defined as "a) cultural events which are already well established at European level, such as European City of Culture, the EC Youth Orchestra, the EC Baroque Orchestra, etc.; b) cultural events organized jointly by the Member States to mark Europe Day on 9 May; c) large-scale, high-quality cultural projects with a European dimension which enable the cultural and socio-economic impact of projects carried out in partnership to be assessed". Similarly, the programme Action 2 "Networks and partnerships: Support for events and cultural projects carried out in partnership or through networks" excludes from its scope "cultural cooperation projects of a purely regional, national or bilateral nature" and the "cost of setting up networks" (Ibid., pp. 21–23).

[46] The budgetary allocations previewed under this programme are of a much smaller entity that those previewed for Kaleidoskope 2000 (Ibid., pp. 50–51 and 28–29, respectively).

Member States and the professionals in the field.[47] Furthermore, practical, detailed measures are envisaged to promote cultural diversity including support for activities not only by regional, but also by local authorities.

Other specific provisions concerning minority protection under these proposals are those included in Action II of Chapter II of the amended proposal for the SOCRATES programme,[48] dedicated to the promotion of the intercultural dimension of learning and improvement of the quality of education for the children of migrant workers, children of gypsies and children of occupational travellers. In addition, a certain scope for minorities' contribution to the design and implementation of the programme could be derived from the references to: (a) the requirement for consultation with the Committee of the Regions under Article 126 EC Treaty; (b) the granting of financial assistance to groups of universities at regional, cross-border and other levels for joint development of activities in co-operation with regional or local communities and interested parties from the economic and social spheres; (c) action to promote equitable participation of schools at Community, national and regional level; (d) equitable participation by schools in the Member States; (e) equitable participation by universities in less-favoured regions; and (f) balanced distribution of networks between the various disciplines, regions and universities. The enhancement of the understanding of European cultures and the learning and teaching of the lesser used languages of the Community are to be given priority and support and to constitute one of the priority criteria for the disbursement of Community funds under the SOCRATES programme.

What might be considered an expression of the states' resistance to Community interference in the cultural domain but may in fact serve as a positive influence for the promotion of minorities' cultures has been the insertion in the TEU, of paragraph d of Article 92(3). State aid "to promote culture and heritage conservation where such aid does not affect trading conditions and competition in the Community to an extent that is contrary to the common interest" shall be compatible with the common market. States may no longer use the competition rules of the Treaty to justify a restrictive attitude regarding the support of minority cultures within their territory. Given that state "aid to promote the economic development of areas where the standard

---

[47] Ibid., p. 45.

[48] Opinion of the Commission pursuant to Article 189b(2)(d) of the EC Treaty, on the European Parliament's amendments to the Council's common position regarding the proposal for a European Parliament and Council Decision establishing the Community Action Programme SOCRATES, COM (94) 502 final.

of living is abnormally low ..."[49] is considered to be compatible with the competition rules, and with the common interest, there would be no reason to maintain a different approach with regard to state aid in support of the development of minority cultures in a disadvantaged situation.

Another breakthrough has resulted from the introduction of paragraph 4 of Article 128: "The Community shall take cultural aspects into account in its action under other provisions of this Treaty". In connection with the consideration of cultural diversity as a common concern, this implies on the one hand that the Community should not engage in any activity damaging to cultural diversity, and therefore, to minorities' cultures and identities. On the other hand, it is also implied that in every Community action cultural diversity should be promoted. According to the Commission's interpretation: "The point here is that cultural aspects must be taken into account as soon as any new action or policy is devised, subject obviously to Community law".[50] However, the Commission, in its Communication on "European Community Action in Support of Culture", has only contemplated the drawing up of an "inventory" of the cultural dimension of the main Community policies concerned—which will deal in particular with the support given to the cultural sector under Community policies—and the adoption of internal "procedural" measures to ensure that the demands of culture are given due consideration when Community policies are being formulated or implemented.[51] No substantive plan or set of guidelines for an innovative approach in this area have been envisaged.

Finally, the TEU has also made culture a "common concern" in the international field. Emphasis has been placed on the fostering of co-operation in the educational and cultural fields by the Community and by the Member States with third countries and competent international organizations, and in particular with the Council of Europe. Regarding their activities in the international arena, the Member States are under an obligation, not only to take into account the cultural interest of the Union, including minorities' cultures, but also to take positive action to promote that interest. Although no specific international treaty-making power has been granted to the Community, in accordance with the ERTA[52] doctrine the Community can engage in treaty-making for the promotion of minorities' cultures, especially with regard to

---

[49] Art 92(3), para. a.

[50] COM (92) 149 final, p. 7.

[51] COM (94) 356 final, op. cit., note 37, p. 9.

[52] Case 22/70, *Commission* v *Council*, [1971] ECR 263.

transfrontier co-operation in the border areas of the Union. The shared competence between the Member States and the Community in the cultural field could make appropriate the adoption of "mixed agreements".[53] However, in addition to the Member States' resistance to Community interference in the cultural domain, reluctance may be expected on the part of some Member States to have included within cultural mixed agreements "minority specific" provisions. It should be stressed that "the flowering of the cultures" of the Member States has become a common concern and that Member States' action (or omission) should not undermine this commitment under the TEU.

Although the introduction of Title IX has implied a substantial break-through for minority purposes since the protection of minorities' identities and cultures has ceased to be a domain restricted to the competence of the state, the lack of precedents for comprehensive Community action in the cultural field may act as an obstacle to the development of measures for the protection of the cultural identity of minorities. Moreover, the narrow interpretation of the principle of subsidiarity already referred to and the existence within the TEU of provisions still reflecting the states' reluctance to give up their exclusive competence in the cultural field may also act as obstacles.[54] However, it is the responsibility not only of the Member States but also of the Community institutions to respond adequately to the new challenges and opportunities, especially those brought forward by the new technologies, the current Community initiatives in the audiovisual sector and the ongoing processes of media concentration. As the Commission has recently pointed out in its Communication on "Europe's Way to the Information Society, an Action Plan"[55]: "The information society promises to create new jobs, enhanced social solidarity and to promote Europe's linguistic and cultural diversity. However, if not adequately framed, it could create new social and economic discrepancies".[56] The content of the Green Paper and Communication envisaged to cover, respectively, the cultural aspects and linguistic issues

---

[53] Lomman et al., op. cit., note 32, at p. 200. See generally O'Keeffe and Schermers (eds), *Mixed Agreements* (1993). See also Neuwahl, "Joint Participation in International Treaties and the Exercise of Power by the EEC and its Member States: Mixed Agreements", 28 CML Rev. (1991), 717–740.

[54] An example is the unanimity requirement affecting the decision-making process in the cultural field established in Art. 128(5), which has not been established with regard to education.

[55] Communication from the Commission to the Council and the European Parliament and to the Economic and Social Committee and the Committee of Regions, COM (94) 347 final.

[56] Ibid., p. 14

involved in the process may prove crucial for minority protection.[57] The revision of the Directive on "Television without frontiers" may also be relevant.[58] The proper covering of expanding cross-border activities and the defence of the interest of citizens in other Member States able to receive a particular channel, by means of control at source of the licensing, have been used as arguments favouring the option for harmonization of the national rules on media ownership in the context of the consultation process on pluralism and media concentration in the internal market.[59] Although harmonization at Community level may help to overcome disturbances to the operation of the internal market generated by diverging national legislation regarding media concentration, it may lack real consequences for the promotion of genuine cultural pluralism unless decisive steps are taken to this effect.

In conclusion, the European Community must take minorities' cultures into consideration within the wide range of its economic activity and engage in initiatives for the promotion of these cultures, both in the exercising of its internal competence and in the international arena. Especially since the "necessity" to support and supplement the action of the Member States with regard to the protection and promotion of minorities' cultures, as derived from the narrowest possible interpretation of the subsidiarity principle, is not only likely but already long-standing.

5   REGIONAL POLICIES

The subsidiarity principle is treated in Article 3b EC Treaty mainly as a guiding principle for organizing the distribution of competence between the Community and the Member States. This interpretation has prevailed in the approach of the Community institutions.[60] However, Article A of the Common Provisions of the TEU seems to call for the active involvement of

---

[57] Ibid.

[58] Ibid., p. 7.

[59] Communication from the Commission to the Council and the European Parliament on the follow-up to the consultation process relating to the green paper on "pluralism and media concentration in the internal market—an assessment of the need for Community action", COM (94) 353 final, p. 34.

[60] Neuwahl, "A Europe Close to the Citizen? The 'Trinity Concepts' of Subsidiarity, Transparency and Democracy", in Rosas and Antola (eds), *A Citizens' Europe: In Search of a New Order* (1995), pp. 39–57.

communities or levels of government lower than the central one in the decision-making processes of the Union.

Of special relevance is the role played by local and regional authorities in the definition and implementation of the Community's regional policy since, as the European Parliament has acknowledged, "the cultural identity of a region can only exist if the populations are able to live and work in their own area".[61] The survival of minorities in the areas in which they live is determined not only by the possibilities for the development of these areas, but also by the adequacy of this development for the minorities' particular needs. These needs can only be appropriately established and responded to with the active participation of the minorities involved. The functions granted to the Committee of the Regions in the TEU,[62] whose members are elected by the Council, may not suffice to guarantee this.

In the implementation of the reform of the Structural Funds "relations between the Commission and the Member States and local authorities at various levels have been improving all the time" ... with regard to "the regional development objectives (Objectives 1, 2 and 5(b) there could be greater participation by the representatives of local authorities in a large number of cases ...".[63] In a recent Commission paper[64] several draft initiatives have been presented. Under the initiative on "Employment and Development of Human Resources" assistance may be granted directly to decentralized organizations responsible for implementation, including organizations responsible for managing transnational actions, to be designated by the Member State concerned.[65]

Under the "LEADER II" rural development programme a planning and decision-making partnership is to be established "which will include, at a minimum, all those who will provide part-finance at the national level (state, region, other local collective bodies)". The opinions of other local and regional public authorities and the rural partners, whether administrative or professional

---

[61] O.J. 1981, C 287/107.

[62] Arts. 126(4), 128(5), 129(4), 129d(1), 130b(2), 130b(3), 130d, 130d(2), 130e(1), 198c(1), 198c(4).

[63] Fourth Annual Report from the Commission on the implementation of the Reform of the Structural Funds (1992). COM (93) 530 final, pp. 80–81.

[64] "The Future of Community Initiatives under the Structural Funds", COM (94) 46 final, p. 2.

[65] Draft Communication to the Member States laying down guidelines for operational programmes or global grants which Member States are invited to propose within the framework of a Community initiative on Employment and Development of Human Resources aimed at promoting employment growth mainly through the development of human resources. Ibid., at 19.

bodies or associations (in particular in the field of culture), must be secured and attached to the programme.[66] Within the indicative list of eligible measures under this programme the "raising of the awareness of the public, including young people still at school, about the area's identity and prospects and the need for innovation" is included.[67]

The Community initiative concerning cross-border co-operation and selected energy networks (Interreg II) will also accord priority to proposals which are made in co-operation with regional and local authorities in border areas and in internal border areas, and to those which include the establishment or development of shared institutional or administrative structures intended to widen and deepen cross-border co-operation between public agencies, private organizations and voluntary bodies. Where possible, these shared institutional or administrative structures would have the competence to implement jointly determined projects. Measures assisted under this initiative should be designed to have their main development impact on the population of the border areas eligible for participation.[68] The support for structures of transfrontier co-operation not only offers an economic boost for minorities whose population is divided by borders, but also allows for the development of common institutional structures, which help to maintain the existence and development of those communities.

Finally, although the possibility of involvement of regional and local authorities in the monitoring and supervision of the projects and measures adopted under the cohesion financial instrument has been discussed occasionally at the national level,[69] Member States are the beneficiaries of the Cohesion Fund, whose priorities are also established by the states concerned. The need for consultation with the Committee of the Regions seems to offer the only scope for minority involvement. The same seems to apply to the adoption of specific actions which prove necessary and which fall outside the Structural Funds.

From the above we can conclude that progress achieved with regard to minority involvement in the design and implementation of Community regional

---

[66] Draft Notice to Member States laying down guidelines for integrated operational programmes for which Member States are invited to submit applications for assistance in the framework of a Community initiative for rural development. LEADER II Programme. Ibid., at 11.

[67] Ibid., at 17.

[68] Draft Notice to the Member States laying down the guidelines for operational programmes in the framework of the Community initiative concerning cross-border co-operation and selected energy networks (Interreg II). Ibid., at 2.

[69] Annual Report Cohesion Financial Instrument 1993/1994. COM (95) 1 final, pp. 88–89.

policies has been more the result of the search for a coherent approach on the basis of the experience acquired in the different areas than the result of a conscious effort to attend to the specific needs of minorities. The development of these policies will probably call for increasing minority involvement in the future.[70]

6   EXTERNAL ACTION

The association and co-operation agreements between the Community and the countries of Central and Eastern Europe have included suspension clauses applicable in the event of the Community-associated country failing to uphold minority rights. However, it was the conflict in the former Yugoslavia that brought the minority question to the forefront of the external activity of the Union. Not until 28 October 1991 did the Member States give a general evaluation of the results of the Conference on the former Yugoslavia. Then, the principles upon which a general agreement should be based were pointed out: the non-acceptance of the unilateral modification of the frontiers and the protection of human rights and of national and ethnic groups.[71] In an extraordinary meeting held on 16 December 1991 the Ministers of Foreign Affairs adopted a common position on the process of recognition of new states in Eastern Europe and the Soviet Union, requiring, *inter alia*: "guarantees for the rights of ethnic and national groups and minorities in accordance with the commitments subscribed to in the framework of the CSCE".[72] The Badinter Arbitration Committee, created by the Community and its Member States at the same time as the convening of the peace conference on Yugoslavia, ruled that Macedonia and Slovenia fulfilled all the conditions, but made a reservation in the case of Croatia in relation to the rights of minorities.[73]

The difficulties encountered in preserving peace and international security in accordance with the principles established in Article J.1 TEU, as well as the desire of the Union to reaffirm its international authority in the shadow of the conflict in the former Yugoslavia, were factors leading to the launching of the

---

[70] In support of this view, see the fifth annual report on the implementation of the reform of the structural funds 1993. COM (95) 30 final, p. 8.

[71] Lucron, "L'Europe devant la crise Yugoslave: mesures restrictives et mesures positives", 354 RMC (1992), 7–16, at 9.

[72] Bull. EC 12–1991, at 119.

[73] Pellet, "The Opinions of the Badinter Arbitration Committee—A Second Breath for the Self-Determination of Peoples", 3 EJIL (1992), 178–181, at 178.

Balladur *Projet de Pacte sur la stabilité en Europe.*[74] This resulted in a joint action by the Member States of the Union through a Council Decision of 20 December 1993, on the basis of Article J.3 TEU, for the convening of a Conference in Paris[75] to inaugurate an exercise in preventive diplomacy aimed at encouraging good neighbourly relations between the countries concerned, the consolidation of frontiers and the solution of minority problems.[76] The Pact of Stability in Europe, adopted in Paris on 21 March 1995, consists of a declaration and a list of good-neighbourliness and co-operation agreements and arrangements, supplemented by a list of measures taken or planned by the European Union to contribute to the achievement of the objectives of the Pact.

The economic weight of the Union as well as its possession of the means for consolidating stability together with its allies—provided the political will exists—were taken as the bases for the success of the plan. The plan has primarily focused on those European states which have associated status already and to which the possibility of membership has been offered by the Copenhagen Summit, as well as on other Central and Eastern European countries that have approached the European Union and with membership as the ultimate aim: Bulgaria, Estonia, Hungary, Latvia, Lithuania, Poland, the Czech Republic, Romania, and Slovakia. These so-called "interested states" could also invite neighbouring states and international organizations and institutions concerned to join the bilateral and regional round tables where the negotiations have taken place and whose specific composition and agenda were determined by the participating states. Meanwhile, the Presidency of the European Union visited several capitals to promote the objectives of the Pact.

The system of minority protection resulting from the Pact of Stability resembles that of the League of Nations by virtue of its lack of a general character, as it deals only with specific situations in several European countries. Economic, security and political factors seem to be prevailing once more over the human rights and international law aspects of the minority question in Europe. The adoption of such an approach in the past has not led to encouraging results, and has indeed proved disastrous for minority groups in Western Europe. Nevertheless, the economic and geopolitical conditions differ, and as a result of the Pact attention has been focused on the minority

---

[74] In addition, several Council Decisions and Regulations have been adopted in relation to various aspects of the Yugoslav conflict. See e.g., O.J. 1993, L 102/17; O.J. 1993, L 339/3; O.J. 1994, L 134/1; O.J. 1994, L 182/1; O.J. 1994, L 266/1. See also COM (94) 419 final.

[75] This Conference took place on 26–27 May 1994.

[76] O.J. 1993, L 339/1.

question in some Central and Eastern European countries, pending issues being subject to discussion and peaceful settlement. A process for the encouragement of good neighbourly relations and the improvement of transfrontier co-operation has gained momentum and new frameworks for minority protection, including bilateral treaties, have emerged. The transfer of the Pact on Stability to the OSCE, entrusted with following its implementation, opens possibilities for the projection of the objectives and achievements of the Pact in a wider framework providing for international supervision.

International supervision is also provided under the Council of Europe Framework Convention for the Protection of National Minorities.[77] Although the Community itself is not a party to the Convention, at the time of writing ten of the Member States have signed it.[78] The Framework Convention, although not providing a specific catalogue of subjective rights of minorities, contains a set of rules on state action regarding minority protection. However, given the restriction of the subjects protected to *national* minorities, some states may argue that this Convention only applies to minority groups in Central and Eastern European states. The parallel drafting of a protocol complementing the Convention for the Protection of Human Rights and Fundamental Freedoms (European Convention on Human Rights; ECHR) *in the cultural field* by provisions guaranteeing individual rights, in particular for persons belonging to national minorities, also opens new possibilities for international supervision. At the same time it manifests the lack of political will to provide for a *comprehensive* framework for minority protection that would fall under the monitoring system of the ECHR.

Finally, during the recent, Fifty-first Session of the UN Commission on Human Rights, no common statement was made by the EU presidency under Agenda item 20, dealing with minority protection. Finland (on behalf of the Nordic countries), Austria and Italy made separate statements.[79] Under Austrian initiative resolution 1995/24 was adopted. The resolution opens possibilities for positive developments in the international protection of minorities, and in particular, for the practical implementation of the UN Declaration. This resolution builds upon UN General Assembly resolution 49/192, where the promotion and protection of the rights of persons belonging

---

[77] Framework Convention for the Protection of National Minorities and Explanatory Report, Council of Europe Doc. H (94) 10, Strasbourg, Nov. 1994.

[78] These countries are Austria, Denmark, Finland, Ireland, Italy, The Netherlands, Portugal, Spain, Sweden, and the United Kingdom.

[79] Order of the day of the Fifty-first Session of the UN Commission on Human Rights, 18th and 19th meetings.

to national or ethnic, religious and linguistic minorities are considered to "contribute to political and social stability and peace and enrich the cultural heritage of society as a whole" and by which states and the international community are urged, *inter alia,* to promote and protect the rights of minorities, as set out in the UN Declaration, "including through the facilitation of their full participation in all aspects of the political, economic, social, religious and cultural life of society and in the economic progress and development of their country".[80]

7   THE PROTECTION AND SUPERVISION OF THE RIGHTS OF MINORITIES

No specific framework for the protection of the rights of minorities has been provided by Community legislation. The question arises as to whether minority protection could be derived from other sources of Community law besides the limited references in the Protocols to the Accession Treaties.

The widely diverging approaches adopted by the Member States in their national legislation on the minority question[81]—which most Member States have preferred to ignore altogether—make it difficult to establish general principles of law from their common traditions. In several declarations both the Member States and the Community organs have expressed their respect for human rights and their will to safeguard representative democracy,[82] from which their respect for and safeguarding of the rights of minorities may be implied. Additionally, according to Article F TEU, "the Union shall respect fundamental rights ...". However, the concrete content of minority rights is not easy to determine, since common standards have not been spelled out at the Union level.

This is why the analysis of the applicability of existing international standards regarding minority protection acquires special relevance. The Community has not become a party to any international instrument relevant to minority protection. The Community has not become a party either to the ECHR. However, the TEU refers to this Convention as the main source of

---

[80] A/RES/49/192 on "Effective promotion of the Declaration on the Rights of Persons Belonging to National or Ethnic, Religious and Linguistic Minorities", p. 2.

[81] See Frowein, Hofmann and Oeter (eds), *Das Minderheitenrecht Europäischer Staaten* (1993). See also Packer and Myntti (eds), *The Protection of Ethnic and Linguistic Minorities in Europe* (1993).

[82] Duparc, op. cit., note 7.

delimitation of the fundamental rights respected within the Union alongside the constitutional traditions common to the Member States.

Although according to the European Commission of Human Rights a minority group is in principle entitled to claim rights under the ECHR, the human rights protection provided by the ECHR does not guarantee specific rights to minorities.[83] Its Article 14 contains a provision on protection against discrimination "on any ground such as ... association with a national minority" but its application is limited to the enjoyment of the other rights and freedoms set forth in the ECHR. Matters of importance to minorities falling outside the scope of the individual rights granted by the ECHR are not covered by the prohibition on discrimination. The ECHR does not provide for a general framework of positive action for the protection of minority rights. Maybe the proposed protocol complementing the ECHR in the cultural field will provide for positive action.[84] Although its restriction to the cultural field reduces its potential for providing a general framework of minority protection, the relevance of the Protocol will be determined by the quality of its response to the specific needs of minorities. It should be borne in mind that the ECJ uses not only the ECHR but also its Protocols as a basis for deciding human rights issues.[85]

In addition, in the *second Nold* case the ECJ indicated that "international treaties for the protection of human rights on which the Member States have collaborated, or of which they are signatories, can supply guidelines which should be followed within the framework of Community law."[86] References by the ECJ to international legal texts establishing human rights standards have not been restricted to the ECHR and its Protocols but have also included other texts, such as the European Social Charter and the ILO Conventions. More recently, in the *ERT* case, the Court indicated that it must provide the national court with all the criteria of interpretation needed in order to enable it to assess the compatibility of national legislation "with the fundamental rights, the observance of which the Court ensures and which derive *in particular* from the

---

[83] Thornberry and Martín Estebanez, "The Council of Europe and Minorities", Council of Europe, Doc. COEMIN, Strasbourg (Sept. 1994), pp. 20–24.

[84] *Supra*, note 22.

[85] We could mention the classic examples of Case 36/75, *Rutili* v *Minister for the Interior*, [1975] ECR 1219, which refers to Protocol No. 4, and Case 44/79, *Hauer* v *Land Rheinland-Pfalz*, [1979] ECR 3727, at 3740, referring to Protocol No. 1.

[86] Case 4/73, *Nold* v *Commission*, [1974] ECR 491, para. 13 of the judgment. See also Case 44/79, loc. cit., note 85, para. 15 of the judgment.

European Convention on Human Rights".[87] Therefore, the use of sources of fundamental rights in international law alongside the ECHR are not excluded. Other international instruments providing for minority protection should also be analysed, not only because of the effective legal protection they may provide for minorities within the European Union, but also as a source of inspiration for policies concerning minorities in the future.

According to Schermers, the provisions of the Convention on the Prevention and Punishment of the Crime of Genocide, in so far as they are not part of *ius cogens* (and necessarily binding *erga omnes*) were binding on the Member States before they established the Community. As more powers than are possessed cannot be transferred, the Member States were not competent to transfer any powers conflicting with this Convention to the Communities. Any rules made by the Community contrary to the Convention are therefore void.[88] Article 1 of the Convention confirms the international criminal character of genocide and Article 2 enumerates those acts which constitute genocide when "intended to destroy, in whole or in part, a national, ethnical, racial or religious group". The Community must respect the provisions of the Convention on the Prevention and Punishment of the Crime of Genocide and provide for minority protection accordingly.

A similar rule cannot be applied to other international legal texts relevant to minority protection, such as the International Convention on the Elimination of All Forms of Racial Discrimination, the International Covenant on Civil and Political Rights, the UNESCO Convention against Discrimination in Education, or the Declaration on the Elimination of All Forms of Intolerance and of Discrimination Based on Religion or Belief. Neither can it be applied to several conventions adopted within the framework of the Council of Europe which are highly relevant to minority protection such as the Framework Convention for the Protection of National Minorities already referred to.[89] These texts were adopted after the Communities had been constituted. This is relevant especially with regard to Article 26 of the Covenant (which in contrast with Article 14 ECHR contains a general, autonomous provision of protection "for all persons" against discrimination "on any ground such as race, colour, sex, language, religion, political or other opinion, national or social origin,

---

[87] Case C-260/89, *Elliniki Radiophonia Tileorassi (ERT)*, [1991] ECR I-2925, para. 42 of the judgment. Emphasis added.

[88] Schermers, "The European Communities Bound by Fundamental Human Rights", 27 CML Rev. (1990), 249–258, at 251 and 252.

[89] In addition to the Framework Convention, loc. cit., note 77, see Thornberry and Martín Estébanez, op. cit., note 83.

property, birth or other status") and Article 27 (which although not granting any rights to minorities as groups, grants to persons belonging to minorities the right, in community with the other members of their group, to enjoy their own culture, to profess and practice their own religion, or to use their own language). It has been mainly on the basis of these latter provisions and the monitoring of their implementation by the Human Rights Committee established under the Optional Protocol of the Covenant that the rights of minorities have been protected internationally over the last years. Although these texts and provisions relevant to minority protection are not strictly binding upon the Community under public international law, they supply guidelines which should be followed within the framework of Community law. The UN Declaration recently adopted, which provides for a comprehensive framework of minority protection including the minorities' collective right to exist and to see their identity protected, and for the encouragement of the conditions for its promotion, while not contemplating a system to monitor compliance with its provisions, nonetheless provides for an expression of universal consensus on minimum legal standards regarding minority protection and could be used as a source of fundamental rights. The same could possibly apply to the expression of consensus on non-legally binding standards regarding minority protection included in OSCE documents.

In addition, according to the decision of the ECJ in the *ERT* case, as soon as rules of national legislation:[90]

> do fall within the scope of Community law, and reference is made to the Court for a preliminary ruling, it must provide all the criteria of interpretation needed by the national court to determine whether those rules are compatible with the fundamental rights the observance of which the Court ensures and which derive in particular from the European Convention on Human Rights.

This points to the role of the ECJ as guarantor not only of the coherence of Community legislation with international legal standards on minority protection, but also of national legislation as long as it falls within the Community's sphere of action. Given the extended field of Community competence already analysed, this may have far-reaching consequences for minority protection in those states which refuse to provide for it or accept the existence of minorities within their territories, even if they do so on the basis of their constitutional texts.

---

[90] Case C-260/89, loc. cit., note 87.

It has been stressed, however, that:[91]

> in the cases in which the Court has adopted fundamental rights discourse, it has been the general Community rule or the Community objective which has prevailed against claims as to the violation of fundamental rights ... although the Court has increasingly referred to the Convention, international treaties and constitutional principles and traditions, the rights contained have hardly been developed by the Court, and they have rarely been relied on to give concrete protection to an individual.

In the *second Nold* case the ECJ considered that fundamental rights derived from the constitutional traditions of the Member States could "if necessary, be subject to certain limits justified by the overall objectives pursued by the Community, on condition that the substance of these rights is left untouched".[92] If a similar principle were to be applied to the fundamental rights deriving from international texts, the rights of minorities could be undermined on the basis of the Community general interest, given the fact that, as already indicated, the substance of these rights has not been strictly delimited by the Court. This points to the appropriateness of placing, for the time being, minority protection within the Union in a wider framework where human rights protection is not balanced by economic considerations.

Notwithstanding, international texts are applicable within the Union and possibilities for recourse to the ECJ are offered under Article 177 EC Treaty and could also be provided indirectly by the Member States and the Community institutions, according to their particular right of standing before the Court. Grounds for direct recourse by minorities under Community law are provided in Articles 173(4) and 175(3) which refer to "any natural or legal person ...". The requirement of "individual" concern established in Article 173(4) with regard to decisions addressed to other persons does not necessarily imply an additional burden on the limitation of "direct" concern under this article, given the individual aspect that minority rights involve.

Finally, the codification of the right of petition to the European Parliament and the introduction of the Community Ombudsman also seem to be affording new possibilities for the safeguarding of the rights of minorities within the European Union. The possibility of a collective exercise of the right of petition and the lack of a citizenship requirement points to its aptness for

---

[91] Coppel and O'Neill, "The European Court of Justice: Taking Rights Seriously?", 29 CML Rev. (1992), 669–692, at 683. See also Clapham, "Human Rights and the European Community", 10 YEL (1990), 309–366, at 331.

[92] Case 4/73, loc. cit., note 86, para. 14.

minority questions. The principles set forth in regard to the requirement of direct and individual concern in Article 173(4) apply also to the same restriction established under 138d for the right to petition the European Parliament. In contrast, direct concern is not required for the presentation of complaints to the Community Ombudsman. The competence of the latter seems especially relevant with regard to instances of maladministration by the Community institutions and states in Community measures affecting the rights of minorities, given the particularly vulnerable position of minorities *vis-à-vis* administrative action.

8   CONCLUSION

Action in favour of minority protection within the European Union has ceased to be an issue of legal legitimacy and become a question of political will. In spite of the lack of a specific reference to the protection of national or ethnic, religious and linguistic minorities, the TEU includes provisions relevant to minorities, on the basis of which Community legislation providing for minority protection could be developed. We can even speak of the existence of a legal expectation of Community action regarding minority protection in some areas of policy (such as in the field of culture) if the provisions of the TEU are to be applied. Further, Community legislation has been adopted in areas of policy relevant to minority protection, and often the development of Community policies calls for provisions dealing specifically with the needs of minorities. In addition, international texts exist which are entirely devoted to minority protection or contain provisions relevant to this protection which are applicable or provide guidelines which should be followed within the Community legal order. This applies both to action by the Community institutions and by the Member States under Community competence. The experience of other international organizations in the area of minority protection, especially the Council of Europe,[93] can be used by the Community as a basis for the development of its own policies.

Therefore, the lack of appropriate treatment of the minority question within the European Union cannot be explained on the basis of the absence of a minority rights catalogue. In the preceding pages the existing fields of Community competence relevant to the protection of minorities have been established. The Court's jurisprudence establishes its responsibility for guaranteeing that both Community and state action within the fields of

---

[93] Thornberry and Martín Estébanez, op. cit., note 83.

Community competence respect fundamental rights in accordance with the international instruments applicable. Cultivating respect for the rights of minorities will not be an easy task within the Union, given that the negative attitude towards minorities remains strong in some of the Member States. To overcome this reluctance at the present time, the Community institutions should bear in mind that although the TEU does not call for specific policies "on minorities", legal grounds exist for action in protection of the basic interests and concerns of minorities in the different fields of Community competence.

In spite of the weakness of the present international system of minority protection, both the activities already undertaken by the Union in the field of Foreign and Security Policy and the approach of the ECJ to human rights protection so far point to the necessity of placing the treatment of the rights of minorities by the European Union within a wider framework. Progress in the field of minority protection is being achieved in the context of the UN, the Council of Europe and the OSCE, where all the Member States of the Union participate. The possibility of full participation by the Community in the minority protection provided under these frameworks should be grasped. This would facilitate the full compliance of Community action with the existing and future international standards of minority protection in all those areas falling under Community competence and thus contribute to the protection of the rights of minorities within the Union.

8 ELECTORAL RIGHTS AND THE EUROPEAN UNION: A BROADER HUMAN RIGHTS PERSPECTIVE

Allan Rosas

1 INTRODUCTION

One of the central sub-themes in the discussion of a "Citizens' Europe" has been the question of extending electoral rights to non-national residents of a Union Member State. Part Two of the EC Treaty, as introduced by the Treaty on European Union (TEU), deals with "citizenship of the Union", and includes an Article (8b) which provides that every citizen of the Union residing in a Member State of which he is not a national shall have the right to vote and to stand as a candidate at municipal (local) and European elections in the country where he resides, under the same conditions as nationals of that state.

The discussions of granting voting rights to non-citizens date back to the 1960s. A specific Community context is, of course, provided by Article 138(3) EC Treaty, with its reference to direct elections of the European Parliament, including a still abortive reference to "a uniform procedure in all Member States".[1] Some of the pronouncements of the early 1970s on granting "special rights" to nationals of EC Member States included references to the right to vote in municipal elections.[2] The Commission in 1988 put forward a proposal for a Council Directive on voting rights in local elections, invoking Article 235 as a legal basis.[3] The reference in Article 138(3) to direct elections of the European Parliament was again conducive to bringing these elections under the prohibition of discrimination on grounds of nationality contained in the then Article 7 of the EEC Treaty (now Article 6 EC Treaty).

---

[1] For commentaries on Art. 138 and its follow-up see, e.g., Kovar et al. (eds), *Traité instituant la CEE: Commentaire article par article* (1992), pp. 814–819; Smit and Herzog, *The Law of The European Community: A Commentary on the EEC Treaty* (1994), 5–45 – 5–53.

[2] Van den Berghe, *Political Rights for European Citizens* (1982), p. 31.

[3] Proposal for a Council Directive on voting rights for Community nationals in local elections in their Member States of residence, COM (1988) 371 final 11.07.1988, O.J. 1988, C 246/3.

N. A. Neuwahl and A. Rosas (eds.), The European Union and Human Rights, 165–184.

These interpretations did not go uncontested, as Member States tended to exclude political rights from the ambit of Community law.[4] The matter was only solved with the adoption of Article 8b of the Maastricht version of the EC Treaty. During this process, it has almost been taken for granted that electoral rights associated with Union citizenship could cover local and European elections only, while national elections and referenda are so intimately linked to popular sovereignty in a state sovereignty and nation-state context that electoral rights in these elections should continue to be a matter for the exclusive jurisdiction of the Member States.[5]

Rather than discussing the fine print of Article 8b, this chapter will put the question of electoral rights in the European Union in a broader human rights perspective. The expansion and deepening of European integration has brought in its wake some overlapping of, and tension between, Community action and the protection of human rights.[6] This has been especially apparent for such "traditional" rights as the right to privacy, property rights and rights related to the administration of justice. A few cases have involved what can be termed political freedoms,[7] but political rights in the narrow sense—meaning electoral rights and other rights of political participation[8]—have been outside potential collision avenues. The situation could have been otherwise had the Council gone forward with the above-mentioned Commission proposal of 1988 for a Directive on electoral rights in local elections.[9]

With the Maastricht Treaty, then, the Communities have taken a further step in the delicate field of political rights and freedoms, albeit still within the

---

[4] Closa, "The Concept of Citizenship in the Treaty on European Union", 29 CML Rev., 1137–1169, at 1149.

[5] Rosas, "Union Citizenship and National Elections", in Rosas and Antola (eds), *A Citizens' Europe: In Search of a New Order* (1995), pp. 135–155.

[6] See, e.g., Mendelson, "The European Court of Justice and Human Rights", 1 YEL (1981), 125–165; Ghandi, "Interaction between the Protection of Fundamental Rights in the European Economic Community and under the European Convention on Human Rights", (1981) LIEI, 1–33; Foster, "The European Court of Justice and the European Convention for the Protection of Human Rights", 8 HRLJ (1987), 245–272; Clapham, *Human Rights and the European Community: A Critical Overview* (1991), pp. 45–55; Krogsgaard, "Fundamental Rights in the European Community after Maastricht", (1993) LIEI, 99–113.

[7] Case 36/75, *Rutili v Minister for the Interior,* [1975] ECR 1219; Case C-260/89, *Elliniki Radiophonia Tileorassi (ERT),* [1991] ECR I-2925.

[8] Steiner, "Political Participation as a Human Right", 1 *Harvard Human Rights Yearbook* (1988), 77–134.

[9] Closa, loc. cit., note 4, at 1149, refers to the opinion of the British Home Office, according to which the Community lacked jurisdiction to legislate in the field of political rights.

limited context of electoral rights for Union citizens residing in a country other than their country of nationality. This step, which is not insignificant as a matter of principle, merits further consideration from the more general perspective of internationally recognized political rights. Moreover, the dynamic nature of the case law of the Court of Justice of the European Communities (ECJ), and the evolution clause of Article 8e(2) EC Treaty, suggest that additional steps may be taken in the future with respect to the political rights of Union citizens.

We shall first take a brief look at the history of political rights *qua* human rights and relate this historical and ideological background to the EU context. Second, the relationship between Article 8b and political rights provisions in universal and European human rights and other instruments will be explored. Third, we shall look more specifically at the question of the division of jurisdiction in the field of electoral rights between the ECJ and the human rights control bodies, notably the European Commission and Court of Human Rights. At the end, there will be an effort to sum up the discussion, partly from a *de lege ferenda* point of view.

2   HISTORICAL BACKGROUND

To understand why introducing even some modest elements of political rights into the concept of Union citizenship has been such a contentious issue, it is useful to take a brief look at the historical and ideological background of political rights *qua* human rights. In everyday human rights parlance, a basic distinction (which is also reflected in the existence of two separate human rights Covenants of 1966[10]) is usually made between civil and political rights on the one hand and economic, social and cultural rights on the other. It is often then taken for granted that "civil and political rights" go historically together, being children of the American and French Revolutions and the Western liberal democracy that has followed in their footsteps.

A closer look will reveal a much more diverse and complex picture.[11] Electoral reforms introducing universal suffrage based on the principle of

---

[10] International Covenant on Economic, Social and Cultural Rights and International Covenant on Civil and Political Rights, the latter with two Additional Protocols.

[11] Rosas, "Democracy and Human Rights", in Rosas and Helgesen (eds), *Human Rights in a Changing East-West Perspective* (1990), pp. 17–57; idem, "Article 21", in Eide et al. (eds), *The Universal Declaration of Human Rights: A Commentary* (1992), pp. 299–317.

political equality have only been carried out during the present century.[12] At the level of constitutional law, there has been a tendency to deny the status of political rights *qua* fundamental (constitutional) rights.[13]

After the Second World War, there was reluctance among many Western countries to include electoral rights in the Universal Declaration of Human Rights of 1948, the Convention for the Protection of Human Rights and Fundamental Freedoms of 1950 (European Convention on Human Rights; ECHR) and the International Covenant on Civil and Political Rights of 1966 (CCPR). While electoral rights were included at the end, this was with regard to the ECHR possible only in the separate Protocol No. 1 of 1952. Moreover, Article 3 of this Protocol is worded as an obligation of the state rather than as an individual right. The nature of this provision as an individual right and a right giving an entitlement to universal suffrage has only been confirmed in more recent case law, and by the European Court of Human Rights in a case decided in the 1980s.[14] One still comes across statements—not necessarily well-founded in law—that "political rights" and "human rights" are two separate things.[15]

This reluctance to recognize political rights as human rights can be historically explained by the emphasis in classical human rights discourse on individual property rights, freedom of movement and other freedoms "from" state interference. Traditionally, property rights are rights "of" rather than a rights "to" property, that is, protection of existing property rather than an

---

[12] The first European electoral reform involving universal suffrage and eligibility for all adults took place in Finland in 1906 (when also a unicameral parliament was established). Switzerland made this move as late as in the 1970s and South Africa only recently.

[13] Nowak, *Politische Grundrechte* (1988), p. 39 et seq.

[14] Eur. Court H. R., *Mathieu-Mohin and Clerfayt* judgment of 2 March 1987, Series A no. 113, at pp. 22–23 (paras 46–51), where reference is also made to the evolving case law of the Commission.

[15] For instance, this argument was advanced in the Finnish Parliament in 1991 in support of introducing a longer period of residence as a requirement for electoral rights of non-Nordic foreigners in local elections, as compared to voting rights of Nordic nationals, see Rosas, loc. cit., note 5, p. 146. The present author has also come across this argument in relation to the political rights of the Russian-speaking populations of Estonia and Latvia, large numbers of which have not yet been granted Estonian or Latvian nationality (on this problematique see, e.g., Öst, "Who is Citizen in Estonia, Latvia and Lithuania?", in Dahlgren (ed.), *Human Rights in the Baltic States* (Publications of the Advisory Board for International Human Rights Affairs, No. 6, 1993), pp. 43–86.

entitlement to redistribution.[16] Freedom of movement, again, served the purpose of enabling a flexible labour force to work for the property-owners within a given national market. Property was accumulated in the hands of a minority, who saw the idea of democracy based on universal suffrage and the majority principle as a threat to their "acquired rights".[17]

As markets, in Western Europe in particular, have developed beyond national borders, the principle of freedom of movement has been lifted to the European level and been granted a prominent place in the European Communities and now in the Maastricht version of Article 8a EC Treaty. As to property rights as such, it is true that they can be seen as a "forgotten issue" under Community law[18] and, to some extent, also under the ECHR. There is no denying, however, that Community law and European integration processes in general are ultimately based on a *system* of private property, market economies and a supportive rule of law.

Political rights, on the other hand, have historically been more in the nature of *concessions* granted by ruling elites to preserve the legitimacy of the nation-state rather than perceived as genuine entitlements. The previous reluctance within the nation-states to recognize political rights as human rights has been followed by a reluctance within the Communities to give them a human rights dimension and/or to make them a central piece of Union citizenship. Article 8b EC Treaty, like all the provisions on Union citizenship, is restricted to nationals of Member States, and even for those nationals it merely regulates the use of electoral rights (introducing residence instead of nationality as one of the criteria) among the Member States rather than establishing and defining rights of political participation. Moreover, there is, of course, the limitation of the elections covered to local and European elections, excluding national and regional elections as well as referenda.

Nevertheless, there is no denying that the European Union has entered the field of political rights. This impression is reinforced by Article 138a EC Treaty, which refers to "political parties at European level" and states that they

---

[16] Rosas, "Property Rights", in Rosas and Helgesen (eds), *The Strength of Diversity: Human Rights and Pluralist Democracy* (1992), pp. 133–157.

[17] According to John Locke, taking away and destroying "the property of the people" put the legislators into a state of war with the people, who are left with a right of resistance (Locke, *Two Treatises on Civil Government* (1690), 1984 edn, II § 222). The "people" probably comprised male property-owners only; on the other hand, Locke's concept of property was here a broad one, to include life and liberty.

[18] See Chapter 13 in this volume.

"contribute ... to expressing the political will of the citizens of the Union".[19] The fact that some of the ideas and proposals for Union citizenship which preceded the Treaty of Maastricht included a broader spectrum of political rights than those ultimately adopted,[20] should also be mentioned in this context. These ideas and proposals illustrate some of the thinking behind the concept of Union citizenship and may well surface again, especially considering the possibility of a dynamic interpretation of Article 8b as well as the evolution clause contained in Article 8e(2).[21] There is thus a case for discussing the relationship between the elements of political rights contained in the Maastricht Treaty and internationally recognized political rights as human rights.

3   ARTICLE 8B OF THE EC TREATY AND INTERNATIONALLY RECOGNIZED POLITICAL RIGHTS

The main provisions expressing internationally recognized political rights are contained in Article 21 of the Universal Declaration of Human Rights, Article 3 of Protocol No. 1 to the ECHR, Article 25 of the CCPR and Article 23 of the American Convention on Human Rights.[22] The two latter provisions specify that the beneficiaries of the right—unlike the general human rights approach—are citizens. The Universal Declaration speaks somewhat more vaguely about the right of "everyone" to take part in the government of "his country", while Protocol No. 1 of the ECHR merely refers to "the opinion of

---

[19] On this provision, see, e.g., Tsatsos, "Europäische politische Parteien?", 21 Eu GRZ (1994), 45–53.

[20] The European Commission proposal on Union citizenship put forward during the initial phase of the Intergovernmental Conference included a provision on not only electoral rights but also the right to be a member of a political association or group (Corbett, *The Treaty of Maastricht. From Conception to Ratification: A Comprehensive Reference Guide* (1993), p. 232). See also the Spanish proposal of 21 Feb. 1991, Laursen and Vanhoonacker (eds), *The Intergovernmental Conference on Political Union: Institutional Reforms, New Policies and International Identity of the European Community* (1992), p. 327.

[21] The dynamic nature of the concept of Union citizenship is acknowledged by, e.g., O'Keeffe, "Union Citizenship", in O'Keeffe and Twomey (eds), *Legal Issues of the Maastricht Treaty* (1994), pp. 87–107, at p. 107. But see d'Oliveira, "European Citizenship: Its Meaning, Its Potential", in Monar, Ungerer and Wessels (eds), *The Maastricht Treaty on European Union: Legal Complexity and Political Dynamic* (1993), pp. 81–106, who (at p. 99), claims that the dynamism of the concept is "pie in the sky".

[22] On these and other similar provisions on political participation see, e.g., Rosas, "Democracy and Human Rights", loc. cit., note 11, pp. 23–30.

the people". The drafters of the latter instruments probably had in mind the people of a given nation-state, meaning as a general rule the citizens of the state as defined under its domestic law, but the wording does not seem to settle the question for good.[23]

Be that as it may, it is obvious that international human rights law does not contain a clear-cut requirement to grant electoral rights to non-citizens. There have been no authoritative assertations to this effect. Rather, the decision of many states to grant electoral rights to resident foreigners have, first of all, usually been limited to local elections. Secondly, they have been seen as additional benefits, sometimes tied to the condition of reciprocity or—as is the case with respect to Union citizenship or the Nordic framework[24]—to a particular community of states. The recent Council of Europe Convention on the Participation of Foreigners in Public Life at Local Level (Convention No. 144 of 1992) is a further step in this regard, but the Convention is at the time of writing binding only on two states.[25]

With respect to local elections, it should be noted that they are, at best, on the margin of the international human rights agenda. This is especially relevant for purposes of Article 3 of Protocol No. 1 of the ECHR, which speaks about the "choice of the legislature". The European supervisory bodies have interpreted this to mean the constituent states of federal states and regional councils vested with legislative powers, whereas there has been a tendency in the case law of the Commission to exclude regional councils devoid of constitutionally anchored legislative powers and local governments competent to adopt by-laws only.[26]

As to the elections for the European Parliament, they too have been previously considered as falling outside the ambit of Article 3 of Protocol No.

---

[23] Van Dijk and van Hoof, *Theory and Practice of the European Convention on Human Rights* (1990), pp. 483–484; Rosas, loc. cit., note 5, p. 137. See further below.

[24] On electoral rights in local elections for "Nordic citizens" see Rosas, loc. cit., note 5, pp. 144–148.

[25] Norway and Sweden, Chart showing signature and ratifications of conventions and agreements concluded within the Council of Europe, signatures and ratifications between 1 Jan. 1989 and 19 May 1994. It should be noted that Norway and Sweden, as a result of discussions taking place in the Nordic Council (see the preceding note), have granted foreign residents local electoral rights since the 1970s, that is, well before the Council of Europe Convention came into being.

[26] *Mathieu-Mohin and Clerfayt,* loc. cit., note 14, p. 23 (para. 53). For the case law of the Commission see, e.g., *Digest of Strasbourg Case-Law*, Vol. V, pp. 864–865; van Dijk and van Hoof, op. cit., note 23, pp. 485–487; de Meyer, "Electoral Rights", in Macdonald, Matscher and Petzold (eds), *The European System for the Protection of Human Rights* (1993), pp. 553–569, at pp. 554–555.

1. In its earlier case law, the European Commission of Human Rights stated that the "European Parliament has no legislative power in the strict sense", although this did not exclude the possibility that it could gradually assume the powers and functions of national legislatures.[27] This has become a debatable opinion, especially after the entry into force of the Single European Act of 1986.[28] With the TEU, it is obvious that the previous line of interpretation must be reconsidered, taking into account the absolute veto power given to the Parliament under Article 189b EC Treaty and the determination of the Parliament as a law-making body in Article 189.[29]

In so far as the elections for the European Parliament are covered by Article 3 of Protocol No. 1 to the ECHR, the question arises as to whether "the people" referred to in this article could include non-nationals who reside in the country. In an authoritative commentary to the ECHR,[30] it is indicated that such an interpretation is possible, but that on the other hand "it may hardly be expected that the Strasbourg case law will force a breakthrough on this point".

Article 8b EC Treaty thus seems to enter new ground in subjecting electoral rights both at the local and European level to European regulation and providing expressly for the extension of such rights to non-nationals residing in a Union Member State. This can be seen as a positive contribution to the efforts to make democracy as *inclusive*[31] as possible, meaning the inclusion

---

[27] Application No. 8364/78, *Lindsay v. United Kingdom*, Decisions and Reports 15 (1979), p. 247; Application No. 8612/79, *Alliances des Belges de la Communauté Européenne v. Belgium*, Decisions and Reports 15 (1979), p. 259. In the first case, the Commission nevertheless "assumed" that Article 3 was applicable in the case (p. 251), whereas it in the second case stated that "the question raised above does not require an immediate answer" (p. 262). See also de Meyer, loc. cit., note 26, p. 554.

[28] In Application No. 11123/84, *Tête v. France*, Decisions and Reports 54 (1987), p. 52; and Application No. 11406/85, *Fournier v. France,* Decisions and Reports 55 (1988), p. 130, the Commission acknowledged the increasing role of the European Parliament, particularly as a result of the entry into force of the Single European Act of 1986, but held nevertheless that "the European Parliament does not yet constitute a legislature within the ordinary meaning of the term" (Decisions and Reports 54 (1987), p. 68). It added, however, that these developments were as yet incomplete and that the Commission therefore considered it unnecessary to answer the question, taking also into account the fact that the applicant's complaints were inadmissible on other grounds.

[29] According to Art. 189 EC Treaty, as amended by the TEU, "the European Parliament acting jointly with the Council, the Council and the Commission shall make regulations and issue directives, take decisions, make recommendations or deliver opinions".

[30] Van Dijk and van Hoof, op. cit., note 23, pp. 483–484.

[31] On the concept of inclusiveness see Dahl, *Polyarchy: Participation and Opposition* (1971), p. 7.

into the electorate of all persons who have residence in a country, regardless of the formal criteria of nationality and citizenship.

On the other hand, the scope and meaning of Article 8b is limited in various ways. To sum up the provision:

— excludes regional and national elections;
— excludes non-EU nationals (third-country nationals);
— does not explicitly address the political freedoms necessary for the effective realization of electoral rights (e.g., freedom of association);
— allows for "derogations where warranted by problems specific to a Member State".

The exlusion of regional and national elections, while not being free from problems,[32] is understandable in view of the present state of European integration.[33] It is perhaps less understandable why third-country nationals are excluded, as they enjoy a widening freedom of movement in an internal market without borders, have in Articles 138d and 138e EC Treaty been given the right to submit petitions to the European Parliament and complaints to the new Ombudsman, and are covered by the Council of Europe Convention on the Participation of Foreigners in Public Life at Local Level referred to above. Some of the proposals for the 1996 Intergovernmental Conference purport to broaden the concept of Union citizenship to include persons who have been lawfully residing in the territory of a Member State for a certain period of time.[34]

As far as the political freedoms (freedom of expression, freedom of association, etc.) are concerned, there were, as noted above,[35] proposals to

---

[32] Rosas, loc. cit., note 5.

[33] See generally Rosas and Antola (eds), op. cit., note 5.

[34] See, e.g., Standing Committee of Experts on International Immigration, Refugee and Criminal Law, *Proposals for the Amendment of the Treaty on European Union at the IGC in 1996* (1995), p. 11. The European Parliament already in a Resolution of 14 June 1990 (O.J. 1990, C 175/180) mentioned the possibility of extending the rights of migrant workers to include, *inter alia,* the right to vote in local elections. The sensitivity of the issue, on the other hand, is reflected in Art. 1(2) of Council Directive 94/80/EC of 19 Dec. 1994 (see note 37 below), according to which nothing in the Directive "shall affect each Member State's provisions concerning the right to vote or to stand as a candidate ... of third country nationals who reside in that State". On the status of third-country nationals generally, see, e.g., Hailbronner, "Third-Country Nationals and EC Law", in Rosas and Antola, op. cit., note 5, pp. 182–206.

[35] See note 20.

make some references to them in the amended Maastricht version of the EC Treaty. These ideas were dropped, however, and now the question as to whether the principle of effectiveness requires some respect for the freedom of association (political parties) and freedom of expression is a matter of interpretation.[36]

Finally, it should be noted that the possibility of derogations provided for in Article 8b is of a rather limited practical significance, because subsequent secondary legislation rendered it applicable to Luxembourg and possibly some Belgian local government units only.[37] Nevertheless, the derogation clause seems to underline the secondary status being given to Article 8b *qua* a provision on political rights. The Article is seen as an additional benefit open to "derogations"[38] rather than as a fundamental entitlement called for by the principle of inclusive democracy.

---

[36] Lundberg, "Political Freedoms in the European Union", in Rosas and Antola, op. cit., note 5, pp. 113–134.

[37] See Art. 12 of Council Directive 94/80/EC of 19 Dec. 1994, laying down detailed arrangements for the exercise of the right to vote and to stand as a candidate at municipal elections by citizens of the Union residing in a Member State of which they are not nationals. Luxembourg is covered by the clause in paragraph 1 of Art. 12 concerning a Member State where the proportion of citizens of the Union of voting age who reside in it but are not nationals of it exceeds 20 per cent of the total number of citizens of the Union residing there, while Belgium is specifically mentioned in paragraph 2. In an annexed Statement in the minutes, Belgium stated that "if it were to make use of the derogation provided for in Article 12(2) that derogation would be applied to only some of the local government units in which the number of voters within the scope of Article 3 exceeded 20 % of all voters where the Belgian Federal Government regarded the specific situation as justifying an exceptional derogation of that kind". In Council Directive 93/198/EC of 6 Dec. 1993 laying down detailed arrangements for the exercise of the right to vote and to stand as a candidate at elections to the European Parliament for citizens of the Union residing in a Member State of which they are not nationals, there is a similar derogation possibility for Member States where the proportion of citizens of the Union of voting age who reside in it but are not nationals of it exceeds 20 per cent of the total number of citizens of the Union residing there who are of voting age (Art. 14) but no derogation clause expressly applicable to Belgium.

[38] Note that in the human rights discourse, "derogations" imply the possibility of far-reaching deviations in times of public emergency threatening the life of the nation. See, e.g., Rosas, "Public Emergency Regimes: A Comparison", in Gomien (ed)., *Broadening the Frontiers of Human Rights: Essays in Honour of Asbjørn Eide* (1993), pp. 165–199.

4 DIVISION OF JURISDICTION BETWEEN
THE LUXEMBOURG AND STRASBOURG ORGANS

Ever since the EU legal order has come to include "fundamental rights" as general principles of Community law, positive conflicts of jurisdiction between the ECHR and EC control systems have become a real possibility.[39] Several possible situations can be envisaged. An application might be filed with the Strasbourg Commission, alleging violations of the ECHR by the EU organs, by Member States collectively or by individual states. This may take place whether or not the case has been considered by the ECJ. On the other hand, a case may come before the latter Court, most likely as a request for a preliminary ruling by a national court or tribunal (Article 177 EC Treaty), an action for annulment of Community acts under Article 173 or as a claim for compensation of damage under Article 215. The ECJ, of course, is called upon to apply and interpret Community law, but this task may include use of the ECHR and possibly also other human rights instruments as relevant sources.

To begin with the possibility of an application to Strasbourg, some procedural hurdles may arise as to whether non-use of the Luxembourg option (in so far as it would be available in a given case) means that domestic remedies have not been exhausted, as required by Article 26 ECHR, or conversely, whether previous use of the Luxembourg system means that the application to Strasbourg "has already been submitted to another procedure of international investigation or settlement" and "contains no relevant new information", which according to Article 27(1)(b) ECHR should lead to a decision of inadmissibility.

The question of a possible need to exhaust local remedies would normally seem to arise in relation to the institution of preliminary rulings only.[40] It is doubtful, to say the least, that the Luxembourg detour would be considered as a "domestic" remedy that has to be exhausted in order to reach the admissibility stage in Strasbourg.[41] It is another matter that a pending

---

[39] See the literature mentioned in note 6 *supra*. For a more general comparison between European Community and Council of Europe instruments and norms see Dowrick, "Overlapping European Laws", 27 ICLQ (1978), 629–660.

[40] An action for annulment of Community acts under Art. 173 could normally not lead to a successful application to Strasbourg; the Strasbourg organs not considering themselves competent to review the activities of Community organs (see below).

[41] Mendelson, "The Impact of European Community Law on the Implementation of the European Convention on Human Rights", 3 YEL (1983), pp. 99–126 at pp. 110–112; Clements, *European*

request for a preliminary ruling may imply that the *domestic* procedures before the relevant national court have not yet been exhausted.

Concerning the effect of previous or simultaneous use of the Luxembourg option, I would argue that the proceedings before the ECJ in Luxembourg do not normally constitute a "procedure of international investigation or settlement" in the meaning of Article 27 ECHR, at least not for the system of preliminary rulings.[42] If the national court refuses to request a preliminary ruling, there may in exceptional cases be a ground for submitting an application to Strasbourg, alleging a violation of Article 6 (right to fair trial).[43] As far as bringing a case before the ECJ, there seems to be no reason why the fact that the case has already been considered by the Strasbourg organs should as such constitute a bar for the ECJ in Luxembourg to consider the matter.[44]

Human Rights: Taking a Case under the Convention (1994), p. 25. In Eur. Court H. R., *Deweer* judgment of 27 February 1980, Series A no. 35, Belgium did not raise the defence of non-exhaustion of the remedy of preliminary ruling, although this remedy might have been available in the case (see paras 19 and 21 of the judgment and Case 154/77, *Procureur du Roi* v *Dechmann,* [1978] ECR 1573). The decision to request a preliminary ruling rests with the national court and not the applicant (although a court of final instance is, in principle, under a duty to make such a request). The outcome of the preliminary rulings procedure may be highly uncertain in human rights related matters of Community law. One should not exclude, on the other hand, that this institution might in some special cases be considered as offering an effective remedy under Art. 26 ECHR on exhaustion of local remedies. Thus, in Application No. 13539/88, *Dufay v. European Communities,* Decision of 19 Jan. 1989, the Strasbourg Commission held that the internal remedy available for employees of the European Parliament to turn to the ECJ was a "local" remedy to be exhausted by an employee who had been disbanded; failure to comply with a deadline for submitting a case to the ECJ consequently led the Strasbourg Commission to declare the application inadmissible because of non-exhaustion of local remedies.

[42] As van Dijk and van Hoof, op. cit., note 23, pp. 71–72, point out, the two procedures are likely to involve different legal issues. See also Ghandi, loc. cit., note 6, 22. Cf. Mendelson, loc. cit., note 41, 109.

[43] See, e.g., Applications Nos. 17239/90, 20631/92 and 15669/89, which were declared inadmissible by the Commission of Human Rights on 31 March, 12 May and 28 June 1993, respectively, but where the Commission, on the other hand, expressly did not rule out the possibility that a refusal to request a preliminary ruling could in some circumstances raise a question under Art. 6(1) ECHR.

[44] True, Art. 62 ECHR provides that the Contracting Parties, except by special agreement, "will not avail themselves of treaties, conventions or declarations in force between them for the purpose of submitting, by way of petition, a dispute arising out of the interpretation or application of this Convention to a means of settlement other than those provided for in this Convention". This provision is not only limited to interstate disputes (which are rare under the ECHR) but it also seems to be limited to disputes relating specifically to the ECHR rather than disputes relating to Community law where human rights aspects may be involved. See also Mendelson, loc. cit., note

In so far as the above interpretations are accepted, the procedural relationship between the two control systems is quite flexible, increasing the chance of both systems being involved in the same or two similar cases.[45] Moreover, there is with respect to most Union Member States the additional possibility of submitting a communication to the Human Rights Committee, acting under the (First) Optional Protocol to the CCPR. Unless a state adhering to the Optional Protocol has made a reservation,[46] the Human Rights Committee is competent to deal also with cases that have already been decided in Strasbourg (or Luxembourg), while the Strasbourg organs would be barred from taking up cases already considered in the Human Rights Committee.[47] It remains to be seen whether such overlapping jurisdictions will have any substantive effect on the political rights of Union citizens.

A number of situations and possible grievances could be envisaged. First of all, a European Union citizen who is not a national of the country where he lives could argue that the absence of electoral rights in national elections constitutes discrimination, under either Community law, the ECHR or the CCPR. To argue for electoral rights in national elections on an equal footing with nationals, invoking the EC Treaty principles of freedom of movement

---

41, 107–109.

[45] Examples where this has happened are Application No. 6452/74, *Sacchi v. Italy,* Decisions and Reports 5 (1976), p. 42, as compared to Case 155/73, *Sacchi,* [1974] ECR 409 (see van Dijk and van Hoof, op. cit., note 23, at p. 72, note 52), Case 7/78, *Regina v Thompson,* [1978] ECR 2247, as compared to Eur. Court H. R., *Agosi* judgment of 24 October 1986, Series A no. 108 (see Clapham, op. cit., note 6, p. 42), and Case C-159/90, *Society for the Protection of Unborn Children Ireland,* [1991] ECR I-4685, as compared to Eur. Court H. R., *Open Door Counselling and Dublin Well Woman Centre Ltd. v. Ireland* judgment of 29 October 1992, Series A no. 246 (see de Búrca, "Fundamental Human Rights and the Reach of EC Law", 13 OJLS (1993), 283–319). Some links can also be seen between the *Deweer* case decided by the European Court of Human Rights and certain requests for a preliminary ruling by the ECJ, such as *Procureur du Roi v P. Dechmann,* see note 41.

[46] Denmark, France, Iceland, Italy, Luxembourg, Norway, Spain and Sweden have formulated reservations or interpretative declarations to Art. 5(2) of the Optional Protocol making it clear that the Human Rights Committee is also barred from considering a communication which has already been examined under another procedure of international investigation, see United Nations, *Human Rights: Status of International Instruments* (1987), pp. 91–94.

[47] This follows from the difference in wording of Art. 27(2)(b) ECHR and Art. 5(2) of the Optional Protocol (the latter provision prevents the Human Rights Committee from considering a communication only if "the same matter is not being examined" under another procedure of international investigation or settlement).

(Articles 8 and 48) and non-discrimination (Article 6),[48] coupled with the importance for freedom of movement of the social integration of the migrant in the host state,[49] seems after Maastricht to be foreclosed by the wording of Article 8b (which is restricted to European and municipal elections) and its *travaux préparatoires*.

As to the human rights aspect, he or she might invoke not only Article 3 of Protocol No. 1 to the ECHR but also Articles 25 and 26 CCPR, arguing that the latter provisions as well should be considered at least as guidelines in the determination of a general principle of Community law.[50] This would, in fact, imply that Article 8b EC Treaty—assuming that this provision should be understood *e contrario* to exclude national elections—is in violation of human rights. In view of the foregoing, such an argument lacks a basis in existing human rights law. There is clearly no rule requiring states that have extended foreigners' electoral rights to local (and in the case of the EU, European) elections to provide for an additional extension to national elections.

The situation may become a little more problematic if the issue is raised in Ireland or the United Kingdom, which grant electoral rights to each other's citizens—but not to other Union citizens—in national elections as well.[51] But it is possible to argue that the extension of electoral rights in national elections to certain foreign citizens is not a matter regulated by Community law and

---

[48] In Case 186/87, *Cowan* v *Trésor Public*, [1989] ECR 195, the ECJ considered a bar to compensation under a national scheme for compensating victims of crime as an impediment to freedom of movement and thus as falling under the prohibition of discrimination on grounds of nationality.

[49] Cf. Case 59/85, *Netherlands* v *Reed*, [1986] ECR 1283, where the ECJ noted that "the possibility for a migrant worker of obtaining permission for his unmarried companion to reside with him ... can assist his integration in the host State and thus contribute to the achievement of freedom of movements for workers". See also Joined Cases 281, 283 to 285 and 287/85, *Germany, France, Netherlands, Denmark and United Kingdom* v *Commission*, [1987] ECR 3203. As has been pointed out by Evans, "Nationality Law and European Integration", 16 EL Rev. (1991), 190–215, at 210, "from the point of view of the development of Community citizenship ... participation at the national level might be thought to be more important than participation at the local level".

[50] While Art. F(2) TEU, and often the ECJ in its case law, refer to the ECHR only, in some cases (e.g., Case 4/73, *Nold* v *Commission*, [1974] ECR 491, at 506; Case 44/79, *Hauer* v *Land Rheinland-Pfalz*, [1979] ECR 3727, at 3744) the Court has made a broader reference to "international treaties for the protection of human rights on which the Member States have collaborated or of which they are signatories". Such a broadening of the sources may be especially pertinent in matters such as political rights and non-discrimination, where the CCPR (Arts. 25 and 26) are more far-reaching than the corresponding provisions (Art. 3 of Protocol No. 1 and Art. 14) of the ECHR.

[51] Rosas, loc. cit., note 5, p. 140. A similar regime was in the 1980s discussed among the Nordic countries, ibid., pp. 144–148.

thus falls outside its non-discrimination principle.[52] This seems to be the reasoning underlying Article 14(2) of the 1993 Directive on European elections and Article 12(3) of the 1994 Directive on municipal elections, where express reference is made to the possibility that the laws of a Member State prescribe that the nationals of another Member State who reside there have the right to vote for the national Parliament of that state.[53]

Apart from Community law, could one—either before the Strasbourg organs or the ECJ—argue that the Irish–UK regime contravenes the prohibition of discrimination in human rights law? The answer to this question is not necessarily a definitive "no", as Article 26 CCPR has been applied in the field of social rights (which are not otherwise covered by the Covenant at all) and even in a case of nationality being the distinguishing criterion.[54] Also, one could possibly interpret the concept of "people" in Article 3 of Protocol No. 1 to the ECHR as extending to resident non-nationals from all countries, if such resident non-nationals from certain countries have been included in the electorate. This, in combination with the non-discrimination clause in Article 14 ECHR, could then imply that the Irish–UK regime (more precisely, the exclusion of other Union citizens from this regime) would also be doubtful under the European Convention on Human Rights.

Such an interpretation is nevertheless not likely to achieve general acceptance in the foreseeable future. It should be remembered in this context that state practice also allows for privileges for nationals from a special group of states (the Nordic countries, Union Member States, Central American

---

[52] Cf. Case 59/85, loc. cit., note 49, where it was held that The Netherlands, which permitted the unmarried foreign companions of its own nationals to reside in its territory could not refuse to grant the same advantage to a British migrant worker (whose companion's application for a residence permit had been rejected by the Dutch authorities), despite the fact that unmarried couples could not be recognized as "spouses" and thus family members. The Court arrived at this conclusion, however, only after having held that the possibility for the migrant worker of obtaining permission for his unmarried companion was a "social advantage" for the purposes of Art. 7(2) of Council Regulation No. 1612/68 (which provided that migrant workers from other EC countries must enjoy "the same social and tax advantages as national workers") and thus a matter of Community law.

[53] The provisions go on to provide that if the national of the other Member State may be entered on the electoral roll of the host state "under exactly the same conditions as national voters", the host state may, by way of derogation from the respective Directive, refrain from applying certain Articles of the Directive in respect of such persons.

[54] Case of *Gueye et al. v. France*, Communication No. 196/1985, Report of the Human Rights Committee. General Assembly Official Records. Forty-fourth Session, Supplement No. 40 (A/44/40), pp. 189–195. See also Scheinin, "Economic and Social Rights as Legal Rights", in Eide, Krause and Rosas (eds), *Economic, Social and Cultural Rights: A Textbook* (1995), pp. 41–62, at pp. 44–45.

Republics, etc.) when it comes to such a fundamental issue as the conditions for acquiring nationality.[55]

Similarly, few have argued that the exclusion of resident non-Union citizens from the ambit of Article 8b EC Treaty would constitute prohibited discrimination under the CCPR or ECHR. With respect to municipal elections, there is the further consideration that these elections seem to fall outside the ambit of Article 3 of Protocol No. 1 to the ECHR, and may fall outside Article 25 CCPR.[56] But one should note the discussions in the Nordic countries on the electoral rights of foreign nationals in local elections, which have gradually led to an abolition of a distinction initially made in the 1970s between "Nordic" and other nationals. This development has been grounded in general notions of fairness and equal treatment rather than a legal non-discrimination principle, but it may still be a sign of possible future legal developments.[57]

Article 8b EC Treaty, supplemented by the 1994 EC Directive on municipal elections as well as the 1993 Directive on European elections, provides, as already mentioned above, for the possibility of "derogations" "where warranted by problems specific to a Member State". One may discuss whether the derogations specified in the Directives go too far. There also seem to be grounds for questioning the exclusion allowed in the 1994 Directive on municipal elections for the right of non-nationals to "hold the office of elected head, deputy or member of the governing college of the executive of a basic local government unit" (Article 5(3)). This limitation, prompted by French concerns in particular (the French Constitution prohibits non-nationals from holding the office of mayor), applies, in principle, to all Member States and thus does not fall under the express derogation clause in Article 8b EC Treaty. In principle, one could surmise the ECJ declaring this provision, or some aspects of the derogation clauses, of the Directives to be in contravention of Articles 6 and 8b EC Treaty,[58] possibly taking also into account Articles 25

---

[55] See I/A Court H. R., *Proposed Amendments to the Naturalization Provisions of the Constitution of Costa Rica*, Advisory Opinion OC-4/84 of 19 Jan. 1984, Series A no. 4, pp. 106–109; and Rosas, "Nationality and Citizenship in a Changing European and World Order", in Suksi (ed.), *Law under Exogenous Influences* (1994), pp. 30–59, at pp. 43, 54.

[56] Rosas, "Democracy and Human Rights", loc. cit., note 11, p. 47.

[57] See also the 1992 Council of Europe Convention on the Participation of Foreigners in Public Life at the Local Level, *supra* at note 25.

[58] The Committee on Institutional Affairs of the European Parliament in its Opinion for the Committee on Legal Affairs and Citizens' Rights (Report of the Committee on Legal Affairs and Citizens' Rights, A4–0011/94, 6 Oct. 1994, pp. 22–23) argued that the exclusion clause "is in principle contrary to Article 6 of the EC Treaty and to the case law of the Court of Justice ...., which demand absolute equality of treatment with the nationals of the Member State involved for all

and 26 CCPR.[59] In this context, it should be noted that the derogation introduced in the Directive on municipal elections with respect to Belgium, as well as the implementation of this Directive in Spain, has been questioned recently in the European Parliament.[60]

Apart from the above derogation and exclusion clauses, a number of more specific practical and technical problems could be envisaged concerning the way European and municipal elections are run. If Union citizens who are not nationals of the country of election file grievances, complex issues could come up relating to which aspects of the election process are covered by Article 8b EC Treaty and the supplementing Directives and which again by domestic law.[61]

If it is a matter of domestic law, the Strasbourg organs might be competent as far as European elections are concerned (possibly also in case the application is submitted by a non-national[62]), and it is not to be excluded that the Human Rights Committee acting under the CCPR might also be competent with regard to local elections. The competence of the ECJ would also come into play in so far as the situation should be seen as coming under the

---

persons in a situation subject to Community law and which prohibit any discrimination based on nationality; furthermore, there is no justification to be found in Article 8b(1)". See also the Own-Initiative Opinion of the Economic and Social Committee, 14 Sept. 1994, CES(94) 1026, p. 2. In these Opinions, reference was made to the Joined Cases C-92/92 and C-326/92, *Phil Collins* v *Imtrat Handelsgesellschaft* and *Patricia Im- und Export Verwaltungsgesellschaft* v *EMI Electrola,* [1993] ECR I-5145, where copyrights and related rights were deemed to fall within the scope of application of the Treaty "particularly by reason of their effects on trade in goods and services in the Community" (ibid., para. 27).

[59] It will be noted that on this point there would be much less ground for an application to the European Commission of Human Rights, as the mandate of this body is limited to the ECHR, which (Art. 3 of Protocol No. 1) probably does not regulate municipal elections at all, and also in so far as acts of the Community (such as the Directive in question) fall outside the competence of the Strasbourg organs (on the latter question, see below).

[60] Oral Questions to the Council B4–0332/95 and B4–0333/95, to the Commission B4–0334/95 and B4–0335/95. Draft resolution on Oral Question B–0322/95, B4–0405/95.

[61] To take but one example: According to Art. 6(1) of the 1994 Directive non-nationals entitled to stand as candidates because they are Union citizens "shall be subject to the same conditions concerning incompatibility as apply, under the laws of the Member State of residence, to nationals of that State". The substance is then regulated in domestic law, but the formal basis for the rule concerning non-nationals is in EC secondary legislation.

[62] This is linked to the question as to whether the "people" referred to in Art. 3 of Protocol No. 1 to the ECHR includes EU citizens who are not nationals of the state where the European elections are taking place. See *supra,* at note 30.

umbrella of Article 8b, including both its derogations clauses[63] and the relevant Directives.[64] In such cases, there may be overlapping jurisdiction between the Strasbourg and Luxembourg organs.

If there is no available national "court or tribunal" within the meaning of Article 177 EC Treaty, and thus no possibility to request a preliminary ruling, the matter might be raised before the Strasbourg organs as a question of failing national remedies.[65] In so far as the matter at hand is clearly determined by Article 8b EC Treaty and/or one of the two Directives, the question arises as to whether this would preclude the competence of the Strasbourg organs. In theory, Strasbourg jurisdiction cannot be ruled out[66] but on substance, it is

---

[63] Cf. the discussion in de Búrca, loc. cit., note 45, 301–303, on a possible distinction in the case law between EC exceptions to general principles and rules which are based on express Treaty provisions (such as the derogation clause of Art. 8b) and exceptions which are developed by the ECJ itself. Cf. Clapham, op. cit., note 6, pp. 31–55.

[64] In so far as the provisions of the Directives are not given direct effect, there is still the obligation of national courts, developed in Cases 14/83, *Von Colson and Kamann* v *Land Nordrhein-Westfalen,* [1984] ECR 1891; and C-106/89, *Marleasing,* [1990] ECR I-4135, to interpret, as far as possible, the national law in the light of the wording and the purpose of the directive. Failure to implement the Directives could, of course, also lead to legal action against the Member State itself under Arts. 169 to 171 EC Treaty.

[65] Art. 13 ECHR. The applicability of Art. 6 (right to fair trial when it comes to the determination of "civil rights and obligations") is more open to doubt. Recent Strasbourg case law goes far in including rights under public law in the concept of civil rights and obligations, but one of the leading cases, Eur. Court H. R., *Schuler-Zraggen v. Switzerland* judgment of 24 June 1993, Series A no. 263, refers to the fact that the applicant was claiming "an individual, *economic* right flowing from specific rules laid down in a federal statute" (para. 46, emphasis added). But if there *is* an available national court or tribunal, its failure to request a preliminary ruling might become an issue under Art. 6 ECHR as well (see *supra,* note 43).

[66] If the application is directed against the European Communities, the complaint lies outside the Strasbourg Commission's jurisdiction *ratione personae,* as the Communities are not a Contracting Party to the ECHR, Application No. 8030/77, *C.F.D.T. v. European Communities,* Decisions and Reports 13 (1979), p. 231, Application No. 13539/88, *Dufay v. European Communities,* Decision of 19 Jan. 1989. But if the application is directed against a State Party to the ECHR, the transfer of powers to the European Communities "does not necessarily exclude a state's responsibility under the Convention with regard to the exercise of the transferred powers", Application No. 13258/87, *M & Co. v. Federal Republic of Germany,* Decisions and Reports 64 (1990), p. 138, at p. 145. See also Application No. 21090/92, *Heinz v. Contracting States also Parties to the European Patent Convention,* Decisions and Reports 76-A (1994), p. 125. In such cases a kind of presumption seems to have been established. which would respect decisions taken by an international organization "provided that within that organisation fundamental rights will receive an equivalent protection" (*M & Co v. Federal Republic of Germany,* Decisions and Reports 64 (1990), at p. 145). In such cases the European Commission of Human Rights will normally declare the application incompatible with the provisions of the Convention *ratione materiae.*

hard to imagine cases where Article 3 of Protocol No. 1 to the ECHR could offer concrete assistance to an applicant.[67]

5   CONCLUDING REMARKS

The preceding discussion has shown that Article 8b EC Treaty and the two supplementing Directives of 1993 and 1994 cannot be viewed in isolation but should be seen in the framework not only of European political integration in general but also political rights as human rights. The significant restrictions of Article 8b EC Treaty, excluding national elections and electoral rights for third-country nationals, can be seen as signs of the lower status that political integration and political rights as human rights enjoy as compared to the economic and social aspects of European integration.

It has, on the other hand, also been demonstrated that there may, in some instances, arise situations of overlapping jurisdictions between the Strasbourg and Luxembourg organs with respect to electoral rights and also that, at least in theory, a number of procedural and substantive problems can be envisaged in this respect. The pending idea of the Communities acceding to the ECHR[68] would probably not add much to the substantive law in this field but could clarify issues of jurisdiction and procedure.

As to the basic ideological issues involved, and looking at things in a more long-term perspective, it is the view of the present author that we should move in the direction of including in the electorate all those who have been allowed by the state to take up residence in the country.[69] This would, at least in the long run, involve a broadening of the concept of "people" appearing in

---

[67] In the sphere of electoral rights, Member States are granted a wide margin of appreciation. See *Mathieu-Mohin and Clerfayt,* loc. cit., note 14; and Rosas, "Democracy and Human Rights", loc. cit., note 11, pp. 41–42; de Meyer, loc. cit., note 26, pp. 553–569.

[68] Communication by the Commission of 3 Dec. 1990 on Community Accession to the European Convention on Human Rights, SEC(90)2087; Report of the Committee on Legal Affairs and Citizens' Rights of the European Parliament, 8 Dec. 1993, A3–0421/93. An Opinion requested in April 1994 by the Council is pending before the ECJ, Opinion 2/94 (The Proceedings of the Court of Justice and Court of First Instance of the European Communities, No. 14/1994).

[69] Michael Walzer goes further and asserts as a moral principle that every person allowed to enter the state territory should be offered the opportunity of nationality/citizenship (Walzer, *Spheres of Justice: A Defence of Pluralism & Equality* (1983), p. 62). See also Rosas, loc. cit., note 55, pp. 55–57; Rosas, loc. cit., note 5, pp. 152–153.

Article 3 of Protocol No. 1 to the ECHR.[70] One should not, on the other hand, assume that states will readily agree to such developments, at least as far as national elections are concerned.[71]

What is imaginable, as a first step, is that Article 8b EC Treaty be amended at the 1996 Conference, so as to include third-country nationals residing in the EU area in the electorate of the European elections and/or the municipal elections held in the 15 Member States. Such an amendment could be undertaken without amending Article 8 on the concept of European citizenship. Admittedly, this would underline a multifaceted nature of nationality and citizenship (various "citizenships") and could be said to further increase the complexity of these issues. But perhaps such a pluralist approach is called for in an increasingly complex and multi-layered world?

---

[70] As has been pointed out by van Dijk and van Hoof, op. cit., note 23, pp. 483–484, "it can hardly be argued that those aliens who have been residents of a given country for a long time and as such contribute to the economic, social and cultural life of that country, without, for whatever reasons, having been naturalized, do not belong to the 'people' of that country". See also *supra* at note 30.

[71] Rosas, loc. cit, note 5, pp. 135, pp. 148–155. Even as far as local elections are concerned, the German Constitutional Court held in judgments of 31 Oct. 1990 (BVerfGE 83, 37; BVerfGE 83, 60), that is, before the Maastricht amendments to Art. 28 of the German Constitution, that the inclusion of foreigners in the electorate was unconstitutional, as foreigners could not be included in the concept of the German people.

9 WORKERS' RIGHTS OF PARTICIPATION

Catherine Barnard

1 INTRODUCTION

Rights and the founding Treaties of the European Community have traditionally been unhappy bedfellows. The Treaty of Rome, particularly in the context
of social policy, was not couched in the language of rights. Article 2 EEC
Treaty contained the general aspiration that the Community should have as its
task an "accelerated raising of the standard of living". However, this was only
to be achieved as a direct consequence of economic growth caused by the
creation of a common market and the progressive approximation of the
economic policies of the Member States.[1] Thirty-five years later, with the
signing of the Treaty on European Union (TEU), there has been no radical
shift in emphasis. Article 2 EC Treaty now also talks of achieving "a high
level of employment and social protection" resulting from the establishment
of a common market *and an economic and monetary union*. This economic
neo-liberalism has nipped "rights-speak" in the bud. While a title of the Treaty
on social policy does exist,[2] its provisions are largely exhortatory and confer
little by way of direct rights on Community citizens.[3] Article 119 is the
exception to this but, far from talking in the language of rights conferred on
the individual, it is drafted in terms of a governmental obligation. It requires
that "Each *Member State* shall ... maintain the principle that men and women
should receive equal pay for equal work" (emphasis added).

The only genuine "rights" found in the Treaty relate to the fundamental
economic freedoms: the right for workers to move freely within the Community to accept offers of employment, the right to stay in the Member State
during employment, the right to remain in the territory of the Member State

---

[1] Shanks, "Introductory Article: The Social Policy of the European Community", 14 CML Rev.
(1977), 375–383.

[2] Title VIII.

[3] Hallstein, *Europe in the Making* (1972), p. 119, cited in Watson, "The Community Social
Charter", 28 CML Rev. (1991), 37–68, at 39.

N. A. Neuwahl and A. Rosas (eds.), The European Union and Human Rights, 185–206.

after having been employed[4] and the right of establishment for the self-employed.[5] However, even these rights were not originally conceived as social provisions but rather as a means of facilitating movement of one of the factors of production to areas where work was available.[6] It required action by the Court of Justice of the European Communities (ECJ) to invest these economic rights with a social element.[7] Thus, in *Kempf*,[8] for example, the Court did not limit the exercise of the right of free movement to financially independent full-time workers but extended it to part-timers whose income fell below the minimum level of subsistence and who required financial assistance provided out of public funds. Moreover, the ECJ has even been prepared to extend the rights conferred on workers to their family members, explaining that this encourages workers to exercise their rights of free movement[9] and furthers the integration of workers and their families into the host Member State.[10]

The social dimension of these economic rights was made more explicit in the earlier case of *Defrenne (No. 2)*,[11] concerning the application and interpretation of Article 119. The ECJ expressly recognized that Article 119 pursued a double aim. First, it was designed to avoid a situation in which undertakings established in states which have implemented the principle of equal pay suffer a competitive disadvantage in intra-Community competition as compared with undertakings established in states which have failed to eliminate discrimination against women workers as regards pay.[12] Secondly, the Court said that Article 119 formed part of the social objectives of the

---

[4] Art. 48(3)(a)–(d).

[5] Art. 52(2).

[6] Spaak Report, Rapport des Chefs des Délégations, Comité Intergouvernemental, 21 April 1956, at 19–20 and 60–61. Arts. 48–51 were complemented by Art. 123 setting up the European Social Fund which was designed to increase the geographic and occupational mobility of workers.

[7] Case 41/74, *Van Duyn* v *Home Office*, [1974] ECR 1337 (Art. 48); and Case 2/74, *Reyners* v *Belgium*, [1974] ECR 631 (Art. 52). These rights were developed further by subsequent secondary legislation, e.g., Regulation 1612/68/EEC (O.J. Sp. Ed. 1968, L 257/2, 475), Directive 68/360/EEC (O.J. Sp. Ed. 1968, L 257/13, 485), Regulation 1251/70/EEC (O.J. Sp. Ed. 1970, L 142/24, 402).

[8] Case 139/85, *Kempf* v *Staatssecretaris van Justitie*, [1986] ECR 1741.

[9] Case 94/84, *ONEM* v *Deak*, [1985] ECR 1873.

[10] See, e.g., Joined Cases 389 and 390/87, *Echternach and Another* v *Minister for Education and Science*, [1989] ECR 723.

[11] Case 43/75, *Defrenne* v *Sabena*, [1976] ECR 455.

[12] Art. 120 EC Treaty on paid holiday schemes was also introduced largely at the behest of the French who feared that the very specific protection afforded to workers by French labour law would put France at a competitive disadvantage.

Community "which is not merely an economic union, but is at the same time intended ... to ensure social progress and seek the constant improvement of living and working conditions of their people". The ECJ then concluded, with a direct reference to the language of rights, that:[13]

> the fact that certain provisions of the Treaty are formally addressed to the Member States *does not prevent rights from being conferred at the same time on any individual* who has an interest in the performance of the duties thus laid down.

It was therefore able to decide that "Article 119 is directly applicable and may thus give rise to individual rights which the courts must protect".

The constitutional[14] role of the ECJ, converting international obligations into effective rights enforceable by individuals,[15] is perhaps one of the greatest achievements of the Community legal system. The development of the combined doctrines of supremacy[16] and direct effect[17] revolutionized the notion of rights, particularly in the employment context. Employees could now enforce their "rights" to non-discriminatory dismissal,[18] to equality in occupational pension age,[19] and to have their contractual rights transferred on a transfer of an undertaking.[20]

In addition to ensuring the effectiveness of substantive rights the ECJ has also sought to ensure that the rights it has recognized are effectively enforced

---

[13] Para. 31 (emphasis added). See also Case 26/62, *Van Gend en Loos* v *Nederlandse Administratie der Belastingen,* [1963] ECR 1, where the ECJ stated: "Community law therefore not only imposes obligations on individuals but is also intended to confer upon them rights which become part of their legal heritage. These rights arise not only where they are expressly granted by the Treaty, but also by reason of obligations which the Treaty imposes in a clearly defined way upon individuals as well as the Member States".

[14] See Chapter 10 in this volume.

[15] For the ECJ's recognition of this see *Opinion 1/91, Re the Draft Treaty on a European Economic Area,* [1991] ECR I-6079, [1992] 1 CMLR 245, para. 21: "the EEC Treaty, albeit concluded in the form of an international agreement, none the less constitutes the constitutional charter of a Community based on the rule of law".

[16] See, i.a., Case 6/64, *Costa* v *ENEL,* [1964] ECR 585.

[17] See, i.a., Case 26/62, loc. cit., note 13; and Case 152/84, *Marshall* v *Southampton and South-West Hampshire Area Health Authority,* [1986] ECR 723.

[18] Art. 5(1) of Directive 76/207 and Case 152/84, loc. cit., note 17.

[19] Art. 119 and Case C-262/88, *Barber,* [1990] ECR I-1889.

[20] Art. 3(1) of Directive 77/187 and Case 105/84, *Foreningen af Arbejdsledere i Danmark* v *Danmols Inventar,* [1985] ECR 2639.

and remedied by the national system. Relying on Article 5 EC Treaty and the principle of effectiveness, it has required national courts to ensure both that Community law rules take full and immediate effect, and that the rights conferred by Community law on individuals are protected.[21] Moreover, remedies for breach of a Community law right must be genuine and effective.[22] Most recently, in the important judgment in *Francovich*,[23] the ECJ required that Member States are obliged to make good loss and damage caused to individuals as a result of breaches of Community law for which the states can be held responsible. It reasoned that state liability is necessary because:[24]

> the full effectiveness of Community rules would be impaired and the protection of the rights which they grant would be weakened if individuals were unable to obtain redress when their rights are infringed by a breach of Community law for which a Member State can be held responsible.

This judicial activism was precipitated by a reassessment of priorities by the Member States at the Paris Summit in 1972 where they insisted that as much importance was attached "to vigorous action in the social field as to the achievement of economic union ... it is essential to ensure the increased involvement of labour and management in the economic and social decisions of the Community". This change of attitude can be explained in part by the realization that the Community had to be seen as more than a mere device to enable capitalists to exploit the Common Market; the Community needed a human face to persuade its citizens that the social consequences of growth were being effectively tackled.[25] Failure to do so might have jeopardized the whole process of economic integration.

Similar sentiments inspired the Community to draw up the Social Charter 20 years later, on the back of the 1992 programme, in an attempt to secure the

---

[21] Case 106/77, *Amministrazione delle Finanze dello Stato v Simmenthal,* [1978] ECR 629, para. 16; and Case C-213/89, *Factortame and Others,* [1990] ECR I-2433, para. 19.

[22] Case 14/83, *Von Colson and Kamann v Land Nordrhein-Westfalen,* [1984] ECR 1891; Case 222/84, *Johnston v Chief Constable of the RUC,* [1986] ECR 1651; Case C-271/91, *Marshall v Southampton and South West Area Health Authority (Marshall No. 2),* [1993] 3 CMLR 293; and, more specifically on enhancing enforceability see Case C-208/90, *Emmott,* [1991] ECR I-4269.

[23] Cases C-6/90 and C-9/90, *Francovich and Others,* [1991] ECR I-5357. See Lewis and Moore, "Duties, Directives and Damages in European Community Law", (1993) *Public Law,* 151–170; and Steiner, "From Direct Effects to Francovich; Shifting Means of Enforcement of Community Law", 18 EL Rev. (1993), 3–22.

[24] Cases C-6/90 and C-9/90, loc. cit., note 23, para. 34.

[25] Shanks, loc. cit., note 1, 378.

support of the Community's citizens for the Single Market programme. As the Commission observed in its Internal Market White Paper:[26]

> the inevitable restructuring of European industry will be more efficiently achieved and necessary change more readily accepted if all the interests concerned are involved and committed to the process. In particular the role of the social dialogue is a vital one; it is essential that the workers of the Community should be able to recognize the internal market as the one they have helped to create and as one in which their interests are appropriately safe-guarded.

The Social Charter lists twelve "fundamental social rights of workers". These include the right to freedom of movement, the right to be free to choose and engage in an occupation, the right to adequate social protection, the right of association, the right to join or not to join a trade union, the right to conclude collective agreements and the right to strike. Drawing on the ILO Conventions and the European Social Charter 1961, the Community Social Charter represented the first attempt, at Community level, to codify social rights. Its effectiveness was, however, significantly undermined by the fact that it was signed by only ten of the twelve Member States,[27] and, in any case was merely a political, rather than a legally binding, declaration.[28] Some commen-tators were disappointed with its content:[29] Vogel-Polsky, for example, described it as putting "non-decision into a concrete form".[30] Others, by contrast, were deeply concerned about the possible anti-competitive effects on community industry.[31]

This tension between rights and competition is the focus of this chapter.

---

[26] COM (88) 320, at 2.

[27] Denmark abstained on a technicality and the UK voted against the Charter.

[28] For a contrary view, see Riley, "The European Social Charter and Community Law", 14 EL Rev. (1989), 80–86; and the reply by Gould, "The European Social Charter and Community Law. A Comment", 14 EL Rev. (1989), 223–226.

[29] See, e.g., Bercusson, "The European Community's Charter of Fundamental Social Rights of Workers", 53 MLR (1990), 624–642; Silvia, "The Social Charter of the European Community: A Defeat for European Labor", 44 *Industrial and Labour Relations Review* (1990–1991), 626–643.

[30] "What Future Is there for a Social Europe Following the Strasbourg Summit?", 19 *International Law Journal* (1990), 65–80.

[31] Addison and Siebert, "The Social Charter: Whatever Next?", 30 *British Journal of Industrial Relations* (1992), 495–514. See also Addison and Siebert, "The Social Charter of the European Community: Evolution and Controversies", 44 *Industrial and Labour Relations Review* (1990–1991), 597–625.

It considers, first, whether workers should have Community law rights and, secondly, how the Commission has addressed this tension in the context of worker participation and, thirdly, the future direction of workers' rights at Community level.

2 WHY SHOULD WORKERS HAVE RIGHTS AT COMMUNITY LEVEL?

The desire to encourage worker participation in the Single Market programme and to confer benefits on them has two purposes: first, to ensure the welfare of workers at work and, secondly, to prevent distortions of competition. As suggested above, the dual purpose of Community legislation was identified at an early stage by the ECJ in *Defrenne (No. 2)* and more recently affirmed by Vasso Papandreou, then Commissioner for social affairs. Community action, she said, may be necessary:[32]

> either because there is no other way—as is the case with the free movement of workers or the provision of minimum requirements for health and safety—or because the necessary deregulation at national level requires some kind of Community framework so as to avoid unfair competition—as may be the case with the provisions governing work contracts.

Such mixed motives are not unique to the European Community: broadly speaking the same justifications were advanced for international labour standards by Robert Owen more than 170 years ago.[33]

As far as the welfare aspect of Community social policy is concerned, the necessity for such action is recognized by Article 117 which provides that "Member States agree upon the need to promote improved working conditions and an improved standard of living for workers" and supported by statistics—in the field of health and safety Community figures reveal that 7,617 fatal accidents occurred at work in 1989 and that 10 million people from a

---

[32] Vasso Papandreou, "Moving On", *Social Europe* 1/90, 8–9. See also the Opinion of the Economic and Social Committee on the Social Aspects of the Internal Market (87/C 356/08) which talked of the need for basic social rules to "avoid market distortions and provide industrial and economic decision-makers with a stable basis making it possible to extend social dialogue".

[33] See Wedderburn, "The Social Charter in Britain—Labour Law and Labour Courts", 54 MLR (1991), 1–47, at 15; and Ramm, Chapter 7, in Hepple (ed.) *The Making of Labour Law in Europe* (1986).

workforce of 138 million suffer occupational accidents and diseases every year.[34] Consequently, Community legislation based on Article 118a has been adopted on a wide range of health and safety matters, including a general framework directive,[35] directives prescribing minimum health and safety standards of the workplace,[36] and directives laying down minimum standards for the use by workers of machines and equipment,[37] personal protective equipment,[38] manual handling of loads,[39] and visual display units.[40] More controversial directives have also been passed giving protection to pregnant workers and workers who have recently given birth[41] and limiting the working time of large groups of workers.[42] Not only are these forms of worker protection morally justifiable, they are also supported by economic necessity: the total figure for compensation and medical costs arising from occupational accidents and diseases is ECU 20 billion every year to which can be added indirect costs in the form of wages, material costs, consultants' fees and legal fees.[43]

Such economic justification for action is equally applicable at the micro-level of individual businesses and, on a macro-level, across the Community. Community wide action in the employment field has been necessary to avoid distortions of competition caused by a liberalized and integrated internal market but a deregulated and decentralized European labour market. The desire to create a level playing field across the Community has been prompted in part by concern over social dumping, the phenomenon of standards of social protection being depressed, or at least prevented from rising, by increased competition after 1992 from states with substantially lower standards.[44] The fear is that a liberalized internal market without a floor of employment rights

---

[34] Commission of the European Communities, "Health and Safety at Work: A Challenge to Europe".

[35] Directive 89/391/EEC, O.J. 1989, L 183.

[36] Directive 89/654/EEC, O.J. 1989, L 393.

[37] Directive 89/655/EEC, O.J. 1989, L 393.

[38] Directive 89/656/EEC, O.J. 1989, L 393.

[39] Directive 90/269/EEC, O.J. 1990, L 156.

[40] Directive 90/270/EEC, O.J. 1990, L 156.

[41] Directive 92/85/EEC, O.J. 1992, L 348.

[42] Directive 93/104/EC, O.J. 1993, L 307/18.

[43] Commission of the European Communities, loc. cit., note 34.

[44] Mosely, "The Social Dimension of European Integration", 129 *International Labour Review* (1990), 147–163, at 160.

might lead peripheral Member States, such as Spain, Greece and Portugal, to take advantage of the freedom to regulate their own social policy, in particular their relatively low wage status *vis-à-vis* Germany and the other northern European countries (see Table 1), to attract inward investment. This would simply lead to potential domestic unemployment being exported to other Member States[45] and potentially exerting a downward pressure on wages and working conditions in the more prosperous states.

Table 1: Hourly labour costs in industry in the EC, 1990, in ECUs

Germany	20.08
Belgium	19.30
Netherlands	17.47
Denmark	17.19
France*	15.27
Luxembourg+	14.48
Italy*	14.24
UK	12.20
Ireland	11.64
Spain	11.30
Greece*	5.24
Portugal	3.57

* 1988 figures
\+ 1989 figures

Source: Eurostat (1992)

The prophets of doom warning of social dumping appeared vindicated by the much publicized Hoover affair. In January 1993 Hoover, the vacuum cleaner manufacturer, announced that it was closing its factory in Dijon with a loss of 600 of the 700 jobs and relocating its activities, not to one of the Mediterranean States, but to Cambuslang in Scotland. The United Kingdom's determination to regulate its own labour policies—or rather to deregulate its labour

---

[45] Teague, "Constitution or Regime? The Social Dimension to the 1992 Project", 27 *British Journal of Industrial Relations* (1990), 310–329, at 322.

market ensuring maximum flexibility of the workforce,[46] in line with Japanese and American models[47] had prompted its refusal to sign either the Social Charter 1989 or the Social Chapter of the TEU. This was widely cited as the reason for Hoover's decision.[48]

The Commission has recognized that the risk of social dumping exists but has attempted to minimize its significance. It argues that social dumping can arise in specific sectors, particularly those involving relatively unskilled activities—certain food processing industries, transport, building and public works—and other cases which are "at all events very much in the minority".[49] Nevertheless, the emphasis on the desire to prevent distortions of competition seems to have eclipsed the welfarist motive, prompting Davies to observe that subservience to the process of market integration fatally hinders the development of a rationale for Community action in the social field.[50] The proposed directives on atypical work provide a good example of the Commission's overriding concern for a level playing field.[51] In the context of *indirect* costs (for example dismissal protection, social security contributions and taxation), but, surprisingly, not in the context of direct wage costs,[52] the Commission argued that if a Member State could produce with lower labour costs than the other Member States "it will have a comparative advantage which cannot be considered permanent and runs counter to Commission interests".[53]

---

[46] *Hansard,* 23 July 1993, at 630. See also Gospel, "The Single European Market and Industrial Relations: An Introduction", 30 *British Journal of Industrial Relations* (1992), 483–494, at 488. The British Prime Minister, John Major, in the House of Commons at the time of the British parliamentary debate on the ratification of the Treaty on European Union, argued that "Europe must compete with the United States and Japan as well. All across Europe people know that Europe is losing competitiveness at present. Twenty years ago the unemployment debate across Europe was 60% of that of the United States. Today it is 60% above the United States."

[47] See further, "Employment: The Challenge to the Nation", Cmnd 9474.

[48] For a comprehensive analysis of the issues relating to the Hoover affair, see "The Hoover Affair and Social Dumping", 230 EIRR, 14.

[49] The Social Dimension of the Internal Market, *Social Europe,* Sp. edn 1988, at 66; Bull. EC 9–1988, at 8.

[50] Davies, "The Emergence of European Labour Law", in McCarthy (ed.), *Legal Intervention in Industrial Relations: Gains and Losses* (1992), pp. 313–359, at p. 346.

[51] COM (90) 228 final, SYN 280, SYN 281, 12.

[52] For a criticism of this approach see Davies, loc. cit., note 50, pp. 346–347; and Deakin, "Integration through Law? The Legal and Economic Foundations of European Social Policy", forthcoming in a collection of essays edited by Addison and Siebert.

[53] Para. 25.

3   WHY SHOULD WORKERS NOT HAVE RIGHTS AT COMMUNITY LEVEL?

In much academic literature written by labour lawyers it is taken as read that workers' Community rights are beneficial and, given the deregulatory stance of certain Member States, the Community's commitment to workers' rights is to be encouraged. There is, however, a growing body of literature which suggests that Community social legislation is detrimental to the Community's long-term interests and, in particular to the development of the poorer, southern states. The most significant criticism levelled at Community social legislation is that it represents an indirect form of social protectionism intended to favour the best placed, largely northern European countries at the expense of their poorer neighbours. As *The Economist* has graphically described it, imposing higher standards on countries such as Greece and Portugal may well result in "killing them with kindness".[54]

Kierman and Beim explain this phenomenon in terms of comparative advantage. They argue that countries with cheap labour have a comparative advantage over wealthier countries in terms of the production of certain types of goods.[55] The figures taken from Eurostat detailing Community labour costs are reproduced in Table 1 above and Table 2 below.

Columns one and two of Table 2 show the earnings of manual and non-manual workers expressed according to the Purchasing Power Standard (PPS). The third column contains a comparison in ECUs of the total labour costs for industry, including both direct costs (all payments to employees including wages, bonuses, payments for days not worked or benefits in kind) and indirect costs (principally social security contributions and other expenses including fees for training). The wide differences in costs between the Member States immediately becomes apparent—Portugal offers the lowest hourly cost value (2.98) and Germany the highest (18.27). This highlights Portugal's comparative advantage: there are clear incentives for companies in need of low-skilled or unskilled labour to open operations in Portugal.

---

[54] *The Economist,* 23 June 1990, 17.

[55] Kierman and Beim, "On the Economic Realities of the European Social Charter and the Social Dimension of EC 1992", (1992) *Duke Journal of Comparative and International Labour Law,* 149–162.

Table 2: Earnings of manual and non-manual workers and a comparison of hourly labour costs

Country	manual workers' earnings (hourly rate)	non-manual workers' earnings (monthly rate)	Comparison of hourly labour costs in ECUs
Belgium	9.90	2489	17.82
Denmark	11.90	2314	15.51
Germany	10.77	2670	18.27
Greece	6.12	1561	n/a
Spain	8.40	2002	n/a
France	7.39	2162	15.27
Ireland	9.16	2448	10.62
Italy	8.91	1981	14.24
Luxembourg	10.65	3283	13.61
Netherlands	10.59	2441	16.37
Portugal	3.76	1076	2.98
UK	10.48	2796	10.87

Source: Eurostat (1992), pp. 126–127

According to Kierman and Beim, such investment paves the way for future prosperity. For example, in 1970 Japanese hourly wages were $0.94. Twenty years later the average wage is over $12 an hour. The relatively low wages and willing workforce gave Japan in the early 1970s a clear comparative advantage in the manufacture of certain goods, particularly cars. Japan was able to offer quality products at relatively low prices. As sales increased there was a concurrent increase in demand for Japanese labour, an increase which has bid up wages and other compensation for Japanese workers. Furthermore, the increased demand for Japanese labour has prompted Japanese companies to invest more time and money into training workers and to purchasing the most up-to-date machinery and technology for these workers to use, making the workforce even more productive. Kierman and Beim conclude that today

Japan has high cost labour, but that the labour is very productive and extremely competitive.

However, they also argue that the incentive to invest in the southern European countries would be lost if, as a result of Community legislation, employers were obliged to pay higher wages or make greater social security contributions which would provide more generous welfare benefits. This would have the effect of undermining Portugal's comparative advantage, thereby hindering its economic development while at the same time reinforcing the position of strength enjoyed by countries such as Germany and Denmark.

While this argument is seductive it is also misleading. For example, the link between low pay and competitiveness has been disputed, not least because low pay and conditions do not foster a commitment to the enterprise.[56] Moreover, the Community has strictly limited competence to regulate wages: provisions relating to pay are expressly excluded from the Social Chapter[57] and thus any measure would have to be proposed under Articles 100 or 235 EC Treaty, both of which require unanimity in Council. So far the Commission has only succeeded in producing a non-binding opinion on an equitable wage.[58]

The focus on direct wage costs also distorts the picture: wage costs form only one element in a decision about where to invest. While labour costs are highly significant in labour intensive industries, their impact is reduced in other sectors. Other factors, such as a good infrastructure, trained workers, technology advances, a good supply network and access to markets, are also important and are not transportable.[59] The productivity of the workforce is another major factor: for example, it was found that in the 1980s German firms were 50 per cent more efficient than their British counterparts where efficiency was measured by labour productivity.[60] This point has also been recognized by the Commission. In its explanatory memorandum accompanying

---

[56] Deakin and Wilkinson, *The Economics of Employment Rights* (Institute of Employment Rights, 1991), esp. pp. 32–33.

[57] Art. 2(6).

[58] COM (93) 388 final.

[59] See, "Europe's Social Insecurity", *The Economist,* 23 June 1990; and Mosely, loc. cit., note 44, at 161.

[60] Hart and Shipman, "The Variation of Productivity within British and German Industries", 40 *The Journal of Industrial Economics* (1992), 417–425. They do, however, point out that while this productivity gap is declining Britain has a longer tail of low productivity plants. These firms will encounter the strongest threat from 1992.

the draft directives on atypical workers,[61] the Commission said that differences between Member States in respect of wage levels, non-wage labour costs and rules on working conditions:[62]

> do not hamper the operation of healthy competition in the Community. The differences in productivity levels attenuate these differences in unit labour costs to a considerable degree. Moreover, other production cost components tend to be higher in the less-developed Member States where nominal costs are the lowest.

Others have recognized the currency of the social dumping debate but argue that while it is possible that high cost producers will be displaced by low cost producers in countries in which wages, social benefits and the direct and indirect costs of social legislation are markedly lower, it is more likely to occur in Korea, Taiwan and China and not in southern Europe.[63] This underlines the importance of *international* labour standards.[64] In recent years the Commission has also recognized the threat posed by the Pacific rim countries to a comprehensive European social policy. Jacques Delors, the former President of the Commission, has acknowledged that there is less difference between Germany and Ireland than between Europe and Korea; social problems, he said, are caused by third countries producing goods at low prices. However, he has argued that this does not mean that the internal market should lead to a reduction in social rights.[65] Instead, the Commission has been forced to reassess the nature of Community action, leading to the development of "a more flexible and pragmatic policy".[66] In other words, the Commission, unlike the UK Government, does not equate flexibility with deregulation,[67] and, as the Social Charter Action programme testifies,[68] the Commission is committed to developing a framework of workers' rights. Recent legislative proposals do, however, contain a considerable degree of

---

[61] COM (90) 228 final.

[62] COM (90) 228, para. 22.

[63] Mosely, loc. cit., note 44, at 160.

[64] See generally, Ewing, *Britain and the ILO* (Institute of Employment Rights, 2nd edn), and minutes of the meeting of the Trade Negotiations Committee at Ministerial Level, Marakesh, 12–15 April 1994, MTN.TNC/MIN(94)/6, 15 April 1994.

[65] Quoted in Hirsch, "Un Volet Social pour le Grand Marché", (1988) RMC, at 371–372.

[66] The Social Dimension of the Internal Market, loc. cit., note 49, at 62.

[67] Hepple, "The Crisis in EEC Labour Law", 16 *International Law Journal* (1987), 77, at 81.

[68] COM (89) 568 final, 29 Nov. 1989.

flexibility which was not found in the social legislation of the 1970s.

4   THE EVOLVING APPROACH OF THE COMMISSION
TOWARDS LEGISLATION: THE CASE OF WORKER PARTICIPATION

The Commission has had a long-standing commitment to worker participation in corporate decision-making.[69] As early as 1970 the Commission made proposals for a European Company Statute (Societas Europea),[70] in the form of a regulation,[71] which included provisions for an obligatory two-tier board with German style worker participation. This combined one-third to one half employee representation on the supervisory board, and the mandatory establishment of a works council. The amended proposal retained the German structure but proposed that the supervisory board be made up of one-third employee representatives and one-third shareholder representatives, with the remainder being co-opted by these two groups.[72]

This proposal was criticized for its detailed prescription and its inflexibility: it prescribed a two-tier board at a time when the company law of Member States such as the United Kingdom and Ireland provided only for a unitary board. It also required the establishment of a works council, at a time when worker participation was not necessarily recognized in this form in other Member States. The United Kingdom and Ireland, for example, adopted an essentially voluntarist approach, leaving the question of the form of worker participation to be determined by employers and employees. As a result, deadlock was reached in Council and discussions were suspended in 1982. A similar fate befell the early drafts of the fifth company law directive, which was also based on the two-tier board system,[73] requiring worker participation on the supervisory board of a public limited company with over 1,000 employees. These early initiatives suggested that exhaustive harmonization which cut so significantly across national tradition would not find sufficient support in the Member States to be adopted.

---

[69] See generally, Kolvenbach, "EEC Company Law Harmonisation and Worker Participation", 11 *University of Pennsylvania Journal of International Business Law* (1990), 709–788.

[70] O.J. No. C 124, 10 Oct. 1970, amended in 1975, COM (75) 150 final.

[71] O.J. 1970, C 124; Bull. EC 8–1970.

[72] Supplement 4/75 – Bull. EC. See also 223 EIRR 25.

[73] O.J. 1972, C 131/44. See Temple Lang, "The Fifth EEC Directive on the Harmonisation of Company Law", 12 CML Rev. (1975), 155–170 and 345–368.

Ten years later the Commission produced an amended and more flexible draft of the fifth company directive which was intended to accommodate the diverse national traditions.[74] It provided for two forms of board structure and a menu of methods of worker participation. Thus, on a two-tier board, it was possible to adopt the German model, where employees elect between one-third and one half of the supervisory board, or the Dutch model, where employee representatives have the right to veto nominations for the supervisory board where the board co-opts its own members. On a unitary board employees could elect between one-third and one half of the non-executive directors. Alternatively, the directive envisaged the establishment of a consultative council or the conclusion of collective agreements guaranteeing a measure of employee participation in the case of either a two-tier or unitary board.

This approach was mirrored in the new draft Regulation on the Statute for a European Company,[75] and the now separate but complementary directive concerning the involvement of employees in the European Company.[76] All of these proposals have been the product of the "company law" approach of DG XV—Financial Institutions and Company Law—of the Commission. Striving towards harmonization of national laws relating to the structure of public limited companies, including participation by employees in the decision-making process, their approach has been relatively detailed and prescriptive.[77] On the other hand, a different "social affairs" approach can be detected in certain legislative proposals by DG V—Employment, Industrial Relationships and Social Affairs—concerning the more limited ambition of informing and consulting the employees of undertakings with complex structures, in particular transnational undertakings.[78] Its approach has been more pragmatic, relying on Member States' existing employee representation arrangements instead of specifying particular models.[79]

The first proposal, known as the Vredeling Directive,[80] required com-

---

[74] O.J. 1983, C 240/2. This was primarily a company law provision, based as it was on Art. 54(3)(g).

[75] O.J. 1989, C 263, amended by O.J. 1991, C 176.

[76] O.J. 1989, C 263, amended by O.J. 1991, C 138.

[77] Hall, "Legislating for Employee Participation: A Case Study of the European Works Council Directive" (Warwick Papers in Industrial Relations, 1992). An expanded version of this paper can be found in Hall, "Behind the European Works Councils Directive: The European Commission's Legislative Strategy", 30 *British Journal of Industrial Relations* (1992), 547–566.

[78] O.J. 1980, C 297; Supplement 3/80 – Bull. EC.

[79] Hall, loc. cit., note 77, at 6.

[80] O.J. 1980, C 297/3.

panies with over 100 employees periodically to disclose company information through local management to employees in subsidiaries or separate establishments. It also provided for consultation with employee representatives over management decisions likely to have a substantial effect on employees' interests. Revised proposals were published in 1983, including a higher workforce threshold (1,000) and wider exemptions for confidential information.[81] Nevertheless both proposals prompted heated opposition and were accused of being on the one hand complicated and unfamiliar, and on the other that they interfered with information and consultation at national level, because the proposal covered large undertakings or groups of undertakings in a single state, and that they would disrupt voluntarist systems of industrial relations.[82] Consequently, in 1986 the Council postponed further consideration of the directive until 1989. Discussions have not since been resumed.[83]

Undeterred, the Commission revised its approach. Recognizing the rapid growth in acquisitions involving Community enterprises from two Member States[84] it decided to focus on the transnational dimension of employee information and consultation,[85] arguing that EC legislation was needed to bridge the gap between increasingly transnational corporate decision-making and workers' nationally defined and nationally-confined information and consultation rights.[86] While this approach was designed to accommodate but not to cut across national practice in respect of employee representation, it seemed to offer, to the Commission at least, the added advantage of providing an acceptable social face to the extensive restructuring associated with the

---

[81] O.J. 1983, C 217. Supplement 2/83 – Bull. EC.

[82] Docksey, "Information and Consultation of Employees: The United Kingdom and the Vredeling Directive", 49 MLR (1986), 281–313.

[83] However, the Council did adopt a resolution relating to the Commission's 1983 proposals which acknowledged the political and economic importance of the problem and emphasized the importance of the social area in the context of the completion of the Community internal market and the need for greater convergence between the rights of employees in the Member States to be informed and consulted about the major decisions in the undertakings concerned. It also urged the Commission to continue its work on the subject, and where appropriate present another proposal on the subject.

[84] In 1988–1989 such operations accounted for 40 per cent of the 492 acquisitions effected by the top 1,000 European industrial enterprises—Commission, The Impact of the Internal Market by Industrial Sector: The Challenge for the Member States, European Economy/Social Europe, Sp. Edn.

[85] See also the Opinion of the Economic and Social Committee on the social consequences of cross-frontier mergers, O.J. 1989, C 329/10.

[86] Gold and Hall, "Statutory European Works Councils: The Final Countdown?", 25 *Industrial Relations Journal* (1994), 177–180.

completion of the internal market.[87]

At first the Commission proposed the establishment of a European Works Council (EWC)[88]—the term used to describe a transnational, pan-European forum of employee representatives within multinational corporate groups for the purposes of information disclosure and consultation with group-level management[89]—in Community scale undertakings[90] or groups of undertakings. Nevertheless, despite the emphasis on the transnational issues that would fall within the EWC's competence and the assertion that EWC was not intended to interfere with existing information, consultation or negotiation rights,[91] the United Kingdom remained implacably opposed to the principle of the directive, arguing that it would undermine existing successful arrangements for consultation particularly at local levels.[92] Consequently, relying on the Social Chapter from which the United Kingdom is excluded the Commission[93] has proposed the establishment of either a "European Committee", the term Works Council having been dropped, *or* a procedure for informing and consulting employees[94] in Community scale undertakings or Community scale groups of undertakings with more than 1,000 employees with at least two establishments in different Member States each employing at least 100 people.[95]

The proposed directive lays down certain minimum or "subsidiary" requirements in the case of failure by the parties to reach an agreement as to the nature, function or powers of the committee, or if management fails to initiate negotiations within six months of the request being made. These requirements are fairly modest and concern the composition and operating

---

[87] "Commission Social Charter Action Programme", *Social Europe* 1/90, 51–76, at 66.

[88] COM (90) 581 final, O.J. 1991, C 39/10, amended proposal COM (91) 345 final. See also, 206 EIRR, at 12.

[89] Gold and Hall, loc. cit., note 86.

[90] Defined as an undertaking with at least 1,000 employees in the EC, and at least two establishments in different Member States with at least 100 employees each.

[91] See, e.g., COM (90) 581, para. 20(iii).

[92] Employment Department, The United Kingdom in Europe: People, Jobs and Progress (Aug. 1993), at 16–17.

[93] 238 EIRR, at 2.

[94] COM (94) 134 final, 13 April 1994.

[95] This transnational requirement is intended to prevent this proposal from having any effect on existing information and consultation procedures in Member States based on national legislation and practices.

methods of the committee, requiring as a minimum one information and consultation meeting per year on the basis of a report drawn up by central management. It is striking that despite the complex legislative history of this directive its substance has remained largely intact. Its provisions draw heavily on the structure of the French and German Works Councils but they lack the sophisticated codetermination principles found in the German system.

When contrasted with the earlier Vredeling Directive the flexibility conferred by the 1994 proposal is striking. In the past the principal criticism of the directive has been that it is too rigid and bureaucratic and incompatible with decentralized management structures. This problem has largely been addressed by the role envisaged for the Member States and the social partners.[96]

This directive is an example of the more recent trend away from rigid and prescriptive measures to more flexibility and choice. The Commission has concentrated on the transnational dimension of information and consultation arrangements, but, using the directive as a vehicle, has conferred power on the Member States to determine the details of the legislation and has encouraged management and employee representatives to negotiate the nature, functions and powers of the information and consultation bodies. This approach does contain sufficient flexibility to allow the integration of European standards into existing national industrial relations frameworks. This is entirely consistent with the application of the principle of subsidiarity, minimizing the normative content of Community legislation and maximizing the scope for devolved regulation by means of national legislation or agreements between the social partners. Moreover, consistent with the notion of a floor of rights the directive lays down minimum requirements upon which Member States are free to improve.[97] This trend was set by Article 118a which provides that the Council shall adopt "by means of directives, minimum requirements" to help encourage improvements especially in the working environment, as regards health and safety and is apparent in the framework directive on health and safety and its daughters. Article 1(3) of Directive 89/391 is typical. It provides that "this directive shall be without prejudice to existing or future national and Community provisions which are more favourable to protection of the safety and health of workers at work". Similarly, Article 10(1) requires that the employer must inform workers and/or their representatives of health and safety risks "in accordance with national laws and/or practices". These practices might differ in each Member State—ranging from formalized works councils

---

[96] Art. 12(3).

[97] Art. 4(3).

to informal information procedures—but, in accordance with the principle of mutual recognition,[98] all national practices are equally valid.

While partial harmonization has secured agreement in areas where legislation might otherwise have been blocked, this approach is not without its drawbacks. First, it is not clear at what level minimum standards are to be set. Since upward harmonization is beyond the financial capacities of poorer countries it is inevitable that minimum standards will be set at a lower level than those found in more prosperous Member States. Thus, instead of seeking out best practice[99] the Community is heading for the lowest common denominator approach which may result in creeping deregulation as firms are able to escape or threaten to escape, statutory or collectively agreed social protection by relocating elsewhere in the Community.[100] Secondly, it is increasingly the case that Member States negotiate significant derogations from the rights conferred by a directive. For example, in the course of the negotiations for the Working Time Directive the United Kingdom ensured that doctors in training would not be covered by the directive and secured the concession that, subject to certain administrative requirements Member States need not apply Article 6 on the maximum 48-hour week.[101] Thirdly, where the drafting of norms or implementation is delegated to the social partners the position of non-unionized members of the workforce remains uncertain. Unlike Belgium, the United Kingdom has no provision which grants *erga omnes* effects to collective agreements.[102]

5   THE WAY FORWARD?

If, as has been suggested, the rationale for Community legislation is uncertain and the legislative approach itself proves unsatisfactory it may be that it is now necessary to reassess the Community's approach to workers' rights. Perhaps the time has come, with the advent of the intergovernmental conference in 1996 and in the wake of the Commission's Green Paper, to demonstrate the

---

[98] This approach was first identified by the ECJ in Case 120/78, *Rewe v Bundesmonopolverwaltung für Branntwein ("Cassis de Dijon"),* [1979] ECR 649 and endorsed by the Commission in its White Paper, COM (85) 310 final.

[99] See further, Hughes, *The Social Charter and the Single European Market* (1991).

[100] Mosely, loc. cit., note 44, at 163.

[101] Art. 18(1)(i).

[102] See generally, Wedderburn, "Inderogability, Collective Agreements and Community Law", 21 *International Law Journal* (1992), at 245.

Community's genuine commitment to employment rights.

One possibility would be to enshrine a body of inderogable fundamental rights in the TEU. These rights could be derived from ILO Conventions, the Convention for the Protection of Human Rights and Fundamental Freedoms (European Convention on Human Rights; ECHR) and the European Social Charter 1961. Indeed a step has already been taken in this direction: the Commission has adopted a request to the Council seeking accession and a mandate to start negotiations with the Council of Europe[103] and the ECJ has been requested to give its opinion under Article 228. However, the most important source of those rights would be the national constitutional traditions, and, indeed, the content of any rights could be determined by reference to these national traditions. For example, the Community could guarantee that all workers should enjoy a minimum wage, but the level of that wage could be determined by reference to national minimum earnings. Similarly, all workers could be guaranteed the right to strike but the conditions under which a strike could take place should be laid down by national law, subject to the *caveat* that the national conditions do not undermine the effective exercise of that right.[104]

The content of these fundamental rights could, where necessary, be supported and supplemented by Community legislation the form and structure of which would follow the more recent pattern adopted by the Commission, providing scope for the involvement of both the Member States and the social partners.[105] However, the exercise of the rights would not be dependent on the enactment of legislation: any fundamental constitutional rights would be free standing and directly effective,[106] much in the same way as Articles 48 and 52.

This rights-based approach might offer the added advantage of helping to reconcile the growing tension between the decentralization of industrial relations in the Member States and the drive towards central regulation by the

---

[103] Bull. EC 11–1990, point 1.3.203. For a discussion on the merits of accession to the ECHR see the Commission's Memorandum, 4 April 1979, Supplement 2/79 – Bull. EC. Clapham, "A Human Rights Policy for the European Community", 10 YEL (1990), 309–366; McBride and Neville Brown, "The United Kingdom, the European Community and the European Convention on Human Rights", 1 YEL (1981), 167–205, at 172–182.

[104] Art. 5 EC Treaty.

[105] Cf. also the Commission's Green Paper COM (93) 551, at 61.

[106] Case 41/74 and Case 2/74, loc. cit., note 7.

Community.[107] While permitting a key role to be played by the states, the unions, the works councils and enterprises, it would also ensure the protection of a clearly identifiable core of rights. This approach would, however, place considerable power in the hands of the ECJ, a power which already the ECJ has not been slow to exploit. Nevertheless, the Court has proved itself a willing champion of promoting and protecting the rights of individuals, as the cases *Van Gend en Loos, Defrenne (No. 2)* and *Francovich* have clearly demonstrated.

Some indication of the success that this approach might enjoy can be gained from examining the precedent of Article 119. Increasingly it has been used to challenge a diversity of discriminatory practices, ranging from discriminatory access to occupational pensions schemes[108] to discriminatory conditions relating to time off for trade union activities.[109] Indeed, the principle of the elimination of discrimination on the grounds of sex has assumed such importance that the ECJ in *Defrenne (No. 3)*[110] in fact raised its status to the category of a constitutional, fundamental norm of Community law—a *lex superior* which cannot be derogated by implementing provisions.[111] This resounding endorsement of the importance of the principle of sex equality has been picked up by domestic tribunals which have shown themselves willing to recognize and enforce these principles.[112]

This rights-based approach would require a radical shift both on the part of the Community and of the Member States. Such a shift is, however, necessary if the Union is to give substance to its commitment in Article B TEU "to strengthen the protection of the rights and interests of the nationals

---

[107] See further, the Commission's Green Paper, loc. cit., note 105; Roberts, "Industrial Relations and the European Community", 23 *Industrial Relations Journal* (1992), 3–13, at 12; Rhodes, "The Future of the 'Social Dimension': Labour Market Regulation in Post-1992 Europe", 30 JCMS (1992), 23–51.

[108] Case C-262/88, loc. cit., note 19.

[109] Case C-360/90, *Arbeiterwohlfahrt der Stadt Berlin v Botel,* [1992] IRLR 423.

[110] Case 149/77, *Defrenne v Sabena,* [1978] ECR 1365, para. 27.

[111] Bengoextea, *The Legal Reasoning of the European Court of Justice: Towards a European Jurisprudence* (1993), p. 247.

[112] For British examples, see *Hammersmith and Queen Charlotte v Cato,* [1988] 1 CMLR 3; *Stevens v Bexley Health Authority,* [1989] ICR 629; *Secretary of State for Scotland v Wright and Hannah,* [1991] IRLR 187; *McKechnie v UBM Building Supplies (Southern) Ltd.,* [1991] IRLR 283, [1991] 2 CMLR 668; *Livingstone v Hepworth Refractories plc,* [1992] 3 CMLR 601.

of its Member States through the introduction of a citizenship of the Union"[113] and if the Community genuinely intends workers to feel a meaningful commitment to the ideals of the Community. Such a suggestion may be utopian, particularly in face of the present stance of the UK administration, but the time must come when the realization dawns that it is not possible for the Community to compete with low cost Pacific rim labour but should concentrate on and develop its own strengths—a highly trained, flexible but motivated workforce.

---

[113] According to Closa, "the distinctive element of the concept of citizenship of the Union is the enjoyment of rights and the subjection to the obligations granted by the Treaty (Article 8(2))"; "The Concept of Citizenship in the Treaty on European Union", 29 CML Rev. (1992), 1137–1170, at 1159.

10 SOCIAL RIGHTS AS GENERAL PRINCIPLES OF COMMUNITY LAW

Erika Szyszczak

1 INTRODUCTION

Although not overtly conceived as such, the constitutive Treaties establishing the European Communities have been construed as constitutional documents by the Court of Justice of the European Communities (ECJ).[1] In *Les Verts* v *Parliament*[2] the ECJ speaks of the (then) EEC Treaty as a "basic constitutional charter" and that:[3]

> The ... Community is based on the rule of law, inasmuch as neither its Member States nor its institutions can avoid a review of the question whether measures adopted by them are in conformity with the basic constitutional charter, the Treaty ...

A point reaffirmed in *Opinion 1/91*[4] when the EEC Treaty is described as "the constitutional charter of a Community based on the rule of law". The coherence of the constitutional charter has, however, been severely threatened as a result of the compromises made at the Maastricht Summit 1991[5] and it could be argued that the Treaty Constitution seems primarily concerned with handling the allocation of competence between the Member States and the EC

---

[1] See Stein, "Lawyers, Judges and the Making of a Transnational Constitution", 75 AJIL (1981), 1–27; Weiler, "The Community System: The Dual Character of Supranationalism", 100 Yale LJ (1991), 2403; Mancini, "The Making of a Constitution for Europe", 26 CML Rev. (1989), 595–614.

[2] Case 294/83, [1986] ECR 1339.

[3] Case 294/83, loc. cit., note 2, para. 23.

[4] *Opinion 1/91, Re the Draft Treaty on a European Economic Area,* [1992] 1 CMLR 245, para. 21.

[5] Curtin, "The Constitutional Structure of the Union: A Europe of Bits and Pieces", 20 CML Rev. (1993), 17–69.

N. A. Neuwahl and A. Rosas (eds.), The European Union and Human Rights, 207–220.

and providing a framework for dealing with inter-institutional conflicts.[6] Individual and collective rights are scarcely mentioned. Neither are human rights or social rights. And yet such issues are now seen as fundamental principles of most modern national and international constitutions. This chapter will look at how social rights have been protected in the constitutional legal order of the EC arguing that while many gains have been made, largely through the case law of the ECJ, the Maastricht "settlement" may have detracted from the special status accorded to social rights.

2   WHAT IS MEANT BY SOCIAL RIGHTS?

Social rights, as understood in EC law, are capable of a wide and varied definition. It is noticeable in the constitutional charter of the Treaties that the provisions relating to social rights are scattered and conceptually diffuse—they are not organized around a single or indeed coherent concept. As a result social rights could be said to embrace socio-economic rights such as the freedom of movement provisions, human rights, citizenship rights, general rights such as the principle of non-discrimination (used as a general principle and specifically defined in relation to nationality in Article 6 EC Treaty), social rights to education and vocational training, the protection of culture, public health, consumer protection, environmental protection. The "widening and deepening" process of European integration has led to new Treaty bases, a plethora of substantive secondary legislation and, inevitably, conflicts between the internal market programme and its flanking policies and the Member States' own domestic policies.

There is one area, generically termed "social policy", where a particular Chapter (Title III) of the Treaty of Rome 1957 identified a set of socio-economic rights based broadly upon labour-market participation. Articles 100, 118, 119, 235 EEC Treaty provided legal bases for substantive provisions of EC social policy law. Articles 2, 3, 117 EEC Treaty provided statements of principle which have assumed importance as interpretive mechanisms for social policy issues, particularly where there are conflicts of interest with national

---

[6] A point most clearly felt in Case C-70/88, *Parliament v Council*, [1990] ECR I-2041, where the ECJ attached great importance to institutional balance within the EC, recognizing this constitutional principle took precedence even over the clear text of the EEC Treaty.

law.[7]

The role of the ECJ has been central to both the substantive development of social rights and the development of those rights into fundamental or general principles of EC law. In order to remedy the individual deficit in the EC legal order the ECJ stepped in with its classic statement, departing from international law, that the EC was as much concerned with individual rights as with relationships between the Member States.[8] The power of the concept of direct effect cannot be underestimated and in recent years we have seen a broadening of the criteria upon which direct effect can be triggered,[9] and the development of the principle of indirect effect,[10] although arguably the underlying purpose of such principles is not so much to enhance the individual enforcement of social rights but to constantly affirm the supremacy of EC law and maintain the viability of the EC legal structure.

The starting-point for the interest in a social dimension to the EC is usually traced back to the (political) Declaration of the Heads of State or Government 1972 when the Member States emphasized "that vigorous action in the social sphere is to them just as important as achieving economic and monetary union".[11]

But the political commitment was weak. Despite the EC Commission's Social Action Programme 1974–76, linking participatory democracy to the evolution of social policy, very few substantive legal measures emerged. Many of the EC Commission's measures were reduced to "soft law"[12] or never saw the light of day. The ECJ picked up the mantle in its statement in *Defrenne* v

---

[7] Case 126/86, *Giménez Zaera v Instituto Nacional de la Seguridad Social y Tesorería General de la Seguridad Social*, [1987] ECR 3697; Joined Cases C-72/91 and C-73/91, *Firma Sloman Neptun Schiffahrts AG v Seebetriebsrat Bodo Ziesemer der Sloman Neptun Schiffahrts AG*, [1993] ECR I-887.

[8] Case 26/62, *Van Gend en Loos v Nederlandse Administratie der Belastingen*, [1963] ECR 1.

[9] Case C-271/91, *Marshall v Southampton and South-West Area Health Authority (Marshall No. 2)*, [1993] 3 CMLR 293. Cf. the attempts by the Advocates General to push the ECJ further into reversing the limitations on horizontal direct effect enunciated in Case 152/84, *Marshall v Southampton and South-West Hampshire Area Health Authority*, [1986] ECR 723: Advocate General Van Gerven in Case C-271/91, *Marshall (No. 2), supra;* Advocate General Jacobs in Case C-316/91, *Vaneetveld*, [1994] ECR I-763; Advocate General Lenz in Case C-91/92, *Faccini Dori*, [1994] ECR I-3325.

[10] Case C-106/89, *Marleasing*, [1990] ECR I-4135.

[11] Bull. EC 10–1972, para. 6.

[12] "Soft law" was declared to be of binding and interpretative value in Case C-322/88, *Grimaldi v Fonds des maladies professionelles*, [1989] ECR 4407.

Sabena (No. 2):[13]

> [Article 119 EC Treaty] forms part of the social objectives of the Community, which is not merely an economic union, but at the same time intended, by common action, to ensure social progress and seek the constant improvement of the living and working conditions [of the people of Europe].

From this turning-point we saw the elevation of certain social rights—notably the free movement of persons and the principle of equal treatment between men and women[14]—into fundamental rights of EC law protected by the ECJ and binding upon the Member States. Temple Lang[15] identifies three situations where the Member States will be bound by EC fundamental rights principles: (1) when they implement EC measures; (2) when they take measures affecting rights given or protected by EC law or in areas specifically regulated by EC; (3) where Member States, even though they no longer have any powers of their own may take measures on behalf of the EC. Few national courts have conceptualized the rights in this way and yet Advocate General Trabucchi in *Eridania* v *Minister of Agriculture and Forestry* made the position clear: "The general principles of Community law ... are binding on all authorities entrusted with the implementation of Community provisions".[16]

So too the development of the general principles of EC law, for example, proportionality, equality, non-discrimination, played an important role in firming up the skeletal social rights provisions in EC law.[17]

In addition to the fleshing out of substantive rights the ECJ also played a key role in developing EC procedural rights and remedies.[18] Most remark-

---

[13] Case 43/75, [1976] ECR 455, para. 10.

[14] See Arnull, *The General Principles of EEC Law and the Individual* (1990); Docksey, "The Principle of Equality between Women and Men as a Fundamental Right under Community Law", 20 *International Law Journal* (1991), 258–280.

[15] Temple Lang, "The Sphere in Which Member States are Obliged to Comply with the General Principles of Law and Community Fundamental Rights Principles", (1991) LIEI, 23–35; Grief, "The Domestic Impact of the European Convention on Human Rights as Mediated through Community Law", (1991) *Public Law*, 555–567.

[16] Case 230/78, [1979] ECR 2749, at 2771.

[17] See Arnull, op. cit., note 14.

[18] Case 14/83, *Von Colson and Kamann* v *Land Nordrhein-Westfalen,* [1984] ECR 1891; Case 222/84, *Johnston* v *Chief Constable of the RUC,* [1986] ECR 1651; Case 222/86, *UNECTEF* v *Heylens,* [1987] ECR 4097; Case C-271/91; loc. cit., note 9. See Szyszczak, "European Community Law: New Remedies, New Directions?", 55 MLR (1992), 690–697; Steiner, "From Direct Effect to *Francovich*: Shifting Means of Enforcement of Community Law", 18 EL Rev. (1992), 3–22.

able of all is the development of direct effect and indirect effect to take the reach of EC law into the national procedural arena, culminating in the *Marshall (No. 2)* ruling.[19]

The ECJ has also taken cognizance of international social rights standards in providing the inspiration for the development of a set of EC based social rights.[20] In *Defrenne* v *Sabena (No. 3)*[21] ECJ declared:

> The Court has repeatedly stated that respect for fundamental personal human rights is one of the general principles of Community law, the observance of which it has a duty to ensure.
>
> There can be no doubt that the elimination of discrimination based on sex forms part of those fundamental rights.
>
> Moreover, the same concepts are recognised by the European Social Charter of 18 November 1961 and by Convention No. 111 of the International Labour Organisation of 25 June 1958 concerning discrimination in respect of employment and occupation.

Similarly in *Blaizot* v *University of Liège*[22] the European Social Charter was used by the ECJ as aid to the interpretation of vocational training in Article 128 EC Treaty. In *Rutili* v *Minister for the Interior*[23] the ECJ explained that the limitations on the powers of the Member States were "a specific manifestation" of similar controls set out in the Convention for the Protection of Human Rights and Fundamental Freedoms 1950 (European Convention on Human Rights; ECHR). The same Convention was referred to in *Johnston* v *Chief Constable of the RUC*[24] where the ECJ explained that the principle of judicial control "reflects a general principle of law which underlies the constitutional traditions common to the Member States ...". Advocate General Van Gerven tried to stretch the ECJ further in *Barber*[25] to suggest that certain provisions of international social law could give rise to direct effect between individuals in the EC legal order, a point not explored by the ECJ in its ruling. The ECJ has asserted that it cannot assess the compatibility with the ECHR of

---

[19] Case C-271/91, loc. cit., note 9. Cf. Case C-338/91, *Steenhorst-Neerings*, [1993] ECR I-5475.

[20] Cf. Clapham, "A Human Rights Policy for the European Community", 10 YEL (1990), 309–366.

[21] Case 149/77, [1978] ECR 1365, paras 26–27.

[22] Case 24/86, [1988] ECR 379.

[23] Case 36/75, [1975] ECR 1219.

[24] Case 222/84, loc. cit., note 18, para. 18.

[25] Case 262/88, [1990] ECR I-1889.

provisions of national law which are not within the limits of EC law.[26] Some commentators[27] have suggested that the EC should accede to international social law conventions but the controversy surrounding *Opinion 2/91,*[28] suggests that this may not be easy to achieve since the Member States are reluctant to give up their sovereignty in this field.

There was a symbolic breakthrough in 1989 with the acceptance by eleven of the Member States of the Community Charter of Fundamental Social Rights of Workers. The ground for the elevation of certain social rights into fundamental rights had been set by the ECJ's case law and also by the inclusion in the Preamble to the Single European Act (SEA) 1986 of the statement that the Member States were:[29]

> Determined to work together to promote democracy on the basis of the fundamental rights recognized in the constitutions and laws of the Member States, in the Convention for the Protection of Human Rights and Fundamental Freedoms and the European Social Charter, notably freedom, equality and social justice.

The United Kingdom opposed such an overtly political acceptance of basic social rights, protecting largely people who have been economically active in the paid labour market. Yet the rights contained in the Community Charter of Fundamental Social Rights of Workers are hardly new or radical and the United Kingdom has recognized many of these rights already in international conventions and charters. Although it is a breakthrough in that it catalogues a set of basic social rights, a number of limitations surround the Community Charter: Its substantive scope is limited—in particular, issues of race discrimination are not addressed and no legal tools or bases are introduced to implement its ideals. The legal status of the Charter is tenuous. It is not a piece of EC law and not even an intergovernmental agreement accepted by the (then) Member States (as is the Protocol on Social Policy, signed together with

---

[26] Joined Cases 60 and 61/84, *Cinéthèque* v *Fédération nationale des cinémas français,* [1985] ECR 2605; Case 12/86, *Demirel* v *Stadt Schwäbisch Gmünd,* [1987] ECR 3719; Case C-260/89, *Elliniki Radiophonia Tileorassi (ERT),* [1991] ECR I-2925.

[27] Vogel-Polsky, "What Future is there for a Social Europe Following the Strasbourg Summit?", 19 *International Law Journal* (1990), 65–80.

[28] *Re Convention No. 170 of the ILO Concerning Safety in the Use of Chemicals at Work,* [1993] 3 CMLR 800. Where the scope of an international convention lies within the exclusive competence of the EC the Member States have no choice but to relinquish sovereignty in that field.

[29] Cf. Wedderburn, "Labour Standards, Global Markets and Labour Laws in Europe", in Duncan, Campbell and Senenberger (eds), *International Labour Standards in the Globalised Economy* (1994).

the Treaty on European Union, TEU, 1992). For its implementation the Charter was reliant upon the existing Treaty provisions relating to social policy. Nielsen and Szyszczak[30] have argued that the Charter should be viewed as a piece of "soft law" by the ECJ and thus be used as an interpretative mechanism to raise the constitutional status of the rights protected within it. By contrast, the EC Commission begins its Second Report on the Implementation of the Community Charter of Fundamental Social Rights of Workers with the words: "The Charter, as a European act, merely states and notes the rights which were the subject of deliberations in the European Council in Strasbourg in December 1989. In itself, it has no effect on the existing legal situation."[31]

The relative paucity of new proposals in the EC Commission's legislative Programme for 1994[32] suggests that the Community Charter's action programme is exhausted and the drive for social policy developments is expected to come from the changes introduced by the TEU.[33]

3 THE TREATY ON EUROPEAN UNION 1992

The TEU adds several new dimensions to the notion of social rights as general principles of EC law. Not all the developments are positive, however, and arguably an element of regulatory law has crept into the social dimension of the internal market which may make it more difficult for the ECJ to elevate this form of social law into fundamental principles of EC law.

3.1 "Mission Statements"[34]

In the Preamble to the Treaty the High Contracting Parties show their willingness:

> to promote economic and social progress for their peoples, within the context of the accomplishment of the internal market and of reinforced cohesion and environmental protection, and to implement policies ensuring that advances in

---

[30] *The Social Dimension of the European Community* (1993).

[31] COM (92) 562 final, 23 Dec. 1992.

[32] COM (93) 588, 24 Nov. 1993.

[33] See the EC Commission's Green Paper *European Social Policy Options for the Union,* COM (93) 551, 17 Nov. 1993.

[34] See in particular Shaw, "Twin-Track Social Europe—the Inside Track", in O'Keeffe and Twomey (eds), *Legal Issues of the Maastricht Treaty* (1994), pp. 295–311.

economic integration are accompanied by parallel progress in other fields.

In Article B TEU one of the objectives of the Union is stated to be "to promote economic and social progress which is balanced and sustainable, in particular through the creation of an area without internal frontiers, through the strengthening of economic and social cohesion ..."
Shaw is dismissive of such statements:[35]

> Since the Paris Summit in 1972, the Member States have been concerned to promote a public rhetoric in which social affairs are accorded equal status with 'pure' economic integration. The rhetoric of the Preamble and of the general principles contained in the TEU and the amended EC Treaty indicates that it is 'neo-liberal business as usual', with these provisions apeing those which have long stood largely unheeded in the Treaty of Rome.

However, one should not underestimate the teleological use the ECJ has made of such statements as interpretative tools, both to increase the substantive content of social rights and, in certain cases, to raise them to fundamental principles of the EC.

3.2 Citizenship

Article 8 EC Treaty introduces the new legal concept of "Citizenship of the Union". At the conceptual level the recognition of "citizenship rights" is an enormous leap forward in terms of a "People's Europe". In the first report from the Commission on the Citizenship of the Union[36] the EC Commission emphasizes the constitutional significance of citizenship:

> The introduction of these new provisions underscores the fact that the Treaty of Rome is not concerned solely with economic matters, as is also plainly demonstrated by the change of name from the EEC to the EC. For the first time, the Treaty has created a direct political link between the citizens of the Member States and the European Union such as never existed within the Community, with the aim of fostering a sense of identity with the Union. As testimony to their importance, the Intergovernmental Conference placed them immediately after the introductory provisions of the Treaty of Rome, such as Article 6 EC, ... which prohibits discrimination on the grounds of nationality, and Article 7a EC, ... which provides for the establishment of the internal market *inter alia* for persons. Thus citizenship of the Union appears in the

---

[35] Ibid., at p. 298.
[36] COM (93) 702 final.

Treaty even before the four freedoms which together make up the internal market.

But the limited nature of the rights has been criticized. The result is disappointing because of the lack of a human rights element to citizenship[37] and because the rights to Union citizenship crystallize around the quality of holding the nationality of a Member State—notwithstanding the ruling in *Michelletti v Delegacion del Gobierno en Cantabria*[38] a concept the Member States have been eager to assert is defined by domestic, not EC law.[39]

3.3 Human rights[40]

The ECJ has attempted to redress the lack of a basic human rights code within the EC constitutional charter by accepting that the protection of human rights is one of the areas it is charged to address. But the extension of the binding nature of human rights to the application of EC law by the Member States in *ERT*[41] is matched by the subordination of human rights to the economic aims of the EC in *Grogan*.[42]

The Treaty aims to consolidate the ECJ's case law in Article F(2):

The Union shall respect fundamental rights, as guaranteed by the European Convention for the Protection of Human Rights and Fundamental Freedoms signed in Rome on 4 November 1950 and as they result from the constitutional traditions common to the Member States, as general principles of Community law.

---

[37] See Closa, "The Concept of Citizenship in the Treaty on European Union", 29 CML Rev. (1992), 1137–1170; O'Keeffe, "Union Citizenship", in O'Keeffe and Twomey (eds), op. cit., note 34, pp. 109–119.

[38] Cf. Case C-369/90, *Michelletti v Delegacion del Gobierno en Cantabria*, [1992] ECR I-4239, where the ECJ ruled that the Member States must exercise the rules relating to nationality in a way which is compatible with EC law.

[39] See the Declaration on Nationality of a Member State attached to the TEU and reaffirmed in the Declaration of the Edinburgh Summit, 12 Dec. 1992: "The question whether an individual possesses the nationality of a Member State will be settled solely by reference to the national law of the Member State concerned."

[40] See in particular Krogsgaard, "Fundamental Rights in the European Community after Maastricht", (1993) LIEI, 99–113.

[41] Case C-260/89, loc. cit., note 26.

[42] Case C-159/90, *Society for the Protection of Unborn Children Ireland,* [1991] ECR I-4685. See de Búrca, "Fundamental Human Rights and the Reach of EC Law", 13 OJLS (1993), 283–319.

However, this article is not enforceable before the ECJ.[43]

Article K.1 requires that Justice and Home Affairs matters be dealt with in compliance with the European Convention on Human Rights 1950 and the UN Convention Relating to the Status of Refugees 1951, but these matters will be dealt with under the intergovernmental pillars of the Treaty with little publicity, no democratic input and the ECJ is not given the jurisdiction to review any conventions which materialize unless such jurisdiction is expressly stipulated therein. Arguably the issues dealt with under the title of "justice and home affairs", touching upon sensitive civil liberties matters, are areas in greatest need of democratic accountability and judicial control.

Thus the outcome of the Maastricht negotiations is disappointing. Twomey argues: "in shifting the focus from the nation State, the proponents of integration have underestimated the extent to which enumerated human rights form the constitutional bedrock of a legal order, be it national or transnational".[44]

3.4 New competences

The Treaty has added new areas of competence for the EC—"flanking policies" to the internal market—in areas such as culture, public health and refined some existing policies, for example, in the areas of education, vocational training, consumer protection.[45] The opportunity to extend EC competence at both the substantive and procedural/remedial level in the area of social rights is therefore increased. But this again has fragmented the notion of a social rights element to the internal market and thus fragmented any attempt to develop a constitutional coherence to social rights. Third-country immigration—an area sadly lacking in social rights[46]—is partly in the new EC Treaty[47] and partly dealt with at the intergovernmental level. Surely a missed opportunity for the development of crucial basic social rights affecting

---

[43] Article L TEU.

[44] "The European Union: Three Pillars without a Human Rights Foundation", in O'Keeffe and Twomey (eds), op. cit., note 34, pp. 121–132.

[45] See Lane, "New Community Competences under the Maastricht Treaty", 30 CML Rev. (1993), 939–979.

[46] Szyszczak, "Race Discrimination: The Limits of Market Equality?", in Hepple and Szyszczak (eds), *Discrimination: The Limits of Law* (1993), pp. 313–327.

[47] Art. 100c EC Treaty enables the Council of Ministers to determine which third-country nationals need a visa in order to enter the EC. Art. 100c(6) EC Treaty provides for the transfer of certain areas relating to immigration policy from the intergovernmental pillar for Justice and Home Affairs to the decision-making framework of Art. 100c EC Treaty.

the operation of the EC?

3.5 Institutional changes

Attempts have been made to redress the democratic deficit of the EC[48] by increasing the European Parliament's powers and introducing a new body, the Committee of the Regions (Article 198a EC Treaty). In relation to the European Parliament the words "advisory and supervisory" have been dropped from Article 137 EC Treaty, showing the anticipated wider role the European Parliament is to play in the running of the EC. A number of powers which either existed under the European Parliament's rules of procedure, for example, Committees of Inquiry, or developed through the ECJ's case law, for example, the amendment to Article 173 EC Treaty allowing *locus standi,*[49] have received Treaty recognition. It will be recalled that the ECJ elevated the co-operation procedure to a "fundamental democratic principle"[50] as the European Parliament flexed its enhanced muscles by challenging the legal base of the Students' Residence Directive.[51] It will be interesting to see if the ECJ accords the same status to the new negative assent procedure contained in Article 189b EC Treaty. The basis of the ECJ's approach is the right of the European Parliament to participate in the legislative process to the full extent envisaged in the Treaty and thus there can be no doubt that a failure to comply with Article 189b EC Treaty would have the same consequences as a failure to comply with Article 189 EC Treaty. Given the broader spectrum of interests and wider political composition when compared with the other EC institutions, the future role of the European Parliament in keeping social rights on the political agenda of the EC is important.

The Committee of the Regions is designed to provide an input from the regional perspective into the EC legislative process. In certain areas there is compulsory consultation of the Committee in areas such as culture (Article 128 EC Treaty), public health (Article 129 EC Treaty), economic and social cohesion (Article 130 a–e EC Treaty), but not in the central area of social policy (Article 118a EC Treaty) or environmental policy (Article 130r–t EC Treaty).

---

[48] See also Article 138a EC Treaty which states: "Political parties at the European level are important as a factor for integration within the Union. They contribute to forming a European awareness and to expressing the political will of the citizens of the Union."

[49] Case C 70/88, *European Parliament* v *Council, (Chernobyl),* [1990] ECR I-2041.

[50] Case C-295/90, *European Parliament* v *Council,* [1992] ECR I-4193.

[51] Council Directive 90/336/EEC, O.J. 1990, L 180. Case C-295/90, loc. cit., note 50.

4 THE SOCIAL POLICY PROTOCOL AND AGREEMENT

Finally we must consider the fragmentation of the social policy base as a result of the Maastricht compromise, taking the revised Chapter of Social Policy out of the main body of the EC Treaty and annexing it as a Protocol and Agreement to the EC Treaty. The UK Government has previously tried to water down the social policy provisions of the EC Treaty by challenging the legal base of proposed measures. Now it will be able to use the principle of subsidiarity (Article 3b EC Treaty) to limit EC competence in areas of social policy law which do not directly impinge upon the operation of the internal market. The United Kingdom's view of subsidiarity is at odds with the EC Commission's interpretation of subsidiarity and also the Edinburgh *Communiqué.*[52] However, the *Communiqué* also states:

> The Community should legislate only to the extent necessary. Other things being equal, Directives should be preferred to Regulations and framework directives to detailed measures. Non-binding measures such as Recommendations should be preferred where appropriate. Consideration should also be given where appropriate to the use of voluntary codes of conduct.

Notwithstanding *Grimaldi,*[53] the use of weaker forms of EC law must surely detract from the gains made under the original EEC Treaty particularly by the use of direct and indirect effect to meet EC standards at the national level.

Turning to the new Protocol and Agreement, although there is an express commitment towards preserving the *acquis communautaire* in the Protocol, there are a number of areas where the Social Policy Agreement deviates from the EC Treaty and the case law of the ECJ.[54] For example, Article 1 of the

---

[52] Annex to the Conclusions of the Presidency of the European Council at Edinburgh 11–12 Dec. 1992. Part One: Overall Approach to the Application by the Council of the Subsidiarity Principle and Article 3b of the Treaty on European Union. Bull. EC 12/92, pt. I.15-I.22.

[53] Case C-322/88, loc. cit., note 12.

[54] For detail see Szyszczak, "Social Policy: A Happy Ending or a Reworking of the Fairytale?", in O'Keeffe and Twomey (eds), op. cit., note 34, pp. 313–327. Cf. Protocol No. 2 on Article 119 EC which "interprets" Case 262/88, loc. cit., note 25—an interpretation followed lamely by the ECJ in Case C-109/91, *Ten Oever,* [1993] ECR I-4879. At a conference, Equality of Treatment Between Women and Men in Social Security, in Oxford, Jan. 1994, Advocate General Van Gerven made the following comments: "By the way in which the ECJ answered the question [concerning the temporal limitations of *Barber*] it has avoided the delicate problem of conflict of laws. Indeed pursuant to Article 239 EC Treaty the Protocol forms an integral part of the EC Treaty and therefore has the same legal force as a provision thereof. A different ECJ ruling on the operation in time of *Barber*

Agreement deviates from Article 117 EC Treaty; Article 2 deviates from Article 118 EC Treaty and would seem to override Article 100a(2) EC Treaty. Article 6(3) must be read in the light of Article 2(4) of the Equal Treatment Directive 76/207/EEC[55] and *Commission* v *France*.[56] Equally the use of collective agreements to implement social policy must be reconciled with the ECJ's guidelines.[57]

A second point is the creation of a "variable geometry" by allowing one Member State to opt-out of EC policy. Such opt-outs are found in other areas, for example, economic and monetary union, but in *ICI*[58] and *Commissionnaires Réunis* v *Receveur des Douanes*,[59] alongside the host of cases affirming the supremacy of EC law the ECJ emphasizes that the uniform application of EC law is imperative and that both the Member States and the EC institutions must use their powers with the unity of the market in mind.[60] This use of the idea of "mutuality of obligations" is seen also in the use of Article 5 EC Treaty to pursue the procedural and remedial aspect of EC law in the national legal systems.

A third point relates to the status of any measures enacted under the Social Policy Agreement. Although the term "directives" is used, the balance of academic opinion seems to be that any new measures would not form part of EC law.[61] It has been argued that the "directives" will be a form of intergovernmental agreement over which the ECJ will not have jurisdiction.

Barber would have led to great confusion, *a fortiori* since the Maastricht Treaty is expressly committed to the *acquis communautaire,* of which the ECJ's judgment in *Ten Oever* (since it was rendered before 1 November 1993) forms a part." One wonders what has happened to Art. 164 EC Treaty and Art. 219 EC Treaty. See also Curtin, loc. cit., note 5.

[55] O.J. 1076, L 39.

[56] Case 312/86, [1988] ECR 6315.

[57] See Adinolfi, "The Implementation of Social Policy Directives Through Collective Agreements", 25 CML Rev. (1988), 291–316.

[58] Case 66/80, *International Chemical Corporation (ICI)* v *Amministrazione delle Finanze dello Stato,* [1981] ECR 1191.

[59] Joined Cases 80 and 81/77, [1978] ECR 927.

[60] See the radical extension of Art. 5 EC Treaty in Case C-2/88, *Zwartveld and Others,* [1990] ECR I-3365.

[61] Vogel-Polsky, "Evaluation of the Social Provisions of the Treaty on European Union agreed by the European Summit at Maastricht on 9 and 10 December 1991", Committee on Social Affairs, Employment and the Working Environment of the European Parliament, 7 Feb. 1992, DOC EC/CM/202155, PE 155.405.I; Whiteford, "Social Policy After Maastricht", 18 EL Rev. (1993), 202–222. Curtin, loc. cit., note 5; Szyszczak, loc. cit., note 54.

This would be unfortunate not only for the continued development of a Community based upon the rule of law but also for the future entrenchment of social rights as constitutional rights. The EC Commission has stated: "the Community nature of measures taken under the Agreement is beyond doubt, which means that the Court of Justice will be empowered to rule on the legality of directives adopted by the Eleven and to interpret them".[62]

Already, many of the measures taken under the Action Programme designed to implement the Community Charter of Fundamental Social Rights of Workers 1989 have taken a purely regulatory form, with little attention being paid to the wider dimension of procedural, remedial and indeed, social rights.[63] There is scope for the ECJ to continue to use the general principles of law to maintain the protection of EC rights in this area but the approach is slow and piecemeal. Perhaps the most salient lesson we have learnt from individuals such as *Defrenne, Johnson, Marshall* and also *Francovich* is that the implementation, enforcement, expansion and coherence of the social rights contained in EC law are heavily reliant upon individual litigants at the national level with access to the ECJ under Article 177 EC Treaty. Unless the new dynamic to social law incorporated fully into EC law and elevated into a special status, the outcome will be disappointing for the constitutional coherence of social rights post-Maastricht.

---

[62] Communication concerning the application of the Agreement on social policy presented by the Commission to the Council and to the European Parliament, COM (93) 600 final, 14 Dec. 1993. See Bercusson, "The Dynamic of European Labour Law After Maastricht", 23 *International Law Journal* (1994), 1–31.

[63] See Hepple, *European Social Dialogue—Alibi or Opportunity?* (1993). The shortcomings of this approach are outlined in Muckenburger and Deakin, "From Deregulation to a European Floor of Rights", 3 *Zeitschrift für ausländisches und internationales Arbeits- und Sozialrecht* (1989), 153–207.

11 A GENDERED PERSPECTIVE ON THE RIGHT TO FAMILY LIFE IN EUROPEAN COMMUNITY LAW

Tamara Hervey

1   INTRODUCTION

Where the European Community (EC) has competence to act, its institutions are obliged to respect the "general principles of Community law", including the protection of fundamental rights.[1] The Treaty on European Union (TEU), Article F(2) expressly requires the European Union (EU) to respect fundamental rights as guaranteed by the Convention for the Protection of Human Rights and Fundamental Freedoms (European Convention on Human Rights; ECHR). Although the competence of the Community is focused upon economic activity, in particular the creation of a Single European Market through the medium of law, the Community may act in spheres which are not purely economic. It is axiomatic to the discussion in this chapter that the European Community is not now (if it ever was) *solely* an economic community; the Community has a "social face". I contend that this assumption is implicit in the original Treaty of Rome[2] and has been developed as the reach of Community law has developed.[3] It follows that the duty of the Community (and of the Union) towards individuals who live and work within

---

[1] See, e.g., Case 29/69, *Stauder v Ulm,* [1969] ECR 419; Case 4/73, *Nold v Commission,* [1974] ECR 491; Case 11/70, *Internationale Handelsgesellschaft* v *Einfuhr- und Vorratstelle Getreide,* [1970] ECR 1125; Case 44/79, *Hauer v Land Rheinland-Pfalz,* [1979] ECR 3727; Joined Cases 46/87 and 227/88, *Hoechst v Commission,* [1989] ECR 2859.

[2] See, e.g., Preamble, "resolved to ensure the economic *and social* progress of their countries; affirming ... the constant improvement of the living and working conditions of their peoples"; Title III Social Policy, Art. 117, Art. 118, Art. 119; provisions for the structural funds.

[3] E.g., the extension of the provisions concerning social and employment law by the Single European Act (SEA) 1986, the Community Charter of Fundamental Social Rights of Workers 1989; the Social Protocol 1994. See also Twomey, "The European Union: Three Pillars without a Human Rights Foundation", in O'Keeffe and Twomey (eds), *Legal Issues of the Maastricht Treaty* (1993), pp. 121–132, at p. 122, citing Toth, "The Individual and European Law", 24 ICLQ (1975), 659–706, at 667.

N. A. Neuwahl and A. Rosas (eds.), The European Union and Human Rights, 221–234.
© 1995 *Kluwer Law International. Printed in the Netherlands.*

its territorial boundaries, and whose lives are affected by Community law, is a duty towards those individuals *as human beings*, not simply as market actors. A significant facet of that duty is the protection of those individuals' fundamental human rights.

Perhaps one of the areas of Community law in which the duty to respect fundamental human rights is most readily apparent is that concerning the free movement of persons. The focus of this chapter is a particular aspect of the free movement of persons provisions, that which might broadly be termed the right to respect for family life. The Court of Justice of the European Communities (ECJ) recognizes the right to family life as part of Community law:[4]

> the respect for family life set out in Article 8 of the Convention for the Protection of Human Rights and Fundamental Freedoms ... is one of the fundamental rights which, according to the Court's settled case-law ... are recognized by Community law.

The concern of this chapter is a relatively narrow topic, the "right to family life" *in Community law*.[5] It is important to stress at the outset that I am not concerned with instruments of general international law, except in so far as they have influenced Community norms. Nor do I intend to discuss national law and policies on family rights.

The fact that "family rights" form a legitimate part of Community law and fall within Community legislative competence originally stems from the role of family rights in the endeavour of the Community to utilize law in order to establish the Single European Market. "Family rights" in this sense denotes a group of substantive rights; a somewhat narrower concept than "the right to family life" in its human rights sense. Creation of the Single Market includes provision for free movement of workers and the self-employed. The rights of the families of workers and self-employed persons who move in the Single Market play an essential role in the creation of that market. Community law on family rights is therefore contingent upon two crucial matters: the status (mover or non-mover) and the nationality of the worker whose family is at

---

[4] Case 249/86, *Commission* v *Germany,* [1989] ECR 1263, para. 10; see also Case 36/75, *Rutili* v *Minister for the Interior,* [1975] ECR 1219, at para. 32.

[5] The EC Commission Communication on Family Policies stresses that most responsibility for the appropriate social, legal and economic protection of families is at the level of Member States. However, Community provisions, such as "free movement of persons, equal opportunities for men and women, equal treatment within the area of social security and professional insertion of the handicapped" have a "family dimension", COM (89) 363 final, at 13–14.

issue. Community law is primarily concerned with Community nationals who move in order to work. Third-country national family members are only included in the legal provisions because to fail to do so might jeopardize the Single Market endeavour.

2   "FAMILY LIFE" IN THE EUROPEAN UNION: A GENDERED CONSTRUCT

Provisions relating to some of the substantive elements of the "right to family life" feature in secondary Community legislation, particularly that relating to the free movement of persons. The specific aspects of the "right to family life" to be considered in this chapter essentially concern the free movement provisions of Community law.[6]

The constituents of the right to family life in the context of Community law[7] essentially focus upon the right of family members to install themselves together,[8] in the family home. Community law is therefore concerned with rights of residence,[9] and adjuncts to these rights, such as the right to "social advantages",[10] including family benefits,[11] and the right of family members to work in the state in which the family is installed.[12] Of particular importance in the enforcement of substantive rights is the principle of non-discrimination on grounds of nationality (Article 6 EC Treaty) according to which non-national[13] workers and their families may not be treated less favourably than nationals.[14]

---

[6] Mention should also be made of the emergent common immigration and asylum policies of the European Union.

[7] There exist in international law other aspects of the right to respect for family life, concerning for example inheritance law, custody of children and legitimacy. These do not fall within Community competence.

[8] Regulation 1612/68/EEC, O.J. Sp. Ed. 1968, L 257/2, 475, Art. 10(1).

[9] Directive 68/360/EEC, O.J. Sp. Ed. 1968, L 257/13, 485.

[10] Regulation 1612/68/EEC, Art. 7(2).

[11] Case 32/75, *Christini* v *SNCF,* [1975] ECR 1085; Case 65/81, *Reina* v *Landeskreditbank Baden-Württemberg,* [1982] ECR 33; but see Case 40/76, *Kermaschek* v *Bundesanstalt für Arbeit,* [1976] ECR 1669; Case 157/84, *Frascogna* v *Caisse des dépôts et consignations,* [1985] ECR 1739.

[12] Regulation 1612/68/EEC, Art. 11.

[13] I.e., citizens of the European Union (nationals of a Member State) who do not hold the nationality of the host state in which they are workers or are established.

[14] See, e.g., Case 59/85, *Netherlands* v *Reed,* [1986] ECR 1283; Case 249/86, loc. cit., note 4; Case C-111/91, *Commission* v *Luxembourg,* [1993] ECR I-817.

The protection of family rights in European Community law may be regarded as inadequate for a number of reasons. One particularly striking criticism which might be levelled at the family rights protection granted by Community law is that the substantive provisions concerned are not applied uniformly as *human* rights, but rather depend upon the status of individuals seeking to enforce the provisions. "Status" in this sense denotes not only the nationality of individuals, in particular whether they are nationals of a Member State of the European Union[15] or "third-country nationals", but also whether individuals have exercised their right to move between the Member States.[16] These considerations might lead one to a conclusion that the provisions of Community law concerning family rights are intrinsically racist,[17] or at least that they bolster "fortress Europe" at the expense of "third-country nationals", who, as human beings, are entitled equally with European Union citizens to respect for their fundamental rights.[18] Another criticism which has been levelled is that the Community provisions concerning families discriminate on grounds of sexual preference.[19]

These concerns, though serious, are not the focus of this chapter. Instead, the chapter seeks to reflect on the gender implications of the Community provisions on family rights. In particular, the idea that family rights in Community law, although predominantly based upon formally gender neutral free movement provisions, are in fact structurally discriminatory against women, is to be explored. As such, the law operates to perpetuate a market

---

[15] Or "citizens of the Union", Art. 8 EC Treaty. Note that the free movement provisions have now also been extended to citizens of EEA states.

[16] The ECJ has consistently refused to apply the non-discrimination principle in Art. 6 EC Treaty to situations where the home state discriminates against its own nationals. See, e.g., Cases 35 and 36/82, *Morson and Jhanjan* v *State of The Netherlands,* [1982] ECR 3723. The situation is mitigated where there is a "Community element" to the conduct of the person concerned. See Case C-370/90, *The Queen* v *Immigration Appeal Tribunal and Surinder Singh,* [1992] ECR I-4265. Nielsen and Szyszczak, *The Social Dimension of the European Community* (1993), 2nd edn, pp. 91–95.

[17] See, e.g., EC Migrants Forum Information and Proposals to the Ad Hoc Immigration Group; *SCORE News,* 1994, published by the Standing Conference on Racial Equality in Europe (SCORE); Szyszczak, "Race Discrimination: The Limits of Market Equality", in Hepple and Szyszczak (eds), *Discrimination: The Limits of Law* (1992), pp. 125–147; Bhabha and Shutter, *Women's Movement* (1994), at pp. 212–227.

[18] Szyszczak, loc. cit., note 17; Weiler, "Thou Shalt Not Oppress a Stranger: On the Judicial Protection of the Human Rights of Non-EC Nationals—A Critique", 3 EJIL (1992), 65–91; Twomey, loc. cit., note 3.

[19] Emmert, "The Family Policy of the European Community", in Waaldijk and Clapham (eds), *Homosexuality: A European Community Issue* (1993), pp. 365–394.

ideology which has a particular construct of the roles of women and men in the Single European Market; a construct which marginalizes, or decommodifies,[20] women as "outside" market activity, and "ancillary" to (male) market actors (workers).

There are three interconnected reasons for the discriminatory impact of provisions protecting the family in Community law. These are, first, that "the family" as a Community concept, reflects a norm which marginalizes alternative forms of family. Alternative forms of family tend to be (although are not exclusively) families with women as head of household.[21] The second, and more crucial, reason is that family rights are protected in Community law for economic ends. According to this model, the law is not concerned with protecting families *qua* families, but only with the economic function of family members, in particular the function of support of movement of workers. The focus of legal protection is the rights (or perhaps "needs") of the (predominantly male) worker to be able to have his family with him in order to move freely as an economic actor in the Single Market. The rights (or needs) of those individuals (predominantly women) whose role is to support or commodify the worker who moves, are subsidiary to the programmatic economic function of the Community provisions. Linked closely to this reason is the third reason that family rights in Community law discriminate against women, that the legal basis for most (if not all) family rights in Community law is the free movement provisions,[22] and family rights are thereby premised upon workers' rights. Given the fact that neither the ECJ nor the provisions of secondary legislation recognize women's domestic and caring work done in private households as work, women are excluded from protection unless they enter the public world of work for pay. This option is simply not open to many women, and, given the current structure of family and work in European society, is not chosen by many others. European Community law concerning family rights perpetuates the structural distinction between work for pay in the market and work in the home; a distinction which reflects the public/private dichotomy familiar in feminist writing.

---

[20] Cf. Langan and Ostner, "Gender and Welfare", in Room (ed.), *Towards a European Welfare State?* (1991), at p. 131.

[21] EC Commission Communication on Family Policies, loc. cit., note 5, at 7.

[22] Arts. 48–66 EC Treaty.

3   THE CONCEPT OF THE FAMILY IN COMMUNITY LAW

There is no Community definition of "the family", although a number of provisions of secondary legislation indicate who is considered to be included. Generally speaking, the matter of definition of "members of the family" is within the competence of the Member States,[23] provided that there is no breach of the non-discrimination principle. In the Community secondary legislation, although precise definitions differ, "family" covers marital and close blood relationships.[24] Descendants (children and grandchildren) tend to be included only until they reach a certain age, unless they continue to be dependants. Likewise, only dependant ascendants are included.[25] As far as marital relationships are concerned, the ECJ has held that only formally married individuals are included within the Community definition.[26]

The ECJ's approach to interpretation of the scope *ratione personae* of provisions protecting family members, at least in so far as it concerns adults, may be characterized as static and conservative. This is surprising, given the usual dynamic approach of the ECJ to interpretation of legislation which brings into effect the Single European Market. In *Reed*, the ECJ was asked whether the term "spouse" in Regulation 1612/68 included a cohabiting partner in a stable relationship, though without the formality of marriage. The ECJ remained unconvinced that a dynamic approach to interpretation, based upon social changes and the considerable numbers of individuals choosing to live

---

[23] See Case 7/75, *Mr and Mrs F.* v *Belgium,* [1975] ECR 679, at 697, *per* Advocate General Trabucchi. See also, e.g., Regulation 1408/71, as amended, O.J. 1983, L 230/6, Art. 1 (f)(i) and (ii).

[24] This definition is similar to that reached by the European Commission of Human Rights and the European Court of Human Rights, who assume "family" to denote "nuclear family", i.e., spouses, parents and dependent children. Cf. Douglas, "The Family and the State under the European Convention on Human Rights", 2 *International Journal of Law and the Family* (1988).

[25] Regulation 1612/68/EEC, Art. 10; Directive 68/360/EEC, Art. 1 and Regulation 1251/70/EEC, Art. 1, which both refer to the definition in Regulation 1612/68/EEC; Directive 73/148/EEC, Art. 1(c) and (d); Directive 75/34/EEC, Art. 1, which refers to the definition in Directive 73/148/EEC, Art. 1; Directive 90/364/EEC, Art. 1(2); Directive 90/365/EEC, Art. 1(2); Directive 90/366/EEC, Art. 1. (Note that the new text of Directive 90/365/EEC, proposed to take account of Case C-357/89, *Raulin* v *Minister van Onderwijs en Wetenschappen,* [1994] 1 CMLR 227, will not alter this provision—see COM (93) 209 final.)

[26] Case 59/85, loc. cit., note 14, at 1296.

together without a formal marriage relationship, would be appropriate.[27] The ECJ's reasoning is based upon the formal legal position in the Member States,[28] rather than the social "presence of millions of unmarried couples in all Member States",[29] and thus reflects (and perpetuates) formal structures rather than the experience of many individuals in the European Union.

In *Diatta*,[30] the ECJ considered the position of a husband (with nationality of an EC Member State) and wife (a non-EC national) who were living separately, although had not formally divorced. The ECJ held that *until the marriage was annulled*, the wife fell within the provisions of Community law granting her residence rights. The implication of the ruling is that the right of installation ceases on the legal dissolution of marriage. The decision has been criticized for its failure to respect the plaintiff's right to human dignity (by giving the husband control over her expulsion) or her right to family life, if the couple had children.[31] Of course, the formal position would be the same if a man who was a non-EC national enjoying rights through his marriage to a woman with Union citizenship divorced. The provisions of Community law are not directly discriminatory. However, once one takes into account the position of women in the labour market,[32] and the particular difficulties faced by migrant women in the EC[33] (remembering that the Community provisions do not come into play until the Union citizen exercises her free movement rights), the indirectly discriminatory impact of the rules is apparent.

Although the traditional model of a family consisting of a husband and wife with one or more children still prevails, other types of families are present in significant numbers in the European Community, for example reconstituted families, single-parent families, and families with no marital or

---

[27] "... any interpretation of [Art. 10 of Regulation 1612/68/EEC] on the basis of social developments must take into account the situation in the whole Community, not merely in one Member State". (Case 59/85, loc. cit., note 14, paras 12–13); O'Higgins, "The Family and European Law", 140 NLJ (1990), 1643–1646, at 1643.

[28] Even though social security and tax laws of many Member States treat married and cohabiting couples in stable relationships in the same way. O'Higgins, loc. cit., note 27, at 1643.

[29] Emmert, loc. cit., note 19, at 373–374.

[30] Case 267/83, *Diatta* v *Land Berlin*, [1985] ECR 567.

[31] See Weiler, loc. cit., note 18; Emmert, loc. cit., note 19, at 373.

[32] See *infra*.

[33] Hecq and Plasman, *La mobilité européenne des travailleurs feminins dans la Communauté* (1991); Jackson, *The Impact of the Completion of the Internal Market on Women in the EC* (1990).

blood ties, including lesbian (and gay) families.[34] Arguably it is desirable for pragmatic reasons alone that the fact that the concept of family in the European Community is fluid rather than static should be reflected in the jurisprudence of the ECJ. Moreover, the ECJ's approach has gender implications. The position of women in the labour market[35] means, for example, that exclusion of divorcees from the protection of Community secondary law concerning family rights leaves women more vulnerable than men to exclusion from the Member State of residence of the family. Single-parent families are predominantly headed by women;[36] where that woman is not even a worker, let alone a migrant worker in the European Community, then the family is unable to benefit from the provisions of Community law.[37] If the woman is a worker, some form of child-care is necessary, and is generally speaking carried out by another woman: grandparents, aunts, or close family friends or associates not related by blood ties.[38] Unless the carer is a dependant ascendant (grandmother), she will not fall within the ECJ's definition of "family". Thus the model of family perpetuated by the ECJ, reflecting a norm which is not experienced by all families, has a disparate impact on women, since it is their experience which it least reflects.

4   FAMILY RIGHTS PROTECTED FOR
ECONOMIC, NOT SOCIAL OR HUMAN ENDS

The jurisprudence of the ECJ on family rights reflects a particular presumption concerning the function of the provisions protecting family rights. The ECJ has consistently stated, in the context of both Regulation 1612/68 and Regulation 1408/71, that the provisions are in place in order to encourage and facilitate

---

[34] See Commission Communication on Family Policies, loc. cit., note 5, at 5–8; Emmert, loc. cit., note 19, at 365.

[35] See *infra.*

[36] Commission Communication on Family Policies, *supra,* note 5, at 7.

[37] See further *infra.*

[38] Glasner, "Gender and Europe: Cultural and Structural Impediments to Change", in Bailey (ed.), *Social Europe* (1992), at p. 84.

the free movement of workers or self-employed persons.[39] The rights of family members are "derived rights",[40] "secondary to those of the worker".[41]

The focus on the economic purpose underpinning family rights in Community law operates to the detriment of the social or human purposes of the right to respect for family life as a *fundamental* right. The elevation of economic rights, and concomitant subordination of social and political rights, is a general criticism of human rights protection in European Community law. Defenders of the ECJ's position would be quick to point out that the Community is an economic community, and the purpose of Community law is to attain and maintain the Single European Market. However, as posited in the introduction, the Community has now "grown up" into the European Union, a supranational organization whose activities affect matters other than purely economic matters. When Community law affects individual *human beings*, as the legal system of a mature democratic society, it has a duty to guarantee respect for fundamental political and social rights. Consideration of those rights as "fundamental" necessarily implies that their protection is more important than promotion of economic goals.[42] Respect for the right to family life is not guaranteed where the enforcement of rights of family members in Community law depends upon a construction of the relevant provisions which reflects their *economic* function in preference to their social and human function.

Weiler is particularly critical of this aspect of the ECJ's protection of the right to family life. In his analysis of the *Diatta*[43] case, he points out that the effect of the ECJ's decision is to "reify" the (woman) spouse, whose rights do not attach to her at all, but are given to her spouse in order to ensure that he can benefit from free movement in the Community. This approach, concludes

---

[39] See, e.g., Case 40/76, loc. cit., note 11, at para. 7; Case 63/76, *Inzirillo* v *Caisse Allocations Familiales Lyon*, [1976] ECR 2057, at para. 17; Case 65/81, loc. cit., note 11, at para. 12; Case 267/83, loc. cit., note 30, at para. 16; Case 157/84, loc. cit., note 11, at paras 15–17; Case 59/85, loc. cit., note 14, at para. 28; Case 131/85, *Gül* v *Regierungspräsident Düsseldorf,* [1986] ECR 1573, at para. 14; Case 249/86, loc. cit., note 4, at para. 11; Case C-370/90, loc. cit., note 16, at paras 19–20. See Weiler, loc. cit., note 18, at 88–89.

[40] Case 40/76, loc. cit., note 11, at para. 7; Case 157/84, loc. cit., note 11, at paras 15–17.

[41] Case 131/85, loc. cit., note 39, at para. 14.

[42] This statement somewhat oversimplifies matters: it would be rare to find a direct and bald conflict between political and social rights on the one hand and economic goals on the other. However, it is asserted that in "hard cases" protection of "fundamental" (political and social) rights should prevail.

[43] Case 267/83, loc. cit., note 30.

Weiler, is "profoundly contradictory from a human rights perspective".[44] The ECJ should "refuse to base its jurisprudence *exclusively* on that basis and it should also refuse to construe any provision of Community law which involves real individuals exclusively on that basis".[45]

The ECJ's economic approach to the protection of family rights also has gender implications. The ECJ's reasoning can be characterized by an extension of Langan and Ostner's use of "commodification" and "decommodification": "men are commodified, made ready to sell their labour power on the market, by the work done by women in the family. Women on the other hand, are decommodified by their position in the family".[46] The Single Market takes into account the commodification of (male) workers, by recognizing that in order to move to work, workers need to take with them the family support structures which enable them to work. The role of supporting and caring for the worker, and dependents of the worker, is predominantly carried out by women. In Community law, migrant workers are further "commodified" by the possibility that their families are able to move with them. Since migrant workers are mostly men,[47] the gendered construct of protection of family rights is perpetuated.

5   FAMILY RIGHTS AS PARASITES ON WORKERS' RIGHTS

All rights of family members in Community law flow from the relationship of the family members with a Union citizen who has exercised his or her free movement rights. The more significant, and costly,[48] rights (to social advantages in accordance with the non-discrimination principle) are reserved for family members of those who have moved in order to work.

"Irrespective of their nationality" the spouse and their[49] descendants who are under the age of 21 years or are dependants, and dependant ascendants of a worker and the worker's spouse have "the right to install themselves" with a worker who is a Union citizen and is employed, or has

---

[44] Weiler, loc. cit., note 18, at 90.

[45] Ibid.

[46] Langan and Ostner, loc. cit., note 20, at p. 131.

[47] See *infra*.

[48] I.e., for the host state.

[49] I.e., of either spouse.

been employed,[50] in a Member State which is not the state of which the worker is a national.[51] The worker must be able to provide "normal housing" for the family.[52] Members of the family of the worker, as defined in Regulation 1612/68, are entitled to residence permits[53] and, if certain requirements are met, are entitled to remain in the host state.[54] No restrictions on the movement or residence of a Union citizen established or providing services in another Member State and that person's spouse and children, and their ascending and descending lines of dependants are permitted.[55] Family members of self-employed persons, as defined in Directive 73/148, are entitled to remain in the host state if the self-employed person has gained that entitlement.[56] Families of students who have moved in order to undertake their education or training are entitled to reside in the host Member State provided that the entire family is covered by sickness insurance, and has sufficient resources to avoid becoming a burden on the host Member State.[57]

For those Union citizens who do not enjoy the right of residence in a state of which they are not nationals under other provisions of Community law, they and their families are entitled to reside in that state, again provided that the entire family is covered by sickness insurance, and has sufficient resources to avoid becoming a burden on the host Member State.[58]

The spouse and children under the age of 21 of a Union citizen worker who has moved have the right to work, regardless of their nationality.[59] In this context, the right to work includes the right to exercise a profession.[60] A Union citizen worker who has moved "shall enjoy the same social and tax

---

[50] See Case C-370/90, loc. cit., note 16.

[51] Regulation 1612/68/EEC, Art. 10.

[52] Regulation 1612/68/EEC, Art. 10(3). See Case 249/86, loc. cit., note 4—the non-discrimination principle applies: once the family are admitted, into "normal" housing, they cannot be removed if another child is born, taking them outside the definition of "normal" housing, where such a sanction would not be applied to German nationals.

[53] Directive 68/360/EEC, O.J. Sp. Ed. 1968 L 257/13, Art. 4(3).

[54] Directive 1251/70/EEC, Arts. 1 and 3.

[55] Directive 73/148/EEC, Art. 1; Art. 4(3)—residence permits.

[56] Directive 75/34/EEC, Arts. 1 and 3.

[57] Directive 90/366/EEC, Art. 1.

[58] Directive 90/364/EEC, Art. 1. "Family members" are defined in Art. 1(2).

[59] Regulation 1612/68, Art. 11.

[60] See Case 131/85, loc. cit., note 39.

advantages as national workers".[61] The term "social advantage" has been given a wide definition as:[62]

> those [advantages] which, whether or not linked to the contract of employment, are generally granted to national workers primarily because of their objective status as workers or by virtue of the mere fact of their residence on the national territory.

Social advantages include family benefits (the term is used in its broadest sense), as these benefits have been interpreted by the ECJ as being in essence benefits granted to the worker.[63] Family members are included in the provisions for the application of social security schemes to migrant workers.[64]

The rights of family members in Community law are thus heavily contingent upon the relationship of the family members to a Union citizen who has moved. Better protection of family rights is given to families of moving Union citizen workers. Moreover, the ECJ has been reluctant to extend the application of the relevant provisions of Community law to all persons whose human right to respect for family life might have been breached, by means of reference to the principle of respect for the right to family life in Article 8 ECHR. The *Demirel* case[65] is illustrative in this respect. The ECJ was called upon to interpret the Association Agreement between the European Community and Turkey, in the context of a Turkish national, married to a Turkish worker in Germany, who did not comply with the provisions of German law on reunification of families. The ECJ simply held that the provision of the Association Agreement did not produce direct effects, and therefore it was not required to consider Article 8 ECHR.[66]

---

[61] Regulation 1612/68/EEC, Art. 7.

[62] Case 207/78, *Ministère Public* v *Even,* [1979] ECR 2019.

[63] Case 32/75, loc. cit., note 11; Case 63/76, loc. cit., note 39; Case 261/83, *Castelli* v *ONPTS,* [1984] ECR 3199; Case 157/84, loc. cit., note 11; see Wyatt and Dashwood, *European Community Law* (1993), 3rd edn, at p. 261.

[64] Regulation 1408/71/EEC, Art. 1(f) and (g). Family benefits are payable even if the family is not resident in the same Member State as the worker—see Case 41/84, *Pinna* v *Caisse d'allocations familiales de la Savoie,* [1986] ECR 1.

[65] Case 12/86, *Demirel* v *Stadt Schwäbisch Gmünd,* [1987] ECR 3719.

[66] The reasoning of the ECJ has been criticized: "This approach might be compared to the instances when *Community* nationals have successfully invoked human rights concepts in the context of freedom of movement [e.g., Case 36/75, loc. cit., note 4]. It may also be compared to the ruling of the European Court of Human Rights in Eur. Court H. R., *Berrehab* judgment of 21 June 1988, Series A no. 138, where a Moroccan migrant in the Netherlands successfully argued that deportation

The contingency of family rights upon workers rights has a gendered impact. Migrant workers in the European Union are predominantly male.[67] Although the ECJ has been at pains to give a wide definition to "worker" in the context of the free movement provisions,[68] the definition is nevertheless firmly rooted in the prevailing model of work and family in Western European society.[69] The model reflects a particular construct of "work".[70] "Work" is a public, market-related concept, legally (and socially) constructed as an economic activity undertaken in the public sphere, for pay. Work carried out by women, in particular migrant women, such as domestic service, petty trade, jobs with high seasonal variations and home-working, is often outside the formal economy[71] and does not fall within the construct. The construct of "work" reflects certain assumptions about "workers", for example that they are independent, supported by a spouse, without significant caring responsibilities in the private world of the family. Those assumptions skew the concept of worker towards men, whose position more readily fits the norm.

The trend in all Member States towards informal, private and largely unpaid welfare provision[72] exacerbates the position. Women's domestic role

---

after the breakdown of his marriage would deny him the right to see his child and would therefore be an infringement of the right to respect family life contained in Art. 8 of the ECHR 1953." Nielsen and Szyszczak, op. cit., note 16, p. 67.

[67] Hecq and Plasman, op. cit., note 33; Jackson, op. cit., note 33; Schwiewe, "EC Law's Unequal Treatment of the Family: The Case Law of the European Court of Justice on Rules Prohibiting Discrimination on Grounds of Sex and Nationality", 3 *Social and Legal Studies* (1994), 243–265, at 249.

[68] Case 75/63, *Hoekstra v Bedrijfsvereniging voor Detailhandel*, [1964] ECR 177; Case 53/81, *Levin v Staatssecretaris van Justitie*, [1982] ECR 1035; Case 139/85, *Kempf v Staatssecretaris van Justitie*, [1986] ECR 1741; Case 196/87, *Steymann v Staatssecretaris van Justitie*, [1988] ECR 6159; Joined Cases 389 and 390/87, *Echternach and Another v Minister for Education and Science*, [1989] ECR 723.

[69] The model is well documented in feminist legal writing. For comment relating the model specifically to European Community law, see, for example, Hervey, *Justifications for Sex Discrimination in Employment* (1993), at pp. 21–41; Fredman, "European Community Discrimination Law: A Critique", 21 *International Law Journal* (1992), 119–134; Hoskyns, "Women, European Law and Transnational Politics", (1986) Int J Soc L, 299–315.

[70] Meehan describes the neutrality of the terms "migrant" and "worker" as "more apparent than real". Meehan, *Citizenship and the European Community* (1993), at p. 105.

[71] Morokvasic, "Fortress Europe and Migrant Women", 39 *Feminist Review* (1991), 69–84, at 75; Bhabha and Shutter, op. cit., note 17, at pp. 6–8.

[72] See Cochrane and Clarke, *Comparing Welfare States* (1993); Glasner, loc. cit., note 38; Lewis, "Gender and the Development of Welfare Regimes", 2 *Journal of European Social Policy* (1992) 159–173; Ackers, "Women, Citizenship and European Community Law", 16 *Journal of Social*

as carers[73] has implications for their ability to enter the public workforce as workers. The social values concerning the roles and responsibilities of women, and those of men, result in a gendering of the provisions concerning workers in European Community law. That construction is carried over and impacts upon family rights, since family rights are contingent upon workers' rights.

As pointed out above, neither provisions of secondary law nor decisions of the ECJ discriminate directly on grounds of sex. But given the particular position of many women, and the fact that most women's work does not give them worker status, the effect of the rules is to perpetuate a gendered structure of family rights, in which women's rights are subordinate to men's.

6   CONCLUSION

In view of the contribution to equal treatment of women with men made by the ECJ in the area of employment law, in particular by recognition of the concept of indirect discrimination, it would be desirable for similar gendered implications of provisions of Community law concerning family rights to be subjected to equivalent scrutiny. The principle of equality or non-discrimination, *inter alia,* on grounds of sex, is reputed to pervade Community law. Proper protection for human rights depends upon respect for the principle of equality, not only in its formal sense, but also in order to protect human rights of women within the structural inequalities that permeate Western European conceptions of work and the family.

Welfare and Family Law (1994), 391–406.

[73] Glasner, loc. cit., note 38, at 79–85.

12 CULTURAL PROTECTION: A MATTER OF UNION CITIZENSHIP OR HUMAN RIGHTS?

Malcolm Ross

1 INTRODUCTION

> In my opinion, a Community national ... is ... entitled to assume that ... he will be treated in accordance with a common code of fundamental values, in particular those laid down in the European Convention on Human Rights. In other words he is entitled to say *'civis europeus sum'* and to invoke that status in order to oppose any violation of his fundamental rights.[1]

This trenchant espousal of the European citizen, even before the Maastricht Treaty on European Union (TEU) took effect, combines inspiration with aspiration. It is radical enough to have engendered caution and opposition from within the Court of Justice of the European Communities (ECJ) itself.[2] The concept of citizenship of the Union, expressly contained in Article B of the Common Provisions of the TEU and given greater detail in the revised Part Two (Articles 8–8e) of the EC Treaty, concentrates on free movement and civic participation without any further elaboration of potential content.[3] However, the particularly interesting feature of the *Konstantinidis* case is that the argument of the Advocate General utilized a concept of European citizenry to urge the protection of individual identity by requiring accurate transliteration of names. Although the ECJ chose to resolve that case by a narrower and less

---

[1] Advocate General Jacobs' Opinion in Case C-168/91, *Konstantinidis* v *Stadt Altensteig Standesamt,* [1993] ECR I-1191.

[2] In Case C-2/92, *Bostock,* [1994] ECR I-955 Advocate General Gulmann expressly indicated that the views of Advocate General Jacobs were "too far-reaching".

[3] In a legal context, see Closa, "The Concept of Citizenship in the Treaty on European Union", 29 CML Rev. (1992), 1137–1170; O'Keeffe, "Union Citizenship", in O'Keeffe and Twomey (eds), *Legal Issues of the Maastricht Treaty* (1993), pp. 87–107. For a different perspective, see Meehan, *Citizenship and the European Community* (1993).

N. A. Neuwahl and A. Rosas (eds.), The European Union and Human Rights, 235–248.
© 1995 Kluwer Law International. Printed in the Netherlands.

controversial route,[4] the Opinion blazes a trail which others will inevitably follow. In principle, the argument for preserving individual identity is applicable with equal force to group or regional identities and traditions, or to other elements of cultural heritage.

This chapter accordingly examines the link between cultural policy, freshly but loosely articulated as a matter of EC competence and concern in Article 128 of the revised EC Treaty, and the enhanced constitutional development of the Community and Union. At present the Community's survival and progression face at least two broad threats. First, there exists an increasingly variable geometry in terms of decision-making machinery, competences and enforcement processes.[5] This may bring Europe closer to the citizen in one sense but simultaneously threatens to obscure the benefits of membership and distort their uniform application. Secondly, the programme of continuing territorial expansion risks dilution of the substantive content of the rights of citizens. In the light of these threats, the rationale for a supranational Community may perhaps rest upon the identification of a core of values to be rooted and sustained throughout the unit. The search for such values seems likely to trigger an explosion of interest in the relationship between law and culture.

An initial difficulty is that the labels of culture, cultural rights or cultural heritage are not susceptible to tidy or universally meaningful definition.[6] Indeed, there is no attempt at such a definition in either Article 128 or elsewhere in the Treaty. For the purpose of this chapter, references to culture and cultural protection belong at the wider, anthropologically inspired,[7] end of the spectrum of definitions rather than reflecting what might be the narrower approaches of, say, particular international conventions.[8] Put another way, the concept here is not confined to any grand view of culture as a

---

[4] I.e., by a test based on whether the individual's right of establishment would be prejudiced by confusion as to his identity among customers.

[5] See Curtin, "The Constitutional Structure of the Union: A Europe of Bits and Pieces", 30 CML Rev. (1993), 17–69; Harmsen, "A European Union of Variable Geometry: Problems and Perspectives" 45 *Netherlands International Law Quarterly* (1994), 109.

[6] Further discussed in Loman, Mortelmans, Post and Watson, *Culture and Community Law,* (1992), Chapter 1.

[7] See Macdonald, "Identity Complexes in Western Europe: Social Anthropological Perspectives", in Macdonald (ed.), *Inside European Identities* (1993), pp. 1–26. More widely, see Snyder, *Law and Anthropology: A Review,* EUI Working Papers in Law, No. 93/4, European University Institute, Florence.

[8] E.g, Art. 10 of the Convention for the Protection of Human Rights and Fundamental Freedoms (European Convention on Human Rights; ECHR) concerning freedom of expression.

universalized zenith of human achievement and spirit, but instead accommodates a variety of values, practices, contributions and knowledge. The evolving nature of the European Community and Union requires that neither culture nor its values should remain static.

But this very fluidity should not be taken to imply that Article 128 implements what might have been the Member States' intention to take a vacuous or minimalist approach to enjoyment of cultural heritage. First, it is clear from the TEU that the pre-existing *acquis communautaire* is left in place. As explained further below, considerable case law pre-Maastricht reveals culture as a legitimate protectable interest with regard to measures which might otherwise interfere with fundamental freedoms of the Treaty of Rome. Secondly, from an institutional perspective, the ECJ's proven record in translating rhetoric or aspirations into legally enforceable rights supports an expectation that far from being an adjunct to other considerations and interests, cultural heritage may be elevated in the light of national and international experiences together with the ECJ's view of EC Treaty objectives into a fundamental EC law interest. By this route, cultural protection can be seen as an essential element in the constitutionalizing process. Thirdly, especially since the TEU, cultural issues themselves cut across other areas of Treaty activity, making it inadvisable (and indeed impossible) to seal off Article 128 as the sole legal basis relevant to cultural protection. Fourthly, the express affirmation in the TEU of a concept of citizenship, as yet unexplored by the ECJ, may prove the catalyst and justification for a more coherent and principled approach to cultural protection. Finally, attention must be paid to the normative element in shaping cultural development and resolving conflicts between cultures. The human rights perspective dominates this issue. These considerations are examined in turn below.

2   THE PLACE OF CULTURAL HERITAGE
PROTECTION IN THE *ACQUIS COMMUNAUTAIRE*

The place of cultural heritage in existing EC law has been to perform a legitimizing role for Member State activity, rather than as a specific goal for Community level action and protection. In evolving a unitary set of principles with which to evaluate the compatibility of national action with Community freedoms of movement, particularly in relation to goods and services, the ECJ has relied upon various "mandatory requirements".[9] These represent values or interests of sufficient importance to outrank the principles of free movement. Thus cultural characteristics or interests have, for example, supported non-interference by the ECJ in rules affecting the video release of cinema films.[10] However, these interests can only be relied upon if applied in accordance with the general EC law principle of proportionality. Hence the inability of Member States in cases relating to tourist guides[11] and broadcasting privileges[12] to use cultural protection as a justification for measures which operated as restrictions on the freedom to provide those services. As the ECJ observed in the *Greek Tourist Guide* case:

> The general interest in the proper appreciation of the artistic and archaeological heritage of a country and in consumer protection can constitute an overriding reason justifying a restriction on the freedom to provide services. However, the requirement in question contained in the Greek legislation goes beyond what is necessary to ensure the safeguarding of that interest inasmuch as it makes the activities of a tourist guide accompanying groups of tourists from another Member State subject to possession of a licence ...
> It follows that in view of the scale of the restrictions it imposes, the legislation in issue is disproportionate in relation to the objective pursued, namely to ensure the proper appreciation of places and things of historical interest, the widest possible dissemination of knowledge and the artistic and cultural heritage of the Member State in which the tour is conducted, and the protection of consumers.

The importance of these cases lies not just in the function performed by cultural interests, but in the status attached to them by the ECJ. By putting cultural heritage alongside other recognized interests such as protection of the environment,[13] consumers,[14] and workers,[15] the ECJ has isolated cultural heritage as a concern which is protectable by virtue of it being compatible with the goals of the EC. In other words, the effect is not to disable EC level action

---

[9] Originating in Case 120/78, *Rewe* v *Bundesmonopolverwaltung für Branntwein,* [1979] ECR 649, the so-called *Cassis de Dijon* doctrine.

[10] Joined Cases 60 and 61/84, *Cinéthèque* v *Fédération nationale des cinémas français,* [1985] ECR 2605.

[11] Case C-198/89, *Commission* v *Greece,* [1991] ECR I-727.

[12] Case C-288/89, *Collectieve Antennevoorziening Gouda,* [1991] ECR I-4007.

[13] Case 302/86, *Commission* v *Denmark ("drinks containers"),* [1988] ECR 4607.

[14] Case 220/83, *Commission* v *France,* [1986] ECR 3663.

[15] Case C-113/89, *Rush Portuguesa* v *ONI,* [1990] ECR I-1417.

in favour of national measures as a matter of principle, but instead to assert that those measures are only acceptable by reason of meeting legitimate purposes recognized by and contained in the EC Treaty. Although there has been some (much criticized) retrenchment by the ECJ in the area of free movement of goods[16] in favour of a rule-based approach instead of a standard-oriented one,[17] the *Cassis* edifice remains in place as a set of generally applicable values.[18] Those values may change over time, but the crucial point is that when recognized by the ECJ they dictate the application of inferior provisions in the legal hierarchy.

3   CULTURE AND THE CONSTITUTIONALIZING PROCESS

These observations about culture's significance must be related to the pattern of constitutional development engineered by the ECJ. This has consisted in establishing the Treaty as a constitutional charter for a Community based on the rule of law[19] and in identifying a hierarchy of obligations within the Treaty, based not just on the overt objectives set out in Articles 2 and 3 but in the fundamental and general principles revealed by the ECJ's own jurisprudence. The role and effect of Article 5 in this context has been amply demonstrated elsewhere.[20] Its most noticeable contribution has been to legitimize the duties imposed by the ECJ upon institutional actors to promote the efficacy of EC law. Put another way, the product of Article 5 is to focus more upon process and institutional solidarity than upon the content of

---

[16] Joined Cases C-267 and C-268/91, *Keck and Mithouard,* [1993] ECR I-6097. See Chalmers, "Repackaging the Internal Market—the Ramifications of the *Keck* Judgment", 19 EL Rev. (1994), 385–403; Reich, "The 'November Revolution' of the European Court of Justice: *Keck, Meng* and *Audi* revisited", 31 CML Rev. (1994), 459–492. The ECJ's reasoning in *Keck* has been described as "unsatisfactory" by Advocate General Jacobs in his Opinion in Case C-412/93, *Leclerc-Siplec* v *TF1 Publicité and M6 Publicité* (24 Nov. 1994), para. 38, not yet reported.

[17] Wils, "The Search for the Rule in Article 30 EEC: Much Ado about Nothing?", 18 EL Rev. (1993), 475–492.

[18] Cf. the developments in relation to Art. 90(2) in response to the claims of entrusted undertakings to escape the rules of the Treaty. For example, Case C-393/92, *Almelo,* [1994] ECR I-1477.

[19] See *Opinion 1/91, Re the Draft Treaty on a European Economic Area,* [1992] 1 CMLR 245, especially para. 21.

[20] See, i.a., Temple Lang, "Community Constitutional Law: Article 5 EC Treaty", 27 CML Rev. (1990), 645–681; Mancini and Keeling, "Democracy and the European Court of Justice", 57 MLR (1994), 175–190; Ross, "Beyond Francovich", 56 MLR (1993), 55–73.

individual legal rights. This is not to say that Article 5 is incapable of adding to the latter. Indeed, the day that the ECJ reveals that individuals have a right to have the Community (or Union) run in accordance with its constitution will perhaps be the clearest testimony to progress in that direction.[21]

The most clearcut manifestation of the expansion of content has been the ECJ's use of fundamental principles.[22] These have been derived from international conventions and commonality between national constitutions, most obviously in the human rights field.

The debate about cultural rights in the latter at international level has been fierce, both as to their content and their status in comparison with other "generations" of rights.[23] These same difficulties, which must inevitably resurface in the Union context, are likely to be addressed by the ECJ in a fragmented and limited manner.[24] Moreover, the climate surrounding the discussion is one in which a drive for localized identity and decentralization of an alien Community is more rife than ever.

But in this very fact lies opportunity. The precedents for judicial activism in the guise of constraint reinforce the view that aspects of cultural protection may provide the ammunition for the entrenchment and development of allegiance to an EC unit to the extent that it is perceived to offer benefits to regions, groups and individuals. It may be recalled that the ECJ's first recognition of human rights protection[25] was driven by the need to maintain the principle of supremacy in the face of a national constitution which threatened to confer a greater measure of individual protection. The challenge for the ECJ now is how to offer a Community level of individual and local protection as a tangible benefit which in turn generates allegiance and identity. As Meehan has observed,[26] overlapping or multiple layers of citizenship or identity are possible. It would prove a bitter irony for some Member States if the thrust for subsidiarity were to generate a judicial response which vigorously applied it to promote increased reliance upon Community

---

[21] See further Ross, loc. cit., note 20. In the past the ECJ has expressly said that Art. 5 does not have direct effect: Case 9/73, *Schlüter* v *Hauptzollamt Lörrach,* [1973] ECR 1135; Case 44/84, *Hurd* v *Jones,* [1986] ECR 29.

[22] See Coppel and O'Neill, "The European Court of Justice: Taking Rights Seriously?', 29 CML Rev. (1992), 669–692.

[23] See generally, Heffernan (ed.), *Human Rights—A European Perspective* (1994).

[24] Although the pattern of this may largely be influenced by the outcome of the Opinion on EC accession to the ECHR, currently pending before the ECJ.

[25] Case 29/69, *Stauder* v *Ulm,* [1969] ECR 419.

[26] Op. cit., note 3.

instruments and principles for the most effective and efficient achievement of sub-national cultural maintenance and development.

The fate of cultural protection must be seen against the general processes shaping the constitutional development of the Union. To date, this evolution as led by the ECJ has derived from and then perpetuated norms which rely upon hierarchical values and individualized enforcement rather than any philosophical underpinning of human rights. The continuing debate as to the merits and effects of so-called variable geometry points up the need for some discernible and fundamental "core" to be maintained. Whilst there may be room for structural and jurisidictional variations[27] without inflicting terminal damage, it is submitted that a core set of values are indispensable to the survival of the Union as a coherent and democratic unit. The balancing or, where necessary, prioritizing of values is thus an essential task for the ECJ. This has to be undertaken within the objectives and framework of the Treaty so that, for example, securing enjoyment of an identified cultural heritage would be achieved by subjecting competing restrictions or goals to the ECJ's imposed hierarchy of protectable interests. Instead of previous emphasis on limited free movement for factors of production, a post-Single Market agenda might attempt to give effect to economic and social cohesion based on citizenship whilst retaining cultural diversity. In this way, cultural protection as a core value for the Union has then to be pursued and recognized through the effective legal channels already established by the ECJ in its famous constitutionalizing decisions.

For the ECJ, individual enforcement of rights is a paradigm in EC development which has in the past furthered the goal of entrenchment of the new legal order in national contexts. With regard to cultural heritage this same paradigm of effective enjoyment can be directed towards the maintenance of diversity as the basis of allegiance. Furthermore, the decentralizing potential of subsidiarity works to the same end. Indeed, instead of removing or diminishing the relevance of EC law, the combined effect of subsidiarity and solidarity[28] applied to a generalized principle of cultural protection provides a route for individual action independent of the cumbersome and ostensibly minimalist legislative provisions contemplated in Article 128. Once a right to cultural protection is established at EC level, the normal principles of supremacy can then be applied to circumvent some of the difficulties

---

[27] Harmsen, loc. cit., note 5: illustrations of structural geometry being the three pillars of the Union, whilst jurisdictional patterns embrace, for example, the European Economic Area (EEA).

[28] Art. 5 EC Treaty, obliging Member States to facilitate the achievement of the objectives of the Treaty and to abstain from any measure which could jeopardize their attainment.

encountered under national laws in asserting rights to enjoyment of cultural heritage.

But even assuming that individual enforcement of cultural protection is available by this process, there remains the need to consider how the strengthening of *ad hoc* redress falls short of achieving the wider priorities of a Community cultural policy to be established under the Article 128 institutional framework.[29] For even if individuals are able to seek protection outside that provision, any scope for institutional legal action at Community level remains circumscribed by it as a result of the ECJ's jurisprudence on the choice of legal basis for legislative intervention.[30] A curious gulf thus exists between the tools available to individuals to challenge particular threats to cultural heritage and the scope for proactive policy development. The scope of the new Article 128 to support the latter must therefore be examined.

4   CULTURAL POLICY UNDER THE MAASTRICHT TREATY

As a result of the revisions introduced by the TEU, Article 3(p) EC Treaty now provides that one of the objectives of Community action is "a contribution to education and training of quality and to the flowering of the cultures of the Member States". This is then fleshed out by a separate Title devoted to culture, comprising Article 128:

> 1. The Community shall contribute to the flowering of the cultures of the Member States, while respecting their national and regional diversity and at the same time bringing the common cultural heritage to the fore.
> 2. Action by the Community shall be aimed at encouraging cooperation between Member States and, if necessary, supporting and supplementing their action in the following areas:
> — improvement of the knowledge and dissemination of the culture and history of the European peoples;
> — conservation and safeguarding of cultural heritage of European significance;
> — non-commercial cultural exchanges;

---

[29] See "New Prospects for Community Cultural Action", COM (92) 149 final for the Commission's policy proposals and the opinion thereon of the Economic and Social Committee, O.J. C 332/67.

[30] It is clear, for example, that Art. 235 EC Treaty will not be authorized by the ECJ as a general law-making basis in situations where a particular article of the Treaty can be identified instead. See Case C-295/90, *European Parliament (EC Commission intervening)* v *Council*, [1992] ECR I-4193. See generally, Emiliou, "Opening Pandora's Box: The Legal Basis of Community Measures before the Court of Justice", 19 EL Rev. (1994), 488–507.

— artistic and literary creation, including in the audiovisual sector;

3. The Community and the Member States shall foster cooperation with third countries and the competent international organizations in the sphere of culture, in particular the Council of Europe.

4. The Community shall take cultural aspects into account in its action under other provisions of this Treaty.

5. In order to contribute to the achievement of the objectives referred to in this Article, the Council:

— acting in accordance with the procedure referred to in Article 189b[31] and after consulting the Committee of the Regions,[32] shall adopt incentive measures, excluding any harmonization of the laws and regulations of the Member States. The Council shall act unanimously throughout the procedures referred to in Article 189b;

— acting unanimously on a proposal from the Commission, shall adopt recommendations.

Several points are immediately striking about this provision.

First, there is no definition of cultural heritage in this context. It is especially noticeable that the reference is to the cultures of the Member States, a phrase which does not obviously include regions and sub-groups. Nevertheless, the ECJ has an unfettered hand in clarifying the scope of this concept. Secondly, the express rejection of harmonization measures, indicated in paragraph 5, is potentially offset by the general obligation imposed (arguably at least) by paragraph 4. Thirdly, there is an odd internal contradiction in the decision-making processes envisaged, since the device named (Article 189b) is based on qualified majority voting yet Article 128 expressly requires unanimity in its operation. An immediate conflict is opened up between the institutional arrangements for action under Article 128 and the possibilities for individual protection routed through fundamental principles of the Treaty.

Given political sensitivities, it is not surprising that the Commisson's response[33] to Article 128 has stuck closely to its unequivocal scope. Thus there are three priority areas for intervention: heritage,[34] artistic activities[35]

---

[31] I.e., the so-called co-decision procedure; discussed fully by Dashwood, "Community Legislative Procedures in the Era of the Treaty on European Union", 19 EL Rev. (1994), 343–366.

[32] Set up under Art. 198a EC Treaty, consisting of representatives of regional and local bodies, and required to be consulted on various matters under the EC Treaty.

[33] "European Community Action in Support of Culture", COM (94) 356.

[34] Embracing both movable and nonmovable heritage.

[35] The "Kaleidoscope 2000" project, to encourage artistic and cultural creation in Europe in the fields of the performing arts, visual or spatial arts, multimedia arts and applied arts by bringing this creation closer to different European publics: see O.J. 1994, C 324/5.

and books and reading.[36] Each of these is to be promoted by five strategies: enhancement and extension to a wider audience; networks and partnerships; access to culture; research and training; and co-operation with third countries and international organizations. The instruments for these strategies are financial support and technical assistance. These programmes are designed to extend beyond purely emblematic activities to provide a deeper horizontal communication and understanding of culture. Vertical initiatives are also envisaged, particularly in the context of economy and employment in heritage activities, tourism, the environment, research and new technologies.[37]

It is easy to understate these strategies, especially since their effectiveness is not susceptible to immediate or obvious measurement. In the short term such activities should stress that culture is dynamic, and not just the embalming of the past. In the longer term this horizontal strategy touches on the most fundamental elements of a cohesive Union, since it is capable of underpinning both allegiance and tolerance.[38] The former is served by establishing the value in EC law of heritage (whether relating to EC, national or sub-national levels) and creating the legal machinery by which to sustain it. Tolerance, which in turn preserves the dynamic of diversity, is supported by awareness and education. But the relationship between competing allegiances is likely to be in tension, the balance of which is made all the more precarious by many factors, including most obviously patterns of migration.[39] There are too many cultural clashes still giving rise to armed conflict in Europe to make grandiose claims about the magic wand effects of cultural initiatives in promoting tolerance. Nevertheless, it should be noted that the actions envisaged under Article 128 are based on bringing Europe closer to the citizen as a necessary bottom-up principle which is not so evident in other moves to greater integration.

The provision of Article 128 which is likely to prove more contentious legally once sufficient confidence has been acquired to test its scope is paragraph 4. A requirement to "take account of" cultural aspects in other

---

[36] The ARIANE scheme, mainly to support translation as a means to promote knowledge and dissemination of European cultures and literary creation; see O.J. 1994, C 324/11.

[37] See discussion of the Lisbon Meeting of Member States' Directors of Movable and Non-Movable Heritage, 27–29 April 1994.

[38] See Wæver, "Societal Security: the Concept"; and Wæver and Kelstrup, "Europe and Its Nations: Political and Cultural Identities", in Wæver, Buzan, Kelstrup and Lemaitre (eds), *Identity, Migration and the New Security Agenda in Europe* (1993), pp. 61–92. Also Harvie, *The Rise of Regional Europe* (1994).

[39] A tension compounded by the requirement for Union citizenship of Member State nationality.

Community spheres invites a minimalist response from Member States eager to play down internal strife or dissent among different traditions, groups or regions. But the presence of Article 128(4) recognizes two crucial points: that nurturing culture is a genuinely horizontal factor in the development of the Community, cutting across all other activities, and that this in itself is indicative of the fundamental character of cultural protection. The consequences can be discussed at the level of both legal process and individual enjoyment.

As far as process is concerned, there are two key preconditions to safeguard Article 128(4). First, the Commission needs to be sufficiently organized internally to recognize and integrate cultural issues into general policy formulation. This requirement has already been acknowledged in the Commission's proposals regarding the Kaleidoscope and ARIANE programmes,[40] in so far as it is to draw up an inventory of the cultural dimension in what it sees as the relevant Community policies such as regional development, new technologies and external relations. It is less clear what impact cultural considerations are likely to have in other sectors, for example competition and the Single Market. Scenarios are easy enough to devise in which culture could be raised in the context of questions relating to merger control, infrastructure development (such as motorway construction) or commercial arrangements such as the net book agreement.[41] It does not appear to be envisaged that cultural issues which already[42] belong to other specific areas of the Treaty will have their legal base changed as a result of the introduction of the new Title IX.

Secondly, effective dissemination of cultural awareness is of course conditional upon financial assistance and political commitment, the former being forthcoming from the latter. The political attraction of an umbrella EC-level protection of culture is that it can be viewed as a paradigm of subsidiarity: the encouragement and effective use of national and sub-national traditions and styles. In this sense Article 128 forms a counterbalance to the fears associated with myths (or realities) about Single Market homogeneity. A "Euro-sceptic" perspective might portray Article 128 as the harbinger of some equally anodyne European cultural monolith but, as has been argued above,

---

[40] *Supra,* notes 35 and 36.

[41] See Joined Cases 43 and 63/82, *VBVB and VBBB* v *Commission,* [1984] ECR 19; and Case T-66/89, *Publishers' Association* v *Commission,* [1992] ECR II-1995.

[42] For example, measures adopted for the export of cultural goods and the return of cultural property exported illegally: Regulation 3911/92, O.J. 1992, L 395/1 and Directive 93/7, O.J. 1993, L 74/74 respectively.

this view is misplaced. The paradox of EC-level protection in this area is that it maintains faith in the larger unit to protect the interests of sub-groups.

As indicated in the previous discussion of the constitutionalizing process, recognition of the fundamental character of culture implies that the ECJ would use the principles available to it to secure its effective enjoyment by individuals. Actions by disgruntled inhabitants of rural environments laid waste by motorway construction or by speakers of particular regional languages seeking to resist their abandonment could test the relevance of Article 128(4). Might so-called travellers challenge national statutory policing provisions on the basis that their effect is to deprive this group of their way of life?[43] Possibilities such as these illustrate ways in which the ECJ might be fed the opportunity to engage in cementing cultural values at an individual level. However, unlike previous developments in private rights, scope now exists to place them within a more systematic, institutionalized model, that is, citizenship of the Union.

5   CULTURE AND CITIZENSHIP

The essentially horizontal function of Article 128 can only be fulfilled if the content of binding acts or recommendations includes and is informed by the citizens of Europe, as distinct from expert groups merely drawn from heritage managers and the like. Moreover, if the provision is to promote allegiance and tolerance, the necessary empowerment that it confers must be targeted at the appropriate level. Hence the arguments elsewhere in this chapter concerning the cultural content and underpinning of citizenship. The ECJ is just as capable of filling the lacunae left by Articles 8–8e EC Treaty as it can do with other open-textured provisions of the Treaty. However, the point to emphasize is that in this instance (unlike for example the recognition of fundamental principles) citizenship constitutes a vehicle already in existence which can be used to house layers of interests, rights and duties.

The path towards a set of duties arising from citizenship is particularly difficult to chart. The reference in the second paragraph of Article 8 EC Treaty to citizens of the Union being subject to the duties imposed by "this Treaty" is intriguing if somewhat opaque. Are these duties purely generalized negatives (not to disturb or thwart others' rights) or are there specific obligations to be developed? It should be remembered that some suggestions have already been

---

[43] I am indebted to my colleague Estella Baker for drawing my attention to this intriguing view of the Criminal Justice and Public Order Act 1994.

articulated, such as the Commission's proposal to include as a corollary to the right to enjoy a healthy environment a duty to contribute to protecting it.[44] More apposite here is the proposal in the same draft that there should be a "right to cultural expression and the obligation to respect cultural expression by others". The word tolerance may be absent, but that is the result which such a duty seeks to achieve.

Given the lack of specific concretization of citizenship duties,[45] the ECJ could follow its earlier patterns of reasoning and find that generalized duties are inherent in the Treaty.[46] Hence the crucial importance of the existence of cultural values as a protectable and fundamental interest in the *acquis communautaire*. As an alternative source, or as a reinforcement, the same inspirational role may be assigned in this context to provisions of human rights protection.

6   CULTURE AND HUMAN RIGHTS

On one, perhaps heretical view, the relevance of utilizing human rights principles as manifested in the ECHR and the ECJ's fundamental principles of EC law is to strengthen process (especially in the criminal field) rather than content. In so far as the content of individual protection is enlarged by human rights, it is perhaps most appropriately seen as a model which provides an irreducible minimum standard. By fulfilling this normative function, human rights ensure a threshold below which cultural practices and traditions must not descend.[47] In a Community which gives effect by judicial protection to such rights, it might be expected that the latter will themselves inform and become part of the cultural development of its citizens.

Put another way, the role of the human rights machinery in the maintenance of cultural diversity and protection underpins and complements

---

[44] See draft text on citizenship, Supplement 2/91 – Bull. EC.

[45] Leaving aside for the moment the obligations which might arise in the future to pay EC taxes, vote in EC elections, serve in an EC army or on a jury hearing a trial based on putative EC criminal law, since these are all predicated upon establishing the relevant EC element.

[46] Cf. the reasoning in Joined Cases C-6/90 and C-9/90, *Francovich and Others,* [1991] ECR I-5357, at 5403; see Ross, loc. cit., note 20.

[47] Implicit for example in Advocate General Jacobs' illustration in Case C-168/91, *Konstantinidis,* loc. cit., note 1, that cutting off hands as the punishment for theft would violate EC law in any circumstances despite being non-discriminatory. Perhaps more pertinently, this normative model would not see birching as an acceptable cultural value either.

the institution of citizenship. However, it is by being overlaid with the existing judicial principles in EC law of effective individual protection and the addition of duties appertaining to Union citizenship that valuing, preserving and enhancing diverse cultures within the Community becomes a legal prospect.

7   CONCLUSION

Jean Monnet is said to have claimed[48] that if the European project were to be started again from scratch, culture would be its first target. The argument of this chapter has been that a framework now exists, both expressly in Treaty provisions and as constructed by the ECJ, for cultural protection. However, the strands of development are at present unevenly matched between individual enforcement of private rights through judicial process, effective institutional action under Article 128 and the under-explored avenues of human rights and citizenship. Article 128 has the long-term advantage of developing horizontal confidence in the Community but on its own is too embryonic and tentative to withstand possibly determined assault by financial and political deprivation. The concept of citizenship thus occupies a vital role as the legal vessel which, when anchored to a bedrock of human rights standards, can harness the strength of effective protection at the micro level for individuals with the integrative glue provided by a putative duty to sustain cultural diversity and tolerance. Recognition of the fundamental role of culture requires that its legal embodiment is addressed: the debate over citizenship duties which has hardly begun should be taken in that direction.

---

[48] See Schlesinger, *Media, State and Nation: Political Violence and Collective Identities* (1991).

13 PROPERTY RIGHTS: A FORGOTTEN ISSUE UNDER THE UNION

Fiona Campbell-White

1 INTRODUCTION

Neither the EC Treaty nor the Convention for the Protection of Human Rights and Fundamental Freedoms (European Convention on Human Rights; ECHR) mentions property rights in any more than the most peripheral terms. This reticence may be easily enough explained, although the grounds are pragmatic and political rather than principled or philosophical. On the one hand the economic basis of the founding EC Treaties concentrated upon the liberalization of movement. On the other, entitlement to the ownership or enjoyment of private property sits uneasily in any framework seeking to occupy high moral ground or aspiring to egalitarian guarantees.[1]

The prima-facie position of the EC is to be found in Article 222 EC Treaty, which provides that: "This Treaty shall in no way prejudice rules in Member States governing the system of property ownership." This apparent exclusion of interference in private property reflects a general political constraint upon any obvious and wholesale transfers of competences from national to supranational levels. However, rules concerning property interests are inevitably touched upon in order to achieve many Community goals, especially the Single Internal Market. As will be discussed below, the Court of Justice of the European Communities (ECJ) has minimized the impact of Article 222 in several ways. In particular, assaults upon property ownership have been dressed in the guise of subtle distinctions between the existence and exercise of rights, the latter being assailable to the extent that they restrict or undermine other Treaty objectives. The changes wrought by the Treaty on

This chapter is based upon a dissertation which won the 1994 May Fund Prize in the Leicester University Law Faculty. I am grateful for the advice and editorial assistance of Malcolm Ross.

[1] See Schermers, "The International Protection of the Right to Property", in Matscher and Petzold (eds), *Protecting Human Rights—The European Dimension: Essays in Honour of G.J. Wiarda* (1990), 2nd edn, pp. 565–580.

N. A. Neuwahl and A. Rosas (eds.), The European Union and Human Rights, 249–263.
© 1995 Kluwer Law International. Printed in the Netherlands.

European Union (TEU) have not removed this tension. Indeed, the treatment of property rights remains dictated by the demands of other, specific, priorities and competences.

As far as the ECHR is concerned, the only mention of property occurs in Article 1 of Protocol No. 1, which states that:

> Every natural or legal person is entitled to the peaceful enjoyment of his possessions. No one shall be deprived of his possessions except in the public interest and subject to the conditions provided for by law and by the general principles of international law.
> The preceding provisions shall not, however, in any way impair the right of a state to enforce such laws as it deems necessary to control the use of property in accordance with the general interest or to secure the payment of taxes or other contributions or penalties.

Many criticisms have been levelled at this provision,[2] although it is sufficient for the moment to note that it only appears to protect enjoyment rather than a right to own.[3] This invites the speculation that such limited goals, avoiding recourse to the entrenchment of property rights, can be adequately met by indirect rules, such as general freedom from discrimination.

The discussion below focuses on the ways in which certain property rights have been subjected to control by judicial interpretation of EC law, and highlights the extent to which the treatment of property remains a corollary to the pursuit of other objectives. It will emerge that the typical level of intervention occurs in relation to Member State measures affecting competition rather than individual enjoyment of private property. The position of entrusted undertakings under Article 90 EC Treaty, intellectual property and timeshare regulation are examined in turn.

---

[2] See Kingston, "Rich People Have Rights Too? The Status of Property as a Fundamental Human Right", in Heffernan (ed.), *Human Rights: A European Perspective,* pp. 284–298.

[3] Cf. Art. 43 of the Irish Constitution which acknowledges the "natural right, antecedent to all positive law, to the private ownership of goods".

2   THE DILUTED STATUS OF ARTICLE 222: LIMITS TO EXCLUSIVE RIGHTS

In the areas of intellectual property and exclusive or special rights[4] granted to undertakings, the ECJ has not been able to avoid Article 222. These rights, by their very nature, restrict fundamental European freedoms. The conflicts between protected exclusivity and a free market of undistorted competition are obvious. As Advocate General Tesauro has observed,[5] this is a "fact which the founding fathers of the Community could not have failed to bear in mind". In his view the answer to this conflict is that the Treaty tolerates exclusive rights, but assigns to the Commission the task of ensuring compliance with rules protecting the fundamental freedoms. Put another way, there is a hierarchy of Community objectives and principles, in which exclusive ownership plays only a subservient role. The ECJ in the same case underlined this by observing that although the Treaty might presuppose the existence of undertakings having certain special or exclusive rights, it does not follow that all the special or exclusive rights are necessarily compatible with the Treaty.[6]

This subordination of exclusive property rights can be traced back to early cases such as *Manghera*.[7] It has also been visible ever since the formative cases about intellectual property,[8] so that it is clearly the position today that "free movement of goods and free competition prevail over any use of national intellectual property law in a manner contrary to these principles".[9] This stance has as its consequence the requirement that the restrictions on trade and competition flowing from property rights and measures establishing them must be justified. Not only must such restrictions serve legitimate, that is, Community-compatible purposes, but they must also be proportionate in their application. It is accordingly necessary to examine the extent of such justifications and how readily they are available.

---

[4] This concept is not settled, although in Case C-202/88, *France* v *Commission,* [1991] ECR I-1223 (cited hereafter as the *Telecoms* case), Advocate General Tesauro suggested that it refers to exclusivity granted to a limited class.

[5] Case C-202/88, loc. cit., note 4, at 1247.

[6] Case C-202/88, loc. cit, note 4, para. 22 of the judgment.

[7] Case 59/75, *Pubblico Ministero* v *Manghera,* [1976] ECR 91 in the context of state monopolies under Art. 37 EC Treaty.

[8] Case 24/67, *Parke, Davis* v *Centrafarm,* [1968] ECR 55.

[9] Court of First Instance in Cases T-69/89 *RTE* v *Commission,* [1991] ECR II-485 and Case T-76/89, *ITP* v *Commission,* [1991] ECR II-575, collectively referred to as *Magill.*

Article 90 EC Treaty, referring to public and private undertakings presupposes the existence of special and exclusive rights granted by Member States, to the extent not prohibited by Article 37,[10] but stresses that they are to be subject to other rules in the Treaty, in particular the rules on competition. Thus even here there is no acceptance of the intrinsic legitimacy of property rights (as might be suggested by Article 222) but instead support only for those rights whose use does not conflict with Community goals. This hierarchy of principles is reflected in the Commission's insistence that the conduct of nationalized undertakings "remains entirely subject to the provisions of the European Community Treaty ... notably the competition rules".[11] Exclusive rights may be deemed a breach of Article 86 EC Treaty if their exercise, or indeed existence, is considered to be an abuse of a dominant position, capable of affecting trade between Member States. Derogation is still possible via the justification provisions of Article 90(2).[12]

The antecedents of this approach can be found in *Continental Can*,[13] where the ECJ established the position that Article 86 could be infringed by the extension of an already existing market dominance. This was followed in *Telemarketing*,[14] to the effect that an undertaking holding a dominant position in one market would commit an abuse if it reserved to itself an ancillary activity in a neighbouring market when there was no objective need for the creation of this right. More recently, the ECJ held in *RTT*[15] that whilst it did not question the legality of the monopoly of the public network operator (RTT), it condemned legislation conferring ancillary rights on the utility of export and import of telecommunications equipment and exclusive rights to connect and repair. Such an extension of power without objective justification was labelled abusive.[16]

---

[10] Art. 37 requires the progressive adjustment of state monopolies of a commercial character so as to ensure that exclusive rights to import and export goods are eliminated.

[11] Answer to Question 413/82, O.J. 1982, C 339/6.

[12] See Case C-179/90, *Merci convenzionali porto di Genova,* [1991] ECR I-5889.

[13] Case 6/72, *Europemballage and Continental Can* v *Commission,* [1973] ECR 215.

[14] Case 311/84, *Centre belge d'études de marché—Télémarketing SA (CBEM)* v *Compagnie luxembourgeoise de télédiffusion SA and Information publicité Benelux, SA,* [1985] ECR 3261.

[15] Case C-18/88, *RTT GB-Inno-BM,* [1991] ECR I-5941.

[16] The ECJ uses the imputed artifice approach to overcome the fact that Arts. 85 and 86 are directed at undertakings and not at Member States. See Bright, "Article 90, Economic Policy and Duties of Member States", 4 ECLR (1993), 263. More recently the ECJ applied these articles directly to Member States using the principle of *effet utile*: see Case C-320/91, *Corbeau,* [1993] ECR I-2533, discussed in Giesen, "Statutory Monopolies and EC Competition Law: The Belgian Post

In *Höfner*[17] the question arose as to whether the monopoly over executive recruitment activities was an abuse of the German public employment agency's dominant position. Advocate General Jacobs tried to introduce a general principle[18] that where national law confers an exclusive right on someone who then fails to produce the goods or services covered by the exclusive right, that failure may be considered an abuse of a dominant position, with the result that the exclusive right cannot be enforced any longer. However, the ECJ stuck to a narrower view, and endeavoured to find a justification for the limitation of the provision of executive recruitment services, resulting in an incapacity to satisfy demand. Upon finding no such objective need, the monopoly was deemed an abuse of a dominant position. This conclusion further illustrates the inherent abuse argument, that an exclusive right cannot be structured in such a way as to lead inevitably to an abuse.[19]

The consistently undefined factor in these cases is the reference to an objective need which would be capable of justifying exclusive rights. Even if a direct parallel cannot be drawn between these and real property rights, the answer to this question is of importance to the issue of EC control over real property. Since Article 222 does not operate as an absolute protection, it is to be expected that objective reasoning should apply to such property. Just as restrictions imposed by exclusive rights can be seen as obstacles to free competition, they may also threaten the free movement of goods or services.[20] Where none of the specified grounds of Article 36 are available in the case of restrictions on goods, it is possible to invoke the mandatory requirements criteria of the so-called *Cassis* doctrine.[21]

Monopoly Case", 4 ECLR (1993), 279. See also Taylor, "Article 90 and Telecommunications Monopolies", 5 ECLR (1994), 322.

[17] Case C-41/90, *Höfner and Elser,* [1991] ECR I-1979.

[18] Derived from Case C-238/87, *Volvo* v *Veng,* [1988] ECR 6211, at 6323.

[19] Cf. the language of Case C-260/89, *Elliniki Radiophonia Tileorassi (ERT),* [1991] ECR I-2925, where the ECJ prohibited the granting of exclusive rights to an undertaking where these rights *are liable to* create a situation in which the enterprise is led to infringe Art. 86.

[20] On the question of such threats in the context of establishment, see Ehlermann, "Managing Monopolies: The Role of the State in Controlling Market Dominance in the EC", 4 ECLR (1993), 61.

[21] Case 120/78, *Rewe* v *Bundesmonopolverwaltung für Branntwein ("Cassis de Dijon"),* [1979] ECR 649, expressly establishing effectiveness of fiscal supervision, protection of public health, fairness of commercial transactions and consumer protection. Other additions include environmental protection in Case 302/86, *Commission* v *Denmark,* [1988] ECR 4607, working conditions in Case

In the *Telecoms*[22] case the ECJ took the view that the obstacles imposed by exclusive rights must be justified by a public interest ground of a non-economic nature. Consumer protection was canvassed in *RTT*[23] to protect restrictions on competition in the market of telephone sets. This was rejected on grounds of proportionality, as all that was needed for the protection of consumers was clear specifications for installation. Other justifications which were put forward in the *Telecoms* case concerned the maintenance of the integrity of the network and the security of the network. These remain undeveloped, though their similarity with the public policy exception advanced in *Campus Oil*[24] should perhaps be noted.

A more definite movement towards a more specific list of justifications, rather than the original skeletal rule that a monopoly is justified if it is in the public interest, can be seen in *Höfner*.[25] The plaintiff merely argued that the monopoly over recruitment services was not justified on public interest grounds. However, the Commission argued more precisely that the monopoly was not justified as it failed to satisfy the demand for this type of service. The ECJ also took this pragmatic approach in the *Telecoms* case and asked whether a monopoly could guarantee the terminals equipment service. Upon deciding that it could not, it held in principle that the directive in question[26] was justified in requiring the withdrawal of such exclusive rights. Similarly in *ERT*[27] the ECJ asked whether the monopoly had provided a full range of services in order to decide whether an exclusive right was justified.

The issue of justifications has been further elaborated in the cases involving postal services and electricity supplies. In the context of Spanish courier services,[28] the Commission rejected a defence under Article 90(2) for the reservation of express delivery services to the national postal monopoly. Demand was not satisfied since the monopoly only provided the service to

---

155/80, *Oebel* [1981] ECR 1993 and culture in Joined Cases 60 and 61/84, *Cinetheque* v *Fédération nationale des cinémas français,* [1985] ECR 2605.

[22] Case C-202/88, loc. cit., note 4.

[23] Case C-18/88, loc. cit., note 15.

[24] Case 72/83, *Campus Oil* v *Minister for Industry and Energy,* [1984] ECR 2727.

[25] Case C-41/90, loc. cit., note 17.

[26] Commission Directive 88/301 EEC of 16 May 1988, O.J. 1988, L 131/73.

[27] Case C-260/89, loc. cit., note 19.

[28] O.J. 1990, L 233/19.

large towns. A similar context gave rise to *Corbeau*,[29] where the ECJ went further in its rejection of the derogation. Although a general postal service can be seen as a service of general economic interest for the purposes of Article 90(2), specific courier services meet a demand of a number of enterprises rather than the public. However, a signal was given by the ECJ to the effect that there might be circumstances in which a general service could be defended.

Indeed, it was this point which was exploited in the *Almelo*[30] case, surrounding electricity distribution. Advocate General Darmon indicated four "essential criteria" to be fulfilled before the market in electricity supply could be opened up. Thus, an operator seeking to invoke the protection of Article 90(2) could do so by demonstrating to a national court that the fulfilment of these criteria could be ensured only by means of the ban on imports and the exclusive purchasing obligations in question. The four criteria identified by the Advocate General were: the obligation to provide an uninterrupted supply to all users, equal treatment of those users, the prevention of distortions of competition between producers and the effective protection of the environment. In its judgment, the ECJ observed that the entrusted undertaking:[31]

> must ensure that throughout the territory in respect of which the concession is granted, all consumers, whether local distributors or end-users, receive uninterrupted supplies of electricity in sufficient quantities to meet demand at any given time, at uniform tariff rates and on terms which may not vary save in accordance with objective criteria applicable to all customers.
>
> Restrictions on competition from other economic operators must be allowed in so far as they are necessary in order to enable the undertaking entrusted with such a task of general interest to perform it. In that regard, it is necessary to take into consideration the economic conditions in which the undertaking operates, in particular the costs which it has to bear and the legislation, particularly concerning the environment, to which it is subject.

This view is more equivocal than that expressed by the Advocate General. In particular, it appears to focus more on the economic environment in which the operator must work rather than upon the development of a *Cassis*-type rule of reason set of values.

The question posed by these developments is whether property rights are therefore to be viewed purely in economic contexts or whether they can be

---

[29] Case C-320/91, loc. cit., note 16.

[30] Case C-393/92, *Almelo*, [1994] ECR I-1477.

[31] Ibid., at I-1521.

linked to fundamental rights. This perhaps reflects the familiar debate as to whether ownership and interest in property can properly be regarded as anything other than the reflection of economic values and capitalist ideology. In the past, for example, television and radio monopolies used to be seen as necessary on pragmatic grounds in the light of the shortage of frequencies, but as a result of cable, satellite and other technological developments that justification no longer applies. Of course, other factors may also impinge on the provision of a particular service by a specific agent (such as considerations of the plurality of the media or moral objections to violent and sexual content of broadcasts). But these tend not to affect the concept of the property right itself. The recent case law discussed above comes close to accepting that exclusive rights *per se* are open to attack unless justified. It is the choice of those criteria which determines how significant the inroad is to become. A useful comparison may be made with the earlier assault upon the unfettered creation and use of intellectual property rights.

3   INTELLECTUAL PROPERTY

Although the EC Treaty contains express references to intellectual property, it does not purport to establish a distinct legal regime over it. The common feature of intellectual property rights is that they reserve to a particular entity the enjoyment of some valuable advantage. It was emphasized in the *Parke, Davis* case[32] that this exclusivity permitted by national intellectual property law will inevitably conflict with the Single Market. With progress on harmonization in this complex field being notoriously slow, the problem of compatibility between intellectual property rights and the market goals of the Community has been left for the ECJ to address.

The case law on intellectual property, just as with exclusive rights, shows not only their exercise but their very existence being subject to scrutiny by the ECJ despite frequent observations that the latter was beyond EC competence. Back in the early days of *Consten & Grundig*[33] the reasoning behind drawing this purported distinction was expressed by Advocate General Roemer on the basis that the purpose of Article 222 was "solely to guarantee in a general manner the freedom of Member States to organize their own system of

---

[32] Case 24/67, loc. cit., note 8.

[33] Cases 56 and 58/64, *Consten & Grundig* v *Commission,* [1966] ECR 299.

property but not to provide a guarantee that the Community institutions may not in any way intervene in subjective rights of property".

Without needing to rehearse in detail the well-known case law of the ECJ,[34] it is sufficient to recall that through the development of principles designed to elicit the "specific subject matter"[35] of intellectual property rights in order to ascertain the appropriate exhaustion of such rights, the ECJ has engaged in applying ideas of justification to the existence as well as the exercise of rights. By limiting the exercisable elements of intellectual property to those perceived to be the indispensable core, a value judgment is not only being made about the balance of interests between those rights and wider notions of EC market and competition, but about the intrinsic worth of the rights themselves.

This is most obviously manifested (or perhaps in some cases disguised) in the ECJ's use of the generally applicable principle of proportionality,[36] which demands there to be a reasonable relationship between the end to be achieved and the method of doing so. For example, in *Thetford* v *Fiamma*[37] a national measure (the novelty rule) was compatible with Community law since its aim was to preserve "the actual substance of the patent right". In deciding this, the ECJ is implicitly applying a test of proportionality, as only that which is absolutely necessary is being protected. In a similar vein, the Court of First Instance in the *Magill* cases[38] severed the form of the programme listings from the actual information regarding the programme schedules to conclude that the actual information should not be held by a monopoly. It would be disproportionate to do so given that it is unnecessary to own an exclusive right over the information in order to protect the actual substance of the holder's right, that is, the form of the programme listings. However, on appeal the Advocate General[39] argued for more caution before placing Community objectives before property rights.

---

[34] See generally Whish, *Competition Law* (1993), 3rd edn, Chapter 19.

[35] See Cases 15/74, *Centrafarm* v *Sterling Drug,* [1974] ECR 1147; and 16/74, *Centrafarm* v *Winthrop,* [1974] ECR 1183.

[36] Derived from the German principle of "Verhältnismässigkeit". It now has Treaty blessing in so far as it is included in the third paragraph of the revised Art. 3b EC Treaty.

[37] Case 35/87, *Thetford and Another* v *Fiamma and Others,* [1988] ECR 3585.

[38] *Magill,* loc. cit., note 9.

[39] Opinion of Advocate General Gulmann in Joined Cases C-241/91-P and C-242/91-P, *RTE and ITP* v *Commission* (1 June 1994), not yet reported.

Proportionality is also at the heart of the second sentence of Article 36 concerning arbitrary and disguised discrimination. This can be seen in *Allen & Hanburys* v *Generics*,[40] a case which was prima facie about lack of exhaustion since consent was absent. However, the ECJ did not follow that analysis and instead asked whether the discrimination the right entailed was necessary to safeguard the specific subject matter of the property. In deciding that it was not, the ECJ concluded that the right was disproportionate and so could not prevent imports (a result contrary to the one which would have been achieved by the exhaustion route). This approach can also be seen in the *Warner Brothers*[41] case. Whilst the Advocate General's assessment concentrated upon specific subject matter and exhaustion, the ECJ took a much wider approach and examined whether a Member State could create a right on the rental of a cassette. The ECJ recognized the legitimacy of Warner's right to protect its lending rights in Denmark and deemed that restraining parallel imports from the United Kingdom, where there were no such lending rights, was necessary to prevent Warner's rights from being undermined. Thus again a different conclusion emerges from that which would follow exhaustion; by invoking proportionality and necessity the ECJ concludes that the measure in question is justified.

Thus from this discussion of both exclusive and intellectual property rights, it can be seen that in order to be maintained against higher demands of EC law, such rights require justification either against specific heads of public interest or general requirements of proportionality. It follows that real property rights posing barriers to the achievement of EC goals must be similarly scrutinized.[42] Member States may argue that the rights are necessary on the basis of an objective need, such as being in the interest of consumers for Member States to deal with their own immoveable property rights. However, even if this claim succeeds it must then still stand up to the further test of proportionality in application. Some of these tensions can be seen at work in the example of timeshare regulation which follows.

---

[40] Case 434/85, *Allen & Hanburys* v *Generics,* [1988] ECR 1245.

[41] Case 158/86, *Warner Brothers and Another* v *Christiansen,* [1988] ECR 2605.

[42] See Wilkinson, "The European Property Market", 54 *Conveyancer* (1990), 409; also see Mair, "Betting on Bologna", 138 *Solicitors' Journal* (1994), 1272, for an example of how EC law might impinge on the conveyancer.

4   TIMESHARE: PROPERTY RIGHTS
AS SECONDARY TO CONSUMER PROTECTION

In layman's terms, timeshare is the purchase of a specified property for a person's exclusive use during a specified period, over a specified number of years in return for an upfront payment and an annual contribution to maintenance.[43] The property need not be an apartment or villa; it may be a boat or a yacht for example. This form of holiday property ownership has enjoyed massive expansion in recent years. In 1990 there were 180,000 timeshare owners in the United Kingdom (10 per cent of the worldwide total).[44] The Timeshare Council's figures for 1993 put the number of UK owners at 284,000 out of 709,500 European owners, with total European sales worth in excess of £ 1 billion.

Three reasons explain why there have been constant calls for regulation of timeshare at a European Community level. First, there are the well publicized problems faced by timeshare purchasers, such as unethical business practices, unscrupulous marketing tactics and the inability of authorities to supervise.[45] Secondly, the timeshare market is characterized by its trans-frontier nature. For example, 73 per cent of timeshare owners in Spain are British, 21 per cent Danish, 3 per cent Belgian and 2.6 per cent French. Given that five Member States[46] have specific legislation, none of which is compat-ible or complete, and the others are trying in vain to use existing legislation to cope with the problems, the third justification for EC intervention is the divergence in national legislation. Therefore, in the words of the Consumers in the European Community Group, "Community-wide controls are essential to ensure that those who sell timeshare do not operate in a legal vacuum".[47]

Such calls for intervention nevertheless require a legal basis for action. From the outset opposition was voiced that timeshare legislation was beyond EC competence given the prohibition contained in Article 222. However, the directive as proposed[48] avoided this difficulty for several reasons. First, the

---

[43] Edmonds, *International Timesharing* (1984), at p. 13.

[44] Sources of statistics: EUI Travel and Tourism Analyst No. 2 (1991), at 37.

[45] These problems were highlighted in the OFT Report on Timeshare, June 1990.

[46] I.e., France, Greece, Portugal, Spain and the United Kingdom.

[47] Consumers in the European Community Group, Timeshare in Europe, August 1992, at 1.

[48] 3rd amended proposal presented by the Commission in Oct. 1993 COM (93) 487 final – SYN 419, O.J. 1993, C 299/8. On 4 March 1994 a draft common position was adopted by the Council.

Timeshare Directive states in its amended title that timeshare is a right to utilize rather than a system of property ownership. This is certainly true in many situations where the timeshare is a straightforward contract between the developer and the purchaser, or a licence by the developer in favour of the purchaser. These transactions give the owners of the timeshare a right to use (a personal interest) whilst the developer retains the fee simple. However, in Spain and Portugal timeshare is specifically labelled as a real property right (see below), which somewhat contradicts the directive's title. Furthermore, the Common Position[49] emphasizes that the directive is concerned with "certain aspects of contracts" relating to the purchase of timeshare, thus claiming at least that it does not affect the law applicable to immoveable property as such. Finally, in the light of timeshare's uncertain legal status[50] and this equivocal drafting of the directive, it has been possible to introduce this measure under the banner of consumer protection.[51] As a measure originally drafted before the Maastricht revisions which introduced Article 129 concerning consumer protection,[52] Article 100a was taken as the legal basis.

Thus, on the face of it, this new piece of legislation does not interfere with national property rights, although in practice this hardly seems the case. Often the purchaser may only acquire a right to use, but a developer may grant the purchaser direct shares in the property itself. For example, the Portuguese Timeshare Decree Law[53] provides for a kind of timeshare estate in the land, by creating a new right *in rem,* known as the right to periodic habitation. Similarly, some Spanish resorts use a system of freehold transfer, whereby a legal title deed known as an *escritura de compraventa* is drawn up and registered at the local land registry. Therefore, by implementing the Timeshare Directive the EC will indeed be controlling some state systems of property ownership.

---

[49] Council Doc. 4275/1/94.

[50] See, e.g., the European Consumer Law Group, *Report on Timeshare,* 26 Nov. 1991: "is [timeshare] a consumer good, a service, an immoveable property or a combination of all three?".

[51] See Commissioner Van Miert in COM (92) 220 final, at 48 on the consumer protection objectives.

[52] See Lane, "New Competences under the Maastricht Treaty", 30 CML Rev. (1993), 939–979.

[53] Decree Law 355/81 of 31 Dec. 1981 amended by Decree Law 368/84 of 4 Oct. 1983 and Decree Law 130/89 of 18 April 1989.

5   PROPERTY IN THE UNION—A LOST CAUSE?

It can be seen from the above discussion that where property rights have been subject to supervision or regulation by EC law it has usually been in the context of state activity in entrusting undertakings or granting specific exclusive rights. In other words the focus has been upon the compatibility of state measures and EC goals. The question at the micro level of individual relationships with property in the Union has not been addressed except within the limited arena of timeshare. The expansion of competences post-Maastricht may only serve to maintain the secondary or camouflaged nature of property issues by offering new pegs, such as consumer protection, on which to hang particular controversies without requiring deep involvement in their property underpinnings. Could, for example, regulation of the conditions and obligations of leases now be a Treaty competence because of their consumer protection implications, assuming that tenants are capable of being seen as consumers?

It is not clear how a debate as to the problems posed by divergent property ownership systems within the Union can be opened further at the individual level. The ECJ's use of general principles derived from the ECHR and incorporated into EC law has been limited. In *Hauer*[54] it said no more than that "the right to property is guaranteed in the Community legal order in accordance with the ideas ... reflected in the First Protocol to the European Convention for the Protection of Human Rights".

Moreover, it is still necessary to satisfy a threshold demonstrating a Community dimension[55] before these principles can be invoked, which again makes the presence of consumer protection a significant contribution to the development of a Community approach to property rights. The existing requirement that national legislation must be tested for compliance with fundamental rights when, for example, derogating from a Community freedom will only yield piecemeal discussion in individual cases.

Perhaps a likelier alternative route for legal activity is by development of the presently rather latent concept of citizenship of the Union. Whilst the express provisions of Articles 8–8e EC Treaty emphasize political participation and diplomatic protection, there have been signs in the case law of seeds being sown for a wider vision of the content of citizenship. Importantly, these have occurred in contexts where property issues in some sense have been relevant.

---

[54] Case 44/79, *Hauer* v *Land Rheinland-Pfalz,* [1979] ECR 3727.

[55] The *ERT* case, loc. cit., note 19.

For example, in a recent copyright dispute[56] concerning rules which allowed nationals, but not others, to prohibit bootleg performances given in another state, Advocate General Jacobs couched his Opinion in the following terms:

> the Community is not just a commercial arrangement between the governments of the Member States but is a common enterprise in which all the citizens of Europe are able to participate as individuals. The nationals of each Member State are entitled to live, work and do business in other Member States on the same terms as the local population .... No other aspect of Community law touches the individual more directly or does more to foster that sense of common identity and shared destiny without which the "ever closer union among the peoples of Europe," proclaimed by the preamble to the Treaty, would be an empty slogan.

In a direct reference to Article 222, he observed:

> That Article ... clearly does not authorise Member States to grant intellectual property rights on a discriminatory basis. It might just as well be argued that a Member State could prohibit the nationals of other Member States from buying land for business use.

It must of course be conceded that, just as in the *Konstantinidis*[57] case, the ECJ in *Phil Collins* did not take up the linkage made in the Opinion between citizenship and substantive EC protection. However, to the extent that these discussions of citizenship acknowledge a sense in which it relates to the quality of the conditions of life and goes beyond non-discrimination there may be an interesting connection to the "peaceful enjoyment of property" as a human right to be exploited.

At present, property appears to be the lost element in the expanding compass of EC law. But it is inevitable that national laws, regulations and practices governing the acquisition, enjoyment and disposal of property will come into conflict with recognized Treaty activities relating to establishment, services, taxation and the general principles of non-discrimination and mutual recognition. Perhaps less obviously, such questions may arise under rules of inheritance or in the context of national or local authority policies relating to housing allocations and provision. Such dimensions as are currently tackled by

---

[56] Case C-92/92 and C-326/92, *Phil Collins v Imtrat Handelsgesellschaft and Patricia Im- und Export Verwaltungsgesellschaft v EMI Electrola,* [1993] ECR I-5145.

[57] Case C-168/91, *Konstantinidis v Stadt Altensteig Standesamt,* [1993] ECR I-1191; see further Chapter 12 in this volume.

EC law concentrate only on the discriminatory treatment of migrants.[58] What is not addressed in this way is the place of property in any individual's bundle of human or citizenship rights. This is a highly complex and politically sensitive matter, especially since the arguments are often predicated upon an individual's right to dispose and use existing property rather than the question of whether holding it in the first place is an entitlement. Given the somewhat flimsy foundations of both human rights and citizenship in this context, it is perhaps likely that activity at EC level in developing views of common property interests is most likely to remain a secondary consideration to surface only when highlighted by other trends such as consumerism.

---

[58] E.g., under Regulation 1612/68 a worker enjoys "the same social and tax advantages as national workers" (Art. 7.2), and "all the rights and benefits accorded to national workers in matters of housing, including ownership of the housing he needs" (Art. 9.1).

14 FREEDOM OF EXPRESSION FOR COMMERCIAL ACTORS

Patrick M. Twomey

1 INTRODUCTION

Despite their shared constitutional bed-rock, the rule of law, several factors mitigated against the legal orders of the European Community and the Council of Europe sharing a uniform approach to human rights. These include their different composition in terms of state membership, the lack of a formally structured relationship between their respective institutions and, more fundamentally, the differences in terms of their respective primary objectives. The EC is primarily concerned with economic integration between its Member States, while the Council of Europe is responsible for the safeguarding of individual rights in Western Europe, in particular, through the framework of its civil and political rights document, the Convention for the Protection of Human Rights and Fundamental Freedoms (European Convention on Human Rights; ECHR). Even without the Community extending beyond the economic sphere, or the Council of Europe seeking to legally enforce socio-economic rights, overlap between the two legal orders in the context of human rights is inevitable.

As the EC and, latterly the Union, move into new spheres of competence, the human rights jurisprudence of the Court of Justice of the European Communities (ECJ) grows accordingly and, as it does, the ECJ draws upon the ECHR[1] in developing that jurisprudence. By the same token the ECHR is not a static instrument; its provisions having proved to be reservoirs of previously unimagined rights.[2]

However, both processes raise some questions in the context of commer-

---

[1] See Chapter 1 in this volume.

[2] In Eur. Court H. R., *Tyrer* judgment of 25 April 1978, Series A no. 26, the Court of Human Rights stressed that the ECHR is to be interpreted as a living instrument.

N. A. Neuwahl and A. Rosas (eds.), The European Union and Human Rights, 265–280.

cial expression.[3] Given the connection between such expression and economic activity should the ECJ diverge from the current line taken by the Court of Human Rights and place commercial expression on a par with political, religious and artistic ("core") expression? Is the rationale put forward by the Court of Human Rights for placing commercial expression in a disadvantaged position in comparison with "core" expression consistent with concern for individual autonomy?

With this brief sketch in mind this chapter explores how the ECJ and the European Court of Human Rights have dealt with claims that modern conditions are such that freedom of expression should extend beyond its historical sphere of concern for the political and religious dissenter into the wider and more problematic arena of commercial activity.

2 COMMERCIAL EXPRESSION IN THE COMMUNITY LEGAL ORDER

The principal route by which commercial[4] expression has gained a foot-hold in the Community legal order has been through its fundamental importance to the Community's objective of an integrated market and in particular its relationship to the free movement of goods and services provisions in the Treaty of Rome (Articles 30–36 and 59–66 EC Treaty respectively). Despite the obvious dependence of economic activity on advertising and promotion, it was not until 1981, in the context of free movement of goods, that the ECJ explicitly recognized that interference with commercial expression could constitute a measure having the equivalent effect to a restriction on trade.[5] Subsequently, in the case of *GB-Inno-BM*[6] the Court expanded upon its rationale for reviewing national measures that served to restrict freedom to advertise. The free movement of goods provisions were deemed to have two aspects, the protection of the right to engage in trade, but also the corollary right of consumers, or potential consumers, to have access to such information that might lead them to buy a particular product. Accordingly, attempts to

---

[3] Defined by Lester and Pannick in *Advertising and Freedom of Expression in Europe* (1984), along the lines of the First Amendment, as expression "which proposes a commercial transaction".

[4] The protection of "core" expression may also arise in the Community context, see Joined Cases 43 and 63/82, *VBVB and VBBB* v *Commission*, [1984] ECR 19, where freedom of expression was raised in the context of proceedings against a book resale price fixing agreement designed to ensure the publication of less marketable works such as works of poetry and science.

[5] Case 286/81, *Oosthoek's Uitgeversmaatschappij*, [1982] ECR 4575.

[6] Case C-362/88, *GB-Inno-BM*, [1990] ECR I-667.

prevent the advertising in Luxembourg of products available for sale in Belgium were deemed to breach Article 30 EEC Treaty. This logical approach was subsequently applied in the context of freedom to provide services,[7] however, one problematic decision has served to circumscribe the extent to which commercial expression is protected in Community law.

In *Grogan*[8] the ECJ was faced with a freedom of services question that presented an uncomfortable combination of political and commercial expression. Political, in that the student unions providing information on abortion services available in the United Kingdom were motivated by civil libertarian concerns; commercial, in that the information advertised abortion facilities which, as the ECJ recognized, constituted a service within the scope of Article 60 EEC Treaty. However, the Court proceeded to distinguish its finding in *GB-Inno-BM* that the free movement of goods encompassed both the consumer as well as the provider.[9] The tenuous nature of the economic link between the student unions and the providers of the service concerned meant that the Government's restriction on the former's expression did not fall for consideration under Article 59 EEC Treaty. Despite the obvious economic interest of Irish women in information regarding abortion services in the United Kingdom the Court's narrow reading of Article 59 results in an artificial Community construction of commercial expression which ignores the reality of the market-place.

The ease with which this requirement, that the provider of the information have an economic interest in the service advertised, may be satisfied, is illustrated by an incident that arose six months after the Court's decision in *Grogan*. On 21 May 1992 some 2,000 copies of the British newspaper, *The Guardian*, were met on arrival at Dublin airport by police officers and withdrawn from distribution on the grounds that they contained an advertisement for abortion clinics in the United Kingdom which was illegal under Irish law. As the newspaper's editor stressed this was a commercial advertisement paid for by the clinics and "no part of any organized effort to test Irish opinion on this matter".[10] Such a scenario falls four-square within the *Grogan* "economic interest" test and would necessitate examination along the lines

---

[7] One particular category of commercial expression relating to the provision of professional legal services has given rise to extensive jurisprudence. See Quinn, "The Right of Lawyers to Advertise in the Market for Legal Services: A Comparative Irish, American and European Perspective", 20 *Anglo-American Law Review* (1991), 405–442.

[8] Case C-159/90, *Society for the Protection of Unborn Children Ireland,* [1991] ECR I-4685.

[9] A distinction for which Advocate General Van Gerven could see no basis.

[10] *The Guardian*, 22 May 1992.

adopted by the Advocate General in *Grogan*.

Restrictions on commercial expression that is governed by Community law on free movement of goods or services may be upheld provided they come within the terms of Articles 36[11] and 56[12] and 66 EC Treaty respectively or, more generally, are required on the grounds of "mandatory requirements" or are imperative in the public interest.[13] However, such restrictions are subject to strict scrutiny by the ECJ which requires that they be necessitated by, and proportionate to, a legitimate aim compatible with the objectives of the EC Treaty. Such an examination, which led the Advocate General to uphold the restrictions in *Grogan*,[14] would have required the Court to enter the "woman versus fetus"[15] jurisprudential minefield. Something which, in common with the European Court of Human Rights, it displayed no willingness to do.

A further qualification on the extent to which commercial expression may be curtailed under Community law is provided by the decision in the *ERT* case.[16] In response to the public policy defence put forward for the Greek broadcasting monopoly the ECJ stressed that exceptions to the freedom to provide services must be read subject to fundamental rights and specifically Article 10 ECHR. In addressing this latter point in *Grogan*, the Advocate General's opinion refers to the wide margin of appreciation that is afforded to states under Article 10(2) in limiting freedom of expression. However, apart from noting that commercial expression is included within the guarantee in Article 10(1) and that paragraph 2 affords states a margin of appreciation, the

---

[11] Prohibitions or restrictions on the free movement of goods are permitted on grounds of public morality, public policy or public security: the protection of health and life of humans, animals or plants; the protection of national treasures possessing artistic, historic or archaeological value; or the protection of industrial and commercial property.

[12] Measures, whether legal, regulatory or administrative, restrictive of the freedom to provide services are permissible on the grounds of public policy, public security or public health.

[13] Consumer protection, of particular relevance in respect of restrictions on commercial expression, has been identified as one such "mandatory requirement" and "public interest" issue in Case 120/78, *Rewe* v *Bundesmonopolverwaltung für Branntwein ("Cassis de Dijon")*, [1979] ECR 649, at para. 8; and in Case C-353/89, *Commission* v *The Netherlands*, [1991] ECR 4069 respectively. However, the protection of the consumer's economic interests has been deemed not to come within the public policy exception in Art. 36; Case 113/80, *Commission* v *Ireland*, [1981] ECR 1625.

[14] Albeit in terms "deferential" to the Government's discretion. See de Búrca, "Fundamental Rights and the Reach of EC Law", 13 OJLS (1993), 283–319, at 294.

[15] See Spalin, "Abortion, Speech and the European Community", 1 *Journal of Social Welfare and Family Law* (1992), 17–32, at 30.

[16] Case C-260/89, *Elliniki Radiophonia Tileorassi (ERT)*, [1991] ECR I-2925.

case law of the ECJ has so far failed to discuss the extent to which the margin of appreciation doctrine is awarded a particularly expansive application, by the ECHR organs, in the context of commercial expression.[17]

More surprisingly, perhaps, the Community legal order itself has come to adopt a hierarchical approach to expression, which devalues commercial in comparison with other forms of expression.[18]

While noting that broadcasting serves to promote Community objectives including integration, socio-economic progress, and the promotion of improved living conditions and referring to the free movement of services as "a specific manifestation of the freedom of expression" enshrined in Article 10 ECHR, the "Television Without Frontiers" Directive[19] serves largely to curtail commercial expression. Specific prohibitions relate to the advertising of tobacco products and prescription medication as well as restrictions on alcohol advertising.[20] An insight into the value-laden approach to different types of expression is provided by Article 11(5) of the Directive which provides that political and religious broadcasts of less than thirty minutes duration shall not be interrupted by advertisements and broadcasts of religious services are to be advertisement-free. Furthermore, advertising is to be readily identifiable and kept distinct from other programmes, and advertising which "offends" religious or political beliefs or encourages conduct prejudicial to the environment is not permitted.[21] Certainly in the context of "core" expression such paternalism would for the most part fail to survive the scrutiny of the European Court of Human Rights.[22] However, the position of that Court with regard to expression in the commercial arena is, as outlined below, significantly different.

---

[17] The invocation of Art. 10 ECHR in the case law of the Community has been described as "cosmetic". See Gardner, "Freedom of Expression", in McCrudden and Chambers (eds), *Individual Rights and the Law in Britain* (1994), pp. 209–238.

[18] Art. 5 (Freedom of opinion and information) of the European Parliament's Declaration of Fundamental Rights and Freedoms, O.J. 1989, C 120/51, while guaranteeing the right to freedom of opinion and the right to receive and impart information and ideas as components of free expression, makes particular reference to philosophical, political and religious information and ideas and freedom in the fields of art, science, research and academia.

[19] Directive 89/552/EEC, O.J. 1989, L 298/23.

[20] Arts. 13–15.

[21] Arts. 10 and 12 respectively.

[22] See Eur. Court H. R., *Handyside* judgment of 7 December 1976, Series A no. 24, where the Court of Human Rights stressed its supervisory jurisdiction in the protection of "information or ideas ... that offend, shock or disturb the state or any sector of the population".

3   COMMERCIAL EXPRESSION UNDER THE ECHR

Freedom of expression arises in a number of contexts in the ECHR.[23] Expression in the context of Article 10(1) has therefore a specific meaning, comprising, though not exclusively, the right to hold opinions and to receive and impart information and ideas. The reference to "opinions" and "ideas" point to a classical liberal basis for Article 10, with the value of free expression lying in the facilitation of a "marketplace of ideas" and the end-goal of a democratic society. As stressed by the Court in the case of *Handyside* such a society is marked by pluralism, openness and tolerance and "freedom of expression constitutes one of the essential foundations of such a society, one of the basic conditions for its progress and the development of every man".[24] This interpretation is reinforced by the extent to which other societal interests permit regulation and limitation of expression. By focusing on the *consequences* of free expression, rather than on expression as an exercise in individual autonomy and a goal in itself, a hierarchical model of expression has evolved in the jurisprudence of the Strasbourg organs. In particular, the "marketplace of ideas" model, with "ideas" being afforded a greater level of protection than "information",[25] has led to commercial expression being placed on a lower tier of protection than other forms of expression. However, the analogy "relies too dangerously on metaphor for a theory that purports to be more hard-headed than literary".[26] This statement made by an American commentator in the context of the First Amendment is equally applicable in the context of Article 10.

At the pinnacle of the hierarchy are political "ideas" and consequently the safeguarding of a free press,[27] as it "affords the public one of the best means of discovering and forming an opinion of the ideas and attitudes of political leaders".[28] Somewhat less plausibly the democratic society rationale has also

---

[23] The right to privacy, Art. 8; freedom of assembly, Art. 11; right to vote, Art. 3, Protocol No. 1; freedom of conscience and religion, Art. 9.

[24] *Handyside*, loc. cit., note 22, at 23.

[25] Eur. Court H. R., *Lingens* judgment of 8 July 1986, Series A no. 103, at 34.

[26] Tribe, *American Constitutional Law* (1988), 2nd edn, p. 786.

[27] This requires that freedom of expression is afforded to both natural and legal persons irrespective of profit motive. See Eur. Court H. R., *Autronic AG* judgment of 22 May 1990, Series A no. 178, at para. 47.

[28] *Lingens,* loc. cit., note 26, at paras 41–42.

provided the basis of the Court's recognition that artistic expression is protected by Article 10.[29] In *Müller*[30] it was noted that restrictions on artistic freedom are the hallmark of an undemocratic society and that artistic expression merits protection, not just by virtue of it being expression by the artist, but as "a view of the society in which he lives. To that extent art not only helps shape public opinion but is also an expression of it and can confront the public with the major issues of the day".[31]

Article 10 contains no explicit right to *seek* information,[32] but the failure of attempts to add such a right, by protocol, suggests that it is implicit in the right to *receive* information. There are two aspects to the right to seek and receive information and ideas, first, as a right in itself, an aspect of individual autonomy, and also as a prerequisite for the effective exercise of one's right to freedom of expression. Attempts to bring commercial expression within Article 10 focus primarily, but not necessarily exclusively,[33] on the reference to the freedom to receive and impart information. Support for this contention is also derived from the Convention's guarantee of a right to property.[34]

However, the jurisprudence of the Commission and Court, to the effect that Article 10 is primarily concerned with protecting the expression of political ideas, as well as both the state's authority to prohibit certain categories of advertising broadcasts[35] and the relative weakness of the right to property, which may, *inter alia,* be subject to control in "the general interest", have served to circumscribe the freedom of "information" guarantee and as a consequence commercial expression.

One problematic decision concerning the right to *impart* information has

---

[29] By contrast, artistic expression is explicitly referred to in Art. 19 of the International Covenant on Civil and Political Rights (CCPR).

[30] Eur. Court H. R., *Müller and Others* judgment of 24 May 1988, Series A no. 133.

[31] *Müller and Others*, loc. cit., note 30, at para. 70.

[32] Unlike Art. 19 CCPR.

[33] Commercial expression covers a spectrum ranging from traditional product advertising to its many modern manifestations that have led to the coining of terms such as "infomercial" and "advertorial".

[34] Art. 1 of Protocol No. 1, ECHR.

[35] *X & the Association of Z v. United Kingdom,* Application No. 4515/70, 14 YB ECHR (1971), 538, Commission decision of 12 July 1971 upholding legislation prohibiting the broadcast of party political commercials by the independent broadcast sector on the basis that Art. 10(1) permits the state to license broadcasting.

been the subject of criticism.[36] In *De Geillustreerde Pers N.V. v. The Netherlands*[37] the Commission took the view that the objective of freedom to impart information is to keep the public informed rather than to protect the commercial interests of media organizations.[38] As a consequence, provided that information is adequately available from some other source, or sources, no breach of Article 10 arises where restrictions are imposed on any particular concern involved in the dissemination of information. Aside from the contention that a right to *impart* information should stand protected, independent of any right to *receive* information, this narrow construction of the right to impart information risks imperilling the multiplicity of sources required to give full effect to the right to receive information.

While permitted by paragraph 2, measures interfering with freedom of expression are supervised by the Strasbourg organs in that they must be prescribed by law, have a legitimate aim[39] and be "necessary in a democratic society". Despite the Court's avowal that these exceptions are to be "narrowly interpreted",[40] the evolution of an ever-broadening margin of appreciation within which states determine the necessity of interfering with expression has served to undermine the guarantees of Article 10(1). The development of this doctrine originated in the Court's recognition that the balancing of rights required by emergency situations requires a degree of state discretion in deciding how to respond to the threats faced.[41] However, from the initial context of threats to the life of the nation, the doctrine subsequently came to be applied to interference with expression in the absence of a uniform European conception of morals[42] to the point where its application has now been deemed "essential in commercial matters".[43] Political sensitivity on the

---

[36] See van Dijk and van Hoof, *Theory and Practice of the European Convention on Human Rights* (1990), 2nd edn, p. 414.

[37] Application No. 5178/71, Decisions and Reports 8 (1977).

[38] Such interests, however, do receive some protection under Art. 1 of Protocol No. 1.

[39] The aims listed in para. 2 are the protection of national security, territorial integrity or public safety, the prevention of disorder or crime, the protection of health or morals, the protection of the reputation or rights of others, the prevention of the disclosure of information received in confidence, and maintaining the authority and impartiality of the judiciary.

[40] Eur. Court H. R., *Sunday Times* judgment of 26 April 1979, Series A no. 30, para. 65.

[41] Application No. 332/57, *Lawless* case, 2 YB ECHR (1958–9), 308.

[42] *Handyside,* loc. cit., note 22.

[43] Eur. Court H. R., *markt intern Verlag GmbH and Klaus Beerman* judgment of 20 November 1989, Series A no. 165, at para. 33 in a 9:9 decision upholding the interference following the casting vote of the President.

part of the Commission and Court has culminated in a virtual abrogation of their supervisory obligations in the context of forms of expression deemed less worthy of protection.[44]

The first examination of commercial expression in the context of Article 10 arose in X. and Church of Scientology v. Sweden.[45] The Swedish courts issued an injunction restricting advertisements in the Church's periodical which offered for sale a device known as an E-meter. The advertisements were restricted in so far as they described the device as "an invaluable aid to measuring man's mental state and changes in it". The Commission pointed to the reference in Article 10 to "enterprises" as a basis for affording the Church, as distinct from its members, the right to freedom of expression.

While the Commission went no further than stating that it "was not of the opinion" that commercial expression fell outside the protection in Article 10(1), some insight regarding the status of such expression was provided in its examination of the *necessity* of limiting commercial expression. Firstly, it noted that such expression merits a lower degree of protection compared with the expression of "political" ideas, the latter being the primary concern of Article 10. It felt that this interpretation was reinforced by the prevalence of legislation restricting such expression in order to protect the consumer in States Parties to the Convention. Having adopted this standpoint the Commission's terse analysis of the issues was influenced by factors which would not be expected to be considered had the expression involved "core" expression. The fact that the national court had found that the advertisement was misleading and directed beyond the Church's membership, and that the injunction only prohibited certain wording and was not issued under penalty of a fine, led to a finding that the interference was not disproportionate to the legitimate aim of protecting the consumer. It is not clear why the expression was not considered to be primarily or at least partly religious in nature, that is, the imparting of religious information on a device was designed to serve a spiritual purpose. In this, the case provides some insight into the dangers of commercial expression standards creeping into examples of "mixed" expression or commercial aspects of "core" expression on the fringe of society being highlighted in order to facilitate easier regulation. It is difficult to envisage the approach in the *Scientology* case being taken with a sales promotion for the Bible or Koran, for example, even if targeted beyond adherents to those faiths.

One case involving "mixed" political-commercial expression, though both

---

[44] See Frowein, "The ECHR as the Public Order of Europe", *Collected Courses of the Academy of European Law* (1990), Vol. 1, Book 2, 273–358, at 347ff.

[45] Application No. 7805/77, Decisions and Reports 16 (1979), 68–81.

the Commission and the Court did not advert to its commercial aspect, which does not fit within the thesis of over-zealous application of the margin of appreciation doctrine by the Strasbourg organs is the *Open Door Counselling*[46] case. The injunctions granted in the Irish courts against the applicants' provision, for a fee, of non-directive pregnancy counselling, as well as information on abortion services in the United Kingdom, were dealt with by the Commission and the Court without recourse to the margin of appreciation doctrine.[47] The fact that Ireland's stance on the provision of abortion information was unique amongst the States Parties to the ECHR appears to have been decisive in a case that, had the commercial aspect of the clinics' activities been highlighted, might have been expected to have gone against the applicants.

The case of *Barthold v. Germany*[48] also concerned an injunction against expression, in this case against the repetition of views expressed in a newspaper article regarding the necessity of 24-hour veterinary services. In expressing such views to a journalist the applicant gave information regarding the service provided by his own clinic and was, as a result, deemed to have publicized his practice in breach of the veterinary rules of professional conduct. The decision that this expression comprised opinions, and information, protected by Article 10, obviated the need for a full examination of the nature of protection to be afforded commercial expression. However, several instructive points were made regarding the process by which the Commission and Court concluded the expression was not commercial expression. Firstly, it was noted that the publication took the form of a journalistic article rather than an advertisement. The Commission also noted that the applicant had not paid for the publication and stated that its character was not altered by virtue of the fact that the article had, as a side effect, publicity benefits for the applicant's clinic.

Judge Pettiti voted with the majority of the Court in finding the injunction to be an unjustifiable breach of Article 10, but in a separate opinion[49] expressed the wish that the Court had "pushed its reasoning a little

---

[46] Eur. Court H. R., *Open Door Counselling Ltd and Dublin Well Woman Centre Ltd v. Ireland* judgment of 29 October 1992, Series A no. 246.

[47] The Commission, on the grounds that the interference with expression was not sufficiently precise to meet the "prescribed by law" test for legitimate restrictions under para. 2; the Court, on the grounds that the disproportionality between the interference and the aim of protecting morals prevented the injunction from satisfying the "necessary in a democratic society" hurdle.

[48] Eur. Court H. R., *Barthold* judgment of 25 March 1985, Series A no. 90.

[49] *Barthold,* loc. cit., note 48, at 31–32.

further" to consider commercial expression in the context of Article 10. In particular, he noted that commercial expression is directly connected to the right to receive and impart information and ideas in that the revenue generated by advertising is essential to a free market in broadcasting.[50] Accordingly, he asserted that only restrictions which were required by a "pressing social need", as opposed to "mere expediency", were permissible under Article 10(2).

The *markt intern* case[51] addressed the issue of commercial expression more directly but, like *Barthold*, did not involve "pure" advertising. *markt intern,* a publication run by journalists for retailers in the pharmacy trade, published a series of articles that questioned the commercial practices of a cosmetic mail order club, detailed the grievance of one customer and solicited information from others who had negative experiences in their dealings with the club. The German courts prohibited repetition of the allegations on the grounds that they constituted dishonest practice detrimental to the mail order club and favoured other retailers.

A central issue was the fact that the articles were published for a specific commercial area rather than in the regular press. In response to the Government's assertion that the prohibition was, as a matter of competition law, outside the remit of Article 10, the Commission noted that, as with the professional practice matters in *Barthold*, acts of competition, even if primarily within the sphere of economics, did not necessarily preclude the application of Article 10. It specifically rejected the argument that Article 10 is limited to "statements of an artistic, religious, scientific, political and politico-economic content which are part of an ongoing intellectual debate".[52] However, once again it was not called upon to decide the applicability of Article 10 to, what the Commission referred to as, "purely competition-related promotional statements" or the problematic issue of commercial expression being "dressed up" as journalism. On recognizing that the expression concerned fell within the protection of Article 10(1) both the Commission and the Court proceeded to examine the interference for compliance with paragraph 2.

In relation to the limitation of expression the principal difficulty concerns the legitimacy of the aim of the restriction, and its necessity: it raises the issue whether the margin of appreciation afforded to states in determining which aims justify restrictions and the necessity of such restrictions ought to vary between commercial and what has been described as "core" expression. In

---

[50] While addressing himself to the issue of broadcasting and satellite broadcasting in particular, Judge Pettiti's argument applies equally to other media.

[51] *markt intern,* loc. cit., note 43.

[52] *markt intern,* loc. cit., note 43, at 34.

both *Barthold* and *markt intern* the state sought to rely upon several of the grounds set out in paragraph 2, namely, the protection of health, morals and "the reputation and the rights of others" (in both contexts), as well as "prevention of disorder" and the protection of the reputation and rights of others in that context.[53] Without deciding the applicability of the other grounds, the interference was in both cases adjudged to have the legitimate aim of protecting the reputation and the rights of others. The difficulty raised by the terse discussion on this aim is that it is of the essence of most commercial expression that it promotes or favours a particular concern over its competitors. It is difficult to avoid the conclusion that the "necessity" criterion has shifted markedly towards being synonymous with "useful" or "reasonable".[54]

The Commission and Court have now resolved that a profit motive is irrelevant and that Article 10(1) is applicable to commercial expression. However, as with all rights, it is in the application of the permitted limitations that the real extent of the protection is determined. In the application of Article 10(2) the hierarchical model of expression is reinforced and being developed, even to the point of suggesting a distinction between "information of a commercial nature" and "commercials".[55] Similarly, the Court's examination of commercial expression cases involves attempts to determine the "value" of different types of commercial expression, something which it is, understandably, loath to do in cases of political or artistic expression. The impossibility of such a task in turn reinforces the margin of appreciation doctrine at the expense of the Court's supervisory jurisdiction.

4   CONCLUSION

The absence, at both the European Community and Council of Europe level, of a coherent theory for the protection of commercial expression has a negative effect on the circulation of "ideas" and "information" in general and makes prediction of the protection standard to be applied in particular cases difficult. The degree of protection afforded to particular categories of expression reflects long established perceptions of the relative worth of the spheres in which such

---

[53] The German Government did not rely upon the "prevention of disorder" and "protection of morals" grounds before the Court.

[54] Something which the Court was not prepared to countenance in *Handyside,* loc. cit., note 22, at para. 48.

[55] Eur. Court H. R., *Casado Cocoa v. Spain* judgment of 24 February 1994, Series A no. 285-A.

expression takes place and the resulting benefit of such freedom to the wider community.

Despite its economic basis the EC has not given commercial expression the status it might have been expected to be afforded. Instead, consumer protection is raised as a justification for delimiting such expression, with little analysis on the consumer's interest in protected commercial expression. On the other hand, freedom of "core" expression is guaranteed by the ECHR on the largely unquestioned premise that only through the protection of such discourse can individual freedom, cultural diversity and the democratic decision-making process be protected. While the boundaries of politics, religion, art and science may shift or become indecipherable, acceptance of the libertarian rationale for protecting such expression remains largely unchallenged.

Neither the realization that discourse does not necessarily culminate in any "truth", nor the suspicion of an ever-increasing number of dubious "ideas" in circulation undermines faith in the "market-place of ideas" itself. Equally enduring has been the belief that the expression associated with the tawdry world of commerce, the market-place of goods and services, should not be exalted to the level of the metaphorical market-place within which "core" expression finds protection.[56]

> ... it (advertising) has been criticized for playing on emotions, simplifying real human situations into stereotypes, exploiting anxieties, and employing techniques of intensive persuasion that amount to manipulation. Many social critics have stated that advertising is essentially concerned with exalting the materialistic virtues of consumption by exploiting achievement drives and emulative anxieties, employing tactics of hidden manipulation, playing on emotions, maximising appeal and minimising information, trivializing, eliminating objective considerations, contriving illogical situations, and generally reducing men, women and children to the role of irrational consumer. Criticism expressed in such a way may be overstated but it cannot be entirely brushed aside.

Since they may apply to much "core" expression as well,[57] the above alleged attributes do not in themselves provide a satisfactory justification for the relative ease with which commercial expression may be curtailed. Is the gullible consumer any less susceptible to liars and charlatans in his, or her,

---

[56] MacBride Report, *Many Voices, One World*, (UNESCO, 1980).

[57] "If advertising persuades some men to live beyond their means, so does matrimony. If advertising speaks to a thousand in order to influence one, so does the church. If advertising is often garrulous and redundant and tiresome, so is the United States Senate." Bruce Barton speaking in 1927 quoted in Fox, *The Mirror Makers* (1985), at p. 108.

capacity as a political, cultural or spiritual being?

Perhaps pointing to some doubt in this supposed perfidious nature of commercial expression, an array of justifications, primarily in US jurisprudence,[58] have been postulated as grounds for the regulation of such expression. These include the assertion that the imposition of accuracy constraints on commercial expression involves no impediment to expression as, unlike much "core" expression, the commercial actors concerned are invariably in a position to ensure the accuracy of statements made by them. Furthermore, advertising and promotion by economic concerns is seen as being so fundamental to economic activity that regulation is unlikely to chill such expression.[59] However, the former point can really only be applied to commercial expression that purports to provide concrete information; whereas the latter involves a rather dangerous hypothesis; that where a right is vigorously asserted there is little to be feared from the imposition of restrictions.

To the extent that it entails the provision of information, and attempts to persuade the consumer to purchase a particular product or service, the case has been made for the regulation of commercial expression in the same way that contract law governs what the seller may, or may not, assert.[60] A preferable approach to commercial, as with all types of, expression is to place the onus on those proposing to impose restrictions on the right to make out a strong case for doing so.

Some of the arguments for the full protection of commercial expression which focus on individual liberty also involve assumptions that do not fit comfortably with the reality of modern commercial practice. Just as "core" expression does not always broaden individual horizons or fuel democratic debate, an increasing amount of commercial expression cannot be said to involve the individual being:[61]

> encouraged to consider ... competing information, weigh it mentally in the light

---

[58] The literature on commercial expression in the US is a veritable cottage-industry. For an extensive list in the wake of the decision granting First Amendment protection to such expression in *Virginia Board of Pharmacy v. Virginia Citizens Consumer Council Inc.,* 425 US 748 (1976); see Feldman, "Survey of the Literature: Commercial Speech and Commercial Speakers", 2 *Cardozo Law Review* (1981), 659–697. An analysis of the pre-1976 approach is provided in Rotunda, "The Commercial Speech Doctrine in the Supreme Court", (1976) U. Ill. L.F. 1080.

[59] See McGowan, "A Critical Analysis of Commercial Speech", (1990) *California Law Review,* 359–448, at 368.

[60] See Farber, "Commercial Speech and First Amendment Theory", 74 *Northwestern University Law Review* (1979), 372–408.

[61] Redish, *Freedom of Expression: A Critical Analysis* (1984), pp. 60–61.

of the goals of personal satisfaction he has set for himself, counter-balance his conclusions with possible price differentials, and in so doing exercise his abilities to reason and think; ... towards the intangible goal of rational self-fulfilment.

While this is certainly the case, it is equally true that commercial expression includes far more than *direct* advertising of products or services and, more generally, expression by commercial actors has increasingly come to involve a combination of expression types. Exhortations to buy brand X at a particular price are supplanted by an ever-increasing number of more subtle marketing techniques, such as the promotion of the producer rather than the product and corporate sponsorship or campaigning on issues that are of concern for its targeted market or shareholders.[62] By the same token the most effective of commercial expression frequently transcends onto the realm of the artistic. At some point the commercial expression, regardless of profit-motive or of being profit generated, becomes more akin to political, or artistic, expression, with the resulting difficulty of deciding what degree of protection it merits. Neatly drawn demarcation lines and tests such as the "primary purpose test"[63] ignore the extent to which "In the service of selling, mass advertising frequently seizes on our politics, values and even identities, and translates them into commercial talk. This is a marriage between the marketplace of items and the marketplace of ideas."[64]

This "marriage" is also reflected in the degree to which the dissemination of "core" ideas and information is dependent upon commercial expression to reach its audience, whether by media organs dependent upon advertising revenue or the marketing of "core" information and ideas.

These are points that ought to be considered not only by the Strasbourg Court but also by the ECJ as it finds itself in previously unfamiliar jurisprudential territory.

Just as it is the premise from which we approach information and ideas

---

[62] To mark the bicentenary of the American Bill of Rights, the food and tobacco giant, Philip Morris sponsored a series of commercials promoting awareness of the Bill of Rights. While the commercials did not mention any Philip Morris products they undoubtedly had the desired effect of promoting the company, and indirectly its products, as "all-American". Other recent examples include corporate involvement in AIDS awareness and ecological issues in response to the "discovery" of "pink" and "green" spending power.

[63] *Valentine v. Christensen,* 316 US 52 (1942), 122 F.2d 511 (2d Cir. 1942).

[64] Collins and Skover, "Pissing in the Snow: A Cultural Approach to the First Amendment", 45 *Stanford Law Review* (1993), 783–806.

that "offend, shock or disturb",[65] so too should full freedom be the starting-point for the approach to expression that may be materialistic or even exploitative.[66] While the primary concern with the delimitation of commercial expression continues to be the extent to which this has repercussions for the protection of "core" expression, that does not in itself account for the multi-facetted individual, who may well be more interested in commercial information and ideas than "the day's most urgent political debate".[67]

---

[65] *Handyside,* loc. cit., note 22, at 144.

[66] As with the content based approach used to delimit racist or defamatory expression, harmful commercial expression could also be subject to control.

[67] Justice Blackmun, dissenting in *Valentine v. Christensen,* loc. cit., note 63, at 763.

15 EXTRATERRITORIALITY IN HUMAN RIGHTS

Paul Torremans

1 INTRODUCTION

Extraterritoriality is a controversial issue as public international lawyers do not necessarily agree whether this is an acceptable basis of jurisdiction in the first place.[1] It also has important political and diplomatic implications.[2] I do not intend to take part in that ongoing debate, I would rather accept the fact that extraterritoriality is used as a ground of jurisdiction. This is particularly so in competition law, both in the European Union and in the United States.[3] I will attempt to give an overview of the way in which competition laws are applied extraterritorially, derive some general principles from that application and in a second part of my analysis I will examine whether extraterritoriality has also a role to play in the human rights debate on both sides of the Atlantic.

2 EXTRATERRITORIALITY IN US COMPETITION LAW

2.1 The early stages

The purely territorial application of the Sherman Act advocated by Supreme Court Justice Oliver Wendell Holmes in *American Banana Co. v. United Fruit*

---

[1] See Slot and Grabandt, "Extraterritoriality and Jurisdiction", 23 CML Rev. (1986), 545–565; Mann, "The Doctrine of Jurisdiction in International Law", 111 *Recueil des Cours* (1964), 9–162; Akehurst, "Jurisdiction in International Law", 46 BYIL (1972–73), 145–257; Mann, "The Doctrine of International Jurisdiction Revisited after Twenty Years", 186 *Recueil des Cours* (1984), 19–116. See also the *Lotus* case before the Permanent Court of International Justice, P.C.I.J., 7 Sept. 1927, Ser. A No. 10, Ser. C. No. 13–11.

[2] See Demaret, "L'extraterritorialité des lois et les relations transatlantiques: une question de droit ou de diplomatie?", 21 RTDE (1985), 1–39.

[3] See, e.g., Whish, *Competition Law* (1993), 3rd edn, at pp. 368–389; and Rubin, "USA—Commentary—Chapter 5. International Enforcement", in Gijlstra (ed.), *Competition Law in Western Europe and the USA* (1984), at USA.C.

N. A. Neuwahl and A. Rosas (eds.), The European Union and Human Rights, 281–296.

Co.[4] was very soon afterwards abandoned and replaced by the principle that US courts had jurisdiction over foreign undertakings if a direct effect on commerce and some conduct within the United States could be shown.[5] The "effects doctrine" was fully embraced as being part of the "settled law" on extraterritoriality in *United States v. Aluminium Company of America (Alcoa)*[6] when Judge Learned Hand stated that:[7]

> On the other hand, it is settled law ... that any state may impose liabilities, even upon persons not within its allegiance, for conduct outside its borders that has consequences within its borders which the state reprehends, and these liabilities other states will ordinarily recognise.

This judgment contains a double requirement for the application of US antitrust law: the agreement has to be intended to affect US commerce and it must effectively do so. The fact that the undertakings concerned are situated outside the United States and that the agreement is concluded outside the United States is held to be immaterial.[8] It should be noted that the specific intent to affect the foreign commerce of the United States has to be distinguished from the general intent required in domestic cases.[9]

2.2 Timberlane *and* Mannington Mills

The application of the crude *Alcoa* test was unacceptable for a number of countries. This resulted in diplomatic protests and blocking statutes.[10]

Obviously the next step was for an American court to recognize that the *Alcoa* test was not "settled law" and that it was incomplete. The US Court of

---

[4] *American Banana Co. v. United Fruit Co.*, 213 US 347 (1909).

[5] *United States v. American Tobacco Co.*, 221 US 106, 31 S. Ct. 632, 55 L. Ed. 663 (1911); *United States v. Sisal Sales Corp.*, 274 US 268 (1927).

[6] *United States v. Aluminium Corp. of America*, 148 F. 2d 416 (2d Cir. 1945).

[7] *United States v. Aluminium Corp. of America*, loc. cit., note 6, at 443.

[8] Stephens, "'Reasonable' Approaches to the Issue of Extra-Territorial Jurisdiction—the US Anti-Trust Example", in Maitland-Walker (ed.), *International Antitrust Law* (1984), Vol. 2, at p. 103; Rubin, loc. cit., note 3, at USA. C, pp. 114–115; Neale and Goyder, *The Antitrust Laws of the USA* (1980), 3rd edn, at p. 349.

[9] Stephens, loc. cit., note 8, at p. 104.

[10] See Demaret, loc. cit., note 2, at 12; and Cohen-Tanugi, "Les juridictions américaines face aux lois étrangères interdisant la communication de renseignements économiques", 72 RCDIP (1983), 9.

Appeals in the Ninth Circuit did so in the *Timberlane* case,[11] where it read into antitrust law a requirement for the judge to consider and balance the interests of the different governments involved.[12] Establishing a new test, Judge Choy stated:

> A tripartite analysis seems to be indicated. As acknowledged above, the antitrust laws require in first instance that there be some effect—actual or intended—on American foreign commerce before the federal courts may legitimately exercise subject matter jurisdiction under those statutes.
> Second, a greater showing of burden or restraint may be necessary to demonstrate that the effect is sufficiently large to present a cognizable injury to the plaintiffs and, therefor, a civil violation of antitrust laws. [...]
> Third, there is the additional question which is unique to the international setting of whether the interests of and the links to, the United States—including the magnitude of the effect on American foreign commerce —are sufficiently strong *vis-à-vis* those of other nations, to justify an assertion of extraterritorial authority.[13]

The latter step introduces consideration of policy variables and evaluation and balancing of the relevant considerations in each case.[14] This is what Kingman Brewster suggested and what he called "a jurisdictional rule of reason".[15] Brewster's factors to be weighed as part of the decision to authorize foreign antitrust jurisdiction—as retained by Judge Choy and the Second Restatement of Foreign Relations Law[16]—are conduct, nationality, intent, effect and national interest.

It·is, however, not entirely clear whether the rule-of-reason analysis is part of the test establishing subject-matter jurisdiction or if it has to be seen as the expression of a discretionary power of the court once its subject matter jurisdiction has already been established.[17] The first option seems to be the reasonable one because the latter one implies an involvement, even if

---

[11] *Timberlane Lumber Co. v. Bank of America,* 549 F. 2d 597 (9th Cir. 1976).

[12] Stephens, loc. cit., note 8, at p. 105; Neale and Goyder, op. cit., note 8, at pp. 350–351.

[13] *Timberlane*, loc. cit., note 11, at 613.

[14] Rubin, loc. cit., note 3, at USA.C—pp. 122–123; Neale and Goyder, op. cit., note 8, at pp. 350–351.

[15] Brewster, *Antitrust and American Business Abroad* (1958). See also Attwood and Brewster, *Antitrust and American Business Abroad* (1981).

[16] American Law Institute, *Restatement (Second) Foreign Relations Law of the U.S.*, ALI (1965), at 47.

[17] Stephens, loc. cit., note 8, at p. 105.

extremely brief, of the court which could be seen by other concerned countries as a breach of international comity.[18]

The list of factors to be weighed in the balancing test was enlarged in the *Mannington Mills* case,[19] where Judge Weiss set forth a non-exhaustive list including:

- the degree of conflict with foreign law or policy;
- the nationality of the parties;
- the relative importance of the alleged violation of conduct in the United States, compared to that abroad;
- the availability of a remedy abroad and the pendency of litigation there;
- the existence of an intent to harm or affect American commerce and its foreseeability;
- the possible effect upon foreign relations if the court exercises jurisdiction and grants relief;
- if relief is granted, whether a party will be placed in the position of being forced to perform an act illegal in either country or be under conflicting requirements in both countries;
- whether the court can make its order effective;
- whether an order for relief would be acceptable in the United States if made by the foreign nation under similar circumstances;
- whether a treaty with the affected nations has addressed the issue.

2.3 Hartford Fire Insurance

After having avoided to rule directly on the point of extraterritoriality the Supreme Court finally intervened in the debate in *Hartford Fire Insurance Co. v. California*.[20] London based reinsurers were accused of infringing the Sherman Act. Their activity took place outside the United States and complied with UK legislation. The majority found that the Sherman Act applies to such foreign conduct, because it is meant to produce and does in fact produce some substantial effect in the United States.[21] The court rejected the *Mannington Mills* approach in as far as it might have suggested that elements of interna-

---

[18] Ibid.; Concurring opinion of Judge Adams in *Mannington Mills Inc. v. Congoleum Corp.*, 595 F. 1287 (3rd Cir. 1979), at 1299 and 1301.

[19] *Mannington Mills Inc. v. Congoleum Corp.*, loc. cit., note 18.

[20] *Hartford Fire Insurance Co. v. California*, 113 S. Ct. 2891 (1993).

[21] *Hartford Fire Insurance Co. v. California*, loc. cit., note 20, at 2909.

tional comity were part of the rule on the basis of which the court takes jurisdiction.[22] Comity can only be taken into account once the court has established its jurisdiction and only if there is a true conflict between US law and the foreign law. This only arises when the foreign law requires the defendant to act in a fashion prohibited by US law or in any other circumstances where it is impossible for the defendant to comply with both his or her domestic law and with US law. The fact that a certain action or conduct is lawful or even encouraged in the foreign state will not, in itself, lead to the non-application of the provisions of the Sherman Act.[23]

It could be argued that the court's judgment signals a return to a rather crude form of the "effects doctrine". This is even more worrying as the court based its "true conflict" analysis on Sections 403 and 415 of the Restatement (Third).[24] These are general provisions and do not limit the analysis to antitrust law. This "true conflict" analysis seems to contradict earlier judgments of the Supreme Court on the comity issue[25] and bears a striking resemblance to the approach adopted in case the foreign sovereign compulsion defence is raised.[26] It is submitted that the approach taken by the majority is wrong, but as long as it stands, this case will not facilitate things in international antitrust cases. Foreign countries are expected to have substantial difficulties in accepting the extraterritorial application of US antitrust laws on this basis.

3   EXTRATERRITORIALITY IN EUROPEAN COMPETITION LAW

3.1 The Dyestuffs case

The Court of Justice of the European Communities (ECJ) was for the first time invited to give judgment in a case concerning the extraterritorial application

---

[22] *Hartford Fire Insurance Co. v. California,* loc. cit., note 20, at 2910; Justice Scalia dissented strongly on this point and would see international comity as an integral part of the rule on the basis of which jurisdiction is determined.

[23] *Hartford Fire Insurance Co. v. California,* loc. cit., note 20, at 2910–2911. See also Robertson and Demetriou, "'But That Was in Another Country ...': The Extraterritorial Application of US Antitrust Laws in the Supreme Court", 43 ICLQ (1994), 417–425, at 421.

[24] Restatement (Third) of the Foreign Relations Law of the United States (1987).

[25] See *Société Nationale Industrielle Aérospatiale v. United States Dist. Court,* 482 US 522, 543–544 (1987); and *Asahi Metal Indus. Co. v. Superior Court,* 480 US 102, 115 (1987).

[26] Griffin, "US Supreme Court Encourages Extraterritorial Application of US Antitrust Laws", 21 *International Business Lawyer* (1993), 389–393, at 391.

of competition law in the *Dyestuffs* case.[27]

The Commission relied on three arguments to impose a fine on ICI. ICI itself had been engaged in the concerted practices, simply treating its subsidiary as an agent; ICI had been present in the Community because it controlled its subsidiary (the "economic-entity doctrine" leading to jurisdiction based on the territoriality principle); and the actions taken by ICI had produced effects within the Community (the "effects doctrine", on the basis of which competition law rules can be applied extraterritorially). Advocate General Mayras favoured in his opinion the acceptance of the "effects doctrine" and specified the requirements for an effect to trigger the extraterritorial application of Articles 85 and 86. The effect should imply a direct and immediate restriction of competition and should be foreseeable by the infringing undertaking. He did not require the effect to be intentional.[28]

The ECJ based its judgment on the "economic-entity doctrine" and found this was a sufficient basis to uphold the jurisdiction of the Commission in this case:[29]

> The fact that a subsidiary has separate legal personality is not sufficient to exclude the possibility of imputing its conduct to the parent company .... In the circumstances, the formal separation between these companies, resulting from their separate legal personality, cannot outweigh the unity of their conduct on the market for the purposes of applying the rules on competition.

It should be stressed that the ECJ accepted that ICI effectively controlled its subsidiaries without requiring much evidence.[30] It remains, however, possible for a subsidiary to rebut the presumption of *de facto* control by its parent.[31]

3.2 The Wood Pulp *case*

Sixteen years after the *Dyestuffs* case, the *Wood Pulp* case[32] allowed the ECJ to review its position regarding the extraterritorial application of European

---

[27] Case 48/69, *ICI* v *Commission,* [1972] ECR 619.

[28] Case 48/69, loc. cit, note 27, Opinion of Advocate General Mayras, at 687–694.

[29] Case 48/69, loc. cit., note 27; for a severe but not completely impartial criticism of this judgment, see Mann, "The Dyestuffs Case in the Court of Justice of the European Communities", 22 ICLQ (1973), 35–50.

[30] Whish, op. cit., note 3, at p. 380.

[31] Cases 6 and 7/73, *Commercial Solvents* v *Commission,* [1974] ECR 223, at 264, Opinion of Advocate General Warner.

[32] Joined Cases 89, 104, 114, 116–117, 125–129/85, *Ahlström* v *Commission,* [1988] ECR 5193.

competition law.

In its *Wood Pulp* decision[33] the Commission established its jurisdiction over an agreement concluded outside the Community by undertakings that were not situated in the Community. The Commission stated broadly that:[34]

> Article 85 of the EEC Treaty applies to restrictive practices which may affect trade between Member States even if the undertakings and associations which are parties to the restrictive practices are established or have their headquarters outside the Community, and even if the restrictive practices in question also affect markets outside the EEC.

The arguments on the basis of which the Commission established its jurisdiction were clearly based on the "effects doctrine". If the effects of the agreements and concerted practices in the Community are intended, direct and substantial, Article 85 should apply to undertakings situated outside the Community. In the Commission's view the fact that "shipments affected by these agreements and practices amounted to about two-thirds of total shipments of bleached sulphate wood pulp to the EEC and some 60 per cent of EEC consumption" and that "the agreements and practices appear to have applied to at least the vast majority of the sales of the relevant product by the parties during the relevant periods"[35] means that the economic effect was substantial and intended. Concerning the direct effect requirement the Commission noted that the producers were "exporting directly or doing business within the Community"[36] and that the concerted conduct "concerned shipments made directly to buyers in the EEC or sales made in the EEC to buyers there".[37]

The Commission added another requirement to create jurisdiction, probably in an attempt to fashion some form of territorial link. The concerted conduct must be implemented within the Community. Implementation means trading directly into the Community or using sales offices or agents to trade in the Community. The latter form refers to what was decided in the *Dyestuffs* case. Under the first form jurisdiction arises not from the concerted practice of the pulp companies, which is situated outside the Community, but from

---

[33] O.J. 1984, L 27/85.

[34] Ibid.

[35] Ibid.

[36] Ibid.

[37] Ibid.

their conduct (the direct trading) in the Community in implementing the practice.[38] It should also be noted that the "economic-entity doctrine" was unworkable in this case, because there were either no subsidiaries in the EEC or the control exercised over them was not substantial enough.

Advocate General Darmon strongly supports the "effects doctrine" in his Opinion.[39] In his view Article 85 applies whenever there is an effect on interstate trade, without further requirements concerning nationality or geographical location of the undertakings. It is, however, uncertain whether the "effect" referred to in Article 85 constitutes, strictly speaking, a basis of jurisdiction.[40]

As an inflexible territorial approach is no longer suited to the modern economically interdependent world, he suggests a criterion of qualified effect.[41] Such an effect within the Community should be direct and immediate, reasonably foreseeable and substantial.[42]

At first sight the ECJ's judgment[43] seems to endorse the "effects doctrine", dismissing any territorial link as immaterial. But it is extremely important to note that the ECJ did not use the term "effects doctrine" and spelled out an implementation requirement. The implementation of an agreement or a concerted practice in the Community provides jurisdiction to the Commission. An implementation appears to mean engaging in a transaction with a Community customer, an agreement is implemented in the Community when it concerns the price, quantity or quality of a product sold to a Community customer. Thus, the ECJ did not uphold the Commission's decision as far as it concerned the KEA association because it did not engage itself in a transaction with an EEC customer.

So one has to conclude that the ECJ did not endorse the pure "effects doctrine". The KEA passage of the judgment indicates that the effect should be direct, and apart from what is said above, "implemented" seems also to

---

[38] See Lange and Sandage, "The Woodpulp Decision and its Implications for the Scope of EC Competition Law", 26 CML Rev. (1989), 137–165.

[39] Joined Cases 89, 104, 114, 116–117, 125–129/85, loc. cit., note 32, Opinion of Advocate General Darmon, at 5214.

[40] For an affirmative answer see Goldman and Lyon-Caen, *Droit commercial européen* (1983), 4th edn, at p. 872.

[41] The Advocate General refers with approval to Idot, *Le contrôle des pratiques restrictives dans les échanges internationaux* (1981), Dissertation University of Paris II.

[42] Reference is made to the Opinion of Advocate General Mayras in the *Dyestuffs* case, loc. cit., note 27.

[43] Joined Cases 89, 104, 114, 116–117, 125–129/85, loc. cit., note 32.

include the requirements of the effect to be substantial and intentional.[44]

The ECJ's judgment also seems to suggest that Article 85 only applies to non-EEC undertakings if there is an actual effect in the Community. For Community undertakings a conduct having the object or effect of restraining competition creates liability under Article 85.[45] An unexecuted agreement can therefore only create liability for Community undertakings.[46]

In the *Wood Pulp* case the Commission conducted extensive consultations with third countries that had an interest in this case. As the ECJ did not express any point of view as far as these comity-consultations are concerned, it remains unclear if this forms a legal limitation on the Commission's power or if this is just an exercise of discretion.[47]

4   A COMPARATIVE EVALUATION

Both the European Community and the United States apply some form of "effects doctrine". In theory the effects test "European style" seems similar to the effects test "American style". But there are differences. One could describe them very roughly by saying that the Community operates a qualified "effects doctrine". It all comes down to the fact that European competition law contains the implementation requirement. Implementation in the Community affects without doubt competition within it. In this respect trading into the Community is no different from trading in the Common Market. Such an additional requirement is not found in US antitrust law. But it is hard to imagine a case where an effect is shown to be direct and substantial and US law could be applied but where there is no implementation in the United States.[48] All other differences are even less substantial, and I will refrain from analysing them in any more detail, as they are less useful for our actual purposes.

This analysis of the extraterritorial application of competition laws on

---

[44] Cf. Ferry, "Towards Completing the Charm: The Woodpulp Judgment", (1989) ECLR, 58–73. See also Whish, op. cit., note 3, at pp. 381–382.

[45] See Case 123/83, *BNIC* v *Clair,* [1985] ECR 391; and Joined Case 40 to 48, 50, 54 to 56, 111, 113 and 114/73, *Suiker Unie and Others* v *Commission,* [1975] ECR 1663.

[46] Lange and Sandage, loc. cit., note 38.

[47] Ibid., at 164–165.

[48] Cf. Van der Esch, "Some Aspects of 'Extra-Territorial' Infringement in EEC Competition Rules", in Hawk (ed.), *Antitrust and Trade Policy in the United States and the European Community* (1986), at p. 287 et seq.

both sides of the Atlantic provides us with a comprehensive overview of the "effects doctrine" and the other aspects of extraterritoriality. It is in this area that extraterritoriality is most developed. We will now have to analyse which role extraterritoriality can play in the human rights area, be it on the basis of similar principles or on a different basis.

5   A ROLE FOR THE EXTRATERRITORIALITY PRINCIPLE IN HUMAN RIGHTS?

Although one would not necessarily expect extraterritoriality cases in the human rights area, there are a couple of them. Seven days before handing down its judgment in the *Hartford Fire Insurance* case[49] the United States Supreme Court dealt with the extraterritoriality issue in *Sale v. Haitian Centers Council*[50] and denied certain provisions of the UN Convention Relating to the Status of Refugees and the US Immigration and Nationality Act 1952 any extraterritorial application. Although the facts involved would produce effects in the United States, the Court felt no obligation to take a similar approach to the effects based approach taken in antitrust cases. Another important US decision, apparently not influenced by the *Sale* case, is *US v. Chen*.[51] In this case the Court of Appeals (9th Circuit) considered the enforcement powers in relation to US immigration laws. These provisions were given extraterritorial application and the officers of the Immigration and Naturalisation Service were allowed to exercise the powers granted to them outside the United States.

It is submitted that it would not be appropriate for the European Union to follow this contradictory approach. It is submitted that the extraterritoriality issue needs a consistent approach and that the area of law in which it is applied should not be seen as an important distinguishing factor. If extraterritoriality is seen as a choice of applicable law problem, the connecting factor on the basis of which the applicable law is determined could be the found in the "effects doctrine". A national law is applicable whenever effects are produced or felt in that nation. This corresponds with the approach taken in competition law cases both by the United States and the European Community.[52] Such an approach would be transparent and fits in with an existing

---

[49] See *Hartford Fire Insurance Co. v. California,* loc. cit., note 20, and accompanying text.

[50] *Chris Sale, Acting Commissioner, Immigration and Naturalisation Service, et al., Petitioners v. Haitian Centers Council, Inc., et al.,* 113 S. Ct. 2549 (1993).

[51] *US v. Chen,* Court of Appeals (9th Circuit), 62 LW 2133 (US *Law Week,* 14 Sept. 1993). See also *US v. Aguilar* (1989), which was also decided by the Court of Appeals (9th Circuit).

[52] For more details on the type of effect required, see the Section on competition law above.

framework of private international law provisions.

It would of course not avoid the problem that a situation may result in the potentially conflicting application of more than one national law. The same happens in competition law cases and no obvious solution seems to be forthcoming. An attempt to solve, or rather to start addressing the problem was made in an agreement between the European Commission and the US Government,[53] but it seems that the Commission went beyond its powers in doing so,[54] which would render the whole exercise pointless. It is submitted that this problem demonstrates clearly that extraterritoriality is not only a legal problem. Politics and diplomacy are probably as important if we are ever going to solve this particular problem,[55] but it would lead us too far if we were to address this issue fully in the scope of this chapter. This leaves us with the second aspect of extraterritoriality. Should a state be allowed to adopt legislation which is clearly extraterritorial in scope? Without going into any detail, I would just like to refer back to my introductory comment that this is an aspect of public international law on which there is no agreement.[56]

The ECJ has not waited for the Treaty on European Union (TEU) to be ratified to address the issue of human rights though and in one case there are indications pointing towards the extraterritorial application of human rights.

5.1 A European approach

The EEC Treaty contained one clear and specific reference to human rights. Article 7, now Article 6 in the post-Maastricht version of the Treaty, prohibited any form of discrimination on grounds of nationality. The ECJ dealt with the interpretation of this provision in a sports context in *Walrave* v *UCI*.[57] The UCI had introduced a rule that stayers and their pacemakers should possess the same nationality and the plaintiffs considered this rule to be incompatible with the Treaty in so far as it prevented a pacemaker of one Member State from offering his services to a stayer of another Member State. The ECJ ruled that the non-discrimination principle applied to all contracts, not

---

[53] Competition Law Cooperation Agreement 1991, [1991] 4 CMLR 823.

[54] See the Opinion of Advocate General Tesauro in Case C-327/91, *French Republic* v *Commission of the European Communities*, [1994] ECR I-3641. See also Riley, "Nailing the Jellyfish: The Illegality of the EC/US Government Competition Agreement", 3 ECLR (1992), 101–109.

[55] See Demaret, loc. cit., note 2.

[56] See the literature mentioned in note 1.

[57] Case 36/74, *Walrave* v *Union Cycliste Internationale*, [1974] ECR 1405.

only to those entered to in the Community. It even applied the non-discrimination principle to contracts whose only link with the Community it was to produce effects in the Community.[58] This should be seen as a general endorsement of the "effects doctrine". Could this approach be applied to other human rights or, as the Community seems to prefer, fundamental rights? Or is there any reason to restrict this approach to the non-discrimination on the basis of nationality rule enshrined in the Treaty?

The latter option cannot be defended. The ECJ made it clear on numerous occasions that it is empowered to apply general principles of law and fundamental rights[59] which in the ECJ's view form part of Community law as general principles of Community law.[60] In protecting these fundamental rights the ECJ will be inspired by the common constitutional traditions of the Member States and the ECJ will not tolerate any measures which violate these constitutional traditions and fundamental rights.[61] So there is no reason to distinguish between the non-discrimination on the basis of nationality principle and other fundamental rights as they all form part of Community law.[62] This approach allows the ECJ to refer to international human rights conventions to which the Member States are parties.[63] The Convention for the Protection of Human Rights and Fundamental Freedoms (European Convention on Human Rights; ECHR) plays a dominant role in this respect and its provisions are used frequently by the ECJ.[64]

This leads the ECJ to require all Community institutions to take these fundamental rights into account, because no violation of these fundamental rights would be tolerated by the ECJ. Fundamental rights are enforceable at Community level.

The position of fundamental rights in the European Union was further

---

[58] Case 36/74, loc. cit., note 57, at 1420 and 1421.

[59] See, e.g., Case 36/75, *Rutili* v *Minister for the Interior*, [1975] ECR 1219; Case 44/79, *Hauer* v *Land Rheinland-Pfalz*, [1979] ECR 3727; Case 136/79, *National Panasonic* v *Commission*, [1980] ECR 2033; Case 63/83, *Regina* v *Kirk*, [1984] ECR 2689; Case 85/87, *Dow Benelux* v *Commission*, [1989] ECR 3137; and Case C-260/89, *Elliniki Radiophonia Tileorassi (ERT)*, [1991] ECR I-2925.

[60] Case 26/69, *Stauder* v *Ulm*, [1969] ECR 419, at 425. See also Case 11/70, *Internationale Handelsgesellschaft* v *Einfuhr- und Vorratstelle Getreide*, [1970] ECR 1125.

[61] See Case 11/70, loc. cit, note 60; and Case 4/73, *Nold* v *Commission*, [1974] ECR 491.

[62] See Kapteyn and VerLoren van Themaat, *Inleiding tot het recht van de Europese Gemeenschappen* (1987), 4th edn, at pp. 114–121; and Wyatt and Dashwood, *European Community Law* (1993), 3rd edn, at pp. 98–102.

[63] Case 4/73, loc. cit., note 61.

[64] See, e.g., Case 36/75, loc. cit., note 59.

enhanced by the TEU. Article F TEU enshrines the position adopted by the Court into European law. Membership of the Union is linked to a democratic system which respects fundamental rights and the Union must respect the fundamental rights guaranteed by the ECHR, as well as those rights resulting from the constitutional traditions common to the Member States.[65]

It is submitted that, as a combined result of the judgment in *Walrave* v *UCI* and the fact that fundamental rights are now one of the pillars on which the European Union rests, all fundamental rights can now be applied extraterritorially. If a violation of a fundamental right has a territorial link with the European Union, national or European legislation will offer a remedy depending on the circumstances of the case; but we are dealing specifically with the UCI type of case where there is not necessarily a territorial link with the European Union. In this type of case the fundamental rights incorporated in the legislation of the Union can be applied extraterritorially if the conduct which violates one or more of these fundamental rights produces effects in the European Union. A good example can be the case where an organization of which European companies or private individuals are members and which is located outside the Union, adopts a decision which violates certain fundamental rights. Not only could one sue those who implement the decision in the Union, but one would also be allowed to go all the way to the source of the decision on the basis of the extraterritorial application of the fundamental rights involved. This would open the possibility to address the problem at its roots and avoid a partial solution. To allow this option the effect in the European Union should be direct, substantial and intentional. Implementation of the alleged conduct in the European Union will also be required.[66]

These requirements prevent that the extraterritorial application of the fundamental rights recognized by the Union would receive an extremely wide scope. It would clearly be inappropriate and in breach of public international law to dictate the law on fundamental rights in cases where there is only an indirect effect in the Union and/or where the conduct is not implemented in the Union. The fact that eventually the conduct was not intended to cause effect in the Union or that these effects were not substantial would only aggravate such a case. The adoption of the "effects doctrine" American style would mean that the implementation requirement was dropped. This would bring more cases within the scope of these provisions. It is submitted that this change should not be advocated as it would lead to an even more conflicting

---

[65] See Wyatt and Dashwood, op. cit., note 62, at p. 656.

[66] See Joined Cases 89, 104, 114, 116–117, 125–129/85, loc. cit., note 32; as discussed above.

application of the rules on extraterritoriality in an international context. Implementation is essential in justifying the action of the Union; without this requirement the link with the Union would be insufficient. An example of a case with a very weak link would be an action against the importation into the Community of products manufactured by Chinese human rights prisoners. Such matters should rather be addressed in trade agreements.

It must be clear that under public international rules the European Union is in no position to sue a foreign state on the basis of the "effects doctrine". The "effects doctrine" cannot solve the problem of a violation of fundamental rights by a foreign state. Here the European Union is left with the possibility to include the respect of fundamental rights as a prerequisite in development and cooperation treaties. The Union makes increasingly use of this possibility.[67] The problem associated with this possibility is that it is less clear which sanctions are linked to a violation of certain of these fundamental rights by the foreign partner.[68] It is assumed that the implementation of the agreement can be suspended or that the agreement could eventually be denounced by the European Union.[69] The Union has also adapted measures to allow trade sanctions in cases in which no agreement exists.[70]

Even in situations where the extraterritorial application would be possible and can be an appropriate tool one difficulty remains. Which sanctions will apply and how is the decision going to be enforced? *Walrave* suggests that a decision deprives the infringing conduct of its legal validity.[71] This makes it also unenforceable in the European Union. This will, however, not be an appropriate remedy in a number of situations in which such a decision should be enforced abroad, as many countries will not be inclined to recognize a decision based entirely on the extraterritorial application of fundamental rights. The same lack of appropriate sanctions has already been raised in the context of international agreements concluded by the European Union. It is clear that this is the weak point of the Union's international action on human rights and further measures are required in this area to equip the Union with a fully

---

[67] See Kuyper, "Trade Sanctions, Security and Human Rights and Commercial Policy", in Maresceau (ed.), *The European Community's Commercial Policy after 1992: The Legal Dimension* (1993), pp. 387–422.

[68] Ibid.

[69] For a national example see Lindemann, "Die Auswirkungen der Menschenrechtsverletzungen in Surinam auf die Vertragsbeziehungen zwischen den Niederlanden und Surinam", 44 ZaöRV (1984), 64–93.

[70] Kuyper, loc. cit, note 67.

[71] Case 36/74, loc. cit., note 57.

effective set of rules in this area.[72]

6   *SALE* AND *CHEN*: AN AMERICAN EXAMPLE?

Both cases which were mentioned previously are concerned with immigration, political and economical refugees. They could have been solved following the approach outlined above. The influx of refugees would have created a substantial intentional and direct effect in the United States. The US immigration legislation, which takes into account the UN Convention Relating to the Status of Refugees, could have been applied extraterritorially. This is indeed the conclusion reached by the Court of Appeals (9th Circuit) in *US v. Chen*. The Supreme Court adopted a different analysis in *Sale v. Haitian Centers Council.*[73]

The Court refers to the presumption that all laws are territorial in scope and on the basis of its examination concludes that that presumption had not been rebutted in this case. It is indeed a good starting-point to accept that normal legislation is territorial in scope, but it must be clear that certain principles are so essential that the laws incorporating them cannot be territorial in scope as that would allow foreign infringements of these principles which have effects in the state adhering to these principles to escape all sanctions. As this would constitute an unacceptable, indirect deviation from essential principles such as the rules on free competition the laws incorporating these provisions must be applied extraterritorially as well. It is submitted that the same applies to human rights provisions, as they too are part of a body of essential rules.

The *non-refoulement* principle which is enshrined in the UN Convention and the corresponding provisions of the Immigration and Nationality Act are part of these essential rules. They should be applied extraterritorially. It is submitted that it is impossible to arrive at a different conclusion as these provisions apply to "any alien" and allowing a state to escape the *non-refoulement* principle by setting up a net preventing these aliens from reaching the national borders with the intention to send them back without allowing them to file an application for political asylum and without a proper examination of their case results in depriving the *non-refoulement* principle of

---

[72] See also Kuyper, loc. cit, note 67.

[73] *Chris Sale, Acting Commissioner, Immigration and Naturalisation Service, et al., Petitioners, v. Haitian Centers Council, Inc., et al.*, loc. cit., note 50.

all meaning.[74] It is a pity that the Supreme Court refused to overturn the territoriality presumption and I would agree with Justice Blackmun, dissenting, that this conclusion could not be achieved without the court straining to sanction the politically motivated conduct of the Executive described above.[75]

This example should not be followed by the European Union in a similar situation. The Union should stick to one systematic approach for all areas of law. Fortress Europe style exceptions should be avoided. Apparently there is already an influx of refugees from Turkey. These refugees arrive on the nearest Greek isles. The two Nordic countries (Finland and Sweden) having become members of the European Union a similar influx across the Baltic Sea can be expected. The rights of these refugees should be respected, even when that implies applying our relevant legal provisions extraterritorially on the high seas. It should be irrelevant whether the extraterritorial application of its fundamental rights provisions suits the European Union or not.

7   CONCLUSION

I hope to have been successful in taking a slightly provocative approach. Why would one advocate the application of a controversial principle such as extraterritoriality to human rights issues in the European Union? In my view there is an easy answer. If we accept that the principle is applied to our rules on free competition on the basis that these are so essential to our European Union that we cannot avoid any form of infringement, not even infringement located outside the European Union which produces effects in the Union, then we should apply it also to the human rights norms, that other fundamental aspect of our Union. It is in my view a logical consequence of the incorporation of a human rights provision in the TEU.

Extraterritoriality is not a magical tool, though. It can only assist in certain circumstances and even then sanctions and enforcement could create problems. But it can be a small step forward and every improvement in the European Union's human rights record needs to be welcomed.

---

[74] *Chris Sale, Acting Commissioner, Immigration and Naturalisation Service, et al., Petitioners v. Haitian Centers Council, Inc., et al.,* loc. cit., note 50, 2558, submission for the respondents by Professor Harold Hongju Koh.

[75] *Chris Sale, Acting Commissioner, Immigration and Naturalisation Service, et al., Petitioners, v. Haitian Centers Council, Inc., et al.,.* loc. cit., note 50, dissenting opinion filed by Justice Blackmun, 2567, at 2568.

16 THE EUROPEAN UNION'S FOREIGN POLICY AND HUMAN RIGHTS

Daniela Napoli

1   INTRODUCTION

Human rights, as defined in the Universal Declaration of 1948, are an essential part of humanity's shared heritage, and where they are not genuinely respected, there can be no question of a lasting peace.

This is generally held to be a sovereign issue, as it embraces all the economic, social, political and cultural aspects of a country's existence, fields in which states tend to be extremely sensitive and vigilant since they perceive them to be their vital interests.

This creates a knot which unravels in the relationships that develop between states. Initially based entirely on economic interests, it is only at a later stage in such relationships that the recognition of shared values allows countries to establish objectives of a political nature which go beyond the merely economic, such as respecting and protecting human rights. The integration process initiated by the European Community has followed this pattern, and the Treaty on European Union (TEU) which entered into force on 1 November 1993 represents a particularly important step forward, as it provides a legal legitimacy for the incorporation of human rights as a key element of the Union's internal and external policies.

This chapter will chart the different stages of this legitimacy through the Treaties and highlight the roles played by the different institutions and by the instruments at their disposal.

2   REFERENCES TO HUMAN RIGHTS

One of the TEU's major innovations is the explicit reference made in different parts of the text to human rights, fundamental freedoms and respect for democratic principles and the rule of law.

N. A. Neuwahl and A. Rosas (eds.), The European Union and Human Rights, 297–312.
© *1995 Kluwer Law International. Printed in the Netherlands.*

2.1 References in the Treaty on European Union

Preamble, third recital:

> Confirming their attachment to the principles of liberty, democracy and respect for human rights and fundamental freedoms and the rule of law ...

Title 1, Common Provisions:

Article F(1):
The Union shall respect the national identities of its Member States, whose systems of government are founded on the principles of democracy;

Article F(2):
The Union shall respect all fundamental rights, as guaranteed by the European Convention for the Protection of Human Rights and Fundamental Freedoms signed in Rome on 4 November 1950 and as they result from the constitutional traditions common to the Member States, as general principles of Community law.

Title XVII EC, Development Cooperation:

Article 130u(2):
Community policy in this area shall contribute to the general objective of developing and consolidating democracy and the rule of law, and to that of respecting human rights and fundamental freedoms.

Title V, Common Foreign and Security Policy:

Article J.1(2), fifth indent:
The objectives of the common foreign and security policy shall be to develop and consolidate democracy and the rule of law, and respect for human rights and fundamental freedoms.

Title VI, Cooperation in the Fields of Justice and Home Affairs:

Article K.2(1):
The matters referred to in Article K.1 shall be dealt with in compliance with the European Convention for the Protection of Human Rights and Fundamental Freedoms of 4 November 1950 and the Convention relating to the Status of Refugees of 28 July 1951 and having regard to the protection afforded by Member States to persons persecuted on political grounds.

Besides such references to respect for basic rights, the expression of those rights at Community level is given greater emphasis by the introduction of new areas of competence, such as citizenship of the Union (Articles 8–8e).

2.2 References as they have evolved through the Treaties

To appreciate the true significance of the incorporation of references to human rights in the body of the TEU text, it is important to retrace the history of European integration since the signing of the Treaties establishing the European Communities. There is no explicit reference to human rights and international measures to safeguard them either in the Treaty of Paris of 18 April 1951, establishing the European Coal and Steel Community (ECSC), or in the Treaties of Rome of 25 March 1957, establishing the European Economic Community (EEC) and the European Atomic Energy Community (EAEC).

The absence of such references reflects the primarily economic substance of these Treaties, which required the Member States to transfer national sovereignty in economically and socially sensitive sectors to common institutions. This process entailed radical changes in the relations between Community Member States in a post-war environment that made it impossible to extend this process to other, more politically charged spheres. This is borne out by the failure, just three years on from the Treaty of Rome, of the proposals for a European Defence Community, which demonstrated the importance, for the time being, of sticking to sectors that would engender a *de facto* solidarity.

In fact, it probably did not occur to the six founder members of the European Economic Community to make some provision for human rights and fundamental freedoms. As Members of the Council of Europe, set up in 1949, they had recently taken part in the drafting of the Convention for the Protection of Human Rights and Fundamental Freedoms (European Convention on Human Rights; ECHR), which was signed on 4 November 1950 and entered into force in 1953, and which was to provide a particularly detailed instrument for the protection of human rights and fundamental freedoms in Europe, with binding force in national legislation.

The absence of references to basic rights in the Treaties establishing the European Communities might be held to be balanced by the EEC Treaty's provisions on freedom of movement for workers (Articles 48–58) and the ban on discrimination on the grounds of nationality (Article 7 in particular) or sex (Article 119). However, these socio-economic rights are included in the Treaty only as elements of a system designed with purely economic objectives in mind. The coverage given to them makes no mention of international or regional instruments for the protection of human rights, and therefore the mechanisms set up to monitor compliance with the texts concerned are not applicable. It is the Court of Justice of the European Communities (ECJ) that is responsible for monitoring the implementation of these texts in Community legislation, in line with the objectives and principles laid down in the Treaties.

It was not until some thirty years later, with the Single European Act (SEA) of February 1986, that explicit reference was made to fundamental rights. The Act, which also formally launched Political Cooperation, incorporates two paragraphs on this issue in the Preamble: one, recital 3, with regard to internal policy, the other, recital 5, concerning external relations:

> Determined to work together to promote democracy on the basis of the fundamental rights recognised in the constitutions and laws of the Member States, in the Convention for the Protection of Human Rights and Fundamental Freedoms and the European Social Charter, notably freedom, equality and social justice (recital 3);
> ... in particular to display the principles of democracy and compliance with the law and with human rights to which they are attached, so that together they may make their own contribution to the preservation of international peace and security in accordance with the undertaking entered into by them within the framework of the United Nations Charter (recital 5).

3   HISTORICAL AND POLITICAL BACKGROUND: ACTORS AND INSTRUMENTS

3.1 Actors

It was the key actors of European integration that were also responsible for the series of developments that culminated in the adoption of legally binding rules on the protection and promotion of basic rights: on the one hand, the ECJ, which produced a body of case law incorporating references to fundamental rights not covered by the Treaties and, on the other, the Community institutions, the European Political Cooperation and the European Council, which publicly declared their commitment to respecting and promoting human rights, and launched specific initiatives along those lines.

The ECJ, Parliament, the Commission, the Council, the European Council. The period between the Treaties of Paris and Rome and the SEA was not devoid of developments in the field of fundamental rights. During that time, the Community institutions and the Member States launched a number of initiatives that bore witness to the need to bring activities in this field together under universal, regional and national umbrellas.

The institutions' pronouncements on the subject paved the way for the incorporation of human rights into the Treaties. From a hesitant and inauspicious start, these declarations developed in parallel to the Community's integration process, becoming progressively more detailed and being adopted at increasingly high level. They were the first indications of the need felt not only within the Community but also at international and regional level to strengthen the ties that bind states together by paying more than lip service to the concept of human rights.

This was a considerable task, given that the lack of Community fundamental rights legislation was liable in the first instance to provoke clashes between nationally enshrined laws based on regional and international systems for the protection of human rights, and Community law, which at the time made no such provision. This state of affairs threatened to sap the Community's legal foundations, particularly in respect of the fundamental principles of the primacy of Community law and its uniform application in all the Member States.

The *ECJ* was confronted with the legal repercussions of this deficit in a case brought before a national court in October 1967. The German Supreme Court, observing that the transfer of powers to the Community threatened to deprive German citizens of their constitutionally protected rights, contested the democratic legitimacy of Community law and rejected its primacy over national law. The Italian Constitutional Court expressed similar doubts a few years later.

The ECJ responded by developing an original praetorian system which enabled it to extend the Community's framework of references beyond the basically economic content of the Treaties of Paris and Rome, by gradually incorporating the fundamental rights traditionally recognized under national constitutions and the relevant regional and international bodies.

This was achieved in three decisive stages: first, two judgments delivered in 1969 and 1970[1] referred for the first time to the constitutional traditions common to the Member States; next, the *Nold* judgment of 1974[2] declared inadmissible measures that are not compatible with the international human rights instruments to which the Member States have affiliated or with which they have co-operated; and finally, in the *Rutili* judgment of 1975[3], the ECJ referred directly to the ECHR. These judgments establish the constitutional principles later given legitimacy in the SEA, as reflected in a 1989 case.[4] Given the many effects of Community activity on the fundamental freedoms

---

[1] Case 29/69, *Stauder* v *Ulm*, [1969] ECR 419; Case 11/70, *Internationale Handelsgesellschaft* v *Einfuhr- und Vorratsstelle Getreide*, [1970] ECR 1125.

[2] Case 4/73, *Nold* v *Commission (second Nold Case)*, [1974] ECR 491.

[3] Case 36/75, *Rutili* v *Minister for the Interior*, [1975] ECR 1219.

[4] Case 249/86, *Commission* v *Germany*, [1989] ECR 1263.

enacted in the ECHR, the ECJ was obliged to consider the rights guaranteed by this instrument. For this reason, the ECJ has been called upon to deliver opinions on such rights as the respect for privacy, religious freedom, freedom of expression and the right to property.

Meanwhile, the *European Parliament* was demonstrating its commitment to respecting and promoting fundamental rights. The introduction of direct universal suffrage for the election of its Members, in 1979, lent Parliament democratic legitimacy and hence a moral authority which, in the 1980s, enabled it to step up its initiatives in the field of fundamental rights and democratic principles.

Despite Parliament's limited influence, it has nonetheless played a key role in providing impetus. Through reports, resolutions, recommendations and written and oral questions submitted to the Council or the Commission, Parliament has acquired the status of tribune for the defence and promotion of human rights, thus encouraging Community policy makers to take these fundamental rights into account. By organizing public conferences on specific human rights issues, Parliament has stimulated and deepened the institutions' debates in this area. It has also made itself the spokesman for individuals who, using a procedure now enshrined in the Maastricht Treaty, submit petitions which can culminate in Parliament approaching the Commission, the Council or national governments with a view to their taking the requisite action.

It was also due to Parliament that, on 5 April 1977, the institutions formally issued a joint declaration recognizing the vital importance of fundamental rights to their own working practices. This document stresses "the prime importance [the institutions] attach to the protection of fundamental rights, as derived in particular from the constitutions of the Member States and in the European Convention for the Protection of Human Rights and Fundamental Freedoms" and they undertake "to respect these rights ... in the exercise of their powers and in pursuance of the aims of the European Communities".

On 12 April 1989, on the basis of the Treaties' first explicit references to fundamental rights, in the SEA, and seeking to anchor the integration process to the common values of the people of Europe, Parliament adopted a declaration on fundamental rights and freedoms, with a view to filling the void left by the lack of written rules in this field.

As guardian of the Treaties, invested with the power of initiative, the *Commission* was also directly confronted with this deficit in its pursuit of the objective of a Single European Market. In 1979 this led to a Memorandum proposing that the institutions' legal acts be scrutinized by the monitoring mechanism of the ECHR. This suggestion was welcomed by the European

Parliament and the Economic and Social Committee but was not taken up by the Council of Ministers. In 1990, the momentum generated by the SEA prompted the Commission to relaunch the debate by formally requesting Council authorization to negotiate the Community's accession to the ECHR.[5] Four years later the issue is still current. The entry into force of the Maastricht Treaty and its explicit references to the ECHR in Articles F(2) (Common Provisions) and K.2(1) (Title VI) have not altered the situation, and the issue of accession is still pending. The Council has just asked the ECJ for a formal opinion on the procedures and implications of possible accession.

In the field of external relations, the Commission initiated a broad-ranging debate on the links between development, human rights and democracy.[6]

The Commission also undertook an in-depth analysis to take stock of the situation with regard to fundamental rights in the context of the completion of the Single Market. To that end a seminar was organized in November 1989 at the occasion of the bicentennial of the *Déclaration des Droits de l'Homme et du Citoyen* on the theme "Human Rights and the European Community: Towards 1992 and Beyond", with the backing of Parliament and the co-operation of the European University Institute in Florence.[7]

The formal institution of Political Cooperation in the SEA which reinforced the importance of human rights in relations with third countries was followed shortly afterwards, on 21 July 1986, by a declaration by the European Community Foreign Ministers meeting in the framework of European Political Cooperation and of the Council, reaffirming "their commitment to promote and protect human rights and fundamental freedoms" and emphasizing "the importance in this context of the principles of parliamentary democracy and the rule of law". This text provides the first elements of a strategy to promote human rights around the world.

On 28 November 1991, the eve of the conclusion of the Maastricht Treaty negotiations, the Council and the Member States meeting within the Council adopted a major new resolution on the theme of human rights, democracy and development. Echoing the broad debate that was then going on in the international fora concerned, this text was the fruit of an assessment

---

[5] Commission Communication of 19 Nov. 1990 on "Community Accession to the European Convention for the Protection of Human Rights and Fundamental Freedoms and Some of its Protocols", SEC (90) 2087 final.

[6] Commission Communication to the Council and to Parliament of 25 March 1991 on "Human Rights, Democracy and Development Cooperation Policy", SEC (91) 61 final.

[7] Cf. the series *European Union—The Human Rights Challenge* (1991), 3 vols.

conducted by the Community institutions which had highlighted the need to integrate development co-operation and the promotion of human rights and democracy into an overall strategy with common objectives. The Council resolution prescribed guidelines, procedures and practical action, and included a (non-exhaustive) list of priorities.

The commitments entered into by the institutions of the Community and in the framework of Political Cooperation are complementary of those at the highest level by Heads of State or Government, starting with the Paris Summit of October 1972, where they undertook to base the development of the Community on the principles of democracy, freedom of opinion, the free movement of individuals and ideas, and the full participation of the people of Europe through their freely elected representatives. A year later, at the Copenhagen Summit of December 1973, the Heads of State or Government adopted a document which identified respect for human rights as one of the fundamental values making up the European identity. Again in Copenhagen, this time at the European Council meeting of April 1978, they endorsed the joint declaration of Parliament, the Council and the Commission expressing their solemn undertaking to respect fundamental rights in the exercise of their powers.

After the entry into force of the SEA, and with the Union in prospect, the European Council meeting in Luxembourg on 27–28 June 1991 adopted a declaration which, based on the declaration of 1986 by the Council of Ministers and Political Cooperation, established the main planks of a political platform committing the Community and its Member States to the active promotion of human rights and democratic principles.

The Heads of State or Government again emphasized that the EC's policy in this field was anchored to a global frame of reference, and that the human rights to which they were committed were universal and indivisible. They gave a definition of the principle of non-interference compatible with the universal duty to respect human rights as enshrined in the international instruments in force. The declaration also covered certain specific issues, such as the protection of minorities and the interdependence of development, human rights and democracy; a few months later, the latter point was taken up in the resolution adopted by the Council and the Member States meeting within the Council which provides the operational basis for all action in this area.

The institutions have also taken stance on specific issues. For example, in response to growing signs of hostility towards immigrants, the Council, Parliament, the Commission and the representatives of the Member States' governments issued on 11 June 1986 a joint declaration condemning racism and xenophobia. The European Council also spoke out on these issues at its meetings in Dublin (June 1990), Maastricht (December 1991), Edinburgh (December 1992) and Copenhagen (June 1993), going well beyond statements of principle by announcing practical measures to stimulate and complement initiatives taken at national level.

The institutions have been and continue to be prime movers when considering human rights in the context of Community policies, but they would never have obtained the desired result without non-governmental organizations, which have played a determining role in the protection of human rights and are particularly valuable partners for the European Community in this field.

Co-operation with non-governmental organizations (NGOs). One of the main reasons why the NGOs are so important is that they promote awareness of human rights issues at national, regional and international level. Their role as representatives of the aspirations and concerns of individuals gives a democratic fillip to international fora where the decisions are taken by governments.

Their relations with the European Community have mirrored its evolution from an economic to a political entity, and have followed a different model of partnership than that used by the United Nations and the Council of Europe in that no specific consultative status is assigned to them.

However, NGO involvement in the implementation of Community priorities has grown in a steady and original manner, extending the scope of that co-operation from the promotion of economic, social and cultural rights to that of civil and political rights, including electoral assistance, the independence of the judiciary, improving the prison system, setting up and bolstering democratic institutions, promoting the rule of law and defending vulnerable groups.

3.2 Instruments

Respect for the Community's commitments is essential for its credibility both in relation to its own citizens and in the wider international community. Implementation of policies is achieved by the allocation of financial resources and the insertion of specific references to human rights in agreements.

Budget resources. The Community's increasing preoccupation with human rights is also reflected in the steady growth of the budget resources allocated to the promotion of human rights and democratic principles. The first dedicated budget heading was introduced in 1978, with an allocation of ECU 200,000. Other headings were added in subsequent years, with ever-increasing allocations that in 1993 reached a total of ECU 45 million. The entry into force of the TEU was marked by a major innovation: at Parliament's prompting, in the 1994 budget all headings relating to the promotion of human rights and democratic principles were brought together in a single chapter entitled "European initiatives in support of democracy and the protection of human rights", with a total allocation of ECU 59.1 million. The aim of this reorganization was to ensure the coherence and transparency of Community support for the promotion of human rights and democracy.

In addition to these specific resources, other financial instruments are also available in support of action having a considerable impact on the promotion of human rights and democracy.

References to human rights in contractual relations with third countries. A new instrument for the promotion of human rights and democratic principles was introduced with the incorporation of "human rights" clauses into agreements with third countries.

Initially, references to human rights and/or international instruments were included in a fairly haphazard way in the preamble of some agreements.

The fourth Lomé Convention, concluded in 1989 with 69 Asian, Caribbean and Pacific (ACP) countries, was the first to include a specific reference to human rights in the body of the text.[8] Article 5 expresses the signatories' shared commitment to respecting human rights and provides for the allocation of part of the funds made available under the Convention to measures to promote human rights.

This approach was the subject of careful analysis on the part of the Community institutions, based on the principle that "all lasting development should be centred on man as the bearer of human rights and beneficiary of the process of development".[9] The outcome of this analysis was the resolution adopted on 28 November 1991 by the Council and the Member States meeting within the Council which, among other more general guidelines and priorities, opted for the insertion of human rights clauses in the texts of development agreements, thus giving tangible and visible form to a binding commitment to shared and universal values.

In the spirit of the Council resolution, these provisions reflect a positive approach, and should not be seen as introducing an element of conditionality. Nevertheless:[10]

---

[8] Fourth ACP/EEC Convention, signed on 15 Dec. 1989, O.J. 1991, L 229.

[9] Declaration on Human Rights, Luxembourg European Council, 28–29 June 1991, in Duparc, *The European Community and Human Rights* (1992), pp. 48–50.

[10] Resolution of 28 Nov. 1991, para. 6, in Duparc, op. cit., note 9, pp. 51–54, at p. 52.

in the event of grave and persistent human rights violations or the serious interruption of democratic processes, the Community and its Member States will consider appropriate responses in the light of the circumstances, guided by objective and equitable criteria.

This insistence on a graduated response, tailored to the specifics of each different situation, is rooted in the desire to maintain an open dialogue and to avoid punishing a country's people for their government's actions. Co-operation activities are, where necessary, adjusted in such a way as to continue providing a minimum of humanitarian or emergency aid to the destitute.

The tenor of the references to human rights has been made progressively more firm, with the use of three different wordings. The first, which stipulates that the provisions of the agreement are based on "respect for democratic principles and human rights", is used in the agreements with Argentina,[11] Chile,[12] Paraguay,[13] Uruguay,[14] Macao[15] and Mongolia.[16] The second formula, which stipulates that respect for democratic principles is an essential element of the agreement, has been used in all co-operation agreements concluded since June 1992, namely: Brazil, 24 June 1992; Central American countries, 22 February 1993; Andean Pact countries, 23 April 1993; India, 20 December 1993.

From October 1992, the "essential element" clause was also included in the association and partnership agreements concluded with the (then) CSCE (Conference on Security and Cooperation in Europe) countries, which also saw the introduction of a third, complementary formula which can take the form either of an explicit suspension clause providing specifically for the immediate suspension of all or part of the agreement where the partner is in serious breach of the key provisions, or of a more general non-execution clause, which provides for "appropriate measures" where the parties fail to comply with their main obligations. The explicit suspension clause was first used in the agreements with the Baltic States,[17] Albania[18] and Slovenia,[19] while the

---

[11] 2 April 1990 (O.J. 1990, L 295).

[12] 20 Dec. 1990 (O.J. 1991, L 79).

[13] 19 Oct. 1992 (O.J. 1992, L 313).

[14] 16 March 1992 (O.J. 1992, L 94).

[15] 14 Dec. 1992 (O.J. 1992, L 404).

[16] 8 Feb. 1993 (O.J. 1993, L 41).

[17] Estonia, Latvia and Lithuania, 21 Dec. 1992 (O.J. 1992, L 403).

[18] 26 Oct. 1992 (O.J. 1992, L 403).

general non-execution clause was used in the agreements with Romania[20] and Bulgaria.[21] The agreement with the Republic of Czechoslovakia signed in May 1990 did not contain this formula, but non-execution clauses were inserted when two separate agreements were subsequently re-negotiated with the Czech Republic and Slovakia.[22]

The virtue of this third formula is that it uncouples the procedure from that laid down by the Vienna Convention on the Law of Treaties, allowing for an immediate response in emergencies by limiting the scope for legally contesting such measures.

The European Commission now "automatically" proposes the inclusion of a clause making human rights and democratic principles an essential element of agreements with all third countries in its draft negotiating directives. This includes trade and co-operation agreements as well as association and partnership agreements. The same approach has recently been suggested for the negotiation of the mid-term review of Lomé IV.

The inclusion of specific clauses in all agreements concluded with third countries is a cornerstone of the Union's policy on the promotion of human rights and democratic principles. This new departure places the European Union in the vanguard of the international community in this field.

The process continues. As in other international circles, the Community institutions are now pondering the inclusion of a "social" clause in future agreements, especially to combat various forms of forced labour and child exploitation.

Relations with the United Nations (UN), the Organization for Security and Cooperation in Europe (OSCE) and the Council of Europe. The European Union makes a significant contribution to the work of the UN, the OSCE and the Council of Europe in terms of their regulatory activities, the strengthening of reference instruments and preventive and protective mechanisms, and the implementation of specific measures.

(a) United Nations: The Union's contribution to the various UN permanent bodies concerned with human rights has gradually gained in substance and impact. At sessions of the UN General Assembly and the Human Rights Commission, co-ordination between the Member States has improved, enabling them to adopt a united front at various stages of the

---

[19] 20 July 1993 (O.J. 1993, L 189).

[20] Signed on 1 Feb. 1993.

[21] Signed on 8 March 1993.

[22] Both signed on 4 Oct. 1993.

procedure. The speech given by the Union Presidency on point 12 of the Human Rights Commission's agenda—Human rights violations in any part of the world—has become a standard reference text for the international community.

The European Union presented a wide-ranging paper setting out the key principles of its human rights policy to the UN-sponsored international conference on human rights held in Vienna in June 1993.[23] This document, which provided much of the basis for the conference's final statement, focuses on fundamental principles such as the universality, indivisibility and interdependence of all human rights as well as the duty of non-interference. It also puts forward proposals on children's rights, education in the field of human rights and the campaign against intolerance in all its guises. Amongst other things, the Union's input was a contributory factor in the creation of the post of High Commissioner for Human Rights.

(b) Organization for Security and Co-operation in Europe (OSCE):[24] The CSCE was one of the first issues to be dealt with by European Political Cooperation in the 1970s. The introduction of a "Human Dimension in January 1989 coincided with the Community institutions" growing preoccupation with human rights.

The Charter of Paris, which codifies the main principles of the Human Dimension was signed by the President of the European Commission on the same footing as the Heads of State or Government as a visible sign of the European Community's commitment to the (then) CSCE Process.

The Union also contributed actively to the creation and then reinforcement of the Office for Democratic Institutions and Human Rights and the High Commissioner on Minorities, both of which were manifestations of a new phase focusing on the application of the principles of the Human Dimension. In the OSCE fora, the Union's high-profile role in this crucial phase for the future of Europe includes participation in the implementation of mechanisms to monitor compliance with obligations and, where necessary, taking part in fact-finding missions.

Recent developments testify to the willingness of the European institutions to join forces and seek out synergy. For example, there were several fruitful exchanges during the preparatory phases of the International

---

[23] Position paper of the European Community and its Member States (A/Conf.157/PC/87), April 1993.

[24] The Conference on Security and Cooperation (CSCE) changed its name into Organization for Security and Cooperation in Europe (OSCE) as of 1 Jan. 1995 on the basis of a decision of the CSCE Summit Meeting in Budapest in Dec. 1994.

Conference on Human Rights. The Human Dimension of the OSCE plays a similar role, and the inaugural conference of the Stability Pact, held in Paris on 26 and 27 May 1994 at the Union's initiative, also demonstrated that body's ability to mobilize resources and initiatives from all quarters of the European spectrum in the interests of common objectives.

(c) Council of Europe: Bearing in mind that six Member States of the Union were founder members of the Council of Europe, it is not surprising that the Union maintains close relations with the Council. Membership of the Council of Europe and particularly the ECHR has become one of the unspoken conditions for membership of the European Union.

A number of Community projects involving the support of the democratic process are done in co-operation with the Council of Europe. This is itself a significant example of the various international institutions using their skills and resources together. This is an "end of century phenomenon", since years ago, the pattern would have been for organizations to be inward-looking. This change can be exemplified by the fruitful work done together to prepare the World Conference on Human Rights. This co-operation is paralleled by the work done in the Human Dimension "basket" of the OSCE. More recently, Edouard Balladur, the Prime Minister of France, launched the initiative, which was taken up by the European Union, of a Stability Pact which is designed to re-enforce the structures of the Council of Europe and the OSCE. The Pact is particularly concerned with the key issues of minorities and national frontiers in Central and Eastern Europe; it bears witness to the resources and energy being devoted to the solution of common problems throughout Europe.

Specific aspects of EU support for the democratic process. The defence and promotion of democratic values are central to the policies of the European Union in the international fora. In this context, electoral assistance can be singled out as being increasingly important since it occurs at a key moment in the process of maturation of civil society and institutional reform in the country concerned.

Community support in this field involves observer missions aimed at guaranteeing free and fair elections. In addition technical and material support is given and, if appropriate, civic courses and legal advice on the formulation of electoral law in accordance with democratic criteria.

This area of activity is increasingly important. In the period 1992–94, forty-one developing and associated countries benefited from the Community assistance in this field, that is, both developing countries and countries with association agreements with the Union. A number of financial instruments have been developed for this type of assistance. The most frequently used are "Human Rights and Democracy in Developing Countries", "Support for

Democratization in Latin America" and the Phare and Tacis Programmes designed to encourage the process of democratization in Central and Eastern Europe and the former Soviet countries.

The European Parliament was committed in this field as early as 1984 when it sent an observation team to Nicaragua and again in 1987 in Turkey. Further missions followed in a more systematic manner during the 1990s. To date, the Parliament has covered elections in thirty different countries.

The political nature of this type of action fits into the framework of the Common Foreign and Security Policy and its so-called "joint actions". Three of the first Joint Actions identified by the European Council held in Brussels in October 1993 were concerned with electoral assistance. The first of these was the sending of observers to the elections in Russia in December 1993. The second exercise of this nature in South Africa was more ambitious in scope, involving complementary assistance and the development of an over-all strategy for co-operation to support the democratic process. And finally, a joint action concerning the Middle East peace process involves assistance for the preparation and monitoring of elections which are scheduled in the autonomous Palestinian territories. In fact, this project encompasses wider issues as well and is aimed at initiating a phase of new relations with the countries of the region and the encouragement of regional co-operation.

4   THE FUTURE?

The role assumed by human rights in the Union's policies clearly results from a combination of the application of political will, initiatives of the different institutions and pressure of public opinion. The void in the original treaties has been filled by references to human rights in the TEU, and human rights have found a place in agreements with third countries. Furthermore, considerable financial resources have enabled the implementation of concrete projects.

Does this mean that the situation cannot be improved? Should we expect further action on the part of the Union in this field? Should there be an effort to define common political attitudes and develop strategic thinking so that the Union can anticipate situations rather than simply react to them? And should we be wary about a weakening of political will to the detriment of what has already been achieved?

The Intergovernmental Conference in 1996 will certainly be the moment of truth for the European Union since it will be asked to consider some fundamental issues. If these are not addressed there is a risk of slippage not only as regards the future but also for what has already been accomplished.

The next step does not merely depend on the views taken by the Member States nor on the work of the Union's institutions. These in turn depend on each individual's willingness to encourage public opinion to be responsible, active and committed.

SELECT BIBLIOGRAPHY

Md. Parvez Sattar

Ackers, "Women, Citizenship and European Community Law: The Gender Implications of the Free Movement Provisions", 16 *Journal of Social Welfare and Family Law* (1994), 391–406.

Addison and Siebert, "The Social Charter of the European Community: Evolution and Controversies", 44 *Industrial and Labour Relations Review* (1991), 597–625.

Addison and Siebert, "The Social Charter of the European Community: Whatever Next?", 30 *British Journal of Industrial Relations* (1992), 495–514.

Addo, "Some Issues in European Community Aid Policy and Human Rights", (1988) LIEI, 55–85.

Alexander, "Free Movement of Non-EC Nationals: A Review of the Case-Law of the Court of Justice", 3 EJIL (1992), 33–64.

An-Na'im (ed.), *Human Rights in Cross-Cultural Perspectives* (1992).

Arlett and Sallnow, "European Centres of Dissent", 61 *Geographical Magazine* (1989), 6–9.

Arnull and Jacobs, "Applying the Common Rules on the Free Movement of Persons—The Role of the National Judiciary in the Light of the Jurisprudence of the European Court of Justice", in Schermers et al. (eds), *Free Movement of Persons in Europe* (1993), pp. 272–285.

Balibar, "Es gibt keinen Staat in Europa: Racism and Politics in Europe Today", 186 *New Left Review* (1991), 5–19.

Barzel, *Economic Analysis of Property Rights* (1989).

Bayfield, "The Challenge of Xenophobia: Reflections on the Heart of the Stranger", 26 *Month* (1993), 298–303.

Belloni, "A Common Policy on Migration: A Step Towards Citizens' Europe", 3 *Politico* (1987), 437–451.

Bercusson, "The European Community's Charter of Fundamental Social Rights of Workers", 53 MLR (1990), 624–642.

Betten (ed.), *The Future of European Social Policy* (1991).

Bhabha and Shutter, *Women's Movement: Women under Immigration, Nationality and Refugee Law* (1994).

Bieber, "Democratic Control of European Foreign Policy", 1 EJIL (1990), 148–173.

Bingham, "'There is a World Elsewhere': The Changing Perspectives of English Law", 41 ICLQ (1992), 513–529.

Blackburn, "The Right to Vote", in Blackburn (ed.), *Rights of Citizenship* (1993), pp. 75–98.

Boeles, "Schengen and the Rule of Law", in Meijers (ed.), *Schengen—Internationalisation of Central Chapters of the Law on Aliens, Refugees, Security & the Police* (1991), pp. 135–146.

Den Boer, "Trends in Refugee Policy and Cooperation in the European Community", 26 *International Migration Review* (1992), 668–675.

Bogdanor, "Direct Elections, Representative Democracy and European Integration", 8 *Electoral Studies* (1989), 205–216.

Boumans and Norbart, "The European Parliament and Human Rights", 7 *Netherlands Quarterly of Human Rights* (1989), 36–56.

Brochmann, "'Fortress Europe' and the Moral Debt Burden: Immigration from the 'South' to the European Economic Community", 26 *Cooperation and Conflict* (1991), 185–195.

Browne Wilkinson, "The Infiltration of a Bill of Rights", (1992) *Public Law,* 397–410.

De Búrca, "Fundamental Human Rights and the Reach of the EC Law", 13 OJLS (1993), 283–319.

Callovi, "Regulation of Immigration in 1993: Pieces of the European Community Jig-Saw Puzzle", 26 *International Migration Review* (1992), 353–372.

Cassese, Clapham and Weiler (eds), *Human Rights and the European Community: Methods of Protection.* Vol. II of *European Union—The Human Rights Challenge* (1991).

Cassese, Clapham and Weiler (eds), *Human Rights and the European Community: The Substantive Law.* Vol. III of *European Union—The Human Rights Challenge* (1991).

Clapham, "A Human Rights Policy for the European Community", 10 YEL (1990), 309–366.

Clapham, *Human Rights and the European Community: A Critical Overview.* Vol. I of *European Union—The Human Rights Challenge* (1991).

Claussen, "Incorporating Women's Reality into Legal Neutrality in the European Community. The Sex Segregation of Labour and the Work-Family Nexus", 22 *Law and Policy in International Business* (1991), 787–813.

Coppel and O'Neill, "The European Court of Justice: Taking Rights Seriously?", 29 CML Rev. (1992), 669–692.

Curtin, "The Constitutional Structure of the Union: A Europe of Bits and Pieces", 30 CML Rev. (1993), 17–69.

Dallen, "An Overview of European Community Protection of Human Rights, with Some Special Reference to the UK", 27 CML Rev. (1990), 761–790.

Dauses, "The Protection of Fundamental Rights in the Community Legal Order", 10 EL

Rev. (1985), 398–419.

Davies, "The Emergence of European Labour Law", in McCarthy (ed.), *Legal Intervention in Industrial Relations: Gains and Losses* (1992), pp. 313–359.

Van Dijk, "Free Movement of Persons: Towards European Citizenship. Netherlands Report on Theme 3 of the 15th FIDE Colloquium", 40 *Sociaal Economisch Weekblad* (1992), 277–307.

Doogan, "The Social Charter and the Europeanisation of Employment and Social Policy", 20 *Policy and Politics* (1992), 167–176.

Dowling, "Workers' Rights in the Post-1992 European Communities: What 'Social Europe' Means to United States-Based Multinational Employers", 11 *Northwestern Journal of International Law and Business* (1991), 564–620.

Drzemczewski, "The Domestic Application of the European Human Rights Convention as European Community Law", 30 ICLQ (1981), 118–140.

Drzemczewski, *The European Rights Convention in Domestic Law* (1983).

Dumon, National Family Policies in EC Countries in 1991.

Dundes Renteln, "The Unanswered Challenge of Relativism and the Consequences for Human Rights", 7 *Human Rights Quarterly* (1987), 514–540.

Edmonds, *International Timesharing* (1991), 3rd edn.

Emmert, "The Family Policy of the European Community", in Waalkijk and Clapham (eds), *Homosexuality: A European Community Issue* (1993), pp. 361–194.

Van der Esch, "Some Aspects of 'Extra-Territorial' Infringement in EEC Competition Rules", in Hawk (ed.), *Antitrust and Trade Policy in the United States and the European Community* (1986), pp. 285–289.

The European Dimensions of Collective Bargaining after Maastricht. II. WORKING DOCUMENTS. European Trade Union Institute (ETUI). Brussels (1992), 53–109.

"Europe's Women: How the Other Half Works", *The Economist*, 30 June 1990, 21–24.

Evans, "Expulsion under the 1971 Immigration Act", 46 MLR (1983), 433–452.

Evans, "Nationality Law and European Integration", 16 EL Rev. (1991), 190–215.

Eyal, "Bordering on Chaos", *The Independent*, 6 November 1992, 19.

Fernandes, "The Free Movement of Persons: The Ever Changing Face of Europe", 3 *European Business Law Review* (1992), 327–330.

Fernhout, "'Europe 1993' and Its Refugees", 1 *Ethnic and Racial Studies* (1993), 492–506.

Foster, "The European Court of Justice and the European Convention for the Protection of Human Rights", 8 HRLJ (1987), 245–272.

Frowein, Schulhofer and Shapiro, "The Protection of Fundamental Rights as a Vehicle of Integration", in Cappelletti, Seccombe and Weiler (eds), *Integration through Law* (1984),

Vol. I, Book 3, p. 231.

Gardner, "Freedom of Expression", in McCrudden and Chambers (eds), *Individual Rights and the Law in Britain* (1994), pp. 209–238.

Gearty, "The European Court of Human Rights and the Protection of Civil Liberties: An Overview", 52 CLJ (1993), 89–127.

Germer, "Administrative Secrecy under the European Convention on Human Rights", in *Secrecy and Openness: Individuals, Enterprises and Public Administration* (1988), pp. 61–75.

Ginn and Arber, "Towards Women's Independence: Pension System in Three Contrasting European Welfare States", 2 *Journal of European Social Policy* (1992), 255–277.

Glasner, "Gender and Europe: Cultural and Structural Impediments to Change", in Bailey, (ed.), *Social Europe* (1992), pp. 70–105.

Gospel, "The Single European Market and Industrial Relations: An Introduction", 30 *British Journal of Industrial Relations* (1992), 483–494.

Gould, "The European Social Charter and Community Law—A Comment", 14 EL Rev. (1989), 223–226.

Grief, "The Domestic Impact of the European Convention on Human Rights as Mediated through Community Law", (1991) *Public Law,* 555–567.

Hall, "The European Convention on Human Rights and Public Policy Exceptions to the Free Movement of Workers under the EEC Treaty", 16 EL Rev. (1991), 466–488.

Hall, "Behind the European Work Council's Directive: The European Commission's Legislative Strategy", 30 *British Journal of Industrial Relations* (1992), 547–566.

Harvie, *The Rise of Regional Europe* (1994).

Heaton, "The European Community After 1992: The Freedom of Movement of People and Its Limitations", 25 *Vanderbilt Journal of Transnational Law* (1992), 643–679.

Hepple, "The Implementation of the Community Charter of Fundamental Social Rights", 53 MLR (1990), 643–654.

Hepple, *European Social Dialogue—Alibi or Opportunity?* (1993).

Higgins, "Human Rights and Foreign Policy", (1987) *Rivista Di Studi Politici Internazionali,* 563–580.

Hoogenboom, "Integration into Society and Free Movement of Non-EC Nationals", 3 EJIL (1992), 36–52.

Jacobs, "The Protection of Human Rights in the Member States of the European Communities—The Impact of the Court of Justice", in O'Reilly (ed.), *Human Rights and Constitutional Law. Essays in Honour of Brian Walsh* (1992), pp. 243–250.

Jacquemin, "The International Dimension of European Competition Policy", JCMS (1993), 91–101.

Kamminga, "Human Rights and the Lomé Conventions", 7 *Netherlands Quarterly of Human Rights* (1989), 28–35.

Kempeneers and Lelievre, "Women's Work in the EC: Five Career Profiles", 9 *European Journal of Population* (1993), 77–92.

King, "The Impact of Western European Border Policies on the Control of 'Refugees' in Eastern and Central Europe", 19 *New Community* (1993), 183–199.

Kingston, "Rich People Have Rights Too? The Status of Property as a Fundamental Human Right", in Heffernan (ed.), *Human Rights: A European Perspective* (1993), pp. 284–298.

Kofman and Sales, "Towards Fortress Europe?", 15 *Women's Studies International Forum* (1992), 29–39.

Korthals Altes, "Towards a European Response to Terrorism: National Experiences and Lessons for 1993", 4 *Terrorism and Political Violence* (1992), 237–244.

Krogsgaard, "Fundamental Rights in the European Community after Maastricht", (1993) LIEI, 99–113.

Kuyper, "Trade Sanctions, Security, Human Rights and Commercial Policy", in Maresceau (ed.), *The European Community's Commercial Policy after 1992. The Legal Dimension* (1992), pp. 387–422.

Lane, "New Community Competence under the Maastricht Treaty", 30 CML Rev. (1993), 939–979.

Langan and Ostner, "Gender and Welfare", in Room (ed.), *Towards a European Welfare State?* (1991), pp. 127–150.

Laske, "The Impact of the Single European Market on Social Protection for Migrant Workers", 30 CML Rev. (1993), 515–539.

Laws, "Is the High Court of Justice the Guardian of Fundamental Constitutional Rights?", (1993) *Public Law,* 59–79.

Lenaerts, "Fundamental Rights to be Included in a Community Catalogue", 16 EL Rev. (1991), 367–390.

Lester, "Rebalancing Lomé: Human Rights, South Africa and the Future", (1991) *Journal of World Trade,* 21–35.

Lester and Pannick, *Advertising and Freedom of Expression in Europe* (1984).

Leuprecht, "Fortress Europe and Human Rights", 3 *Contemporary European Affairs* (1990), 44–53.

Lewis, "Border Controls", 142 NLJ (1992), 1584–1586.

Lewis, "Gender and the Development of Welfare Regimes", 2 *Journal of European Social Policy* (1992), 159–173.

Lingle, "The EC Social Charter, Social Democracy and Post-1992 Europe", 14 *West European Politics* (1991), 129–138.

Lodge, "Social Europe", 13 *Journal of European Integration* (1990), 135–150.

Loman, Mortelmans, Post and Warson, *Culture and Community Law* (1992).

Macdonald, "The Margin of Appreciation in the Jurisprudence of the European Court of Human Rights", *Collected Courses of the Academy of European Law: The Protection of Human Rights in Europe* (1990), No. 1(2), pp. 95–162.

Macdonald, "Identity Complexes in Western Europe: Social Anthropological Perspectives", in Macdonald (ed.), *Inside European Identities* (1993), pp. 1–26.

Mancini, "The Making of a Constitution for Europe", 26 CML Rev. (1989), 595–614.

Marsh, "Freedom of Expression and Official Secrets: The Impact of the Official Secrets Act 1989 in the United Kingdom", 43 *Review of the International Commission of Jurists* (1989), 57–59.

McGowan, "A Critical Analysis of Commercial Speech", (1990) *California Law Review,* 359–448.

McNamara, "How Europe Must Block the Terrorist Bolt-Holes", *The Times,* 20 June 1990, 14.

Mendelson, "The European Court of Justice and Human Rights", 1 YEL (1981), 125–165.

Mendelson, "The Impact of European Community Law on the Implementation of the European Convention on Human Rights", 3 YEL (1983), 99–126.

Merritt et al., "Dossier: Towards a European Immigration Policy", Discussion Paper, Philip Morris Institute for Public Policy Research. Brussels. No. 1. (October 1993), 1–57.

Moller, "Europe: The Coming of the 'Nonmaterial' Society", 27 *Futurist* (1993), 23–28.

Morgenstern, "From the Particular to the General: Limitations to the Judicial Treatment of Social Policy Issues", 130 *International Labour Review* (1991), 559–567.

Morokvasic, "Fortress Europe and Migrant Women", 39 *Feminist Review* (1991), 69–84.

Mowbray, "Reform of the Control System of the European Convention on Human Rights", (1993) *Public Law,* 419–426.

Nielsen and Szyszczak, *The Social Dimension of the European Community* (1993).

Niessen, "Community Policies in the Fields of Migration and Asylum after Maastricht", (1992) ECAS (*Euro Citizen Action Service*), No. 16, 7–8.

Niessen, "European Community Legislation and Intergovernmental Cooperation on Migration", 26 *International Migration Review* (1992), 676–684.

O'Higgins, "The Family and European Law", 140 NLJ (1990), 1643–1646.

O'Keeffe, "The Free Movement of Persons and the Single Market", 17 EL Rev. (1992), 3–19.

Paul, Miller and Paul (eds), *Property Rights* (1994).

Pecoraro, "Defense of the Artistic Heritage by European Organisations", (1984) *Mezzogiorno d'Europa*, 93–104.

Pescatore, "The Content and Significance of Fundamental Rights in the Law of the European Communities", 2 HRLJ (1981), 295–308.

Pinto, *La liberte d'information et d'opinion en droit international* (1984).

Pipkorn, "La Communauté Européenne et la Convention Européenne des Droits de L'Homme", 14 *Revue Trimestrielle des Droits de L'Homme* (1993), 221–241.

"Pregnant Workers Directive Adopted", 226 EIRR (1992), 16–18.

Prondzynski, "The Social Situation and Employment of Migrant Women in the European Community", 17 *Policy and Politics* (1989), 347–354.

Quintin, "An Analysis of the Proposition of Accession of the European Communities to the European Convention on Human Rights (ECHR)", 16 *Vanderbilt Journal of Transnational Law* (1983), 887–911.

Rishikesh, "Extraterritoriality Versus Sovereignty in International Antitrust Jurisdiction", 14 *World Competition* (1991), 33–66.

Robertson, "Extradition, Inhuman Treatment and the Death Penalty", 154 *Justice of the Peace* (1990), 231–232.

Robertson, "Which European Court?", 154 *Justice of the Peace* (1990), 184–185.

Rosas, "Union Citizenship and National Elections", in Rosas and Antola (eds), *A Citizens' Europe: In Search of a New Order* (1995), pp. 135–155.

De Salvia, "La Protezione dei diritti dell'uomo nel quadro della Convenzione Europea e seconda il diritto Communitario: Interferenze e Problemi di Coordinamento", (1979) *Diritto Comunitario e degli scambi internazionale,* 489.

Schermers, "The European Communities Bound by Fundamental Human Rights", 27 CML Rev. (1990), 249–258.

Schermers, "The International Protection of the Right of Property", in Matscher and Petzold (eds), *Protecting Human Rights—The European Dimension: Essays in Honour of G.J. Wiarda* (1990), 2nd edn, pp. 565–580.

Schermers, "The Scales in Balance: National Constitutional Court v. Court of Justice", 27 CML Rev. (1990), 97–105.

Schermers and Waelbroeck, *Judicial Protection in the European Communities* (1987), 5th edn.

Schutte, "Schengen: Its Meaning for the Free Movement of Persons in Europe", 28 CML Rev. (1991), 549–570.

Schweiwe, "EC Law's Unequal Treatment of the Family: The Case-Law of the European Court of Justice on Rules Prohibiting Discrimination on Grounds of Sex and Nationality", (1994) *Social and Legal Studies,* 243–265.

Sermet, *The European Convention on Human Rights and Property Rights* (1990).

Shaw, "The Scope and Content of European Community Social Law: A Review of Progress and a Bibliographical Note", 1 *Journal of Social Welfare and Family Law* (1992), 71–84.

Shaw, "Twin-Track Social Europe—The Inside Track", in O'Keeffe and Twomey (eds), *Legal Issues of the Maastricht Treaty* (1994), pp. 295–311.

Silvia, "The Social Charter of the European Community: A Defeat for European Labor", 44 *Industrial and Labour Relations Review* (1990–1991), 626–643.

Slot and Grabandt, "Extraterritoriality and Jurisdiction", 23 CML Rev. (1986), 545–565.

Steiner, "From Direct Effect to *Francovich*: Shifting Means of Enforcement of Community Law", 18 EL Rev. (1993), 3–22.

Storey, "The Right to Family Life and Immigration Case-Law at Strasbourg", 38 ICLQ (1990), 328–344.

Szyszczak, "Race Discrimination: The Limits of Market Equality?", in Hepple and Szyszczak (eds), *Discrimination: The Limits of Law* (1993), pp. 125–147.

Szyszczak, "Social Policy: A Happy Ending or a Reworking of the Fairy tale?", in O'Keeffe and Twomey (eds), *Legal Issues of the Maastricht Treaty* (1994), pp. 313–327.

Teague, "Constitutional Régime? The Social Dimension to the 1992 Project", 27 *British Journal of Industrial Relations* (1990), 310–329.

Temple Lang, "The Sphere in Which Member States are Obliged to Comply with the General Principles of Law and Community Fundamental Rights Principles", (1991) LIEI, 23–35.

"Time Off for Family Responsibilities: Maternity/Paternity Leave". I. 186 EIRR (1989), 13–19.

Tomuschat, "Quo Vadis, Argentoratum? The Success Story of the European Convention on Human Rights and a Few Dark Stains", 13 HRLJ (1992), 401–406.

Towers, "Two Speed Ahead: Social Europe and the UK After Maastricht", 23 *Industrial and Labour Relations Review* (1992), 83–89.

Vogel-Polsky, "What Future Is There for a Social Europe Following the Strasbourg Summit?", 19 *International Law Journal* (1990), 65–80.

Waever and Kelstrup, "Europe and Its Nations: Political and Cultural Identities", in Waever, Buzan, Kelstrup and Lemaitre (eds), *Identity, Migration and the New Security Agenda in Europe* (1993), pp. 61–92.

Webber, "Europe 1992", 31 *Race and Class* (1989), 78–81.

Weber, "Environmental Information and the European Convention on Human Rights", 12 HRLJ (1991), 177–185.

Wedderburn, "The Social Charter in Britain—Labour Law and Labour Courts?", 54 MLR (1991), 1–47.

Weiler, "Eurocracy and Distrust", 61 *Washington Law Review* (1986), 1103.

Weiler, "The European Court at a Crossroads: Community Human Rights and Member State Action", in Capotorti et al (eds), *Du Droit International au Droit de l'intégration Liiber Amicorum Pierre Pescatore* (1987), pp. 821–842.

Weiler, "Thou Shalt Not Oppress a Stranger: On the Judicial Protection of the Human Rights of Non-EC Nationals—A Critique", 3 EJIL (1992), 65–91.

Weiler, "Journey to an Unknown Destination: A Restrospective and Prospective of the Court of Justice in the Arena of Political Integration", 31 JCMS (1993), 417–446.

Weiler and Lockhart, "'Taking Rights Seriously' Seriously: The European Court of Justice and its Fundamental Rights Jurisprudence", 32 CML Rev. (1995), 59–94 (Part I) and 579–627.

Whiteford, "Social Policy After Maastricht", 18 EL Rev. (1993), 202–222.

De Witte, "Community Law and National Constitutional Values", (1991) LIEI, 1–22.

Van den Wyngaert, "Applying the European Convention on Human Rights to Extradition: Opening Pandora's Box?", 39 ICLQ (1990), 757–779.

Zagari, "Combating Terrorism: Report to the Committee of Legal Affairs and Citizens' Rights of the European Parliament", 4 *Terrorism and Political Violence* (1992), 288–300.

Zch, "The European Business World and the Extraterritorial Application of United States Economic Regulations", 35 *Wirtschaft und Recht* (1983), 71–247.

Zwamborn, "Human Rights Promotion and Protection Through the External Relations of the European Community and the Twelve", 7 *Netherlands Quarterly of Human Rights* (1989), 11–27.

Zwamborn, "Human Rights, a Community Concern?", (1991) ECAS (*Euro Citizen Action Service*), No. 9, 9–12.

TABLE OF CASES

This table of cases does not include national cases.

European Patent Convention, Decisions and Reports 76–A (1994)

INDEX

International Studies in Human Rights

International Studies in Human Rights

20. A. Bloed and P. van Dijk (eds.): *The Human Dimension of the Helsinki Process*. The Vienna Follow-up Meeting and its Aftermath. 1991   ISBN 0-7923-1337-2

21. L.S. Sunga: *Individual Responsibility in International Law for Serious Human Rights Violations*. 1992   ISBN 0-7923-1453-0

22. S. Frankowski and D. Shelton (eds.): *Preventive Detention*. A Comparative and International Law Perspective. 1992   ISBN 0-7923-1465-4

23. M. Freeman and P. Veerman (eds.): *The Ideologies of Children's Rights*. 1992
          ISBN 0-7923-1800-5

24. S. Stavros: *The Guarantees for Accused Persons Under Article 6 of the European Convention on Human Rights*. An Analysis of the Application of the Convention and a Comparison with Other Instruments. 1993   ISBN 0-7923-1897-8

25. A. Rosas and J. Helgesen (eds.): *The Strength of Diversity*. Human Rights and Pluralist Democracy. 1992   ISBN 0-7923-1987-7

26. K. Waaldijk and A. Clapham (eds.): *Homosexuality: A European Community Issue*. Essays on Lesbian and Gay Rights in European Law and Policy. 1993
          ISBN 0-7923-2038-7; Pb: 0-7923-2240-1

27. Y.K. Tyagi: *The Law and Practice of the UN Human Rights Committee*. 1993
          ISBN 0-7923-2040-9

28. H.Ch. Yourow: *The Margin of Appreciation Doctrine in the Dynamics of European Human Rights Jurisprudence*. 1995   ISBN 0-7923-3338-1

29. L.A. Rehof: *Guide to the* Travaux Préparatoires *of the United Nations Convention on the Elimination of All Forms of Discrimination against Women*. 1993
          ISBN 0-7923-2222-3

30. A. Bloed, L. Leicht, M. Novak and A. Rosas (eds.): *Monitoring Human Rights in Europe*. Comparing International Procedures and Mechanisms. 1993
          ISBN 0-7923-2383-1

31. A. Harding and J. Hatchard (eds.): *Preventive Detention and Security Law*. A Comparative Survey. 1993   ISBN 0-7923-2432-3

32. Y. Beigbeder: *International Monitoring of Plebiscites, Referenda and National Elections*. Self-determination and Transition to Democracy. 1994 ISBN 0-7923-2563-X

33. F. de Varennes: *Language, Minorities and Human Rights*. 1994.   ISBN 0-7923-2728-4

34. D.M. Beatty (ed.): *Human Rights and Judicial Review*. A Comparative Perspective. 1994   ISBN 0-7923-2968-6

35. G. Van Bueren, *The International Law on the Rights of the Child*. 1995
          ISBN 0-7923-2687-3

36. T. Zwart: *The Admissibility of Human Rights Petitions*. The Case Law of the European Commission of Human Rights and the Human Rights Committee. 1994
          ISBN 0-7923-3146-X; Pb: 0-7923-3147-8

37. H. Lambert: *Seeking Asylum*. Comparitive Law and Practice in Selected European Countries. 1995   ISBN 0-7923-3152-4

International Studies in Human Rights

This series is designed to shed light on current legal and political aspects of process and organization in the field of human rights.

MARTINUS NIJHOFF PUBLISHERS – THE HAGUE / BOSTON / LONDON